NEWSPEAK in the 21st Century

NEWSPEAK
in the 21st Century

David Edwards and David Cromwell

PLUTO PRESS
www.plutobooks.com

First published 2009 by Pluto Press
345 Archway Road, London N6 5AA and
175 Fifth Avenue, New York, NY 10010

www.plutobooks.com

Distributed in the United States of America exclusively by
Palgrave Macmillan, a division of St. Martin's Press LLC,
175 Fifth Avenue, New York, NY 10010

British Library Cataloguing in Publication Data
A catalogue record for this book is available from the British Library

ISBN   978 0 7453 2894 2   Hardback
ISBN   978 0 7453 2893 5   Paperback

Library of Congress Cataloging in Publication Data applied for

This book is printed on paper suitable for recycling and made from fully managed
and sustained forest sources. Logging, pulping and manufacturing processes are
expected to conform to the environmental standards of the country of origin.
The paper may contain up to 70 per cent post-consumer waste.

10   9   8   7   6   5   4   3   2   1

Designed and produced for Pluto Press by
Chase Publishing Services Ltd, 33 Livonia Road, Sidmouth, EX10 9JB England
Typeset from disk by Stanford DTP Services, Northampton, England
Printed and bound in the European Union by
CPI Antony Rowe, Chippenham and Eastbourne

Don't you see that the whole aim of Newspeak is to narrow the range of thought? In the end we shall make thoughtcrime literally impossible, because there will be no words in which to express it.

George Orwell, *Nineteen Eighty-Four*, 1949

The sinister fact about literary censorship ... is that it is largely voluntary. Unpopular ideas can be silenced, and inconvenient facts kept dark, without the need for any official ban.

George Orwell, from his proposed preface to *Animal Farm*, 1945

Contents

Acknowledgements

Media Lens is a far more collaborative effort than the two names on the cover of this book suggest. Numerous friends – journalists, academics, specialist researchers, even lawyers! – continuously, and freely, provide us with expert assistance. Our website message board also hosts a vibrant community of activists who unpick the media's propaganda puzzles on a daily basis. Their insightful analysis – which shames the work of most professional commentators – often inspires or informs our media alerts. Olly Maw does a wonderful job of maintaining our website with extremely limited resources.

We would like to thank Noam Chomsky, Edward Herman, David Peterson, Jonathan Cook, Les Roberts, Gilbert Burnham, John Tirman, Mike Albert, Chris Spannos, Douwe and Alexander Korff, Gen Kelsang Chonden, Fairness and Accuracy in Reporting, the Venezuela Information Centre and the Gandhi Foundation. We would particularly like to thank John Pilger, whose generosity and support have made all the difference to us.

We would like to thank our families and friends for their love and support. David Cromwell would like to give special thanks to Foske, Sean and Stuart. David Edwards would like to thank M and H.

We gratefully acknowledge financial assistance from the Amiel and Melburn Trust, and Artists for Project Earth, as well as the many individuals who have kindly sent us donations over the years.

Finally, we would like to thank the numerous mainstream journalists who have taken the time to respond to our emails. A fair few have responded to criticism with integrity and honesty. Examples include Andrew Buncombe, Peter Barron and Peter Wilby – we salute them!

1
No Conspiracy:
Solving the Propaganda Puzzle

David Edwards: 'Have you heard of the British historian Mark Curtis?'
Jon Snow: 'I don't know.'
DE: 'He argues that there's a pattern to post-1945 British and US interventions, basically defending profits and installing people like the Shah in Iran...'
JS: 'Oh this is bollocks! Total bollocks!'
DE: 'Do you think so?'
JS: 'Utter bollocks!'[1]

THE NEED TO BELIEVE

Understanding the media is not like understanding maths or physics. We have no great urge to believe that 2 + 2 = 5. We are happy to believe that 2 + 2 = 4, if the evidence adds up. But we do like to believe that the newspaper we read is basically honest. Buying the *Independent* or the *Guardian* may give us a sense that we are involved and informed; that we care. This single act may be the only gesture we make towards democratic responsibility – we can even view it as a kind of vestigial activism. On a more mundane level, we may be proud that we are brainy enough to take the 'high-brow' *Times* (and do the crossword), and sneer at lesser minds that wallow in the *Mail* or ogle at the *Sun*. We want to believe these media when they tell us that Britain and America are attacking other countries out of humanitarian concern. We want to believe that the people in control are decent and rational. The alternative is disturbing, frightening; it can give rise to painful feelings of powerlessness. Above all, it can lead us to question whether we should assume moral responsibility for the state of our country and world – a burden many of us would rather avoid.

In December 2008, the *Times* leader writer, Oliver Kamm, described Media Lens as 'a sinister and ridiculous organisation'.[2] On the face of it, the claim that we are 'ridiculous' would certainly appear to have merit. Since sending our first media alert on July 9, 2001, we have published more than 2,500 pages of material – just under 1 million words. If the media were as honest as we are led to believe, this level of criticism could only be the result of some exotic, shared neurosis. But if we have learned one lesson in the last eight years, it is that there is very much more to the corporate media than meets the eye. The 'free press', truly, is not what it seems.

To understand why the appearance is so different from the reality, we need to understand how the public is deceived. Specifically, we need to understand how our hopes and fears are manipulated in the cause of our own deception. Consider, for example, our vulnerability to small gestures in the direction of truth. The journalist Jonathan Cook addressed the point in a fascinating reply to one of our media alerts in October 2008. Cook, who previously worked for the *Guardian* and the *Observer*, agreed with us that honest voices are systematically filtered out of the mainstream. But he posed a crucial challenge: 'How is it then, if this thesis is right, that there are dissenting voices like John Pilger, Robert Fisk, George Monbiot and Seumas Milne who write in the British media while refusing to toe the line?'[3] In answering his own question, Cook noted the remarkable fact that this small group pretty much exhausts the list of writers who can be said to seriously confront the mainstream consensus: 'That means that in Britain's supposedly leftwing media we can find one writer working for the *Independent* (Fisk), one for the *New Statesman* (Pilger) and two for the *Guardian* (Milne and Monbiot). Only Fisk, we should further note, writes regular news reports. The rest are given at best weekly columns in which to express their opinions.' With the exception of Pilger, none of these journalists 'choose or are allowed to write seriously about the dire state of the mainstream media they serve'; and in truth, even Pilger is heavily constrained in what he can write about the mainstream in the mainstream (as are we). It is also crucial, Cook added, that we recognise both the positive and negative roles these individuals play:

> However grateful we should be to these dissident writers, their relegation to the margins of the commentary pages of Britain's 'leftwing' media serves a useful purpose for corporate interests. It helps define the 'character' of the British media as provocative, pluralistic and free-thinking – when in truth they are anything but. It is a vital component in maintaining the fiction that a professional media is a diverse media.

Cook examined the case of Fisk in more detail:

> All the evidence is that the *Independent* might have folded were it not for his inclusion in the news and comment pages. Fisk appears to be one of the

main reasons people buy the *Independent*. When, for example, the editors realised that most of the hits on the paper's website were for Fisk's articles, they made his pieces accessible only by paying a subscription fee. In response people simply stopped visiting the site, forcing the *Independent* to restore free access to his stories.

It is also probable that the other writers cited above are among the chief reasons readers choose the publications that host them. It is at least possible that, were more such writers allowed on their pages, these papers would grow in popularity. We are never likely to see the hypothesis tested because the so-called leftwing media appear to be in no hurry to take on more dissenting voices.

There is a deep irony here: the public is eager to read the honest and courageous work of writers like Fisk, Monbiot and Pilger. But it is precisely *because* their work is so valued that we perceive the media as more open, free and inclusive than it really is. Focused on this tiny dissident group, we fail to notice the ocean of distortion and distraction that surrounds them and by which they, and we, are overwhelmed. Fisk and Pilger are tiny specks of light, all but invisible to the public in the intellectual murk that is 24/7 media output.

So this is one of the big lessons we have learned about the media: first impressions cannot be trusted.

FACTS ARE NOT SACRED

We have also learned that the media's famed obsession with 'balance' is in fact a powerful support for *biased* reporting. *Guardian* journalist Nick Davies offered a rare honest analysis in his book *Flat Earth News*:

> The great blockbuster myth of modern journalism is objectivity, the idea that a good newspaper or broadcaster simply collects and reproduces the objective truth. It is a classic Flat Earth tale, widely believed and devoid of reality. It has never happened and never will happen because it cannot happen. Reality exists objectively, but any attempt to record the truth about it always and everywhere necessarily involves selection.[4]

Thus, former *Guardian* editor C.P. Scott's famous dictum, 'Comment is free, but facts are sacred',[5] is as naïve as it is misleading. Facts are *not* sacred, pristine, untouchable – they are gathered by human beings guided by mundane, earthy, often compromised beliefs and motives.

To choose 'this' fact over 'that' fact is already to express an opinion. To highlight 'this' fact over 'that' fact is to comment.

The great claim of professional journalistic impartiality – the idea that 'When I joined the BBC, my Organs of Opinion were formally removed',[6] as the BBC's then political editor, Andrew Marr, put it – is a lie. It serves to camouflage a deep bias that consistently mistakes 'impartial' for 'officially approved'. If the Iranian president makes a claim, media 'impartiality' demands that his claim be balanced by an opposing view. But if the American president makes a claim, no such balance is deemed necessary. Time and again, we are given just the Bush, Blair, Brown, Obama view. The unwritten understanding is that news reporters should not express bias by passing judgement on our democratically elected leaders. Doing so is deemed almost a subversion of democracy – news reporting should offer the public a neutral service. And yet, when the same reporters praise our leaders to the skies, it is considered entirely unproblematic. In practice, 'balance' tends to involve presenting a 'spectrum' of views ranging from those heavily supportive of state policy to those mildly critical. Strongly critical views are dismissed as too 'extreme' to be included.

The myth of balance is used to justify the imposition of an 'editorial line' requiring journalists to conform to this structural bias favouring power. After all, as an alternative to editors imposing their version of 'balance', journalists might simply be allowed to present the version of events that strikes them as most rational and honest. And this is exactly what the best journalists do – it is why people love the journalism of Pilger and Fisk. Readers and viewers could then be invited to vote with their feet.

For example, the media present domestic elections as serious exercises in democracy offering a meaningful range of political choices. But there is nothing intrinsically 'professional' or 'balanced' about presenting such a view as being obviously true. It is not 'impartial' to present opinions offered by the leading two or three political parties as the only views that matter. If a journalist's intelligence tells him or her that extremely important opinions are *not* being represented by the big parties, he or she should be allowed to say so. Rational thought should not be subordinated to the idea that we have a properly functioning democracy when that is clearly not the case. The three-time US presidential candidate, Ralph Nader, describes the American political system as 'a two-party dictatorship in thraldom to giant corporations'.[7] An alternative at election time would be for journalists to present evidence indicating that 'democracy' is a charade serving privilege and power. This would be not a subversion but a defence of democracy.

If we accept that it is 'balanced' and 'professional' for a journalist to fail to respond as a thinking, rational human being, we are deferring to a mindless and very dangerous conformity.

LORDLUVADUCK! VULLIAMY GRASSES UP ALTON

If consistent distortions are found right across the supposed 'media spectrum', how can they appear with such consistency? Could it all be, in fact, the result of some kind of conspiracy? Consider, after all, the events that took place in the *Observer* newsroom in 2002. In the autumn of that year, Ed Vulliamy, one of the newspaper's leading reporters, was talking with Mel Goodman, a former senior CIA analyst. Although Goodman had left the agency, he retained his high security clearance and remained in communication with senior former colleagues. He told Vulliamy that, in contradiction to everything the British and American governments had claimed, the CIA were reporting that Saddam Hussein had *no* weapons of mass destruction. And Goodman was willing to go on the record as a named source.

This was an incredibly important scoop at a time when the British and US governments were doing everything they could to persuade the public of the need for war. And yet the *Observer* refused to publish the story. Over the next four months, Vulliamy submitted seven versions of his article for publication – his editors rejected every one of them.

Other people paid the price. In March 2003, eleven days after Vulliamy's story was rejected for the seventh time, the first bombs fell on Baghdad. In January 2003, the *Observer's* then editor, Roger Alton, had told his staff: 'We've got to stand shoulder to shoulder with the Americans.'[8] Three years later, the *Evening Standard* reported that Alton had been on 'something of a lads' holiday' in the Alps. His companions included Jonathan Powell, 'Tony Blair's most trusted aide', as well as staunch Blairite MP and propagandist Denis MacShane.[9]

In February 2008 we wrote to Vulliamy, and asked him: 'Did you try to publish the pieces elsewhere? Why did you not resign in protest at these obvious acts of censorship on such a crucial matter?'[10] We received a series of anguished replies to the effect that Vulliamy had not tried to publish the article elsewhere; that he had been naïve, complacent, fearful of harming his career (he asked us not to publish these emails). But we received nothing that explained why he had failed to get such an important story out somewhere, somehow. We also repeatedly asked him to describe the reasons the *Observer* had given for rejecting his story so many times, but he failed to answer and then stopped replying altogether.

We also wrote to Roger Alton, on April 21, 2008. We asked why seven versions of Ed Vulliamy's story were rejected over a period of four months. Alton replied on April 25:

> ... so it was my old pal Ed who grassed me up eh?? Lordluvaduck, what a surprise ... like Falstaff and Prince Hal eh??
>
> Now, I don't know anything about this tale ... while I think an editor should read, or try to read, all the 250,000-odd words that go into an edition of the *Observer*, I would not expect them to read all the several million words that are submitted eaxh [*sic*] week ... as I understand it, this story was not used by the desk, on journalistic grounds, and indeed this was a decision taken by a very anti-war executive...
>
> There was an article setting all this out in a recent edition of Press Gazette, which I am sure you can easily find...

How remarkable that Alton could be so unaware of the Mel Goodman 'tale'. When we checked, we found nothing in *Press Gazette*, a trade journal for the media industry, to explain why Vulliamy's article had been repeatedly rejected.

We approached Vulliamy and Nick Davies (who wrote about the story in his book *Flat Earth News*) for comment on Alton's bland, mocking response, but received no replies. The *Independent*'s media commentator, Stephen Glover, had perhaps already provided an explanation when he wrote of the *Observer* in 2006: 'one looks in vain to its heart for that old voice of principle and conviction, as well as intellectual distinction. I am not sure that Mr Alton, charming and gifted man though he unquestionably is, believes in very much.'[11]

COMPLICIT ENABLERS

In similar vein, Scott McClellan, George W. Bush's former White House press secretary, described how Bush relied on a 'political propaganda campaign' rather than the truth to sell the Iraq war to the American public. McClellan argued that the invasion was 'unnecessary', a 'strategic blunder', with Bush having made up his mind early on to attack Saddam Hussein. McClellan added: 'In the permanent campaign era, it was all about manipulating sources of public opinion to the president's advantage.'[12] The media had played the role of 'complicit enablers' in Bush's campaign to manipulate public opinion.[13]

In May 2008, CBS news anchor, Katie Couric, revealed that while working as a host of NBC's *Today* programme, she had felt pressure from 'the corporations who own where we work and from the government itself to really squash any kind of dissent or any kind of questioning of it [the Iraq war]'.[14] Howard Kurtz, the host of CNN's *Reliable Sources*, commented: 'Couric has told me that while she was at NBC ... she got what she described as complaints from network executives when she challenged the Bush administration.'[15] Jessica Yellin, who worked for MSNBC in 2003 and now reports for CNN, also said that journalists had been 'under enormous pressure from corporate executives, frankly, to make sure that this was a war presented in a way that was consistent with the patriotic fever in the nation'. Yellin added: 'And my own experience at the White House was that, the higher the president's approval ratings ... the more pressure I had from news executives to put on positive stories about the president.'

She explained that media bosses 'would edit my pieces. They would push me in different directions. They would turn down stories that were more critical and try to put on pieces that were more positive, yes. That was my experience.'[16]

Phil Donahue was host of *Donahue* on MSNBC from 2002 to 2003. Despite having the highest ratings of any show on MSNBC, the programme was cancelled on February 25, 2003. A leaked NBC memo described how the show presented a 'difficult public face for NBC in a time of war ... He seems to delight in presenting guests who are anti-war, anti-Bush and skeptical of the administration's motives.'[17] Bill Moyers interviewed Donahue in 2007:

> Moyers: 'You had Scott Ritter, former weapons inspector. Who was saying that if we invade, it will be a historic blunder.'
> Donahue: 'You didn't have him alone. He had to be there with someone else who supported the war. In other words, you couldn't have Scott Ritter alone. You could have Richard Perle alone.'
> Moyers: 'You could have the conservative.'
> Donahue: 'You could have the supporters of the President alone. And they would say why this war is important. You couldn't have a dissenter alone.

Our producers were instructed to feature two conservatives for every liberal.'
Moyers: 'You're kidding.'
Donahue: 'No this is absolutely true.'
Moyers: 'Instructed from above?'
Donahue: 'Yes. I was counted as two liberals.'[18]

Senior journalists rarely admit that their employers pressure them to follow a political line; it is a pressure that is supposed not to exist. And yet (or perhaps, for that very reason) there has been only one mention of Yellin's comment (in the *Independent*), and none of Couric's, in the entire UK press.

PLEASE REFRAIN FROM EMAILING LITERARY EDITORS

Is this, then, how the media is controlled: by simple suppression of facts based on elite collusion? Is it a conspiracy? Elite interests do collude, as was clearly the case in the run up to the invasion of Iraq, and this does explain some aspects of media performance. But this factor alone is not remotely sufficient to account for the consistently distorted, power-friendly performance of the media at all levels. In reality, this performance is shaped by a variety of factors that are all important jigsaw pieces in the propaganda puzzle.

Martin Tierney was one of a tiny number of mainstream journalists willing to review our previous book, *Guardians of Power*. Although John Pilger described it as 'The most important book about journalism I can remember', it has never been mentioned in any national UK newspaper, let alone reviewed. In June 2006, Tierney published an accurate outline of our argument in the *Herald*. His conclusion: 'It stands up to scrutiny.' He added that we 'do not see conscious conspiracy but a "filter system maintained by free market forces". After all it wouldn't be appropriate to show the limbs of third world children during Thanksgiving as it would only remind consumers who was really being stuffed.'[19] Exactly so. But if no conspiracy is involved, how on earth does the market manage to filter dissident views with such consistency? As baffled Channel 4 News reader, Jon Snow, once told us: 'Well, I'm sorry to say, it either happens or it doesn't happen. If it does happen, it's a conspiracy; if it doesn't happen, it's not a conspiracy.'[20] In 1996, Noam Chomsky attempted to explain the point to an equally bemused Andrew Marr (then of the *Independent*):

Marr: 'This is what I don't get, because it suggests – I mean, I'm a journalist – people like me are "self-censoring"...'

Chomsky: 'No – not self-censoring. There's a filtering system that starts in kindergarten and goes all the way through and – it doesn't work a hundred per cent, but it's pretty effective – it selects for obedience and subordination, and especially...'

Marr: 'So, stroppy people won't make it to positions of influence...'

Chomsky: 'There'll be "behaviour problems" or ... if you read applications to a graduate school, you see that people will tell you "he doesn't get along too well with his colleagues" – you know how to interpret those things.'

Chomsky's key point: 'I'm sure you believe everything you're saying. But what I'm saying is, if you believed something different you wouldn't be sitting where you're sitting.'[21] So what happens when a professional journalist does express 'something different'? Is their office seat just yanked away from them and rolled under a more reliable rear end?

Consider the fate of Tierney, who wrote for the Saturday *Herald* for seven years. In August 2008, he reviewed Barbara Ehrenreich's book *Going To Extremes*.[22] With his usual uncompromising style, he wrote:

It is essentially a tirade against every method used against US citizens to ensure that their wealth is systematically transferred to government and corporate elites. This is done, she claims, via abuse of the tax system, scapegoating immigrants; denial of Unions and Gestapo tactics used by the likes of ... [a large US supermarket] to ensure this and a perennial 'Warfare State' where taxpayers' money is merely used to enrich arms dealers while bludgeoning them into a unnecessary paranoia.[23]

Notice that Tierney merely *reported* claims made by Ehrenreich in her book regarding the use of 'Gestapo tactics'. It seems the *Herald*'s initial response to the review was positive – the piece was excellent, he was told.[24] But someone else on the *Herald*'s editorial staff informed Tierney that the reference to the supermarket's 'Gestapo tactics' had caused great anger in the office. One senior editor in particular was deeply unamused. This last reaction appears to have been decisive. As a result, Tierney was asked to relinquish his column. The reasoning? His editor felt she could not be sure that he would not make similarly 'extreme' comments in future – comments that might slip undetected into the paper.[25] The employer's reference to Tierney's extreme comment was ironic indeed given the nature of the horrors exposed in Ehrenreich's book – titled, after all, *Going To Extremes*.[26]

If you've ever wondered why the press finds it so hard to find 'space' for the multitude of excellent, radical analyses produced, this incident gives an idea of the real reasons. The unwritten corporate media rule is that you can say what you like about the powerless – they can be treated with contempt, smeared and slandered without limit. But when the powerless attempt to challenge the powerful, a different rule applies. Thus, in July 2002, we noted that John Pilger's new book, *The New Rulers of the World*, had by then been granted just two (negative) reviews in the entire UK national mainstream press. With Pilger's support, we invited readers to ask literary editors why they had smeared, or failed to review, the book. To our surprise and amusement, we received the following email from Fiona Price, the Marketing Manager of Verso Press, the publisher of Pilger's book. The email (of July 30, 2002) was copied to the review editor of the *Independent on Sunday*:

> Dear Editor
>
> Please could you ask the people who visit your website to refrain from emailing the literary editors of national newspapers questioning why they have not reviewed John Pilger's book, *The New Rulers of the World*. The *Independent* has a review waiting to be published but after receiving a number of unpleasant emails, all copied in to your email address, they are seriously thinking of pulling the review.
>
> I am working hard to get other national newspapers to review the book and do not appreciate having my efforts undermined by people who do not understand the pressure of space for reviews in newspapers. A paper's failure to review a title is not always politically motivated.
>
> I cannot stress strongly enough how much damage these people are doing to both John Pilger's and Verso's reputation and how counterproductive this campaign (if it is as orchestrated as that) is being.
>
> Fiona Price
> Marketing & Publicity Manager
> Verso

It turned out that the *Independent* had received a grand total of two emails of complaint from our readers!

It should be amazing that a leading radical publisher, and a major 'liberal' literary editor working in one of a tiny number of newspapers that might be willing to give Pilger's books a fair hearing, could adopt such an intolerant stance in response to the tiniest expression of dissent and democratic challenge from the public. Even politicians respond more honourably to criticism!

This is only one small example of the extreme anti-democratic pressures constantly at work in the media, as in all corporations. It is important to be clear that this kind of episode would never normally reach the public. To speak out as we did means career death, and so professional journalists hold their tongues no matter how extreme the abuses directed against them. Our initial media alert, for example, would have been reckless in the extreme had we hoped to be published by the *Independent* or Verso.

THE DAY THE *GUARDIAN* ADS DEPARTMENT WENT APESHIT

All around us, unseen, our media are being continuously cleansed, pore-deep, of important rational reporting and commentary, for the simple, crude reason that they threaten profits. In September 2008, Nick Clayton, a columnist at the *Scotsman* for twelve years and formerly its technology editor, reported that advertisers were leaving the paper in favour of online media. He wrote: 'Whether you're looking for work or a home, the web's the place to go.' On being fired for writing this, Clayton commented: 'I really don't understand why I've been fired ... I was merely reporting what estate agents had said to me about advertising in newspapers.'[27]

This recalls an infamous case from 1988 involving the *Guardian*, considered Britain's most liberal newspaper. An article by *Guardian* journalist James Erlichman covered a Greenpeace campaign to name and shame Ford motor company – then by far the country's biggest advertiser – because it lagged behind other car manufacturers in adapting engines to take unleaded petrol. A Greenpeace poster showed exhaust fumes in the shape of a skull and crossbones with the slogan: 'Ford Gives You More'.

Greenpeace tried to publish the poster as an advertisement in *The Times*, the *Guardian* and the *Independent* – all refused. The conclusion to Erlichman's piece contained one of the great bombshells in the history of British journalism:

Greenpeace booked 20 hoardings for its poster campaign. But then the advertising agency was informed that most of the sites – those owned by Mills & Allen – had been withdrawn.

Carl Johnson, who is handling the account, said: 'We were told that the posters were offensive, but I am sure someone was afraid of losing a lot of Ford advertising.'

Mr Johnson attempted to book the 'skull and crossbones' advertisement with *The Times*, the *Guardian* and the *Independent*. 'I have no doubt that they all feared losing Ford's advertising if they accepted ours,' he said.[28]

Erlichman was thus openly suggesting that his own paper, the *Guardian*, had rejected a Greenpeace advert in order to protect its fossil-fuel advertising revenues. We contacted Steve Elsworth, who organised the Greenpeace campaign. We asked him what he remembered about the fallout from Erlichman's article. Elsworth responded:

> He [Erlichman] told me afterwards that the ads department went apeshit when they saw the story, and that they put pressure on his boss, saying that the *Guardian* was being used as a propaganda machine for Greenpeace. The clear implication was that they didn't mind paid-for propaganda, but resented doing it for free – and like all the papers, were very aware of, and careful about, the economic clout of car advertising. James did get a lot of heat for the story from senior editorial staff, though I couldn't say who.[29]

Freelancers aren't fired or chastised, just waved away. In September 2008, Greg Philo of the prestigious Glasgow University Media Group submitted a powerful article, 'More News Less Views', to the *Guardian's* Comment is Free (CiF) website. Philo wrote:

> News is a procession of the powerful. Watch it on TV, listen to the *Today* programme and marvel at the orthodoxy of views and the lack of critical voices. When the credit crunch hit, we were given a succession of bankers, stockbrokers and even hedge-fund managers to explain and say what should be done. But these were the people who had caused the problem, thinking nothing of taking £20 billion a year in city bonuses. The solution these free market wizards agreed to, was that tax payers should stump up £50 billion (and rising) to fill up the black holes in the banking system. Where were the critical voices to say it would be a better idea to take the bonuses back? Mainstream news has sometimes a social-democratic edge. There are complaints aired about fuel poverty and the state of inner cities. But there are precious few voices making the point that the reason why there are so many poor people is because the rich have taken the bulk of the disposable

wealth. The notion that the people should own the nation's resources is close to derided on orthodox news...

At the start of the Iraq war we had the normal parade of generals and military experts, but in fact, a consistent body of opinion then and since has been completely opposed to it. We asked our sample [of TV viewers] whether people such as Noam Chomsky, John Pilger, Naomi Klein and Michael Moore should be featured routinely on the news as part of a normal range of opinion. Seventy three per cent opted for this rather than wanting them on just occasionally, as at present.[30]

Matt Seaton, the CiF editor, rejected the article on the grounds that 'it would be read as a piece of old lefty whingeing about bias'.[31] This from the same website that had just published Anne Perkins' analysis of the merits of different political leaders' wives: Sarah Brown, wife of prime minister Gordon, and Samantha Cameron, wife of Tory leader David, were doing so much better than 'that awful Cherie' Blair, it seemed: 'Brown is unflashy and sincere. Cameron is cool and elegant. The joke is they could be sisters, with pretty but unacademic Samantha and the older, not quite as pretty but dead brainy Sarah.'

Samantha 'keeps her mouth shut and looks cool and stylish', although there have been gaffes: 'no one mentions those packs of Smythson's Christmas cards (£5.70 each, £57 for 10)'.[32] And so on...

We found this within seconds of visiting the site – there are limitless comparable examples.

As we ourselves know, where dissidents cannot be sacked, patronised or ignored, legal action is always an option. On June 28 and July 3, 2008, Media Lens received repeated threats of both legal and police action from Alastair Brett, legal manager of News International's Times Newspapers. Noam Chomsky described the threats, pithily, as 'pretty sick'.[33] David Miller, professor of sociology at the University of Strathclyde and founder member of Spinwatch (www.spinwatch. org), commented:

> The response from *The Times* is an absolutely outrageous attempt to bully and censor you. It is not – unfortunately – surprising though, as the Murdoch empire is determined to attempt to snuff out those voices which try to bear witness to the truths of our age. Those that unmask naked power will be targeted by the Murdoch empire and its hench people.[34]

Brett claimed that *Times* journalist Bronwen Maddox had been subject to 'vexatious and threatening' emails from Media Lens readers, which constituted 'harassment'. If this did not stop, Brett told us, he would notify the police who might wish to investigate the matter with a view to bringing a criminal prosecution. As former *New Statesman* editor Peter Wilby noted in his *Guardian* article on *The Times'* threat, this was no joke – prosecution for criminal harassment 'can lead to six months' imprisonment or, if a court order is breached, up to five years'.[35]

Maddox claimed to have received 'dozens of emails, many abusive or threatening'.[36] Many of these emails were copied to us. We saw only one that could remotely have been described as 'vexatious'. This was from a high-spirited but harmless Australian reader who had sent similar emails to other media, and indeed to us. The typical gist of his messages was that if journalists failed to do what he demanded of them by a given date, they could consider themselves 'fired'. These were not very pleasant, but not very serious, threats from someone who obviously had no power to sack anyone.

We deleted Maddox's email address from our archived media alert, as requested – a trivial gesture since the alert had already been sent out to thousands of people and had been posted on innumerable websites.

THE ART OF SELF-DECEPTION

The more we have studied the media and the more we have exchanged views with journalists, the less it has seemed to us that media deception can be explained by a conspiracy theory. Instead, it seems clear to us that a key force driving the propaganda system is the human capacity for *self*-deception.

When a shoal of fish instantly changes direction, it looks for all the world as though the movement was synchronised by some guiding hand. Journalists – all trained and selected for obedience by media all seeking to maximise profits within state-capitalist society – tend to respond to the same events in the same way. This can also look like an orchestrated response, but many journalists clearly believe everything they are saying and clearly have no awareness that they are conforming to the needs of power.

In 1999, dozens of British journalists appeared to conclude independently that war on Serbia was a rational, justified response to a 'genocide' in Kosovo that had not in fact taken place. In 2002–03, many journalists concluded that war was necessary to tackle an Iraqi threat that did not exist. And yet, to our knowledge, in 2009, not a single journalist proposed military action in response to Israel's staggering, very visible crimes against the besieged civilian population of Gaza. It is clear that, in all these cases, journalists allowed the British and American governments to define the parameters of 'reasonable', 'rational', 'required' action.

At a politically crucial time in November 2002, the leading liberal commentator, George Monbiot, wrote in the *Guardian*: 'if war turns out to be the only means of removing Saddam, then let us support a war whose sole and incontestable purpose is that and only that'.[37] We asked him: 'Can you explain why you would prioritise the support of such a war ahead of a war to remove the Algerian generals, the Turkish regime, the Colombian regime, or maybe Putin? Would you also support a war to remove these regimes, if this turns out to be the only way?'[38] Monbiot replied the same day:

> The other nations you mention have some, admittedly flimsy, domestic means of redress: in other words, being democracies, or nominal democracies, citizens can, in theory, remove them without recourse to violent means. There is no existing process within Iraq for removing the regime peacefully. Like many of those who oppose this war with Iraq, I also want to help the Iraqi people to shake off their dictator...
>
> As I suggest in my article, we must try the non-violent means first, and there are plenty which have not been exhausted. But if all the conditions which I believe would provide the case for a just war are met – namely that less violent options have been exhausted first, that it reduces the sum total of violence in the world, improves the lives of the oppressed, does not replace one form of oppression with another and has a high chance of success – then it seems to me that it would be right to seek to topple Mr Hussein by military means.[39]

Monbiot failed to notice that 'we' could not satisfy the conditions for 'a just war' for the simple reason explained by the late Harold Pinter: 'the notion that this "we" has the right to act presupposes a moral authority of which this "we" possesses not a jot! It doesn't exist!'[40] Imagine, after all, if a journalist under Saddam Hussein had suggested that 'we' would be 'right' to attack another country 'if all the conditions which I believe would provide the case for a just war are met'.

We asked Monbiot if he thought Iraq was a special case to be singled out for this kind of treatment. He replied: 'I do not believe that Iraq is a special case, or, rather, I do not believe that it is any more special than a number of other cases.'[41] So why single out Iraq, just then, when the British and American governments were clearly intent on attacking Iraq? He replied: 'why did I write that column about Iraq, rather than about Burma or West Papua? The answer is that Iraq is the issue over which the ideological battles of the moment are being fought. Yes, of course the reason for this is that the hawks in the US have put it on the agenda.'[42]

The disturbing truth is that mainstream politics and media have an astonishing capacity to make just 'this' issue seem urgent and real while consigning other issues to oblivion. The temptation for a professional journalist is to be 'relevant', to 'matter', to accept the parameters of debate set by powerful interests, and to ignore the human costs of his or her actions. By late 2002, political and media propaganda had succeeded in making the need to take action against Saddam Hussein 'real' – we believe Monbiot was swept up in the wake of that propaganda.

Journalists, then, deceive others by conforming to the needs of power while deceiving *themselves* that they are responding solely on the basis of independent, rational thought. In his book *Vital Lies, Simple Truths*, psychologist Daniel Goleman examined the mechanics of self-deception. According to Goleman, we build our version of reality around key frameworks of understanding, or 'schemas', which we then protect from conflicting facts and ideas. The more important a schema is for our sense of identity and security, the less likely we are to accept evidence contradicting it. Goleman writes:

> Foremost among these shared, yet unspoken, schemas are those that designate what is worthy of attention, how it is to be attended to – and what we choose to ignore or deny ... People in groups also learn together how not to see – how aspects of shared experience can be veiled by self-deceits held in common.[43]

He concluded: 'The ease with which we deny and dissemble – and deny and dissemble to ourselves that we have denied or dissembled – is remarkable.' Psychologist Donald Spence noted the sophistication of this process: 'We are tempted to conclude that the avoidance is not random but highly efficient – the person knows just where not to look.'[44] This tendency to self-deception appears to be greatly enhanced when we join as part of a group. This creates a sense of belonging, a 'we-feeling', that provides an even greater incentive to reject conflicting truths. As psychologist Irving Janis reports, the 'we-feeling' lends 'a sense of belonging to a powerful, protective group that in some vague way opens up new potentials for each of them'.[45] Members are thus reluctant to say or do anything that might lessen these feelings of security and empowerment. In this situation, even pointing out the risks surrounding a group decision may seem to represent an unforgivable attack on the group itself. This is 'groupthink'. Individual self-deception, combined with groupthink, helps explain why journalists are able to ignore even the most obvious facts.

It is painful for a journalist to be aware of both his or her employer's shortcomings and his or her powerlessness to remedy them. As Goleman has noted, 'when one can't do anything to change the situation, the other recourse is to change how one perceives it'.[46] This, finally, is the human trait that empowers 'brainwashing under freedom'. As we will see in the chapters that follow, journalists are somehow able to perceive only that which allows them to thrive as successful components of the corporate system. As Norman Mailer noted, the price is high: 'There is an odour to any Press Headquarters that is unmistakeable ... the unavoidable smell of flesh burning quietly and slowly in the service of a machine.'[47]

A NOTE ON READING THIS BOOK

Our aim with this book is not to tell you everything there is to know about the war in Iraq, about Venezuela, climate change, the Israel–Palestine conflict, and so on. All of these issues would require separate volumes to do them justice, and a depth of knowledge that we do not possess. Instead, our aim is to challenge the deeply entrenched view that the media present us with a more or less honest version of the world. In particular, we are keen to counter the lethal conceit that while some media (on the right) are just awful, other media (on the 'left') are much better and provide an honest, compassionate balance. Our goal is to offer evidence for a profound, consistent bias favouring powerful interests stretching right across the media 'spectrum'. For this reason, the topics under discussion are actually not the main focus; they are a means to an end.

This transforms the significance of what we have written. For example, at first sight, our chapter on the leaking of a Downing Street memo from 2002 might not initially strike the reader as particularly compelling. Many readers may have decided already that the Iraq war was obviously based on a pack of lies – the whole thing was a disaster, Bush and Blair are gone, so why go over it all again? But we think that to compare carefully the reality of what the memo had to say with the *media* version of what the memo had to say is to reveal modern corporate journalism as a deceptive and highly destructive sham.

From our perspective, the propaganda performance of the media is a weird and wonderful phenomenon, an astonishing product of human society. We do not write out of anger – we hold no grudges against the journalists mentioned in the chapters ahead. The causes of media deceptiveness are too interesting and strange, too rooted in unconscious self-deception, to allow the crude response of anger and hatred.

2
BBC Balance:
The Magnificent Fiction

To deal first with your suggestion that it is factually incorrect to say that an aim of the British and American coalition was to bring democracy and human rights, this was indeed one of the stated aims before and at the start of the Iraq war – and I attach a number of quotes at the bottom of this reply.

Helen Boaden, director, BBC News

GROWING UP WITH AUNTIE

We grew up with the BBC, or 'Auntie Beeb'. We watched *Watch With Mother* with our mothers; we walked the walk and talked the talk with Bill and Ben, the Flower Pot Men. The excitement of childhood at Christmas is forever linked in our minds with the lighting of advent candles on *Blue Peter*, and the *Morecambe and Wise Christmas Show*. And then there were *Top of the Pops*, *Tomorrow's World*, *The Sky At Night*. These were more like old friends than TV programmes. Even the BBC voiceovers were a source of comfort – calm, reassuring (if conspicuously well-spoken), gently guiding us between programmes.

A dentist once asked one of us: 'So what do you write about?' Through a tangle of drills, clamps and tubes, Edwards gurgled: 'Thought control in democratic society.' The answering micro-expressions – impossible to misread at a distance of six inches – signalled anxiety and confusion. A momentary curl of the upper lip unmistakably communicated disdain, as though the word 'Marxist' had flitted darkly, like a bat, across the good dentist's mind.

What micro-expressions are likely to register, now, among our readers – people like us, people who grew up loving the Beeb – when we argue that the BBC is part of a system of thought control complicit in the deaths of millions of people abroad, in severe political oppression at home, and in the possible termination of human life on this planet. Are these fantastic claims? Or is it in fact possible to justify them?

THE SELECTION IN PERCEPTION

The BBC's grand conceit is that it stands neutrally between all contending views. Its journalists will describe the full range of opinions of others, but will never, ever reveal their own. This even-handedness is said to be firmly established in BBC guidelines, which declare a 'commitment to impartiality', requiring that journalists 'strive to reflect a wide range of opinion and explore a range and conflict of views so that no significant strand of thought is knowingly unreflected or under represented'.[1] We are reminded of *Star Trek*'s 'Prime Directive' – the policy of non-interference, ostensibly guiding the crew of the Starship Enterprise. Captain Kirk would often discourse earnestly on the need to avoid interfering in the development of alien cultures, even as he and his crew blasted the self-same aliens to atoms.

Richard Sambrook, the former BBC director of news, told one newspaper: 'People sometimes ask me what I'm going to do after the BBC. And the answer is that I'm going to have opinions again. They've been repressed for so long. In dinner party conversations, I find it quite hard to have an opinion, because I'm so used to the "on-the-one-hand, on-the-other" outlook.'[2] The problem is that while BBC journalists may stand neutrally between the range of views presented, the range itself inevitably reflects their value judgements. Consider an item on the Six O'Clock News of March 20, 2006. Diplomatic Correspondent Bridget Kendall declared solemnly: 'There's still bitter disagreement over invading Iraq. Was it justified or a disastrous mis-calculation?' What ten-year-old could fail to see through the claim that Kendall was not thereby offering an opinion?

The assertion that the alternative to the pro-war justification was to argue that the war was merely a 'disastrous miscalculation' offered a deeply personal, and in fact outrageous, view. The anti-war movement has always argued that the war was *not* just a 'miscalcula-tion', but a deliberate and criminal war of aggression. Would Kendall describe the Nazi Holocaust as a 'disastrous miscalculation'? Were the 9/11 attacks on America a 'misjudgement'? Many people, including former UN Secretary-General Kofi Annan and numerous specialists in international law, are clear that the invasion of Iraq was an 'illegal' war of aggression. Many argue, along with the prosecutors at the Nuremberg trials after the Second World War, that the launching of a war of aggression is 'the supreme international crime, differing only from other war crimes in that it contains within itself the accumulated evil of the whole'.[3] So by what right does the BBC airbrush from reality the swath of informed public opinion that sees the invasion as a crime, rather than as a mistake? By what right does it declare this framing of the topic to be 'impartial', 'balanced', 'objective' reporting?

As noted in the previous chapter, while working as the BBC's political editor, Andrew Marr declared: 'When I joined the BBC, my Organs of Opinion were formally removed.' And yet in April 2003, speaking of Tony Blair as Baghdad fell to American tanks, Marr told a national audience on prime-time TV:

> He said that they would be able to take Baghdad without a bloodbath, and that in the end the Iraqis would be celebrating. And on both of those points he has been proved conclusively right. And it would be entirely ungracious, even for his critics, not to acknowledge that tonight he stands as a larger man and a stronger prime minister as a result.[4]

Just this single comment makes a mockery of the BBC's claims to impartiality and freedom from personal bias. What could more obviously have reflected Marr's personal opinion, his personal sympathy for both Blair and the invasion? Marr has himself commented on his role in his book, *My Trade*: 'Gavin Hewitt, John Simpson, Andrew Marr and the rest are employed to be studiously neutral, expressing little emotion and certainly no opinion; millions of people would say that news is the conveying of fact, and nothing more.'[5] Millions of people would be deceived – Marr most conspicuously among them!

Or consider this, by comparison, innocuous example of bias. A BBC website article reported: 'US President George W. Bush has arrived in Israel to take part in celebrations for the country's 60th anniversary. He also hopes to inject some momentum into the current peace talks between Israel and the Palestinians.'[6] How did the BBC know what Bush *truly* hoped? Why was it 'neutral' to present Bush's claimed 'hopes' as the uncontroversial reality? Given his record, it would have been far more reasonable to assert that Bush's claim was bogus, that his intention was to continue to obstruct the international consensus on the need for a just and equitable settlement.

As American political scientist Norman Finkelstein has noted, the US has consistently opposed a peaceful resolution to the conflict. Except for the US and Israel (and the occasional US client state), an international consensus has backed what is called the 'two-state' settlement for the past 30 years. The US cast the only veto, blocking Security Council resolutions in 1976 and 1980 calling for a two-state settlement that was endorsed by the Palestine Liberation Organization (PLO) and front-line Arab states. A December 1989 General Assembly resolution along similar lines was passed by 151 votes to 3 (no abstentions) – the three negative votes were cast by Israel, the US and Dominica. Finkelstein commented:

> The problem with the Bush administration, we are repeatedly told, is that it has been insufficiently engaged with the Middle East ... But who gave the green light for Israel to commit the massacres [in the West Bank in 2002]? Who supplied the F-16s and Apache helicopters to Israel? Who vetoed the Security Council resolutions calling for international monitors to supervise the reduction of violence?
>
> Consider this scenario. A and B stand accused of murder. The evidence shows that A provided B with the murder weapon, A gave B the 'all-clear' signal, and A prevented onlookers from answering the victim's screams. Would the verdict be that A was insufficiently engaged or that A was every bit as guilty as B of murder?[7]

The BBC *could* have approached commentators like Finkelstein for a dissenting challenge to Bush's claim, but that is unthinkable – it is simply understood that Western leaders are to be portrayed as men and women of peace. If the BBC had provided a contrary view, it would have been interpreted as a sign that the BBC was 'anti-American'. To be balanced is 'biased' – propaganda is 'neutral'.

Critics might argue that the examples we have provided above were isolated slip ups. But in fact, as we will see, they are the norm. Sceptics might also have a case if examples could be cited exaggerating facts and opinions in a way that *harmed* powerful interests. But when did we ever hear the BBC report in 2002 or early 2003: 'Saddam Hussein hopes to inject some momentum into the current peace talks'? This, after all, is what Saddam Hussein claimed, so why could the claim not be presented at face value? In fact, as we know, Saddam Hussein *was* very keen to avoid war in 2003 for very good reasons having to do with self-preservation. He was the only actual peace-seeker in 2002 – Bush and Blair were determined to go to war. But these are unthinkable conclusions for the Western media, the BBC very much included.

PINK ELEPHANT BLUES: THE FABLE OF BBC INDEPENDENCE

The audacity and self-contradiction do not end with claims to impartiality. The BBC also claims that it is invulnerable to external pressures, that its senior management is unbiased and neutral. Helen Boaden, the BBC's director of news, told one viewer: 'People trust the BBC because they know it is an organisation independent of external influences. We do not take that trust lightly.'[8] We are to believe, then, that the BBC is independent of the external influence of the British government that appoints its senior managers!

Remarkably, Boaden's comments came *after* the January 2004 Hutton Report which saw BBC chairman Gavyn Davies, director-general Greg Dyke and journalist Andrew Gilligan all lose their jobs as the result of a ferocious government assault. This, even though Gilligan's news report claiming that the government had knowingly 'sexed up' a dossier on Iraq's supposed weapons of mass destruction was substantively correct, and indeed conservative. The claim that Iraqi WMD could be launched within 45 minutes of an order being given was not 'sexed up' intelligence; it was an invention. It is not 'sexing up' the facts to claim that a pink elephant is flying over Downing Street.

The British government initiated an inquiry on the absurd assumption that a Law Lord had the right to pass judgement on the merits of Gilligan's journalism. Not only did the BBC take this attack on press freedom seriously, it collapsed in a wave of self-recrimination and resignations. As the press observed, the BBC's royal charter was up for review in 2007, allowing the government to apply pressure by threatening to abolish the licence fee that funds the organisation. Ironically, in seeking to defend the BBC against this attack, 'liberal' commentators reinforced the myth of BBC independence. Liberal Democrat leader Menzies Campbell told the audience on the BBC television programme, *Question Time*: 'Andrew Gilligan got it wrong. But just ask yourself: how many hundreds of programmes, how many thousands of hours of broadcasting, and of news broadcasting, have gone out, none of which have been able to be criticised?' Johann Hari, an *Independent* columnist, warned that '[t]he extent of the BBC's problems can be exaggerated', adding: 'The BBC's best journalists – Andrew Marr, John Simpson, the Panorama team – still set an international gold standard.'[9]

This might easily have been mistaken for an attempt at humour. We have already discussed Marr. Similarly, in November 2002, when the British government was doing everything it could to hype the case for war, John Simpson joined with the Panorama team to produce a documentary with the title, 'Saddam: A Warning from History' (BBC1, November 3, 2002). This was a straight steal from an earlier BBC series entitled, 'The Nazis: A Warning from History'. Like the contents, the title was propaganda gold for the Blair government, not 'gold standard' reporting. Two months after the film aired, for instance, Blair said: 'What does the whole of our history teach us, I mean British history in particular? That if when you're faced with a threat you decide to avoid confronting it short term, then all that happens is that in the longer term you have to confront it and confront it in an even more deadly form.'[10] In other words, the Nazis provided us with a warning from history about how to respond to Saddam Hussein in 2003. Six years later, it is almost impossible to credit that Blair could have persuaded anyone to believe this fantastic nonsense. Simpson and Panorama helped make it possible.

The fact that BBC journalists perform as they do without overt external interference is offered as proof of their independence. The BBC's North America editor, Justin Webb, rejected the charge that he is a propagandist for US power, saying: 'Nobody ever tells me what to say about America or the attitude to take towards the United States. And that is the case right across the board in television as well.'[11] Webb began a radio programme from the Middle East thus:

June 2005. US Secretary of State Condoleezza Rice flies to Cairo and at the American University makes a speech that will go down in history: 'For sixty years, my country, the United States, pursued stability at the expense of democracy in this region, here in the Middle East; and we achieved neither. Now we are taking a different course. We are supporting the democratic aspirations of all people.'

Webb told his listeners in all seriousness: 'I believe the Bush administration genuinely wanted that speech to be a turning point; a new start.'[12] Nobody had to tell Webb to say these words; he really believed them.

Newsnight editor Peter Barron – one of the BBC's most reasonable and thoughtful journalists (who has since left the organisation) – declared without irony: '[W]e come under surprisingly little pressure either from within the BBC or from those in positions of power to constrict our coverage. If we fail to be sufficiently challenging I think we only have ourselves to blame.'[13] And yet, even journalists within the liberal mainstream are able to unpick the obvious self-deception. The *Guardian*'s editor, Alan Rusbridger, told us in an interview: 'If you ask anybody who works in newspapers, they will quite rightly say, "Rupert Murdoch", or whoever, "never tells me what to write", which is beside the point: they don't have to be told what to write.'[14]

ARCHITECTURE OF ESTABLISHMENT: WHO TRUSTS THE TRUST?

When challenged on the obvious contradiction that is a corporate 'free press', media professionals commonly refer to the counter-balancing influence of the BBC. Thus Jon Snow told us in an interview: 'Your big problem is that you're dealing with a multi-media activity in Britain, in which there is a huge non-corporate involvement ... I'll give you the BBC as an example.'[15] But in an age when powerful business interests strongly influence state policy and public affairs, how 'non-corporate' can the BBC really be? Consider, for example, that the BBC's upper echelons are largely populated by senior corporate and government figures.

In 1997, prior to becoming BBC chairman (2001–04), Gavyn Davies was touted as the next Governor of the Bank of England. At the time, Davies was chief economist of the bank Goldman Sachs, with an estimated personal fortune of £150 million. Davies' predecessor as BBC chairman, Sir Christopher Bland, left the BBC to become chairman of British Telecom. The *Observer*'s Sarah Ryle noted of Davies' 'non-corporate' agenda: 'those at the BBC prepared to comment only off the record say the Davies appointment is a good one. Broadcasting is as much about business as it is about content, today more than ever before.' Ryle noted that it was impossible to ask the 'secret panel' why they had chosen Davies – the identity of only one of the panel was known. 'But we may guess that Davies's credentials as chief economist of the powerful global bank Goldman Sachs and his undisputed financial acumen played a significant part in the debate.'[16]

Both Davies and his director-general, Greg Dyke (2000–04), were not just supporters of, but donors to, the Labour Party. Personal links also abounded – Davies' wife ran Gordon Brown's office; his children served as pageboy and bridesmaid at the Brown wedding. Tony Blair had stayed at Davies' holiday home. 'In other words,' columnist Richard Ingrams noted, 'it would be hard to find a better example of a Tony crony.'[17] The revolving door that links the BBC, the government and big business has been turning for a very long time. In 2001, Steve Barnett commented in the *Observer*:

> back in 1980, George Howard, the hunting, shooting and fishing aristocratic pal of Home Secretary Willie Whitelaw, was appointed [BBC chairman] because Margaret Thatcher couldn't abide the thought of distinguished Liberal Mark Bonham-Carter being promoted from vice-chairman.

Then there was Stuart Young, accountant and brother of one of Thatcher's staunchest cabinet allies, who succeeded Howard in 1983. He was followed in 1986 by Marmaduke Hussey, brother-in-law of another Cabinet Minister who was plucked from the obscurity of a directorship at Rupert Murdoch's *Times* Newspapers. According to Norman Tebbit, then Tory party chairman, Hussey was appointed 'to get in there and sort the place out, and in days not months.' Those were the days of nods and winks, of unbridled political collusion – not so much Tony's cronies as Maggie's baggage.[18]

As we saw above, commentators warned of the dangers to public broadcasting when the BBC's royal charter came up for renewal in January 2007. Since then, a BBC Trust has been appointed the task of upholding standards after the dissolution of the BBC's governors system. The public knows as little about the Trust as it did about the governors, the charter, or its renewal. And that is as it should be, from the point of view of power – the establishment is to be accepted, not understood. To encourage understanding is to invite challenge.

In reality, former BBC chairman Gavyn Davies was appointed by the British government. So was Greg Dyke. So were the BBC governors. And so were the current BBC Trust members and the current figures at the head of the BBC, establishment figures all. The BBC website lists the names of the Trustees and sketches out their backgrounds. But there is next to no public debate about who they are, whose interests they represent, and the influence of the political and economic networks to which they belong. At time of writing (March 2009), the Trustees are:

1   Sir Michael Lyons, Chair, who has held a number of executive and non-executive media and local government positions.
2   Dr Chitra Bharucha, Vice-Chair, a former consultant haematologist who now chairs General Medical Council panels that decide on the fitness of doctors to practise medicine, and who was previously a member of the Advertising Standards Authority (Broadcast) Council (2004–07).
3   Anthony Fry, senior managing director in the investment banking boutique, Evercore Partners. As Global Head of Media Business and European Head of Telecoms at Credit Suisse, he worked with a number of media organisations including the BBC, BSkyB and Vivendi.
4   Richard Tait, CBE, previously Editor-in-Chief of ITN (1995–2002) and Editor of Channel 4 News (1987–95).

5 Jeremy Peat, previously Group Chief Economist at the Royal Bank of Scotland (1993–2005).

6 Diane Coyle, an economist, member of the Competition Commission and former economics editor of the *Independent*.

7 Alison Hastings, a former regional newspaper editor who served on the Press Complaints Commission from 1999 to 2002.

8 Dame Patricia Hodgson, a former Chief Executive of the Independent Television Commission and a member of the Committee on Standards in Public Life.

9 Rotha Johnston, CBE, 'an entrepreneur in commerce and property' and a non-executive Director of Allied Irish Bank (UK) plc.

10 Janet Lewis-Jones, a trustee of the Baring Foundation and chair of the Membership Selection Panel of Glas Cymru (Welsh Water).

11 David Liddiment, a former Director of Programmes at ITV.

12 Mehmuda Mian, a solicitor and Independent Police Complaints Commissioner since 2004.[19]

There are no representatives from the trade unions, green pressure groups, development charities, child poverty groups or other grass-root organisations. We are to believe there is no reason to doubt that these Trust members are independent from the government that appointed them, and from the elite corporate and other interests that employ them. We are to believe, instead, that these privileged individuals will uphold fair and balanced reporting which displays not a hint of bias towards state ideology or economic orthodoxy in a world of rampant corporate power. Some thoughts are unthinkable; obviously true, but too threatening to be discussed.

'THEY KNOW THEY CAN TRUST US NOT TO BE REALLY IMPARTIAL'

The BBC was founded by Lord Reith in 1922 and immediately used as a propaganda weapon for the Baldwin government during the General Strike, when it was known by workers as the 'British Falsehood Corporation'. During the strike, no representative of organised labour was allowed to be heard on the BBC. Ramsay McDonald, the leader of the opposition, was also banned.

In their highly respected study of the British media, *Power Without Responsibility*, James Curran and Jean Seaton wrote of 'the continuous and insidious dependence of the Corporation [the BBC] on the government'.[20] Thus, at the start of the Second World War, an official wrote that the Ministry of Information 'recognised that for the purpose of war activities the BBC is to be regarded as a Government Department'. He added: 'I wouldn't put it quite like this in any public statement.'[21] For 40 years, from an office in Bush House in London, home of the BBC World Service, a brigadier passed on the names of applicants for editorial jobs in the BBC to MI5 for 'vetting'. John Pilger has reported: 'Journalists with a reputation for independence were refused BBC posts because they were not considered "safe".'[22]

In the leaked minutes of one of the BBC's weekly Review Board meetings during the Falklands war in 1982, BBC executives directed that the weight of their news coverage should be concerned 'primarily with government statements of policy'. An impartial style was felt to be 'an unnecessary irritation'. Prior to the opening of hostilities, a Peruvian plan for a negotiated settlement came close to success. On May 13, 1982, the former British prime minister, Edward Heath, told the broadcaster ITN that the Argentineans had requested three minor amendments to the peace plan. According to Heath these were so trivial they could not possibly be rejected, but prime minister Thatcher rejected them out of hand. The Heath interview was the only time the peace plan was mentioned on British television – the story was blanked.

More recently, a 2003 Cardiff University report found that the BBC 'displayed the most "pro-war" agenda of any broadcaster' on the Iraq invasion. Over the three weeks of the initial conflict, 11 per cent of the sources quoted by the BBC were of coalition government or military origin, the highest proportion of all the main television broadcasters. The BBC was less likely than Sky, ITV or Channel 4 News to use independent sources, who tended to be the most sceptical. The BBC also placed least emphasis on Iraqi casualties, which were mentioned in 22 per cent of its stories about the Iraqi people, and it was least likely to report on Iraqi opposition to the invasion.

On the eve of the invasion of Iraq, Andrew Bergin, the press officer for the Stop the War Coalition, told Media Lens: 'Representatives of the coalition have been invited to appear on every TV channel except the BBC. The BBC have taken a conscious decision to actively exclude Stop the War Coalition people from their programmes, even though everyone knows we are central to organising the massive anti-war movement...'.[23] David Miller of Strathclyde University, and co-founder of Spinwatch, concluded: 'BBC managers have fallen over themselves to grovel to the government in the aftermath of the Hutton whitewash ... When will their bosses apologise for conspiring to keep the anti war movement off the screens? Not any time soon.'[24] In a speech at New York's Columbia University, John Pilger commented:

> We now know that the BBC and other British media were used by MI6, the secret intelligence service. In what was called 'Operation Mass Appeal', MI6 agents planted stories about Saddam Hussein's weapons of mass destruction – such as weapons hidden in his palaces and in secret underground bunkers. All these stories were fake.[25]

In truth, the BBC's relationship with the establishment was accurately summarised long ago, in a single diary entry made by the BBC's own founder, Lord Reith: 'They know they can trust us not to be really impartial.'

THE BIAS IN DEFINING BALANCE

A key feature of BBC reporting is its selective labelling of bias. This is detected when powerful interests – notably the government and powerful corporations – are subject to criticism. By contrast, journalism that faithfully echoes the government line is viewed as neutral. Thus, the assumption that the US and UK governments are motivated by humanitarian concern in Iraq is a 'neutral' view – this can be asserted ad nauseam without provoking the slightest controversy. On the other hand, the idea that US policy is driven by strategic and economic considerations – regional influence and control of oil – is a 'biased' view that needs to be balanced or, more likely, ignored.

This understanding is so engrained in BBC journalists that they are barely able to comprehend the suggestion that government claims should be challenged. Thus, the BBC's Paul Reynolds wrote from Washington in 1999 of the NATO assault on Serbia:

> One often wonders why America bothers. Kosovo, after all, is a far away place of which they know little. And yet the crisis shows that there is room in this great land for a sense of justice and responsibility, just as there was in imperial Britain ... Great powers are capable of great oppressions, but also of great gestures. The Balkans, it seems, have not lost their fascination for the West, though luckily, this time round, the powers are not pitching in against each other as they did in 1914. Some progress has been made in this violent century.[26]

This would appear to suggest, would it not, that, unlike with Marr, the BBC surgeon had missed some of Reynolds' organs of opinion? And yet, when we later asked Reynolds if he thought George Bush hoped to create a genuine democracy in Iraq, he replied with admirable BBC discipline: 'I cannot get into a direct argument about his policies myself! Sorry.'[27] Reynolds explained to one of our readers: 'You are asking for my opinion about the war in Iraq yet BBC correspondents are not allowed to have opinions!'[28] But if Reynolds thought that, post-Serbia, the American obliteration of Iraq had provided further confirmation 'that there is room in this great land for a sense of justice and responsibility', who could possibly object to his reiteration of this neutral non-opinion?

Over footage of fighting between Iraqi militias, BBC reporter Paul Wood commented on the BBC's flagship News at Ten: 'This is not promising soil in which to plant a western-style open society.' Wood told his audience: 'The coalition came to Iraq in the first place to bring democracy and human rights.'[29] When we asked the BBC's director of news, Helen Boaden, if she thought this version of US–UK intent perhaps compromised the BBC's commitment to impartial reporting, she replied: 'Paul Wood's analysis of the underlying motivation of the coalition is borne out by many speeches and remarks made by both Mr Bush and Mr Blair.'[30] But as a matter of simple logic, it is clear that Wood was not merely describing Bush and Blair's version of events. That would have involved him saying: 'The coalition claim that it came to Iraq in the first place to bring democracy and human rights.' Instead, he was stating an opinion, his own, on why the 'coalition came to Iraq'. And if we are to take Boaden's comments at face value, she was arguing that Bush and Blair *must* have been motivated to bring democracy to Iraq, because they said so in speeches! Again, 'impartial' reporting means that we should take our leaders' claims on trust – to challenge the idea that they mean what they are saying is to stray into unprofessional bias.

Not only were Wood and Boaden's comments obviously biased in favour of a government that appoints their senior management and in which BBC journalists often go on to find employment; they were biased against the undeniable facts. When British and American forces 'came to Iraq in the first place' – a polite euphemism for what was actually an illegal invasion, a war crime – the stated reason was to disarm an alleged 'serious and current threat' to the West from Iraq's weapons of mass destruction. This was the 'single question' that mattered according to President Bush, Secretary of State Colin Powell and others.[31] Bush and Blair were careful to emphasise this purpose for one very good reason – they knew that to wage war in order to remove a sovereign government is a war crime. There could be no conceivable legal justification for such an act. Thus, the parliamentary motion Tony Blair supported in the House of Commons on 18 March 2003, on the eve of the invasion, concerned the proposal 'that the United Kingdom should use all means necessary to ensure the disarmament of Iraq's weapons of mass destruction'. From the perspective of international law, the overthrow of tyranny and its replacement by a democracy promoting Iraqi human rights were *not*, and could not have been, the issue.

When Boaden was challenged again, she replied: 'To deal first with your suggestion that it is factually incorrect to say that an aim of the British and American coalition was to bring democracy and human rights, this was indeed one of the stated aims before and at the start of the Iraq war – and I attach a number of quotes at the bottom of this reply.'[32] Remarkably, Boaden supplied no less than 2,700 words of quotes filling six pages from George Bush and Tony Blair to prove her point. It was an occasion when the argument was so foolish that further discussion seemed pointless. We wrote back anyway:

Dear Helen
Many thanks. It's an interesting argument. I look forward to the following opening statement on BBC's News at Ten: 'A recorded message believed to have been made by Al Qaeda leader, Osama bin Laden, has surfaced tonight. Bin Laden, whose forces originally attacked the United States on September 11, 2001 to bring freedom and human rights to the Middle East, said...'. Given that, like Bush and Blair, bin Laden has indeed claimed these goals in speeches, do you see any inherent problem with broadcasting this comment? If so, what?[33]

Boaden replied:

We have on numerous occasions sought to elucidate the motivation of Al Qaeda and Osama bin Laden. We have also on innumerable occasions examined the role, reasoning and the outcomes of US and UK actions in Iraq. The range of our reporting and programmes enables audiences to make up their own minds about the issue, just as you have done.[34]

Again, almost unbelievably, Boaden missed the point. The BBC would never dream of delivering bin Laden's benign claims as fact, although this is second nature where Western leaders are concerned. And this was no isolated example. The BBC news director even told one viewer who had challenged *Newsnight*: 'it is simply a fact that Bush has tried to export democracy [to Iraq] and that this has been troublesome'.

In a 2003 Panorama special, the BBC's Washington editor Matt Frei asserted: 'There's no doubt that the desire to bring good, to bring American values to the rest of the world, and especially now to the Middle East ... is now increasingly tied up with military power.'[35] When we challenged *Newsnight* editor, Peter Barron, to tell us whether he thought Frei's analysis was objective and balanced, he replied: 'I don't think it's right to challenge the assumption that he [Bush] wants democracy in Iraq.'[36] And yet, a year later, Helen Boaden wrote to a Media Lens reader: 'I think the key point that I would make in response is that it is not for the BBC to take a view about the legality of the war in Iraq ... it is not for the BBC to take a stance on the issue.'[37]

We asked Hugh Sykes, a BBC journalist reporting from Baghdad, for his opinion on the issue of legality in relation to the invasion of Iraq. He replied: 'The Americans et al always say they are here "at the invitation of the democratically elected Iraqi government". It certainly WAS an illegal occupation before the elections in 2005, but is it still illegal?'[38] Imagine a comparable comment from a BBC journalist in the 1980s: 'The Soviets et al always say they are here "at the invitation of the democratically elected Afghan government". It certainly WAS an illegal occupation before ... but is it still illegal?'

On his Sunday morning television show of September 25, 2005, Andrew Marr observed: '25,000 civilians have died in Iraq over the last two years.' We are supposed to believe that Marr, then the BBC's political editor, was expressing no personal opinion when he continued: 'About a third of those people were killed, no doubt in absolutely legitimate operations, by British and American soldiers.' At time of writing, 'absolutely legitimate operations' have made a major contribution to the deaths of around 1 million Iraqis as part of an illegal invasion.

An assistant editor on the BBC Radio 4 *Today* programme told one listener: 'You may well disagree, but I think there's a big difference between the aggressive "invasions" of dictators like Hitler and Saddam, and the "occupation" – however badly planned and executed – of a country for positive ends, as in the Coalition effort in Iraq.'[39] A February 1, 2006 BBC Radio 5 live phone-in discussion on Iraq, advertised the topic for the programme thus: 'Are 100 British soldiers' lives too high a price to pay for democracy in Iraq?'

We propose two thoughts for reflection here. First, observe the really amazing failure of BBC editors and journalists to notice how they continuously contradict their own claims to impartiality in a way that is almost comically biased in favour of powerful interests. Second, and a more deeply troubling point: these editors and journalists are referring to one of the most brazen, cynical and destructive acts of state violence the world has seen. So while we might find ourselves chuckling at the Keystone Cops-style confusion, we need to bear in mind that this performance in fact closely resembles the servility to power found in fascist and other totalitarian political systems. No threat of physical violence is involved; just a threat to career progression and financial security. The BBC's servility to power is mostly the product of a professional mindset that shares the values and assumptions of elite power. Auntie Beeb does not need Big Brother to keep her mind right.

THE REAL PROBLEM: LEFT BIAS

Despite a mountain of evidence suggesting the contrary – the material offered above and in the next chapter amounts to merely a tiny sample – the big discussion at the BBC concerns how to correct its malign tendency to be overly critical of powerful interests. In June 2007, the press described how a disturbing internal BBC report had revealed that the organisation was guilty of 'institutional left-wing bias' and, worse still, of 'being anti-American'.[40]

The *Daily Mail* reported the sombre news that 'senior figures at the corporation were forced to admit it was guilty of promoting Left-wing views and an anti-Christian sentiment'.[41] Understandable revulsion was expressed at the fact that a Christmas edition of the BBC1 comedy show, *The Vicar Of Dibley*, had featured a minute-long clip of a Make Poverty History video. This hardly advocated communist revolution, but it was bad enough. Tory MP Philip Davies was quoted: 'This report merely confirms what a load of people have thought for a long time, that the BBC does have an institutional Left-wing bias.'[42] Senior BBC managers and journalists were happy to expose the enemy within. The BBC's Justin Webb 'accused his own employers of being anti-American, saying they treated the nation with scorn and derision and "no moral weight"'.[43] Digging deep, former political editor, Andrew Marr, generated a personal opinion. He noted that the BBC is 'a publicly-funded urban organisation with an abnormally large proportion of younger people, of people in ethnic minorities and almost certainly of gay people, compared with the population at large'. All this, he said, 'creates an innate liberal bias inside the BBC'.[44] And who better to ask than Marr? Tim Luckhurst, a former BBC reporter and producer, wrote in the *Daily Mail* in 2005:

> Andrew Marr has dismayed licence-payers with apologias for New Labour in general and Tony Blair in particular. His repeated insistence that the Prime Minister did not lie about the legal advice he was given on the Iraq War has taken political coverage to a new low. Such conscientious rewriting of history deserves a place in George Orwell's 1984, not on a national television station funded by the taxpayer.[45]

It was, after all, Marr who wrote in the *Observer* of Blair: 'I am constantly impressed, but also mildly alarmed, by his utter lack of cynicism.'[46] Can it be a surprise that Blair shares Marr's views on journalism? In a speech at Reuters' headquarters in London, Blair condemned 'the increasingly shrill tenor of the traditional media'. The problem, he observed, is that it is not enough for journalists to expose the errors of public figures: 'It has to be venal. Conspiratorial.' Media scepticism is focused not just on the judgement of politicians, but on their motivation. The effect of this cynicism is devastating, Blair claimed: 'The damage saps the country's confidence and self-belief; it undermines its assessment of itself, its institutions; and above all, it reduces our capacity to take the right decisions, in the right spirit for our future.'[47]

Comments that can all be applied to Blair's own political performance.

AND DEFENDING THE BBC FROM THE LEFT

Environmental activist and *Guardian* columnist, George Monbiot, once commented: 'there is a very limited number of outlets that I would broadly describe as "free". By free I don't mean that the product is given away. I mean that it is free from the direct influence of private proprietors. I will give you a couple of examples from my own country. The most famous is the BBC.' Monbiot clarified: 'It is not free of all influence, by any means. It is run by the state and financed by a tax on the ownership of televisions, called the licence fee. From time to time it is spectacularly and disastrously disciplined by the government, generally acting in concert with the right-wing press.' He added: 'It [the BBC] operates in a hostile environment, and the perspectives of its enemies – the enemies of free speech – often inform its coverage of the world's affairs. But there is no proprietor to tell it "you cannot do such and such because that offends the interests of my shareholders".'[48]

Monbiot's observation that the BBC 'operates in a hostile environment' portrays the broadcaster as a valiant hero doing its best to provide a fair and impartial news service, while surrounded by corporate news beasts in every direction. As we have seen, the reality could hardly be more different. The BBC is a cornerstone of the establishment; the absence of a direct corporate proprietor makes no discernible difference at all.

In similar vein, Danny Schechter, director and founder of the news site MediaChannel.org, harbours a soft spot for 'Auntie Beeb'. Schechter's credentials as a robust media critic are near-legendary. And yet he wrote wide-eyed of a visit to London where he had been invited to tour the offices of BBC Online: 'With 170 staff members, it provides quality and credible news and information that does not rely on or simply relay the droppings of the two principal news agencies [Associated Press and Reuters]. All of the content is original, with frequent use of audio and video drawn from BBC reports and archives.' Schechter praised the 'savvy BBC veteran' responsible for the creation of the online BBC news service and quoted him, unchallenged, saying that the service has 'in-depth background reports' and boasts 'the kind of breadth and depth that we try to produce on all substantial international stories'. 'In short,' said Schechter, 'they [the BBC] take pains to explain news and respect the intelligence of their readers.' He praised 'this valuable service' as being of benefit to the millions of daily visitors to the BBC's site who want 'real news.'[49]

There is an understandable temptation to use another country's media as a club with which to beat the media of one's own country. The temptation is to be resisted, however. Instead, we need to consider the kind of evidence presented in this and the next chapter, and come to a rational judgement based on the facts.

3

Back-to-Back Bias:
An A–Z of BBC Propaganda

Our collection of BBC propaganda is sufficient to fill several volumes. The distortion is systemic, rooted in the very structure of the BBC – who it employs, how they are chosen, who does the choosing, and so on. Pick a topic and you will find the same bias, without fail, every time. Here, then, is our A–Z of BBC mendacity.

Andrew Marr's Meltdown Moment

We're cheating by using his first name, but Andrew Marr really does deserve to lead out the parade. One of us maintained a lonely vigil before a video recorder in the first half of 2003, taping a huge number of programmes: the lunchtime, early evening and late news on BBC1, BBC2, ITV and Channel 4. Unfortunately for Marr, our video was running when he made the following remarks outside Downing Street on the evening BBC1 News at Ten. The date was April 9, 2003 and US tanks were thundering into Baghdad. Marr said: 'Frankly, the main mood [in Downing Street] is of unbridled relief. I've been watching ministers wander around with smiles like split watermelons.'[1] Marr delivered this with his own happy smile, suggesting not just that he felt the same, but that we should all feel the same. He explored the significance of the fall of Baghdad:

> Well, I think this does one thing – it draws a line under what, before the war, had been a period of ... well, a faint air of pointlessness, almost, was hanging over Downing Street. There were all these slightly tawdry arguments and scandals. That is now history. Mr Blair is well aware that all his critics out there in the party and beyond aren't going to thank him – because they're only human – for being right when they've been wrong. And he knows that there might be trouble ahead, as I said. But I think this is very, very important for him. It gives him a new freedom and a new self-confidence. He confronted many critics. I don't think anybody after this is going to be able to say of Tony Blair that he's somebody who is driven by the drift of public opinion, or focus groups, or opinion polls. He took all of those on. He said that they would be able to take Baghdad without a bloodbath, and that in the end the

Iraqis would be celebrating. And on both of those points he has been proved conclusively right. And it would be entirely ungracious, even for his critics, not to acknowledge that tonight he stands as a larger man and a stronger prime minister as a result.

In his 2007 TV series, *Andrew Marr's History of Modern Britain*, Marr showed video footage of him making these comments and described it as an example of someone getting 'carried away'. Wikipedia suggested that it was 'perhaps an oblique acceptance' of the criticism we had made in our media alerts.[2] But although this was certainly a low point, it did not seem particularly extreme at the time in the context of Marr's, and the BBC's, reporting more generally (see 'Teflon Tony', below).

Beating the Bad Guys

On January 4, 2007, the press reported that nine British soldiers filmed beating 'Iraqis' – in fact, children or youths – would not face charges. The BBC commented: 'The footage showed Iraqis allegedly being kicked, punched and head-butted.'[3] In our dictionary, 'allege' is defined as: 'declare to be the case, especially without proof'. The public was able to decide for themselves if there was proof that British troops kicked, punched and head-butted the Iraqis.[4] The video evidence was impossible to deny.

An earlier BBC website article had reported: 'The Labour Deputy Prime Minister, John Prescott, has punched a protester who threw an egg at him during a visit to Rhyl in north Wales.'[5] We wrote to BBC online editor, Steve Herrmann, on January 5, 2007, and asked: 'Why was Prescott's punch not an 'alleged' punch? What is the difference in terms of proof?' Herrmann replied on January 12:

> Thanks for your recent note about our story 'No charges over Iraq video riots' http://news.bbc.co.uk/1/hi/uk/6230711.stm. When there are questions surrounding the provenance of material such as this video footage and when investigations are being conducted we tend in principle to be cautious in our use of language. However in this story the use of the word allegedly is, we agree, unnecessary and will be removed from our report. Thank you for bringing it to our attention.

Clones R Us

On June 18, 2002, we published a second media alert on the BBC series *The Century of the Self*. On the same day, we received this reply from Adam Curtis, writer and producer of the series: 'I don't know whether it occurred to you that I might have been away – instead of stamping your little feet and trying to whip up an attack of the clones. I've just read your piece – thanks and I'll reply to it on Thursday if that's ok? I've got to be filming before then.'[6]

Dalet: Plan D

It is not possible to understand the Israel–Palestine conflict without knowing that more than half of Palestine's native population, around 800,000 people, were uprooted by forces that were to become the Israeli army. The goal of 'Plan Dalet', or 'Plan D', in 1948 was to expel large numbers of Palestinians from Palestine. Israeli historian Ilan Pappé wrote that the Jewish leadership had a map showing clearly which parts of Palestine were coveted as the future Jewish state. The problem was that within the selected areas, the Jews were a minority of 40 per cent (660,000 Jews and 1 million Palestinians):

> But the leaders ... had foreseen this difficulty at the outset of the Zionist project in Palestine. The solution as they saw it was the enforced transfer of the indigenous population, so that a pure Jewish state could be established. On 10 March 1948, the Zionist leadership adopted the infamous Plan Dalet, which resulted in the ethnic cleansing of the areas regarded as the future Jewish state in Palestine.
>
> Palestine was not divided, it was destroyed, and most of its people expelled. These were the events which triggered the conflict that has lasted ever since.[7]

In his final ever political statement, Bertrand Russell wrote in January 1970:

> The tragedy of the people of Palestine is that their country was 'given' by a foreign power to another people for the creation of a new state. The result was that many hundreds of thousands of innocent people were made permanently homeless. With every new conflict their numbers increased. How much longer is the world willing to endure this spectacle of wanton cruelty? It is abundantly clear that the refugees have every right to the homeland from which they were driven, and the denial of this right is at the heart of the continuing conflict. No people anywhere in the world would accept being expelled en masse from their own country; how can anyone require the people of Palestine to accept a punishment which nobody else would

tolerate? A permanent just settlement of the refugees in their homeland is an essential ingredient of any genuine settlement in the Middle East.[8]

Few BBC viewers, listeners or readers have any idea of the ethnic cleansing at the heart of the conflict. The words 'Plan Dalet', for example, do not appear anywhere on the BBC website. We managed to find a single article mentioning the words 'Plan D'.

Embedded/Inbedded

In a BBC online article, *Newsnight* diplomatic editor Mark Urban was full of admiration for the US occupiers: 'You can marvel at the Americans' can-do spirit, as some British soldiers do. You can see it in terms of America, the world's hyper power, staring failure in the face and refusing to accept it. But in the sergeant's case the will to carry on comes from a sense of responsibility towards the people of Iraq.'[9] Urban was actually discomfited by the quality of the men he met:

> From the odd glimpse or overheard remark, I do not doubt that the second platoon contains the odd bad apple or loud-mouth, but as my time with them went on I became aware of an uncomfortable feeling.
> When eventually I was able to identify it, I realised my unease concerned British soldiers, and how they compared with these Americans. Carlisle, Perez and the rest seem brighter, stronger and more committed.[10]

In the same month that Urban's report was broadcast, a Pentagon survey of US troops in combat in Iraq found that less than half of soldiers and marines said they felt they should treat non-combatants with respect. Only about half said they would report a member of their unit for killing or wounding an innocent civilian. More than 40 per cent supported the idea of torture.[11] In testifying for Iraq Veterans Against the War, Jon Turner, who fought with the Marine Corps, described how he had personally killed several innocent Iraqis. He noted that he and other marines killed innocent civilians even when CBS journalist Laura Logan was nearby, visiting a different section of his unit. Turner reported:

> we went ahead and took out some individuals because we were excited by a firefight we had just gotten into. And we didn't have a cameraman or woman with us. Anytime we did have embedded reporters with us, our actions changed dramatically. We never acted the same. We were always on key with everything, did everything by the book.[12]

Mark Urban is a professional journalist with the huge resources of the BBC at his disposal for research, analysis, contacting veterans, seeking experts' views. But it was somehow beyond him to imagine that just maybe he was being sold an illusion by the US military in Iraq. Unintended dark humour was provided by the fact that Urban's depiction of the American army as a benevolent peacekeeping force was presented from an armoured Humvee, call sign: 'Hellstorm Seven'.

Fallujah: Evidence-Based Journalism (Sometimes)

When challenged about the BBC's skewed coverage of the brutal US assaults on Fallujah, Iraq, the BBC's director of news, Helen Boaden, declared: 'We are committed to evidence-based journalism. We have not been able to establish that the US used banned chemical weapons and committed other atrocities against civilians in Falluja last November [2004]. Inquiries on the ground at the time and subsequently indicate that their use is unlikely to have occurred.'[13] In fact, atrocities *had* taken place and banned chemical weapons – specifically, white phosphorus (WP) – had been used. It took internet bloggers, rather than mainstream journalists, to discover that the March 2005 edition of the US journal *Field Artillery* contained these comments from officers of the US 2nd Infantry's fire support element, describing their role in the November 2004 attack on Fallujah:

> WP proved to be an effective and versatile munition. We used it ... as a potent psychological weapon against the insurgents in trench lines and spider holes when we could not get effects on them with HE [high explosive]. We fired 'shake and bake' missions at the insurgents, using WP to flush them out and HE to take them out.[14]

The BBC had consistently overlooked credible testimony from multiple sources strongly suggesting that this was the case. Fallujah had been placed under 'a strict night-time shoot-to-kill curfew' with 'anyone spotted in the soldiers' night vision sights ... shot'.[15] Male refugees were prevented from leaving the combat zone. A health centre was bombed, killing 60 patients and support staff. Refugees claimed that 'a large number of people, including children, were killed by American snipers' and that the US had used cluster bombs and white phosphorus weapons in the offensive.[16] A Red Cross official estimated that 'at least 800 civilians' were killed in the first nine days of the November 2004 assault on Fallujah.[17] Dr Rafa'ah al-Iyssaue, the director of Fallujah's main hospital, said that most of the dead were women and children.[18]

BBC correspondent Paul Wood, who had been embedded with US forces in Fallujah, and who had failed to report their crimes, excused himself and the BBC with these words: 'We didn't at the time, last November, report the use of banned weapons or a massacre because we didn't see this taking place – and since then, we haven't seen credible evidence that this is what happened.'[19] Wood had earlier dismissed reports of the use of banned weapons in Fallujah on the grounds that no 'reference [was] made to them at the confidential pre-assault military briefings [I] attended'.[20] When we pressed Helen Boaden, citing further independent reports of atrocities committed against civilians, she abruptly ended the correspondence: 'I do not believe that further dialogue on this matter will serve a useful purpose.'[21]

In 2008, Wood returned to the topic of Fallujah in a 40-minute BBC Radio 4 documentary that again displayed bias towards the US military. The independent US journalist Dahr Jamail told us he was particularly appalled to hear Wood report: 'If children were killed in Fallujah, it was because fathers had stayed behind to defend their homes.'[22] Jamail asked: 'How can this kind of "journalism" be taken seriously?'[23]

Gaza: No – Kosovo: Yes

On December 27, 2008, Israel began a 22-day attack on Gaza killing upwards of 1,400 people and wounding 5,000. To many witnessing the massacre, this appeared to be an act of state sadism. Israeli forces repeatedly bombed schools (including UN schools), medical centres, hospitals, ambulances, UN buildings, power plants, sewage plants, roads, bridges and civilian homes. The *Observer* reported that between 35 and 60 per cent of the agriculture industry in Gaza was wrecked by the Israeli attack. Scores, perhaps hundreds, of wells and water sources were damaged and several hundred greenhouses flattened, as well as severe damage inflicted on between a third and one-half of Gaza's farmable land.[24]

Despite this carnage, and despite the fact that 89 per cent of Gaza's 1.5 million residents had received no humanitarian aid since Israel began its assault, the BBC refused to broadcast a national humanitarian appeal for Gaza by the Disasters Emergency Committee (DEC), an umbrella organisation for 13 aid charities. By refusing to give free airtime to the appeal, the BBC made a rare decision to breach an agreement dating back to 1963. Other broadcasters then also rejected the appeal. A January 22 BBC website article defended the

BBC's refusal: 'The BBC decision was made because of question marks about the delivery of aid in a volatile situation and also to avoid any risk of compromising public confidence in the BBC's impartiality in the context of an ongoing news story.'[25]

And yet, in 1999, the BBC had allowed its own high-profile newsreader, Jill Dando, to present a DEC appeal for Kosovo at the height of NATO's 78-day bombing campaign against Serbia. This, also, was an ongoing and highly controversial conflict, one that involved fraudulent US–UK government and media claims of a Serbian 'genocide' in Kosovo (claims which have since been quietly abandoned). Shortly after broadcasting the appeal, with bombing still underway, the BBC reported: 'Millions of pounds of donations have been flooding in to help the Kosovo refugees after a national television appeal for funds.'[26] This article linked to related reports on the conflict, which included comments from then prime minister Tony Blair: 'This will be a daily pounding until he [Serbian leader Slobodan Milošović] comes into line with the terms that Nato has laid down.'[27]

The BBC apparently had no concerns that this might damage its alleged reputation for impartiality.

Hiroshima

The deliberate targeting of civilians in war is deemed a heinous crime by most sane people. Few would argue that the slaughter of 52 civilians in London on July 7, 2005 was a justifiable act of war in response to British and US atrocities in Iraq, Afghanistan and elsewhere. Who, then, would seek to justify the destruction of an entire city of civilians in Hiroshima, the equivalent of nearly 2,700 July 7 attacks? And yet, on the day marking the sixtieth anniversary of the bombing, the BBC reported blandly: 'There is continuing controversy over whether the bomb constituted a war crime, but many commentators believe the US attack helped bring an early end to World War II in the Pacific.'[28]

If igniting an atomic fireball in the heart of a city that kills around 100,000 men, women and children is not a war crime, then what is?[29] And in fact 'many commentators' also *challenge* both the view that the bombing brought an early end to the war, and the claim that, even if it had, this would have provided moral justification for incinerating a city full of civilians. Historian Gar Alperovitz has long argued that the atomic bombings of Hiroshima and Nagasaki were an obscenity of realpolitik intended primarily to intimidate the

Soviet Union.[30] There is considerable evidence that a major concern for President Truman was that Stalin would shortly enter the war in the Pacific region against Japan and make important strategic gains in Asia, thus threatening US interests.

Tsuyoshi Hasegawa, professor of history at the University of California at Santa Barbara, has written that 'one cannot escape the conclusion that the United States rushed to drop the bomb without any attempt to explore the readiness of some Japanese policymakers to seek peace'.[31] He added: 'Justifying Hiroshima and Nagasaki by making a historically unsustainable argument that the atomic bombs ended the war is no longer tenable.'[32]

Iran: Official Enemy

States designated as official enemies by Washington and London quickly become targets for the BBC. The BBC1 lunchtime news on January 20, 2005, saw diplomatic correspondent James Robbins declare that US relations with Iran were 'looking very murky because of the nuclear threat'. There was then (as now), zero evidence that Iran was developing nuclear bombs, much less that it presented a nuclear threat. An April 2006 BBC online article reported: 'Mid-East executions are condemned':

> Amnesty International has said that Iran executed 94 people in 2005, while 86 were executed in Saudi Arabia. Iran, the rights group said, was the only country known to have executed juvenile offenders in 2005. At least eight people were killed for crimes committed when they were children, including two who were still under 18 at the time of execution. Some detainees in Saudi Arabia had been tried and sentenced in a language they did not speak or read.[33]

But the Amnesty report in question focused collectively on China, Iran, Saudi Arabia and the United States, before focusing in separate paragraphs on China – 'the country that accounts for almost 80% of all executions' – on Saudi Arabia, on the United States, and only *then* on Iran. Unlike Amnesty, the BBC chose to highlight the record of Iran – a country under serious threat of attack by the United States, Britain and Israel.

Johns Hopkins University: Out of Line

In 2005, the BBC made a few sceptical mentions of the November 2004 *Lancet* report of 100,000 excess Iraqi deaths since March 2003.

The BBC preferred instead to cite the far less credible, and much lower, number from Iraq Body Count (IBC). In October 2005, a year after the *Lancet* report appeared, the BBC News website noted: 'Unofficial estimates put Iraqi civilian deaths since the war at about 25,000.'[34] This was a reference to IBC's figure. And yet IBC only recorded civilian deaths as the result of violence, and only as reported by at least two media sources – it was not attempting to provide an estimate for *all* civilian deaths. When asked why this low figure was used when the 100,000 figure from the *Lancet* report was available, the BBC responded: 'The figures it [the *Lancet* report] details are now around one year old where as those produced by Iraq Body Count are continually updated.'[35] This was apparently not an attempt at humour.

That same month, Tarik Kafala, Middle East Editor of the BBC News website, wrote to one of our readers:

> We do not usually use the Lancet's figure in standard news stories because it is so far out of line with other studies on the same issue. There are also some questions over the validity of the Lancet study in the case of measuring casualties in Iraq. The technique of sampling and extrapolating from samples has been criticised in this case because the pattern of violence in Iraq has been so uneven.[36]

It is hard to believe, but Kafala was here writing of a study led by Johns Hopkins University in Baltimore, Maryland – one of the world's premier research organisations – and published in one of the world's most highly respected science journals.

Kosovo

Exposed, a BBC documentary on the alleged Serbian genocide of Kosovar civilians, broadcast on January 27, 2002, was billed as a programme marking Holocaust Memorial Day. Imagine the BBC showing a documentary on the Hiroshima and Nagasaki attacks to mark Holocaust Memorial Day. As we discussed in *Guardians of Power*, following the war, NATO sources reported that 2,000 people had been killed in Kosovo on all sides in the year prior to bombing. By contrast, the American atomic attacks on Hiroshima and Nagasaki had killed perhaps 220,000 men, women and children by the end of 1945.[37]

Lebanon: Crushing the 'Scorpions'

BBC online reported US–UK obstruction of attempts to halt Israel's 2006 assault on Lebanon in an article entitled '"World backs Lebanon offensive"', quoting the Israeli view as the title. The article reported: 'Israel says diplomats' failure to call for a halt to its Lebanon offensive ... has given it the green light to continue.' The BBC cited Israel's Justice Minister Haim Ramon: 'We received yesterday at the Rome conference permission from the world ... to continue the operation.'[38] Not only did the BBC's title give credence to this outrageous lie but no contradictory viewpoints were provided anywhere in the piece. Ramon was even given space to argue, again without challenge: 'All those now in south Lebanon are terrorists who are related in some way to Hezbollah.' Three days later, 28 of these 'terrorists', including 16 children, were bombed to death in Qana.

The BBC's security correspondent Frank Gardner reported that Israeli critics likened the Israeli army's campaign against Hezbollah to someone 'using a sledgehammer to kill a scorpion' – 'quite a good analogy', Gardner observed.[39] Imagine if a BBC journalist expressed approval for a Hezbollah description of Israeli forces as vermin to be crushed. But Hezbollah, like Hamas, and like insurgents in Iraq and Afghanistan, are consistently treated as less than human by our media. For example, it almost never occurred to journalists to bother to estimate Hezbollah's military casualties in 2006. Every Israeli, British or American military death is worthy news – but not the dead on the other side.

Massacre in Haditha

The title of a 2006 BBC news report by Washington correspondent, Matt Frei, on the massacre of Iraqi civilians at Haditha was suitably 'balanced': 'Iraqi Deaths'. Not 'US Massacre'. Not 'Haditha Massacre'. Not 'US Civilian Killings'. Just 'Iraqi Deaths'. News anchor George Alagiah introduced the piece: 'The US military is preparing to announce charges against a group of marines accused of killing Iraqi civilians. More than 20 people, some of them children, died in Haditha a year ago. But it's not clear whether they were killed deliberately.'[40] As even the report that followed this introduction made clear, this last sentence was a lie – it *was* very clear that civilians were deliberately killed in Haditha. The previous May, the *New York Times* reported that the slaughter had been 'methodical in nature'.[41] The *Los Angeles Times* reported that month that many of the victims had been killed 'execution-style', shot in the head or in the back. Even a US government official accepted that the US marines had 'suffered a total breakdown in morality and leadership, with tragic results'.[42]

Eman Waleed, aged nine, a survivor of the atrocity, was interviewed by *Time* magazine. She said she had 'heard a lot of shooting, so none of us went outside. Besides, it was very early, and we were all wearing our nightclothes.' US marines then entered her family's house: 'First, they went into my father's room, where he was reading the Qur'an', she said, 'and we heard shots'. Next, the marines entered the living room: 'I couldn't see their faces very well – only their guns sticking into the doorway. I watched them shoot my grandfather, first in the chest and then in the head. Then they killed my granny.'[43]

Two days before Alagiah's introduction to Frei's report, Iraqi prime minister Nuri al-Maliki had called the Haditha killings a 'terrible crime'.[44] None of this was sufficient for the BBC which, as BBC online editor Steve Herrmann noted, likes 'to be cautious in [its] use of language'. Flatly contradicting the BBC's own introduction to his report, Frei reported: 'November 2005, the aftermath of a massacre in Haditha. 24 civilians were slaughtered – the oldest was in his seventies, the youngest three.' Frei concluded: 'Whatever the charges today, Haditha has left the marine corps and America with a very painful question they thought they'd never have to ask: How and why have the liberators ended up killing the liberated?'[45]

As ever, it was not considered biased for a BBC reporter to describe the US superpower army as 'liberators', or the country it had illegally invaded as 'liberated' – no one blinked an eye. The answer to Frei's question was provided by Michael Prysner, who fought with the US 173rd Airborne Brigade in Iraq: 'We were told we were fighting terrorists; the real terrorist was me, and the real terrorism is this occupation.'[46] This would be entirely obvious to BBC journalists like Frei, if they were reporting on any great power other than their own government's leading partner in crime.

Newsnight

As late as September 2008, the BBC's *Newsnight* team felt able to post this message on the BBC website:

> We are producing a special programme tonight called 'Beyond the War on Terror'. We are building this around Mark Urban's interview with General Petraeus in Baghdad, and two films he has done, which ask – is it in any way possible for America to say it has won the war on terror, and how will the fight against terrorism be re-focussed beyond the Bush presidency. There's still a lot for us to do on the day, so let's really try and make this sparkling.[47]

Petraeus was then leading America's occupation of Iraq, and Iraq had nothing whatever to do with the 'war on terror'. The Iraqi government under Saddam Hussein played no part at all in the September 11 attacks, was a bitter enemy of Al Qaeda, and had never attacked America or Britain. But as we have seen, it is 'balanced' reporting for the BBC to allow British and American leaders to frame reality without challenge.

Oil

In 2007, BBC business reporter Robert Plummer gave the standard benign BBC version of US motives in Iraq: 'Now the US wants Iraq to pass an oil law as a means of promoting reconciliation among different religious and ethnic groups.'[48] We emailed Plummer: 'What evidence do you have that the US administration desires the oil law "as a means of promoting reconciliation"? Surely you would agree that is rather different from reporting that the US *claims* that is their aim?'[49] We pointed out that environmental social justice group, PLATFORM, had argued that the 'law has been wrongly described as providing a mechanism for sharing revenue among Iraq's sectarian groups; in fact, this law does not deal with that issue, which will be the subject of a separate law, not yet drafted'.[50]

Plummer told us: 'Never let it be said that we ignore the views of our readers. I have now amended the sentence in question to read: "Now the US wants Iraq to pass an oil law, as *what it says is* a means of promoting reconciliation among different religious and ethnic groups." I trust that meets with your approval.'[51] We replied: 'Many thanks for doing that. It's a small but important difference. After the disaster that has befallen Iraq – and with Iran now in the crosshairs – it's surely vital for all of us to regard any professed government aims and pronouncements with scepticism, and to shine a light on the underlying motivations that drive state policy.'[52]

Pinochet

In December 2006, BBC correspondent Bridget Kendall stunned the nation with her pinpoint pronunciation as she described the death of Chilean tyrant Augusto Pinochet – pronounced 'Pee-nochet' by the BBC reporter. Kendall got the diction right, but everything else was 'a big bowl of wrong': Pee-nochet's rise to power was discussed, as were his crimes, as were the failed attempts to hold him accountable. But of the power behind the throne, the nation that birthed this monster, there was not a word.[53]

In fact Pinochet was a creature of US power. He was trained, financed, armed and installed by the superpower at the behest of US corporations who feared for their profits under the socialist Salvador Allende. It was an ugly, if unexceptional story of mass murder for profit, and deemed unsuitable for the tender minds of the BBC's audience.

Kendall concluded her piece thus: 'To the very end judgements on Augusto Pinochet remained keenly divided.' That can be said of a mass murderer like Pinochet, a Western ally, but not of official enemies. Imagine Kendall pointing out: 'To the very end judgements on Saddam Hussein remained keenly divided.' The point being that opinion is not divided among the people who matter. A BBC online obituary was fractionally bolder: 'It became known later that the CIA had spent millions to destabilise the Allende government.'[54] That, again, was that. Quite what the CIA had spent millions on was left to the reader's imagination. Perhaps opposition politicians were funded. Perhaps propaganda messages were ruthlessly posted around Santiago. Who knows?

Questioning George Galloway

We are to believe that the BBC's 'attack dog' interviewers are the jewel in Auntie Beeb's dissident crown. Dan Sabbagh wrote in *The Times*: 'They are the BBC's "news Rottweilers", the aggressive interviewers and hosts who are popular with the public for refusing to let politicians get away with evasions or pre-rehearsed answers.'[55] The four 'attack dogs' named were John Humphrys, Jeremy Paxman, James Naughtie and David Dimbleby.

This is the conventional media view. In reality, leading politicians are treated with comparative respect and without insinuation that the interviewee is despicable or malevolent. No such considerations apply when the media confront 'rogues' or 'mavericks' who represent a challenge to the establishment.

In the early hours of the morning after Britain's May 5, 2005 general election, viewers were treated to a dramatic exchange between the BBC's principal 'Rottweiler', Jeremy Paxman, and George Galloway, the former Labour MP then representing the anti-war Respect party. Galloway had just deposed the Blairite Labour MP, Oona King, in the Bethnal Green and Bow constituency of East London. Galloway's victory was considerable, overturning a 10,000 majority in the face of the full might of New Labour's political machine. Thousands of London's voters opposed to the Iraq war had clearly made a statement, one shared by millions of people around the country. Paxman somehow missed this salient fact and instead asked:

> Jeremy Paxman: 'Mr Galloway, are you proud of having got rid of one of the very few black women in Parliament?'
>
> George Galloway: 'What a preposterous question. I know it's very late in the night, but wouldn't you be better starting by congratulating me for one of the most sensational election results in modern history?'
>
> JP: 'Are you proud of having got rid of one of the very few black women in Parliament?'
>
> GG: 'I'm not [pause]... Jeremy, move on to your next question.'
>
> JP: 'You're not answering that one?'
>
> GG: 'No, because I don't believe that people get elected because of the colour of their skin. I believe people get elected because of their record and because of their policies. So move on to your next question.'[56]

Moments later, Paxman said: 'I put it to you Mr Galloway that [former local government minister] Nick Raynsford had you to a T when he said you were a "demagogue".' As far as we are aware, Paxman has never 'put it' to any leading pro-war government minister that he or she is a 'demagogue', despite an abundance of evidence that media-amplified propaganda and demagoguery enabled the war on Iraq, as well as earlier attacks on Afghanistan and Serbia.

By contrast, this was Paxman's response to Tony Blair's final, emotional speech to Labour Party delegates: 'Blair's speech was, for my money, the most impressive conference speech in years. In a performance brimming with confidence, flashes of humour and underlain by a clear political analysis (whether you agreed with it or not) he said goodbye to Labour delegates here in Manchester.'[57] One might wonder how a speech that failed to address the staggering catastrophes of Iraq and Afghanistan with even a scintilla of honesty could be deemed 'impressive', as opposed to mendacious, cynical and morally debased.

In a rare *Newsnight* interview with Noam Chomsky in May 2004, Paxman observed: 'You seem to be suggesting or implying, perhaps I'm being unfair to you, but you seem to be implying there is some moral equivalence between democratically elected heads of state like George Bush or Prime Ministers like Tony Blair and regimes in places like Iraq.'[58] This recalled a question posed by the BBC's Michael Buerk when interviewing former UN Assistant Secretary-General Denis Halliday in a BBC radio interview in 2001: 'You can't ...

you can't *possibly* draw a moral equivalence between Saddam Hussein and George Bush Senior, can you?'[59]

Robots R Us

In response to our September 18, 2007 alert, 'The Media Ignore Credible Poll Revealing 1.2 Million Violent Deaths In Iraq', BBC *Newsnight* presenter Gavin Esler sent the following response to one Media Lens reader:

> Sorry but this medialens inspired stuff is very sophomoric. The last time I remember a robotic response from people like this was watching film of the Nuremberg rallies. I always wondered why people marched to another's beat without any obvious thought from themselves. Perhaps you know the answer, or perhaps you merely intend to keep marching.
>
> Please don't write to me again in someone else's words. It is so embarrassing for you. Please learn to think for yourself.

Esler's 'robotic' respondents, in fact, were members of the public who cared enough about the devastating impact of corporate media bias to spend time writing to journalists. The polite and thoughtful email that elicited this response was sent by an MA student at Durham University. You can read his email here: http://www.medialens.org/forum/viewtopic.php?t=2611

Suharto and Saddam

Jonathan Head wrote on the BBC website of the deceased Indonesian dictator and prime Western ally, Suharto: 'His accession to power coincided with the escalation of the Vietnam War, when the United States was desperate for reliable allies in the region and willing to turn a blind eye to his human rights record.'[60] In fact, the United States did far more than 'turn a blind eye'; it played a key role in bringing Suharto to power, and in providing weapons for his genocidal army. The M16 guns Suharto's troops used were American; the Hawk jets that bombed East Timor were British. But East Timor was not so much as mentioned in Head's high-profile BBC report.

When challenged by a reader, Head replied: 'I think it is entirely inappropriate to rank Suharto alongside Sadaam [*sic*] Hussein. There was never anything like the pervasive terror here that existed in Iraq. I in no way wish to diminish the enormous suffering of many Indonesians under his rule.'[61] By contrast, the BBC website's reporting of the judgement to lynch Saddam Hussein was big, bold and more triumphal than neutral: 'Celebrations hail Saddam verdict in Baghdad's Shia-dominated Sadr City'.[62]

The following day, the *New York Times* website echoed the emphasis. But even America's infamous 'newspaper of record' found space for a more realistic version of events than the BBC: 'In a Divided Iraq, Reaction to Saddam Death Sentence Conforms to Sectarian Lines – The guilty verdict was met with carefree celebration in Shiite towns and brooding bitterness in Sunni ones.'[63]

Teflon Tony: Nat And Nick

As US tanks entered Baghdad on April 9, 2003, the BBC's Breakfast News presenter, Natasha Kaplinsky, beamed as she described how Tony Blair 'has become, again, Teflon Tony'. The BBC's royal and diplomatic correspondent, Nicholas Witchell, agreed: 'It is absolutely, without a doubt, a vindication of the strategy.'[64] Much later, Jason Washburn, who fought with the US Marines in Iraq during the invasion, helped put this BBC triumphalism in perspective when he described the 'Rules of Engagement' that were applied to cities containing 'known threats', like Baghdad: 'It was deemed to be a free-fire zone, so we opened fire on everything, and there was really no rule governing the amount of force we were allowed to use on targets during the invasion.'[65]

A week before Kaplinsky and Witchell made their comments, Red Cross doctors reported 'incredible' levels of civilian casualties. Roland Huguenin, one of six International Red Cross workers, said:

> There has been an incredible number of casualties with very, very serious wounds in the region of Hilla. We saw that a truck was delivering dozens of totally dismembered dead bodies of women and children. It was an awful sight. It was really very difficult to believe this was happening. Everybody had very serious wounds and many, many of them small kids and women. We had small toddlers of two or three years of age who had lost their legs, their arms.[66]

So who were these BBC journalists taking the momentous decision of vindicating Blair's war crimes to a national TV audience? Kaplinsky has starred in, and presented, the celebrity ballroom dancing competition *Strictly Come Dancing*. She has also hosted *Making Your Mind Up*, the UK qualifier for the Eurovision Song Contest. In 2005, the BBC reported that the presenter had married investment banker, Justin Bower. Kaplinsky wore 'a white satin gown by Kruszynska Couture'.[67]

The BBC website notes that Witchell was 'the first journalist to broadcast the confirmed news of the death of Diana, Princess of Wales and provided live radio commentary from outside Westminster Abbey at her funeral'. He is a Governor of Queen Elizabeth's Foundation, an Officer of the Order of St John and a Fellow of the Royal Geographical Society. He is also the author of *The Loch Ness Story* (Corgi, 1989). On October 1, 2004, Witchell reported that a series of insurgent car bombs in Baghdad were 'intended to undermine the future'.[68] Not to undermine the intended *American* future for Iraq, notice, but to undermine the future itself.

On the BBC1 News at Ten on September 23, 2004, Witchell said of attempts to crush the Iraqi insurgency: 'Dr. Allawi [leader of the Iraqi interim government] may say, "we're winning," and there may be a time soon when that claim is more obviously justifiable. If that time arrives, there is no doubt that the overwhelming majority of Iraqis will be delighted.' We wrote to him a day later: 'The suggestion that the US-backed interim government has the support of the "overwhelming majority of Iraqis" is remarkable. I have seen no evidence to support this claim. Could you provide sources for this view, please?' Witchell replied the same day: 'The meaning of what I said is perfectly clear: that the overwhelming majority of Iraqis will be pleased if security and stability is established. It was in no way a statement which implies any endorsement of Allawi's interim government.'

Mark Urban: Here To Help

On the May 14, 2007 edition of the BBC's flagship news programme, *Newsnight*, Mark Urban reported from Iraq that the US troop 'surge' was an attempt to 'turn the tide of violence' in Baghdad. Be in no doubt, Urban did not mean the 'surge' was an attempt to turn the tide of violence in America's favour – he meant it was an attempt to *end* the violence. He made his opinion clear, referring to 'Baghdad's sectarian nightmare' and to the 'American struggle to stop [Baghdad's] descent into mayhem'. He added:

> Clearly a lot of people are supporting the insurgents. And that's really the essence of all this – whether the Americans, with all their concerns for their own safety when they go into such dangerous neighbourhoods, can actually communicate the message that they're here to help, and that they *can* turn the tide in one of these really violent districts of the city.[69]

We wrote to Urban on May 15:

> It seems to me that you gave the strong impression that the Americans are essentially a peacekeeping force in Iraq. Of course one might argue that the 'surge' is indeed designed to reduce sectarian violence. But isn't it also unarguable that the 'surge' is part of a US effort to defeat Iraqi armed opposition to its occupation? In other words, isn't it unarguable that the Americans are *not* merely 'here to help', to keep the peace – they are in Iraq to wage war on an insurgency?[70]

Urban's response on May 31 included this point:

> I am clear, on the basis of spending time on operations with the soldiers in Dura, that they sincerely believed their mission to be one of trying to help local people defeat sectarian murder squads as well as turning them against 'al-Qaeda in Iraq' elements in the sunni community. Of course US forces in Iraq have other tasks too, including hunting the al-Qaeda leadership or countering Iranian influence. We report on these other missions as well. On this latest trip, it was my duty to investigate the working on the ground of that surge and security plan – since US and Iraqi authorities all agree that this is their main security priority of the moment.
>
> I know from some of the other comment I have received that embedded coverage with the US Army rankles with many medialens users.

In response to Urban's reply, which we published as part of a media alert, we received this email from a serving British Army officer. The officer gave us permission to publish his message and asked to remain anonymous (we were able to verify his identity):

> I am a serving British Army officer with operational experience in a number of theatres. I am concerned regarding the effect of your recent reports from Baghdad. I have been forwarded the correspondence between yourself and David Edwards of medialens.org, and would like to highlight that it is not merely medialens users who are concerned about embedded coverage with the US Army. The intentions and continuing effects of the US-led invasion and subsequent occupation of Iraq have been questioned by too few people in the mainstream media and political parties, primarily only the Guardian and Independent, and the Liberal Democrats, respectively.
>
> There is a widespread, and well-sourced, belief, based on both experience and evidence, in both the British military and academia, that the US is not 'just in Iraq to keep the peace, regardless of what the troops on the ground

believe. It is in Iraq to establish a client state amenable to the requirements of US realpolitik in a key, oil-rich region. To doubt this is to be ignorant of the motives that have guided US foreign policy in the post-war period and a mountain of evidence since 2003.' (quote from medialens)

That the invasion was 'illegal, immoral and unwinnable', and the 'greatest foreign policy blunder since Suez' – to paraphrase the Liberal Democrats – is the overwhelming feeling of many of my peers, and they speak of loathsome six-month tours, during which they led patrols with dread and fear, reluctantly providing target practice for insurgents, senselessly haemorrhaging casualties, and squandering soldiers' lives, as part of Bush's vain attempt to delay the inevitable Anglo-US rout until after the next US election. Given a free choice most of us would never have invaded Iraq, and certainly would have withdrawn long ago. Hopefully, Tony Blair's handover to Gordon Brown will herald a change of policy, and rapid withdrawal, but skewed pro-US coverage inhibits proper public debate, and is deeply unhealthy; lethally so to many of us deployed to Iraq.

The [inadvertent] dangers of bias of embedded journalism are well known and there is a risk that the 'official line' can be conflated with evidence and facts. Jon Snow graphically demonstrated the effect of this during the initial invasion of Iraq in his programme The True Face of War. I am conscious that reporting independently, outside of the 'green zone' in Iraq, is nigh on impossible, but I would merely request that the 'official line/White House propaganda' be handled with an appropriate degree of scepticism, and be caveated accordingly.[71]

Echoing Urban, James Robbins described the 'surge' as 'a strategy designed to overwhelm the violence'.[72] The illegal American invaders, then, were not themselves engaged in violence; they were engaged solely in preventing violence. The propaganda was boosted by another BBC report: 'The surge was designed to allow space for political reconciliation.'[73] Once again, the BBC was presenting US pronouncements as fact. On September 6, 2007, a piece by BBC business reporter Robert Plummer, entitled 'Little progress on halting Iraq's decay', appeared on the BBC news online website.[74]

Compare these visions of benign US intent to merely reduce violence through the application of violence, with George Bush's actual approach. The *Independent* reported revelations made by Lt Gen Ricardo Sanchez, the US commander in Iraq in 2003–04. In his memoirs, *Wiser in Battle*, Sanchez described how Bush personally ordered Shia leader Moqtadr al Sadr to be captured or killed. During a video conference on April 7, 2004, Bush said: 'The Mehdi Army is a hostile force. We can't allow one man [Sadr] to change the course of the country. At the end of this campaign Sadr must be gone. At a minimum he will be arrested. It is essential he be wiped out.' Bush emphasised the point: 'Stay strong! Stay the course! Kill them! Prevail! We are going to wipe them out! We are not blinking!'[75]

Venezuela: 'Controversial' Chavez

Controlling what we think is not solely a matter of controlling what we know – it is also about influencing who we respect and who we find ridiculous. Western leaders are typically reported without adjectives preceding their names. Obama is simply 'US president Barack Obama'. Gordon Brown is the 'British prime minister'. The leader of Venezuela, by contrast, is 'controversial left-wing president Hugo Chavez' for BBC1 news.[76] He is an 'extreme left-winger', while Bolivian president Evo Morales is 'a radical socialist', according to Jonathan Charles on BBC Radio 4.[77]

Imagine the BBC introducing the former US leader as 'controversial right-wing president George Bush', or as an 'extreme right-winger'. Was Bush, the man who illegally invaded Iraq on fraudulent pretexts, *less* controversial than Chavez? Was Bush less far to the right of the political spectrum than Chavez is to the left?

When Watchdogs Go Walkies: Bring Me the Head of John Humphrys!

While gross examples of pro-government bias pass unnoticed as 'balanced reporting', shudders of horror pass through the BBC when a journalist is perceived to have erred the other way. In 2005, BBC chairman Michael Grade ordered an urgent investigation into press claims that the high-profile Radio 4 *Today* presenter John Humphrys had 'mocked politicians in an after-dinner speech'.[78] Humphrys had poked fun at Labour politicians and said some 'couldn't give a bugger' whether they lied or not.[79]

The Times quoted Humphrys from his speech: '"All you've got to do is say, 'John Prescott' and people laugh." Peter Mandelson, he said, was detested by everyone, Gordon Brown was "the most boring political interviewee I've ever had in my whole bloody life", and Mr Campbell was a "pretty malevolent force ... who has been waging a vendetta against me for a long time"'.[80] Indeed, it soon emerged that Alastair Campbell's former right-hand man Tim Allan might well have been behind the attack on Humphrys:

Mr Allan, who spent four years as Mr Campbell's Downing Street deputy, was sent the only videotape of the veteran broadcaster's controversial after-dinner speech last week. By the next day, the tape had been leaked to the Labour-supporting *Times* newspaper [where Campbell was working] which devoted two pages of its Saturday edition to allegations that Humphrys had 'ridiculed senior Labour politicians and implied that all ministers are liars'.[81]

The Times had originally quoted Allan's enlightened views on press freedom: 'John Humphrys's peculiar brand of folksy nihilism is designed to spread cynicism about politics. The BBC now has to decide whether it is acceptable for their main radio presenter to use his licence fee-created celebrity to earn thousands of pounds telling audiences that all ministers are liars.'[82] It also quoted Tessa Jowell, then Culture Secretary: 'The BBC itself is responsible for ensuring that its codes of conduct for journalists are adhered to.'

Humphrys was unrepentant, insisting that his comments were meant to be 'humorous and knockabout'. He added: 'I do not think anything that I said was out of order.'[83] John Kampfner, then editor of the *New Statesman*, reported that Michael Grade had phoned several BBC executives, demanding that Humphrys be sacked. But Mark Thompson, the new director-general, resisted the pressure when he 'saw the furious reaction to the government's antics in the rest of the media, particularly the *Daily Mail* ... In the end Humphrys was merely rapped on the knuckles.'[84] The *Guardian* reported Thompson's conclusion that he was satisfied that Humphrys 'did not show party political bias ... and that he did not intend to be contemptuous or dismissive about politics or politicians'.

It is 'contemptuous' and 'dismissive', then, to suggest that politicians have lied, when that is clearly the case. 'Objective' journalism involves assuming that the British government is intent on peaceful solutions out of humanitarian concern when the opposite is true. To suggest darker motives is to be 'dismissive' and 'contemptuous'. BBC-approved journalism, in other words, is propaganda. Thompson added: 'However, some specific remarks were inappropriate and ran the risk of calling into question John's own impartiality and, by extension, that of the BBC. We've made it clear to him that this must not happen again.'[85]

According to Kampfner, Grade could barely conceal his annoyance that Thompson had not gone further. The BBC chairman had wanted 'a high-profile casualty to demonstrate to ministers that his new governance strategy has teeth. Humphrys would have been a nice fat plum'.[86] Six months later, the *Daily Mail* reported: 'BBC journalists have been told they could be sacked if they poke fun at politicians in after-dinner speeches.'[87] The report quoted new BBC guidelines: 'If, during a public appearance, a viewpoint expressed turns out to be controversial or one-sided, editors should consider whether to allow the presenter to cover the issue on-air.' 'New guidelines to protect the corporation's impartiality include a crackdown on public speaking engagements. It follows a furious row last year when Radio 4 *Today* presenter John Humphrys made fun of senior Labour politicians during an after-dinner speech.'[88]

Two years after the new guidelines were published, the BBC's impartial North America correspondent, Justin Webb, published a book entitled, *Have A Nice Day – Beyond the Clichés: Giving America Another Chance* (Short Books, 2008). Webb said of his book: 'If you love America and this love has dared not speak its name in recent years, my book is intended to give you ammunition with which to do battle on behalf of the Yanks. But if you hate America, or think that you might, or have a friend who does, please at least give me a chance to change your mind.'[89]

Happily, the viewpoint expressed was not 'controversial or one-sided', so BBC editors have allowed Webb to continue covering American politics on air.

The X-Files: The Need To Believe

At the beginning of every episode of the long-running science fiction series, *The X-Files*, viewers were shown the mysterious words 'I want to believe.' We were to understand that one of the FBI investigators in the show was eager to overcome her scepticism, to be persuaded that aliens and suchlike really exist. BBC journalists also 'want to believe' – in the benevolence of the British government and its leading allies.

In January 2006, Jeremy Bowen, the BBC's Middle East editor, noted that the United States had been the biggest foreign player in the Middle East for 50 years, but that Bush had created 'a much more intimate connection by going to war and occupying Iraq'.[90] 'Intimate' was an interesting adjective to use in describing the relationship between the world's sole superpower and its victims. Bowen added that the US administration justified the enormous human and financial cost of the Iraq war 'by saying that it is spreading democracy to people who deserve it yet have been denied it'.

This was reasonable enough. Bowen, after all, was merely reporting a US government claim. But the meaning was changed by his next comment: 'Voting in itself is not a magic formula to make people's lives better ... Under American protection, Iraq's newly elected politicians now have to show they can build a democracy.' Suddenly, and typically for BBC reporting, Bowen had switched from *reporting* Washington's view to propagandising on its behalf. There was more: 'Critics – enemies – of Washington are still very easy to find in the Middle East. But the irony is that the US intervention in the region, and the way that it is pushing its democracy agenda, has created a political space that dissenters can occupy.' Bowen listed alleged examples of democratisation in the region, before concluding: 'All this does not mean that the dreams that the Bush administration has for the region are coming true.'

This was crude propaganda: Bowen was asserting that the United States and Britain had genuinely benevolent 'dreams' of democracy, freedom, liberty for the Middle East. He was commenting nearly three years after America had launched an illegal military invasion, based on an extensive propaganda campaign to deceive its own population. It had killed, injured and made homeless literally millions of Iraqi people making up a big percentage of the civilian population. This occurred in the aftermath of more than a decade of US-led sanctions that ruthlessly subordinated the welfare of the Iraqi people to US strategic and economic goals. And yet Bowen's version of balanced reporting ascribed benevolent motives to the American government.

On the February 21, 2005 edition of *Newsnight*, Matt Frei reported on problems faced by the US in recruiting to its army as a result of the Iraq war. Frei said: 'The problem, you might say, with a war fought primarily not to defend America, but to create democracy in a distant land.'[91] On March 2, 2006, Jonathan Beale wrote on the BBC News website: 'India is the world's biggest democracy, a shining, though not perfect, example of the kinds of values President Bush wants to spread around the world.'[92] Notice that if Bowen, Frei and Beale had reported that the US was attempting to *subvert* democracy around the world (as indeed it does), intense outrage would have been generated in response to their 'biased' and 'unbalanced' journalism. When the judgement goes the other way, nobody notices.

Yes, Prime Minister! The Art Of Choosing the Interviewer

In 2007, the BBC chose one David Aaronovitch to interview the controversial Christian militant former prime minister Tony Blair for the BBC series, *The Blair Years*, which focused heavily on the Iraq war.

Aaronovitch was the perfect choice for the task. Four years earlier, in January 2003, as the British government was waging a ruthless propaganda campaign to persuade Parliament and public to support war on Iraq, he had written: 'If I were an Iraqi, living under probably the most violent and repressive regime in the world, I would desire Saddam's demise more than anything else. Or do we suppose that some nations and races cannot somehow cope with freedom?'[93] A month later, Aaronovitch responded to the greatest anti-war protest (indeed political protest of any kind) Britain had ever seen: 'Finally, what are you going to do when you are told – as one day you will be – that while you were demonstrating against an allied invasion, and being applauded by friends and Iraqi officials, many of the people of Iraq were hoping, hope against hope, that no one was listening to you?'[94]

In 2005, Peter Wilby, the former editor of the *New Statesman*, noted Aaronovitch's 'unstinting support of new Labour'.[95] Mark Lawson reviewed Aaronovitch's BBC interviews with Blair for the *Guardian*: 'Blair is convinced that he is no Nixon and so, probably, is the interviewer, David Aaronovitch, at least judging from his string of pro-Tony and pro-Iraq columns in *The Times*.'[96] And you do have to wonder why, given his obvious support for Blair over so many years, the BBC would turn to just Aaronovitch to interview Blair. And indeed, all we *can* do is wonder – as with the rest of the media, decision-making at the BBC is a mystery, shrouded in secrecy and silence.

Lawson added sardonically: 'if BBC programmes were allowed to have commercial endorsement, *The Blair Years* would have to be sponsored by Gap'. Like us, Lawson had a sense that 'what we're getting is a televisual equivalent of a personal statement to parliament on Blair's own terms ... although tough questions are asked – did he ever tell Brown to "eff off" over the succession?, did he lie to the public over Iraq? – the ex-PM's first denials are allowed to kill off the topic, without the ping-pong of "come off it" that has come to define being called to account'.

Zzzzzz: Good Night, And Good Luck

For several years, the name above the email address for the BBC's director of news read: zzHelen Boaden Complaints. Slumped in our chairs reading yet another soporific, stupefying response, we would often reflect on how appropriate these zzs were. Like Zen koans, Boaden's emails have the power to stop the mind in its tracks. What is the sound of one hand slow-clapping? Of the US–UK assault on Afghanistan, for example, she wrote:

> But for us to cast doubt on the official policy then we'd probably have to have justification for believing there are alternatives that are possible and probable. In Iraq there are certainly arguments about whether foreign intervention was justified and connected to global terrorism. But in the case of Afghanistan there is not really such debate.[97]

Eventually, Boaden's email address lost its zzs. Francis Elliott explained in the *Independent*:

> Don't bother emailing complaints to BBC head of news Helen Boaden. She was at the launch evening for the Reuters Institute for the Study of Journalism in Oxford last Monday night. Discussion turned to protest groups and lobbying outfits which email their views to senior editors. Boaden's response: 'Oh, I just changed my email address.' So much for the Beeb being accountable.[98]

4
Climate Chaos:
Keeping Madness Mainstream

ADVENTURES IN SHARED MENTAL PATHOLOGY

In *The Sane Society*, published in 1955, the psychologist Erich Fromm proposed that not just individuals, but entire societies 'may be lacking in sanity'. Fromm noted that this social insanity was often kept from awareness by 'consensual validation':

> It is naively assumed that the fact that the majority of people share certain ideas or feelings proves the validity of these ideas and feelings. Nothing is further from the truth ... Just as there is a 'folie a deux' there is a 'folie a millions.' The fact that millions of people share the same vices does not make these vices virtues, the fact that they share so many errors does not make the errors to be truths, and the fact that millions of people share the same form of mental pathology does not make these people sane.[1]

Fromm argued that modern Western society is indeed insane and that its insanity would threaten the very survival of the human species. If this sounds extreme, consider the catastrophic media response to the gravest threat in modern human history: global climate change.

In 2004, a study in the leading science journal *Nature* concluded that by 2050 as many as one-quarter of all plant and animal species could be doomed to extinction as a result of climate change. Climate scientists warn of the risk of at least a five metre rise in sea level should the west Antarctic ice sheet melt. If the Greenland ice sheet were also to melt, that would raise sea levels a further seven metres. In 2006, a study led by scientists at NASA's Jet Propulsion Laboratory concluded that Greenland's glaciers were sliding into the ocean much faster than had previously been believed.[2] Related dangers include an increase in the acidity of the world's oceans, with severe consequences for the marine food web and the ability of the ocean to absorb carbon dioxide emissions. There is also the possible weakening of the North Atlantic 'conveyor belt', a system of ocean currents which includes the Gulf Stream, and which helps to maintain the present, moderate climate in western Europe.[3] In February 2007, a summary of the latest scientific assessment was released by the authoritative UN Intergovernmental Panel on Climate Change.[4] The IPCC noted that: 'Most of the observed increase in globally averaged temperatures since the mid-20th century is *very likely* [i.e. probability greater than 90%] due to the observed increase in anthropogenic greenhouse gas concentrations.'[5]

But even the IPCC's assessment is likely too cautious. Its analyses are based, understandably enough, on established 'peer-reviewed' science: work which has been published in scientific journals after extensive scrutiny by colleagues with expertise in the same fields. However, the process of compiling and agreeing the IPCC reports is so lengthy that by the time they appear they can already be out of date. More recent, post-IPCC research reveals *accelerating* disintegration in the west Antarctic and Greenland ice sheets, rather than a steady, linear decrease, as was assumed in the latest IPCC assessment. James Hansen, the NASA scientist who first alerted the US Congress in 1988 to global warming, has drawn special attention to the danger of 'tipping points'. This is when the climate reaches a state beyond which large, unstoppable and irreversible impacts occur, such as the collapse of an ice sheet.

Hansen notes that observations of the Earth's geological record shows that 'the Earth's climate is remarkably sensitive' to disturbances, such as changes in carbon dioxide concentration. These nudges actually allow 'the entire planet to be whipsawed between climate states'. Indeed, the Earth is already 'perilously close to dramatic climate change that could run out of control, with great dangers for humans and other creatures'.[6] On June 23, 2008, 20 years to the day since he first testified to Congress on global warming, Hansen once again delivered a powerful message to US politicians and the public. The difference between then and now, he said, is that 'we have used up all slack in the schedule for actions needed to defuse the global warming time bomb'. He added that the measures required to protect the planet on which civilisation developed are clear: basically ridding ourselves of fossil fuels, reducing energy needs while shifting massively to clean, renewable energy. But these measures 'have been blocked by special interests, focused on short-term profits, who hold sway in Washington and other capitals'.

Hansen called for the chief executives of oil, coal and other fossil fuel companies to be put on trial for high crimes against humanity and nature. He noted: 'CEOs of fossil energy companies know what they are doing and are aware of long-term consequences of continued business as usual.' Hansen accused them of spreading doubts about global warming in the same cynical way tobacco companies once sought to blur the links between smoking and cancer. These were strong words from a scientist.

Hansen's recent scientific research with colleagues had yielded a 'disturbing conclusion'. A 'safe level' of atmospheric carbon dioxide is no more than 350 ppm (parts per million), and possibly even less. It is deeply worrying that the present level of carbon dioxide is, in fact, already 385 ppm; and rising rapidly at about 2 ppm per year. As Hansen warned: 'the oft-stated goal to keep global warming less than two degrees Celsius is a recipe for global disaster, not salvation'.[7]

In short, the science is compelling: the vast body of evidence now points to the danger that humanity is courting a self-inflicted disaster.

HUNDREDS OF 1p FLIGHTS: LET SANTA PAY

The mainstream media do report the latest scientific findings on climate change; even on occasion using dramatic front-page covers, notably in the *Independent*. But as we will see below, the *content* of these reports and related commentary comes with gaping holes. The material surrounding them also serves to powerfully dissipate their impact.

In considering the sanity of the media reaction there is little point analysing the worst media – the celebrity-packed magazines and tittle-tattle tabloids. Instead, we will consider the performance of the best media on climate change. Consider, for example, this front-page banner headline in the *Independent* of December 3, 2005: 'Climate Change: Time for Action. Today, protestors unite in 30 nations – this is what lies ahead if nothing is done.' Accompanying illustrations and text listed the by now familiar horrors: 'killer storms, rampant disease, rising sea levels, devastated wildlife, water shortages, agricultural turmoil', and 'the X-factor' – the possibility of sudden, devastating climatic phenomena that we cannot even imagine. Page two reported global protests in 33 countries, while page three focused on 'a monument to ecological folly' in Dubai – one of the world's largest indoor ski resorts in the middle of the desert: 'While the outside temperature can reach 50C, the Ski Dubai centre will expend thousands of watts on keeping its indoor climate at minus 1.4C all year round.'[8]

On the same page, the *Independent*'s own 'ecological folly' was visible in the form of an advert for Vauxhall cars. PC World advertised PS2 and X-Box game consoles on page four: 'Game On! This weekend.' Immediately adjacent, the *Independent* listed '10 things you can do at home' to avert climate change, including 'Turn off electrical appliances not in use': 'The power wasted releases an extra one million tons of carbon into the atmosphere every year', we were told.

On page five, flymonarch.com urged readers: 'Let Santa pay – Find hundreds of 1p flights'. Alongside the ad, an emergency appeal from Care International reported: 'Food crisis across Africa', explaining: 'Failed harvests, erratic rains and chronic poverty means millions of people across Africa are at risk of starvation.' This echoed the *Independent*'s own front page, which linked climate change from the burning of fossil fuels to drought in Africa: 'The hundreds of millions of people living in the world's marginal agricultural lands, such as the countries of the Sahel region, already face a desperate struggle to grow food ... The terrifying images of African famine are as nothing to what will come.'

Santa is not alone in picking up the bill for the 1p flights promoted by the *Independent*.

The page that followed the warnings of mass starvation featured a half-page, full-colour advert for Dior Christal watches: '48 diamonds and sapphire crystal chronograph'. Stories of impending climatic collapse had by now dried up. Instead, by way of a bitter irony, a large 'Kodak price crash' was featured on page seven, promising 'The future ... for less.' Page eight featured a full-colour British Airways advert: 'London–Malaga return' for just £59. 'Have you clicked yet?' Had the *Independent*'s readers clicked yet? Page nine was taken up completely by 'Canon Week – great money saving Canon offers' on digital cameras, camcorders, printers and memory cards. Page ten promoted lastminute.com holidays. Pages 12–13 sold British Telecom phones. Page 15 was reserved in its entirety for 'Citroen Happy Deals'. The adverts for cheap holidays, cars, computers and other high-tech goods continued on and on: Comet, Davidoff, Travelodge, Halfords, Currys, bmibaby.com ('the airline with tiny fares'), Sony, 118trades. com, The Link.

After dozens of pages of this relentless propaganda promoting mass consumption, the paper returned to the front-page issue with an editorial on page 40: 'Global warming and the need for all of us to act now to avoid catastrophe': 'Governments must demand greater energy conservation from industry. And action must be taken to curtail emissions from transport. That means extensive investment in the development of alternative fuels and the taxation of air flights.' The editors concluded:

> But it is not just governments that have a responsibility. Individuals must act too. By opting to cycle or walk, instead of driving everywhere, we can all do something to reduce emissions. If more of us turned off electrical devices when not in use and recycled our waste properly, our societies would be hugely less energy inefficient ... A failure to act now will not be forgiven by future generations.

As though these words had not appeared, the rest of the paper returned to adverts, consumer advice and financial news ('bet on easyJet to fly higher'). The *Independent's* holiday supplement, *The Traveller*, urged readers to visit Paris, Brussels, Syria, Panama, Costa Rica, Nicaragua, Aspen, Chamonix, Mallorca, Australia, Dubai, New Zealand, Lapland, Spain, North America, Austria, Germany, the Maldives, and on and on.

More details on newspaper advertising were provided by industry sources (who wished to preserve their anonymity). They told us that between January 1 and October 7, 2005, Independent News and Media PLC, owners of the *Independent* newspapers, received the following revenues from advertisers:

BP Plc	£11,769*
Citroen UK Ltd	£418,779
Ford Motor Company Ltd	£247,506
Peugeot Motor Company Plc	£260,920
Renault UK Ltd	£427,097
Toyota (GB) Ltd	£715,050
Vauxhall Motors Ltd	£662,359
Volkswagen UK Ltd	£555,518
BMI British Midland	£60,847
Bmibaby Ltd	£12,810
British Airways Plc	£248,165
Easyjet Airline Co Ltd	£59,905
Monarch Airlines	£15,713
Ryanair Ltd	£28,543

* This figure rose substantially after October 7, 2005 as a result of the 'Beyond Petroleum' campaign.
Source: Email to Media Lens, December 12, 2005.

Compare these figures with the *Independent*'s suggestion, cited above: 'Individuals must act too. By opting to cycle or walk, instead of driving everywhere, we can all do something to reduce emissions.' At the same time, the *Independent* is continuing to host adverts specifically designed to disarm dissent and pacify the public. It is important to remember (perhaps with a shudder) that the *Independent* is, by some distance, the best, most responsible corporate media source on climate change.

A 2005 Friends of the Earth (FoE) study of car adverts in UK national newspapers discovered that the media were primarily pushing the least fuel-efficient gas guzzlers rather than smaller, greener cars. FoE looked at the best-selling national newspapers and the two best-selling car magazines for the first two weeks of September that year. They found that over one third (35.8 per cent) of adverts promoted cars in car tax band F, the top band, for cars emitting more than 185 g/km CO_2. Over half (57.6 per cent) were for cars in either band E or band F, for cars emitting more than 166 g/km CO_2. Only 3.1 per cent were for cars in bands A and B, the lowest bands, for cars emitting less than 121 g/km CO_2.[9] Environment writer and Spinwatch co-founder, Andy Rowell, made the point that matters:

> Advertising reassures people that it is OK to buy and consume. It provides a safety net to make it acceptable to consume. What makes this so important is the media are often the windows through which we see the world. If we open a paper and see fast cars it makes it acceptable to drive one, if we see cheap flights it makes it acceptable to go on one.[10]

BP: BEYOND PETROLEUM – BEYOND REASON

One day after the *Independent*'s call for 'action' on climate change, the *Independent on Sunday* published two full-page, full-colour adverts on successive right-hand pages promoting BP's 'Beyond Petroleum' campaign. BP's claim to be moving beyond petroleum is a sham. James Marriott, of the environmental social justice group PLATFORM (www.platformlondon.org), told us that BP investments in renewable energy, such as solar and wind power, then constituted around 2 per cent of the company's total investments. Marriott commented: 'The amount of capital being put into renewables is minute. So they *are* going "beyond petroleum", but at this rate it will take several hundred years.'[11]

'Beyond Petroleum' is part of a cynical strategy targeting what the public relations industry calls 'special publics'. Advertising is specifically focused on the *Independent*, the *Guardian*, the *Observer*, the *Financial Times*, *Prospect* magazine, Channel 4 News and the *New Statesman*. Marriott explained:

> The campaign is targeting the liberal intelligentsia. It's not focussed on drivers on the forecourts – it's focussed on changing the opinions of opinion formers. The idea is to bring them on side, to drive a wedge between them and people they perceive as intractable opponents. Shell has used the same tactic with considerable success.

Nevertheless, an article by Saeed Shah in the *Independent* of November 29, 2005, bore the title: 'BP looks "beyond petroleum" with $8bn renewables spend'. An alternative, more accurate title would have been: 'BP *claims* to look "beyond petroleum"...'. On closer inspection, the article revealed that BP's then chief executive, Lord Browne of Madingley, admitted that the company planned to continue raising its production of oil and gas for years to come. Browne said the 'beyond petroleum' marketing slogan was not meant to be taken literally: 'It is more a way of thinking.' Needless to say, that was *not* the impression given by the adverts.

IN THE SPIRIT OF NERO

The Fourth Assessment Report by the Intergovernmental Panel on Climate Change provided 'humanity's loudest warning yet of the catastrophe that is threatening to overtake us', said the *Independent* on February 3, 2007. 'No more excuses', the *Guardian*'s editorial intoned on the same day.

The irony was bitter indeed. While the *Guardian*'s front page that day warned of climate chaos, the centre spread consisted of a two-page full-colour advert for Renault cars: 'Everything is sport.' For good measure, the cover story of the Travel supplement promoted holidays to New York. An astonishing double-page spread was also to be found at the heart of the *Independent*. This consisted of graphs indicating perilously rising temperatures, text explaining the catastrophic impacts, and photographs of climate-related chaos around the world. It also included, bottom left on the same double-page, a large advert for Halfords 'car essentials'. Bottom right was an American Airlines advert for reduced-fare flights to New York – a bargain at just £199.

The cover story of the *Independent on Sunday*'s Review supplement the following day was almost beyond belief. The words on the cover ran: 'Time is running out ... Ski resorts are melting ... Paradise islands are vanishing ... So what are you waiting for? 30 places you need to visit while you still can – A 64-page Travel Special'. It is worth quoting at length from the article by Marcus Fairs, editor of *Icon*, a design magazine:

> I am changing my travel plans this year. Alarmed by global warming, shocked by the imminent mass extinction of species and distraught at the environmental damage wreaked by mass tourism, I have decided to act before it is too late. Yes, carbon-neutral travel can wait. I'm off to see polar bears, tigers and low-lying Pacific atolls while they're still there ... In the spirit of Nero – the Roman emperor who sang to the beauty of the flames while Rome burned to the ground – we are determined to enjoy the final days of our beautiful Earth. We are aware that mass tourism damages the very things we are going to see, but this only increases our urgency. We are aware that we will soon have to act more sustainably, which gives us all the more reason to be irresponsible while we still can.
>
> Not for us the angsty despair of the eco-worriers, nor the stay-home moralising of the greenhouse gasbags. For we are the travel Neroists, and we have spotted a window of opportunity.[12]

Presumably the weight of irony qualifies Fairs' piece as wonderfully 'postmodern'. In his book, *Affluenza*, psychologist Oliver James identified 'an addiction to irony' in modern society: 'saying one thing when another is meant in order to establish a disconnection between the speaker and his listener, or between the speaker and that which is being spoken. Or even between the speaker and himself.'[13] How ironic, how courageously postmodern, to sing 'to the beauty of the flames', to describe mass death, mass destruction, as 'a window of opportunity'.

The World Health Organization has estimated that global warming already contributes to more than 150,000 deaths and 5 million illnesses each year: a toll that could double by 2030. These are real people – this is the real, deteriorating world beyond the computer screens of the paid corporate scribblers.[14] In reality, Fairs is a conformist who doffed his cap to the paper's advertisers in the usual way. Thus he emphasised the mendacious holiday industry perspective:

Travel is often unfairly demonised by the eco-lobby: flying accounts for around 3 per cent of global CO_2 emissions (compared to 20 per cent for domestic heating and a similar amount for road transport). According to the Carbon Trust, of the 11 tonnes of CO_2 emitted each year by the average person in the UK, just 0.68 tonnes comes from flying – whereas a full tonne derives from the manufacture and transport of our clothing. 'Demanding that people stop flying is not the solution to all our problems', says Responsibletravel. com's [Justin] Francis, 'especially when many developing countries rely on responsible tourism as a significant source of income to protect and conserve their environment'.

Fairs neglected to cite any of the development experts and climate scientists who dismiss these arguments as cynical nonsense; as just one more unsubtle attempt to justify inaction in defence of profits.

'OUT-AND-OUT PROPAGANDA':
THE GREAT GLOBAL WARMING SWINDLE

In addition to cognitive dissonance and profit-friendly clichés, there is the problem of straight-out propaganda. In 2007, Channel 4 screened *The Great Global Warming Swindle*, a documentary that branded as a lie the scientific consensus that man-made greenhouse gases are primarily responsible for climate change. The film was advertised extensively on Channel 4 and repeatedly previewed and, thereafter, reviewed in newspapers. Writing in the *Sunday Telegraph*, Christopher Booker declared: 'Never before has there been such a devastatingly authoritative account of how the hysteria over global warming has parted company with reality.'[15] The *Daily Mail*'s Melanie Phillips described it as a 'devastating documentary' that had 'blown an enormous hole in every fundamental claim made to support the climate change obsession'. Phillips concluded of the film: 'Glorious. And terrifying; and shameful.'[16]

Doubtless like many who saw the film, an anonymous *Financial Times* television reviewer was left bewildered: 'Not so long ago, the venerable David Attenborough on the Beeb was telling us that human-driven global warming was real and was coming for us. So that was settled. Now Channel 4, like a dissident schoolboy, is scoffing at the old boy's hobbyhorse and I don't know what to believe.'[17] The film opened with scenes of wild weather and environmental disaster accompanied by dramatic captions:

THE ICE IS MELTING. THE SEA IS RISING.
HURRICANES ARE BLOWING. AND IT'S ALL YOUR FAULT.
SCARED? DON'T BE. IT'S NOT TRUE.

This was immediately followed by a series of equally forthright talking heads: 'We can't say that CO_2 will drive climate; it certainly never did in the past.' 'We imagine that we live in an age of reason. And the global warming alarm is dressed up as science. But it's not science; it's propaganda.' And: 'We're just being told lies; that's what it comes down to.' The commentary added to the sense of outrage: 'You are being told lies.' In an interview, the film's writer and director, Martin Durkin, bluntly explained his agenda:

> I think it [the film] will go down in history as the first chapter in a new era of the relationship between scientists and society. Legitimate scientists – people with qualifications – are the bad guys. It is a big story that is going to cause controversy. It's very rare that a film changes history, but I think this is a turning point and in five years the idea that the greenhouse effect is the main reason behind global warming will be seen as total bollocks.[18]

Compare and contrast this with the aim as described in a letter sent by Wag TV, Durkin's film company, to Professor Carl Wunsch, a leading expert on ocean circulation and climate, who appeared in the film:

> The aim of the film is to examine critically the notion that recent global warming is primarily caused by industrial emissions of CO_2. It explores the scientific evidence which jars with this hypothesis and explores alternative theories such as solar induced climate change. Given the seemingly inconclusive nature of the evidence, it examines the background to the apparent consensus on this issue, and highlights the dangers involved, especially to developing nations, of policies aimed at limiting industrial growth.[19]

Wunsch commented after the film's broadcast:

> I am angry because they completely misrepresented me. My views were distorted by the context in which they placed them. I was misled as to what it was going to be about. I was told about six months ago that this was to be a programme about how complicated it is to understand what is going on. If they had told me even the title of the programme, I would have absolutely refused to be on it. I am the one who has been swindled.[20]

The film presented viewers with an apparently devastating refutation of the 'theory of global warming'. These were not small, esoteric criticisms. Durkin claimed that the world's climate scientists are guilty of the most fundamental error imaginable: increased atmospheric carbon dioxide (CO_2) is not the cause of higher global temperature, as the experts claim. Quite the reverse: increasing atmospheric CO_2 is itself the *result* of rising temperature. As evidence that climate scientists had got it all wrong, Durkin argued that global surface temperature dropped dramatically between 1945 and 1975, at a time when CO_2 emissions were rapidly rising as a result of the postwar economic boom. According to Durkin, if CO_2 emissions were responsible for increasing temperature, then temperature should not have fallen between 1945 and 1975. Clearly, then, some factor other than CO_2 emissions must have caused the subsequent global temperature rise. (This was all leading up to Durkin's argument that solar activity is the culprit.)

In this section of the film, Durkin focused heavily on a graph depicting temperature changes. The graph, whose source was labelled 'NASA', appeared to show a dramatic cooling between the 1940s and 1970s. But an investigation by the *Independent*'s science editor revealed that the plot had been taken from an obscure right-wing-funded journal, and that it referred to just one region of the Northern hemisphere rather than the whole globe.[21] Globally, there was some cooling for *part* of this postwar economic boom, up to the mid 1970s, but also some plateauing, with fluctuations up and down. There was certainly no dramatic continual drop in temperature during this period, as claimed by the film.

But why did the temperature not simply rise in line with the postwar increase in greenhouse gas emissions? In fact, as is well known, the absence of a global rise in temperature between 1945 and 1975 is explained by the release of large amounts of industrial pollutants, called sulphate aerosols, into the atmosphere. These particles have a braking effect on global warming, known as 'global dimming'. By shielding some of the incoming solar energy, sulphate aerosols mask the underlying warming effect generated by rising levels of CO_2. Anti-pollution legislation in a number of countries since the 1970s has reduced the level of sulphate aerosols. The masking effect of global dimming has therefore declined and the warming signal of rising global temperature began to emerge again in 1975, becoming particularly noticeable by the 1990s.

Real Climate, an internet site run by climate scientists, including Gavin Schmidt of NASA and William Connelley of the British Antarctic Survey, described Durkin's discussion of the 1945–75 period as 'deeply deceptive', noting that he was guilty of 'lying to us by omission'.[22] Moreover, the film's claim that solar activity, not greenhouse gas emissions, accounts for recent global warming was without credibility. In September 2006, *The Times* had reported the latest findings published by researchers in *Nature*:

> Scientists have examined various proxies of solar energy output over the past 1,000 years and have found no evidence that they are correlated with today's rising temperatures. Satellite observations over the past 30 years have also turned up nothing. 'The solar contribution to warming ... is negligible', the researchers wrote in the journal *Nature*.[23]

Oceanographer Carl Wunsch of the Massachusetts Institute of Technology – who, as mentioned above, appeared in the film – commented: 'What we now have is an out-and-out propaganda piece, in which there is not even a gesture toward balance or explanation of why many of the extended inferences drawn in the film are not widely accepted by the scientific community.' The documentary makers had, Wunsch said, produced 'pure propaganda'. He added: 'My appearance in the "Global Warming Swindle" is deeply embarrassing, and my professional reputation has been damaged. I was duped – an uncomfortable position in which to be.'[24]

Eight of the scientists in the film – John Christy, Paul Reiter, Richard Lindzen, Paul Driessen, Roy Spencer, Patrick Michaels, Fred Singer and Tim Ball – are linked to American neo-conservative and right-wing think-tanks, many of which have received tens of millions of dollars from Exxon. Journalist Ross Gelbspan noted that in May 1995, Richard Lindzen and Patrick Michaels were hired as expert witnesses to testify on behalf of Western Fuels Association, a $400 million consortium of coal suppliers and coal-fired utilities. Gelbspan said of Lindzen:

> I don't know very many supporters of Mr Lindzen who are not in the pay of the fossil fuel lobby. Dr Lindzen himself, his research is publicly funded, but Dr Lindzen makes, as he told me, $2,500 a day consulting with fossil fuel interests, and that includes his consulting with OPEC, his consulting with the Australian coal industry, his consulting with the US coal industry and so forth. That's not to say Dr Lindzen doesn't believe what he says, but it is to

say that he stands in very sharp distinction to really just about virtually all of the climate scientists around the world.[25]

George Monbiot wrote of Philip Stott, another scientist who appeared in the film: 'Professor Stott is a retired biogeographer. Like almost all the prominent sceptics he has never published a peer-reviewed paper on climate change. But he has made himself available to dismiss climatologists' peer-reviewed work as the "lies" of ecofundamentalists.'[26]

Paul Driessen is a fellow at two right-wing think-tanks in the US, which are part of the anti-green Wise Use movement. One of the think-tanks is headed by Ron Arnold, who has spent the last 20 years attacking the environmental movement. His fellow director is a fundraiser for America's gun lobby. The list goes on...

Following numerous complaints, the UK's official media regulator, Ofcom, ruled that Durkin's film had treated two scientists – Carl Wunsch and former chief government adviser Sir David King – and the Intergovernmental Panel on Climate Change unfairly. Although the ruling dealt a blow to Channel 4's credibility, it also exposed Ofcom's limitations. A detailed 176-page submission, peer-reviewed by leading climate scientists, had presented the regulator with ample evidence showing how *The Great Global Warming Swindle* was itself a swindle packed with bad science.[27] But Ofcom decided it could not rule on the matter of accuracy. While news programmes are expected to be accurate, other factual programmes are not and Ofcom insisted that it 'only regulates misleading material where that material is likely to cause harm or offence'.[28] It decided that Durkin's film had not actually harmed viewers: it is not enough merely to mislead them.

In response to the Ofcom verdict, Hamish Mykura, head of Channel 4 documentaries, was unapologetic: 'Channel 4 believes in engaging with the debate in its fullest form, rather than closing it down. That is why this film was a valid contribution.'[29] But Martin Rees, President of the UK's Royal Society, one of the world's oldest and most prestigious scientific bodies, took a different view, arguing that 'to misrepresent the evidence on an issue as important as global warming was surely irresponsible ... The programme makers misrepresented the science.'[30]

Durkin, *The Great Global Warming Swindle*'s writer and director, has 'form'. In 1997, Channel 4 broadcast Durkin's three-part series, *Against Nature*, which proposed that present-day environmentalists were nothing less than the true heirs of the Nazis.[31] Several interviewees who appeared in the series felt they had been misled about the programme-maker's agenda. Responding to complaints, the Independent Television Commission (ITC) found that the editing of interviews with four contributors had 'distorted or misrepresented their known views'.[32] In addition, the ITC found: 'The interviewees had also been misled as to the content and purpose of the programmes when they agreed to take part.'[33]

As we noted at the start of this chapter, a 2004 *Nature* study warned that by 2050 as much as one-quarter of all plant and animal species could be doomed to extinction as a result of climate change. Recall, too, that the WHO estimates that global warming is a causal factor in over 150,000 deaths and 5 million illnesses annually. Channel 4 performed a huge public disservice by spreading absurd and mendacious arguments guaranteed to generate public confusion. This at a time when a fragile momentum is building on the need to take urgent action on the real threat of catastrophic climate change. Phil Lesly, author of a handbook on public relations, described how big business works to stifle public concern on environmental issues: 'People generally do not favour action on a non-alarming situation when arguments seem to be balanced on both sides and there is a clear doubt. The weight of impressions on the public must be balanced so people will have doubts and lack motivation to take action.'[34]

Ofcom's suggestion that the *Swindle* film had not caused harm was outlandish. In 2008, a poll carried out for the *Observer* found that six out of ten Britons agreed that 'many scientific experts still question if humans are contributing to climate change', and that four out of ten 'sometimes think climate change might not be as bad as people say'.[35] Environment writer Mark Lynas wrote of how he 'blame[d] the media almost entirely for this discrepancy between public understanding and scientific reality'.[36] Durkin's film had surely contributed to this dangerous 'discrepancy'. By sowing confusion, and decreasing the public's will to counter likely catastrophic climate change, polemics like *The Great Global Warming Swindle* increase the likelihood that more people will die in the chaos ahead.

CLIMATE SILENCE: THE FORBIDDEN TOPICS

In 2006, an explosive front-page article in the *Independent* was titled: 'Earth's ecological debt crisis: mankind's "borrowing" from nature hits new record.' Martin Hickman, the newspaper's consumer affairs correspondent, explained the results of a study featured in the story:

Evidence is mounting that rapid population growth and rising living standards among the Earth's six billion inhabitants are putting an intolerable strain on nature. For the first time an organisation – a British think-tank – has sought to pinpoint how quickly man is using the global resources of farming land, forests, fish, air and energy.[37]

By analysing data from the US academic group Global Footprint Network, the think-tank has worked out the day each year when 'humanity starts eating the planet'. Just like a company bound for bankruptcy, the world started falling into ecological debt on October 9 that year. Hickman explained: 'Problems, affecting everything from the seabed to the stratosphere, range from carbon dioxide emissions to the destruction of rainforests to the intensification of agriculture.' The crisis Hickman was describing could hardly be more serious: humanity really is devouring the planet's life-support systems. And yet, typically for mainstream reporting, Hickman's analysis of the causes behind the crisis was lost in unsupported, clichéd assertions about 'rapid population growth' and global 'rising living standards'. It is not just that 'mankind' is '"borrowing" from nature', as Hickman claimed – the problem is rooted in a particular form of politics controlled by wealthy elites.

Consider some of the key issues that *should* be at the heart of any analysis of the looming catastrophe under discussion. And consider how inclusion of these issues is all but inconceivable in any corporate newspaper. These issues include:

1. The inherently biocidal, indeed psychopathic, logic of corporate capitalism, structurally locked into generating maximised revenues in minimum time at minimum cost. As corporations are legally *obliged* to maximise profits for shareholders, it is in fact illegal for corporations to prioritise the welfare of people and planet above private profits. How can this simple fact of entrenched corporate immorality not be front and centre in any discussion of the industrial destruction of global life-support systems?
2. The proven track record of big business in promoting catastrophic consumption regardless of the consequences for human and environmental health. Whether disregarding the links between smoking and cancer, junk food and obesity, Third World exploitation and human suffering, oil exploration and lethal climate change, factory farming and animal suffering, high salt consumption and illness, corporations have consistently subordinated human and animal welfare to short-term profits.

3. The relentless corporate lobbying of governments to shape policies to promote and protect private power.
4. The billions spent by the advertising industry to promote consumer products and services, creating artificial 'needs', with children an increasing target.
5. The collusion between powerful companies, investors and state planners to install compliant dictators in client states around the world.
6. The extensive use of loans and tied aid that ensnare poor nations in webs of debt, ensuring that the West retains control of their resources, markets and development.
7. The deployment of threats, bribery and armed force against countries that attempt to pursue self-development, rather than economic or strategic planning sanctioned by 'the international community'.
8. The lethal role of the corporate media in promoting the planet-devouring aims of private power.

In a powerful book titled *The Decline of Capitalism*, economist Harry Shutt explains how the current system ensures 'the wasteful diversion of economic value added into the pockets of the small minority who also (through their disproportionate wealth) exercise largely unaccountable political power'.[38] As Shutt rightly concludes, global capitalism is 'too dysfunctional to be tolerable in a civilised society'.[39] Forty years ago, Martin Luther King called for 'a radical restructuring of the architecture of American society'. He observed: 'Global capitalism is much more concerned with expanding the domain of market relations than with, say, establishing democracy, expanding elementary education, or enhancing the social opportunities of society's underdogs.'[40] Indeed, King increasingly questioned capitalism towards the end of his life: an aspect of his inspirational speeches that tends to be ignored by establishment commentators who are otherwise keen to praise him. He associated domestic racial and social inequality with US imperialism and social disparity abroad, denouncing what he called 'the triple evils that are interrelated': 'racism, economic exploitation, and war'. In one speech he said:

> A nation that will keep people in slavery for 244 years will 'thingify' them
> – make them things. Therefore they will exploit them, and poor people
> generally, economically. And a nation that will exploit economically will

have to have foreign investments and everything else, and will have to use its military might to protect them. All of these problems are tied together.

King decried the 'evils that are rooted deeply in the whole structure of society' which had 'systemic rather than superficial flaws'. He concluded that 'radical reconstruction of society itself is the real issue to be faced'.[41] But this deep problem, facing anyone hoping for genuine action to combat the environmental crisis, is beyond the pale of mainstream thought and public debate.

Ecologist Franz Broswimmer put it this way: 'At its very core, the prevailing capitalist ethos and liberal world view of the modern industrial era remain expansionary and imperial, involving a calculated form of indifference to the social and ecological order.'[42] The social insanity of this capitalist-fuelled expansionism leads to 'inverted priorities', to adopt the phrase used by the social scientist Immanuel Wallerstein. Hence, dominant features of the economy include a trillion-dollar global arms budget, depletion of the planet's natural resources and a deepening economic apartheid between rich and poor. These features are, in the words of eco-feminist Mary Mellor: 'not the neutral decisions of a market; they are the priorities of powerful people in powerful nations, mostly men whose gender, race, and class interests drive the capitalist political economic system and its worldwide system of accumulation and deprivation'.[43] It is simply not possible to understand, far less to address, the crises facing us without understanding these issues. But, of course, they are simply 'not of this world' from the perspective of mainstream corporate news reporting and commentary.

These are compelling, evidence-based arguments that are buried beneath the complacent clichés favoured by even the best newspapers. We have sketched them only in the briefest detail here – the point is they are hardly ever discussed at all.

ECONOMIC 'GROWTH': THE LAST OF THE UNIVERSAL TABOOS

Hope of a challenge to the discredited folly of economic 'growth' appeared in a front-page article by the *Independent*'s environment editor Michael McCarthy. The paper highlighted 'a different way forward in the struggle to combat global warming. ... It will mean turning established principles of British economic life upside down.' McCarthy was referring to the conclusions of the UK Commons all-party parliamentary climate change group led by Colin Challen MP.

The Commons group had put 'the case for abandoning the "business as usual" pursuit of economic growth, which has been the basis of Western economic policy for two hundred years'.

We place 'growth' in inverted commas because standard measures of economic activity 'externalise' – in plain terms, ignore – the attendant enormous environmental and social costs. As Challen warned: 'No amount of economic growth is going to pay for the cost of the damage caused by a new and unstable climate.' McCarthy expanded: 'the pursuit of growth, which essentially has not changed since Victorian times, is misleading, and the terms need to be redefined. Instead, we need a different policy which looks at how much carbon we can afford to emit.'[44] In an accompanying comment piece, Challen presented the alternative policy; namely, 'contraction and convergence', devised by the London-based Global Commons Institute led by Aubrey Meyer:

> We know that we need to reduce our carbon emissions so that we arrive at a safe concentration in the atmosphere – perhaps 450 parts per million. We also know that without developing countries being part of a global agreement, it won't work. The answer is convergence – we should aim to contract our emissions while converging to a per-capita basis of shared emissions rights.

Challen's warning of the consequences, should contraction and convergence fail to be adopted worldwide as a post-Kyoto climate policy, was expressed in extremely stark terms:

> Our economic model is not so different in the cold light of day to that of the Third Reich – which knew it could only expand by grabbing what it needed from its neighbours. Genocide followed. Now there is a case to answer that genocide is once again an apt description of how we are pursuing business as usual, willfully ignoring the consequences for the poorest people in the world.[45]

This was a crucial and hard-hitting message. So how did the mainstream media respond to the parliamentary climate change group's challenge? The environment editors and commentators at the *Daily Telegraph*, *Financial Times*, the *Guardian* and *The Times* had nothing at all to say. Only the *Times* published a commentary. This was penned by its anti-green columnist, Mick Hume, rubbishing the parliamentary group as a 'cream-puff army' peddling 'irrational' drivel.[46]

What about the *Guardian*, regarded as a key platform for 'green' issues in the eyes of much of the environment movement? Tony Juniper, then director of Friends of the Earth, has even declared the paper 'the voice of progressive and sound environmental thinking both in the UK and in Europe'.[47] In fact, the *Guardian* had nothing at all to say about the parliamentary group's challenge to the primacy of economic 'growth' as a driver of policy. Instead, the *Guardian* continued to perpetuate the myths that 'Britain has at least acted more responsibly than most' on climate, and that Tony Blair and Margaret Beckett – then, respectively, prime minister and environment secretary – 'are certainly sincere on the issue'. The *Guardian*'s editors have yet to ditch the benign blather of far too many years: 'Small measures will help, but big ones are needed too. Some of them will hurt and voters will squeal.' But whatever the measures, it 'does not mean abandoning economic growth'.[48]

Other than the *Independent*, the only British newspaper to report the parliamentary group's challenge was the London-based *Evening Standard*. This took the form of 56 words at the end of an article reporting the Archbishop of Canterbury's comment that George Bush was failing in his Christian duty to tackle global warming.[49]

The public is encouraged to believe that, if anyone 'gets it' on climate change, then it is the environment correspondents and editors of the liberal press. But we cannot rely on corporate environment editors to challenge the elite consensus on the need for relentless economic 'growth', a cancerous process that is killing the planet. As we have seen, the issue is not addressed seriously by journalists, politicians or academics – or even by the major green pressure groups. George Monbiot has rightly called it 'the last of the universal taboos'.[50]

ALWAYS STUCK ON 'SQUARE ONE'

The issues discussed above are hardly new – warnings about global warming have been around for years. One of us (Cromwell) still has a scrapbook he made of old newspaper cuttings from the 1970s. One snippet, from the *Glasgow Herald* of February 3, 1977, is an article entitled, 'Earth may be warming up'. Journalist Robert Cowen reported the view of Academician Mikhail I. Budyko, a Soviet climatologist. Budyko warned that, following a general plateauing of global temperatures since the 1940s, 'substantial warming' was once again kicking off, 'due partly to carbon dioxide pollution'. He added:

'If the present rapid trend towards a warmer climate continues, in five to 10 years, climatic conditions will appear which have not been observed for many centuries.' A decade later, in 1988, concern among the United Nations was such that the Intergovernmental Panel on Climate Change was established.

Depressingly, 20 years on, in June 2007, the *Financial Times* reported a YouGov survey of business leaders that had found that 'Climate change is bottom of the priority list for Britain's largest companies ... and their biggest shareholders are not much more exercised by the issue.'[51] More than half of the companies surveyed said there were more urgent issues, such as brand awareness, marketing strategies and corporate social responsibility. Just 14 per cent of them had a clear plan for tackling climate change. A report from Headland, a communications consultancy, said fund managers 'do not pay much attention to climate change issues when taking investment decisions'. They regarded climate change effects as slow and cumulative and the issue as outside the remit of typical fund managers who 'are not looking at 2012, let alone 2050'. Long term for the investment community was about three years.

Of course, mainstream journalists and editors never tire of insisting that they cover all the issues. They tell us the problem is that readers would be bored to tears if they kept on repeating the kind of arguments discussed above. In reality, the arguments are simply ignored. Instead, the same journalists go on repeating the same empty blather about 'the need for all of us to act now'. Take any number of editorials from the *Independent*, the *Guardian* or any other liberal media outlet from the last 20 years, and almost exactly the same words can be found: governments need to do more – especially the Americans! – but 'we' need to do our bit, too. Something must be done!

Journalists and editors, and perhaps much of the public, fail to notice that the discussion on climate change has somehow managed to stay on 'square one' for the past 20 or 30 years. Our point is that the media are structurally *obliged* to remain on square one. After all, what can a corporate business like the *Independent* possibly say about the impact of corporate advertising of mass consumption on environmental collapse, on the stifling of change? What can it say about the relentless activities of its big business allies working to bend the public mind to their will over decades? What can it say about the historical potency of people power in challenging the entrenched power, to which it, as a part of the corporate media, belongs?

But there is another question that needs to be asked. Why on earth do we, the public, continue looking to corporate media like the *Guardian* and the *Independent* for honest analysis and credible solutions? If we can wake up to the irrationality of our own trust and expectations – if we can become dis-illusioned – we can do something different. We can begin to build our own media, our own sources of information, communication and analysis. This, perhaps more than ever before, is entirely possible. As a result, ideas and action can emerge that are uncompromised by the profit drive. And out of this, in turn, can come hope that is not just one more clever deceit.

AN EXCHANGE WITH THE
INDEPENDENT ON SUNDAY'S REVIEW EDITOR

In response to our alert on Marcus Fairs' article promoting 'the spirit of Nero', discussed above, a large number of readers wrote to the *Independent on Sunday'*s Review magazine editor, Tim Lewis. We also wrote, asking Lewis:

> Given [the] extraordinary and rising level of suffering [associated with climate change], what is the moral justification for today's front cover? Are you not in fact subordinating human welfare to short-term profit by publishing this piece? Fairs links to many travel companies in his article – did the *Independent on Sunday* receive payment for these mentions?[52]

Lewis responded as follows:

> Thank you for your note. I have read it closely, along with your vigorous comments on Media Lens (as well as those of Media Lens readers).
>
> As I'm sure you are aware, the *Independent* and the *Independent on Sunday* have promoted respect for the environment and the impact of climate change more than any other national newspaper group. The subject features frequently – to powerful and uncompromising effect – on the front cover and throughout both newspapers, and recent campaigns (such as criticism of supermarket packaging, for example) have been determined and pursued over the course of a considerable time span (and not just dropped after a couple of days).
>
> We feel that the *Independent'*s credentials as a green newspaper are beyond dispute. This is one of our great strengths and something that our readers look to us for. To describe us as a newspaper that is 'corporate' and one that indulges in 'unrestrained consumerism' is trite and completely

inaccurate. Of course, we need advertising to stay in business – would you prefer that the *Independent* and the *Independent on Sunday* ceased to exist? Who would pick up our high-profile campaigns on climate change? With reference to Marcus Fairs' article, the idea that we received advertising on the back of this feature is untrue and potentially libellous.

Perhaps you are right to question where Fairs' article fits in within the context of the 'green' paper outlined above. The *Independent* was set up to reflect a diversity of opinion in the mainstream press, and, so long as this is not done in a reckless manner, we continue to uphold this belief. While the editorial staff of the *Independent on Sunday* might not share all of Marcus Fairs' opinions, we will defend to the end his right to express them and our right to publish them. The subject matter was provocative, but we do not take our readers for idiots who can't make up their own minds about these issues.

Was it irresponsible? Well, we would argue that the subject is not as straightforward as you make out. Our readers continue to use aeroplanes – as, of course, do environmentalists from Al Gore to Prince Charles – and ripping up our passports and vowing never to fly again will not solve the problem of global warming. One intention of the article was to highlight the rate at which our natural wonders are vanishing, which in turn would prompt our readers to consider the impact of climate change and the precariousness of our planet. We also tried, where possible, to lead our readers towards 'ethical' agencies like responsibletravel.com

We should also not forget the benefits of tourism to local communities, and the impact this can have in leading them to protect their natural resources. I'm sure you will be familiar with various examples – from protected animals to coral reefs – around the world.

The article is certainly not without mistakes. We regret, for example, that we did not mention carbon offsetting to combat the effects of greenhouse gases emitted by taking any journey by aeroplane. Having said that, we would also call into question the approach of Media Lens. Instead of directing your subscribers to the full article to make up their own minds, you printed the most dramatic extracts in an attempt to rabble rouse and bully a response. You say that 'the goal of Media Lens is to promote rationality, compassion and respect for others' – in your response to this article, we have seen little of these qualities.

You are right to be angry about the treatment of environmental issues in the media, but picking a fight with the *Independent* does not seem the most appropriate place to start.

I am happy for you to reprint this letter on your website.

We replied:

Dear Tim

Many thanks for your reply. You write: *'As I'm sure you are aware, the Independent and the Independent on Sunday have promoted respect for the environment and the impact of climate change more than any other national newspaper group ... We feel that the Independent's credentials as a green newspaper are beyond dispute.'*

It is probably true that the *Independent* titles have promoted respect for the climate more than any other newspaper group, which is admirable. But this hardly indicates that the *Independent* is a 'green newspaper' or that its green credentials are 'beyond dispute'. In evaluating such claims we need to consider what an authentically 'green newspaper' would look like and what would characterise acceptable performance.

You write: *'To describe us as a newspaper that is "corporate" and one that indulges in "unrestrained consumerism" is trite and completely inaccurate.'*

To describe the *Independent on Sunday* as a corporate newspaper is a simple statement of fact. Your newspaper is part of Independent News and Media PLC (INMPLC), a public limited company. The company describes itself as: 'a leading international media and communications group, with interests in Australia, Ireland, New Zealand, South Africa, the United Kingdom and most recently, India ... the Group publishes over 176 newspaper and magazine titles with a weekly circulation of over 29 million copies and operates over 70 on-line editorial and classified sites ... The Group has grown consistently over the last 15 years by building a geographically unique and diverse portfolio of market-leading brands, and today manages gross assets of 3.9 billion euros, turnover of over 1.8 billion euros and employs over 11,000 people worldwide.'[53]

The primary focus of your corporate employer is on growing a diverse portfolio of market-leading brands generating gross assets of billions of euros. The wealthy owner of INMPLC, Sir Anthony O'Reilly, is candid enough: 'For the advertiser, the newspaper remains the most effective mechanism to convey to the potential consumer the virtue, value, colour and style of any new product, service or offering that he has.'[54]

O'Reilly forgot to mention the role of the newspaper in overthrowing tyranny, oppression and the suffering that afflicts humanity more generally – perhaps he took that as read.

In our Media Alert we wrote that *Independent* titles are 'crammed with the usual inducements to indulge in unrestrained consumerism'. You respond that this is 'trite and completely inaccurate'. Again, it is a statement of fact. The latest advertisers to appear in the *Independent on Sunday* (February 11) include: Virgin Atlantic, Volkswagen, Ford, Suzuki, Nissan, Vauxhall, Skoda, Saab, Alfa, Barclaycard, Directline Insurance, Abbey, Invesco Perpetual, Nationwide, HSBC, Lloyds TSB, Egg, Boots, Dell, Apple, Sony, BT, Sky, WH Smith, Eurostar, Ebay, Guinness, Greene King IPA, Mornflake, Anglian...

But anyway, how green can the *Independent* and *Independent on Sunday* actually be? In his book, *The Corporation*, Canadian lawyer Joel Bakan notes that the senior managers of corporations are legally obliged, on pain of prosecution, to seek to maximise profits for shareholders. Bakan explains that corporate managers 'must always put their corporation's best interests first and not act out of concern for anyone or anything else (unless the expression of such concern can somehow be justified as advancing the corporation's own interests)'.[55]

Because investment tends to flow to corporations that maximise shareholder returns, the system powerfully selects for irresponsible greed. It is this relentless subordination of people and planet to short-term profit that has so rapidly destabilised the climate. The *Independent* is an integral part of this system: any green initiatives within the paper are constantly compromised by the need to serve its very reason for being – profit-maximisation.

A genuinely 'green newspaper' would be one that not only exposes, not only challenges, but actually seeks to loosen the grip of corporate fundamentalism on modern society. This the *Independent* titles – products of this selfsame fundamentalism – are manifestly powerless to do. It is therefore quite wrong to describe the *Independent* as a 'green newspaper'. Instead the *Independent* titles have provided a powerful platform for their state-corporate allies and sponsors – and those of billionaire owner, Sir Anthony O'Reilly.

There has been positive reporting in the *Independent* but it has been contradicted, in fact buried, by the flood of corporate propaganda acting to stifle serious thought and action on environmental issues. Your papers, for example, happily provide space for BP's mendacious 'Beyond Petroleum' campaign directed at what the public relations industry calls 'special publics'.

You write: '*Perhaps you are right to question where Fairs' article fits in within the context of the "green" paper outlined above.*'

In fact it fits perfectly with the reality that the *Independent* is a corporate shark, red in tooth and fin, with a green tinge around the gills.

You also write: '*The Independent was set up to reflect a diversity of opinion in the mainstream press, and, so long as this is not done in a reckless manner, we continue to uphold this belief.*'

Journalist Hannen Swaffer said it rather better in 1928: '*Freedom of the press in Britain means freedom to print such of the proprietor's prejudices as the advertisers don't object to.*'[56]

In hundreds of Media Alerts over the past five years we have shown how, on issue after issue, the 'diversity of opinion' in the *Independent* strongly reflects elite opinion in this way, with very occasional, token contributions from grassroots or radical commentators (such as Noam Chomsky, who made one of his vanishingly rare appearances in your paper on February 11).

Dramatic front pages are often positive, but they are also a form of niche marketing – one that obscures the deeply reactionary content of much *Independent* reporting and commentary.

You add: '*Instead of directing your subscribers to the full article to make up their own minds, you printed the most dramatic extracts in an attempt to rabble rouse and bully a response.*'

The extracts spoke for themselves. How is it possible to make Fairs' brazen call for irresponsibility less irresponsible? Greg King, an area manager for the sustainable transport charity SUSTRANS, made the point that matters in his email to you. We should emphasise that King was writing in a personal capacity:

'*It beggars belief how such an article can make it into a newspaper. By any assessment this piece is idiotic and absolutely disgraceful. How can you possibly justify printing an article which states (among many other things) that "We are aware that we will soon have to act more sustainably, which gives us all the more reason to be irresponsible while we still can."*

There is already an urgent imperative to act more sustainably. Climate change is already destroying people's lives in the developing world (according to the WHO 150,000 are already dying prematurely as a direct result of climate change) and it is already putting our children's, grandchildren's, and perhaps even our own futures in serious jeopardy.

This article appearing in your paper reflects very poorly on you and your staff.'[57]

Our readers are not a 'rabble' – their rationality often puts mainstream journalism to shame. From the emails you have received, you will know that many of them are the same *Independent* readers you claim are smart enough to 'make up their own minds about these issues'.

As for bullying – media companies are authoritarian institutions in which power flows from the top, and in which journalists are accustomed to unaccountability and public deference. No surprise, then, that public participation – even when limited to the sending of polite, rational emails – feels like bullying. The technical term for what you have experienced is: democracy.

Best wishes
David Edwards and David Cromwell

5
Plan A/Plan B:
The Downing Street Memo

At the Nuremberg war crimes tribunal in 1946, Nazi leaders like Goering, von Ribbentrop, Jodl and Streicher were sentenced to death by hanging for 'Crimes against Peace: namely, planning, preparation, initiation or waging of a war of aggression, or a war in violation of international treaties, agreements or assurances, or participation in a Common Plan or Conspiracy for the accomplishment of any of the foregoing.'[1] It is remarkable, but now indisputable, that in 2003 the leaders of Britain and the United States were responsible for just such a conspiracy.

In Chapter 1, we noted White House press secretary Scott McClellan's description of how Bush relied on a 'political propaganda campaign' rather than the truth to sell the Iraq war to the American public, with Bush having made up his mind early on to attack Saddam Hussein. The way Bush managed the issue 'almost guaranteed that the use of force would become the only feasible option', McClellan added.[2] He also commented: 'In the permanent campaign era, it was all about manipulating sources of public opinion to the president's advantage.'[3] In March 2007, former NATO commander, General Wesley Clark, told *Democracy Now!*:

About ten days after 9/11, I went through the Pentagon and I saw Secretary Rumsfeld and Deputy Secretary Wolfowitz. I went downstairs just to say hello to some of the people on the Joint Staff who used to work for me, and one of the generals called me in. He said, 'Sir, you've got to come in and talk to me a second.' I said, 'Well, you're too busy.' He said, 'No, no.' He says, 'We've made the decision we're going to war with Iraq.'

This was on or about the 20th of September. I said, 'We're going to war with Iraq? Why?' He said, 'I don't know.' He said, 'I guess they don't know what else to do.' So I said, 'Well, did they find some information connecting Saddam to al-Qaeda?' He said, 'No, no.' He says, 'There's nothing new that way. They just made the decision to go to war with Iraq.' He said, 'I guess it's like we don't know what to do about terrorists, but we've got a good military and we can take down governments.' And he said, 'I guess if the only tool you have is a hammer, every problem has to look like a nail.'[4]

Carne Ross, a key Foreign Office diplomat responsible for liaising with UN inspectors in Iraq, said in June 2005 that British government claims about Iraq's weapons programme had been 'totally implausible'. Ross told the *Guardian*: 'I'd read the intelligence on WMD for four and a half years, and there's no way that it could sustain the case that the government was presenting. All of my colleagues knew that, too. There was a very good alternative to war that was never properly pursued, which was to close down Saddam's sources of illegal revenue.'[5]

But an alternative to war was never an option for the Bush–Blair alliance. On May 1, 2005, the *Sunday Times* published a leaked Downing Street memo that hammered the final nails in the coffin of Tony Blair's credibility. The document – minutes of a highly confidential meeting dated July 23, 2002 – was written eight months before the invasion began. John Scarlett, chairman of the Joint Intelligence Committee (JIC), opened proceedings by summarising the intelligence and latest JIC assessment: 'Saddam's regime was tough and based on extreme fear. The only way to overthrow it was likely to be by massive military action.'[6] As Scarlett's initial statement makes clear, it was understood by everyone present that the issue at hand was how best to overthrow Saddam Hussein, not how to neutralise the supposed threat from any weapons of mass destruction. Indeed, remarkably, given the propaganda campaign, little mention was made of WMD. The memo then records the words of Sir Richard Dearlove, the head of the British intelligence service MI6, who commented on his recent visit to Washington where he had held talks with George Tenet, director of the CIA:

There was a perceptible shift in attitude. Military action was now seen as inevitable. Bush wanted to remove Saddam, through military action, justified by the conjunction of terrorism and WMD. But the intelligence and facts were being fixed around the policy. The NSC [US National Security Council] had no patience with the UN route, and no enthusiasm for publishing material on the Iraqi regime's record. There was little discussion in Washington of the aftermath after military action.[7]

This recognition of the inevitability of war is reiterated in comments made in the meeting by foreign secretary Jack Straw: 'It seemed clear that Bush had made up his mind to take military action, even if the timing was not yet decided. But the case was thin. Saddam was not threatening his neighbours, and his WMD capability was less than that of Libya, North Korea or Iran.'[8] But in the absence of a threat – even to Iraq's neighbours, much less to the West – how could war possibly be justified? Straw explained: 'We should work up a plan for an ultimatum to Saddam to allow back in the UN weapons inspectors. This would also help with the legal justification for the use of force.'[9] A further leaked Cabinet Office briefing paper from the same day clarifies that since regime change was illegal under international law it was 'necessary to create the conditions' that would help provide legitimacy for war.

Writing in the *Sunday Times*, Michael Smith noted that the briefing paper asserted the only way the allies could justify military action was 'to place Saddam Hussein in a position where he ignored or rejected a United Nations ultimatum ordering him to co-operate with the weapons inspectors'. But the briefing paper warned this would be difficult. 'It is just possible that an ultimatum could be cast in terms which Saddam would reject', the document said. But if he accepted it and did not attack the allies, they would be 'most unlikely' to obtain the legal justification they needed.[10] Notice the point is not that it was 'just possible' that an ultimatum could be cast in terms which Saddam would *accept* – an outcome that might have allowed a peaceful resolution to the crisis. The aspiration was to cast an ultimatum that Saddam would *reject*, so providing an excuse for war. The goal, clearly, was to lay a trap for a war of aggression and conquest, not to negotiate for peace and security through disarmament. After all, if disarmament had been the concern, an ultimatum would have been superfluous – Saddam was 'not threatening his neighbours, and his WMD capability was less than that of Libya, North Korea or Iran'. Smith accurately commented: 'The suggestion that the allies use the UN to justify war contradicts claims by Blair and Bush ... that they turned to the UN in order to *avoid* having to go to war.'[11]

But the UN trap was merely Plan A of a two-part plan to make war possible. There was also Plan B. As part of the 'attempt to provoke Saddam Hussein into giving the allies an excuse for war', Smith wrote, Britain and America increased bombing raids on Iraq, dropping twice as many bombs in the second half of 2002 as they did during the whole of 2001.[12] By October, with the UN vote still two weeks away, RAF aircraft were dropping 64 per cent of bombs falling on the southern no-fly zone. This aggressive bombing campaign contradicted Foreign Office legal advice appended to the leaked July 23, 2002 briefing paper, which stated that allied aircraft were only 'entitled to use force in self-defence where such a use of force is a necessary and proportionate response to actual or imminent attack from Iraqi ground systems'.[13] The attacks, in other words, were illegal terrorist acts. Smith summarised the two-part plan to generate an excuse for war:

> British officials hoped the ultimatum [for Iraq to readmit UN weapons inspectors] could be framed in words that would be so unacceptable to Hussein that he would reject it outright. But they were far from certain this would work, so there was also a Plan B ... Put simply, US aircraft patrolling the southern no-fly zone were dropping a lot more bombs in the hope of provoking a reaction that would give the allies an excuse to carry out a full-scale bombing campaign, an air war, the first stage of the conflict.[14]

STRAW, BLAIR AND THE BIG LIE

The staggering deceit and criminality of the Blair regime is apparent when we compare the above with public statements made by the government. Despite clearly plotting to ensure a violent outcome at least as early as July 2002, Jack Straw told BBC Radio 4's *Today* programme in January 2003: 'What's important for people to understand is that war is not inevitable.'[15] Responding to comments made by an unnamed government source suggesting that the prospect of conflict had receded from a 60:40 likelihood of conflict to a 60:40 likelihood of peace, Straw commented: 'I think that's a reasonably accurate description.'[16] This was Jonathan Freedland's take on Straw two years later in the *Guardian*:

> To dump Straw would look especially perverse after Sunday's leaked memo revealed not only that Downing Street had set its heart on regime change back in 2002 – as opponents of the war always charged – but also that Straw played a Colin Powell role in those internal deliberations, warning that the case against Iraq was 'thin'. To make him the fall guy would look unfair...[17]

In his May 1, 2005 article, Smith had rightly rejected exactly this benign interpretation: 'Despite voicing concerns, Straw was *not* standing in the way of war. It was he who suggested a solution: they should force Saddam into a corner where he would give them a clear reason for war.'[18] That was obvious to Smith; it is obvious to us. How curious that it was not also obvious to Freedland. Straw was in fact proposing a conspiracy to lure Saddam into actions that would help 'legitimise' a US–UK war of aggression.

In the July 23, 2002 memo, the attorney general, Lord Goldsmith, warned that the desire for regime change was not a legal base for military action. Tony Blair responded that 'it would make a big difference politically and legally if Saddam refused to allow in the UN inspectors'.[19] Blair's comment was made in the context of Straw's points about the lack of a threat and the need for an ultimatum, and of the briefing paper arguing it was 'just possible' that 'an ultimatum could be cast in terms which Saddam would reject'. Blair, then, was also hoping to use UN inspectors, not to disarm Iraq, but to provoke Saddam's refusal to cooperate, so providing an excuse for war.

Blair's criminality in launching a war of aggression, and in lying to Parliament and to the British people, is therefore not in doubt. On November 8, 2002, Blair said: 'Iraq now has a "final opportunity" to comply with its international and legal obligations by giving up once and for all its weapons of mass destruction ... If it does not, then the consequences are clear.'[20] The 'final opportunity' was a fraud, an endgame in a plot to provide an excuse for a war that would devastate an entire country. The consequences, completely regardless of Saddam's response, were guaranteed.

In February 2003, Blair said: 'If we go to war it will not be because we want to, but because we have to in order to disarm Saddam.'[21] As late as February 15, 2003 – just one month before the war began on March 20 – Blair told the Labour Party's spring conference in Glasgow: 'I hope, even now, Iraq can be disarmed peacefully, with or without Saddam.'[22] Blair was lying. He had been plotting to secure a violent outcome since at least July 2002.

The evidence of a conspiracy to lure and goad Saddam into providing an excuse for war is amply corroborated by other sources. Sir Christopher Meyer, the British ambassador to the United States, wrote in a March 18, 2002 memo: 'We backed regime change, but the plan had to be clever and failure was not an option. It would be a tough sell for us domestically.'[23] In March 2005, John Ware reported on the BBC's *Panorama* programme that this 'clever' plan involved getting the UN Security Council to pass a tough new disarmament resolution. Was it intended to achieve peace or provide a trigger for war? Meyer could not be clearer: 'The US could go it alone if it wanted. But if it wanted to act with partners there had to be strategy for building support for military action. I then went through the need to wrong foot Saddam on the inspectors.'[24] As we have seen, the 'wrong footing' involved Saddam being provoked into rejecting the ultimatum – a desired outcome that was considered 'just possible'.

Richard Haass, director of policy planning at the US State Department from 2001 to 2003, also confirmed that war had long been the intended outcome:

> ... the first time I came away persuaded that a war was ninety-nine percent likely was in early July of 2002 during one of my regular sessions with Condoleezza Rice, then the national security advisor ... I was uneasy about it, thought that it raised questions to me at least whether it was worth it ... and when I began to raise these concerns, Condi's reaction was essentially, save your breath, hold your fire 'This decision's pretty much been made, this is where the President is.'[25]

THE REAL NEWS

According to most media accounts, the main revelation of the Downing Street memos centred around the comments made by the then head of MI6, Sir Richard Dearlove: 'Bush wanted to remove Saddam, through military action, justified by the conjunction of terrorism and WMD', and that 'the intelligence and facts were being fixed around the policy'. In an article for the *Los Angeles Times* entitled, 'The real news in the Downing Street memos', Michael Smith challenged this focus: 'Although Blair and Bush still insist the decision to go to the UN was about averting war, one memo states that it was, in fact, about "wrong-footing" Hussein into giving them a legal justification for war.'[26]

Smith's conclusion: 'The way in which the intelligence was "fixed" to justify war is old news. The real news is the shady April 2002 deal [when Bush met Blair in Crawford, Texas] to go to war, the cynical use of the UN to provide an excuse, and the secret, illegal air war without the backing of Congress.'[27] Readers might like to keep Smith's comments in mind as we see how close the corporate media came to communicating the 'real news' of the leaked documents.

MANAGING TO MISS THE POINT: THE MEDIA AND THE MEMO

Writing in the *Guardian*, Sidney Blumenthal focused on the 'old news', making no mention of the 'real news' at all: 'Every revelation of how "the intelligence and facts were being fixed around the policy" for war, as in the Downing Street memo, shatters even Republicans' previously implacable faith.'[28] There was not a word about the Plan A/Plan B conspiracy to provoke a war that is blindingly obvious in the leaked documents published by the *Sunday Times*.

Rupert Cornwell wrote in the *Independent* that the July 2002 memo indicated 'the Bush administration had already made up its mind to invade Iraq, and that intelligence was being "fixed" to fit that policy'.[29] Again, not a word about the 'real news' of Plan A/Plan B. In the same paper one week earlier, Andrew Gumbel had described the memo as being 'about an early decision having been taken to go to war and of the need for justification to be found for the Iraq invasion'.[30] A justification is always needed for war – the point about Smith's revelations is that they show that a trap was actively being sought to make war possible, not merely a justification. It was a conspiracy to *ensure* a war of aggression and conquest would be fought.

The *Evening Standard* wrote that the memo 'showed the PM backed regime change in Iraq as early as July 2002'.[31] This was a tiny fraction of what the memo showed, and was not the 'real news', but it was all the *Standard* had to say. According to the *Express*, the memo 'revealed Mr Blair had already privately committed Britain to help America topple Saddam Hussein and was anxious to find ways of selling the war to the public and Parliament'.[32] Again, the 'old news', this time combined with a distortion. In fact, the conspiracy was to provoke war, not just to sell it to the British people. The same paper added for 'balance': 'But yesterday Mr Blair told BBC1's Breakfast With Frost the decision had not been taken to attack Saddam Hussein by July 2002. He added: "The point is that after that meeting we decided to go back to the UN and give him a last chance."'[33] The *Express* journalists failed to mention the evidence staring them in the face: namely, that the memo itself reveals that Blair's 'last chance' was a fraud designed to 'wrong foot' Saddam into rejecting the ultimatum and so trigger war.

The *Financial Times* wrote that the memo 'revealed that eight months before the conflict, he [Blair] had discussed with colleagues possible invasion scenarios and how to justify military action'.[34] This was a staggering, lobotomised version. In a separate article, one of the same authors wrote that the memo 'suggested that he [Blair] was looking at ways to justify an invasion eight months before the conflict'.[35] In the real world, Blair was looking at ways to provoke, not merely justify, an illegal war of aggression. Remarkably, the FT article added that the memo 'showed Mr Blair giving serious thought to strategy': '"If the political context were right, people would support regime change", the memo said. "The two key issues were whether the military plan worked and whether we had the political strategy to give the military plan the space to work."'[36] One could not possibly guess from this that Blair was in fact giving serious thought to manipulating inspections as part of a campaign of public deception in pursuit of war.

The *Guardian* wrote the day after Smith's May 1, 2005 article that the memo showed 'that, almost a year before the Iraq invasion, Tony Blair was privately preparing to commit Britain to war and topple Saddam Hussein, despite warnings from his closest advisers that it was unjustified'. This was the 'old news'. The article continued: 'The documents show how Mr Blair was told how Britain and the US could "create the conditions" for an invasion, partly, in the words of Jack Straw to "work up" an ultimatum to Saddam even though in the foreign secretary's own words, "the case was thin".'[37] The obfuscation, here, is intensified to the point of incomprehension. The authors could instead simply have explained that the ultimatum was intended to ensure rejection so that war could be launched with a fig leaf of international support and legitimacy. They could have mentioned that Bush and Blair endlessly lied to the public that peace was the desired outcome when they were doing everything in their power to trigger war.

Raymond Whitaker of the *Independent on Sunday* wrote that the contents of the memo 'demonstrate that the Prime Minister had signed up for "regime change" even earlier [than July 2002], when he met President George Bush at his Texas ranch the preceding April. Having promised British backing for war, the Government then set about seeking legal justification'.[38] What could be more innocent than that the government should 'set about seeking legal justification' for war? Whitaker wrote of the conspiracy to lure Iraq to war: 'Mr Straw's suggestion of an ultimatum on weapons inspections seemed to be the most promising way to allow Britain to join the US in its move towards war.' This is truth stripped of all meaning so that the appalling revelations in the memo are obscured from view. Whitaker quoted from the memo:

> 'The Prime Minister said that it would make a big difference politically and legally if Saddam refused to allow in the UN inspectors', the minutes recorded. 'Regime change and WMD were linked in the sense that it was the regime that was producing the WMD ... If the political context were right, people would support regime change.'

This marked the beginning of the Government's campaign to find a legal basis for the war in the alleged threat from Iraq's illegal weapons, marked by the notorious WMD dossier published two months later.[39]

Again, not a word about 'the cynical use of the UN to provide an excuse' for war described by Michael Smith.

According to the *Sunday Telegraph*, the memo 'revealed that Mr Blair explicitly raised the possibility of "regime change" as early as July 2002 – eight months before military action began – and discussed with senior ministers how to "create" the conditions necessary to provide the legal justification for war'.[40] Again, the real issue was buried out of sight. Jonathan Freedland wrote in the *Guardian*:

One [memo] shows that Britain and the US heavily increased bombing raids on Iraq in the summer of 2002 – when London and Washington were still insisting that war was a last resort – even though the Foreign Office's own lawyers had advised that such action was illegal. These 'spikes of activity' were aimed at provoking Saddam into action that might justify war.[41]

Here, at least, Freedland mentioned that increased bombing was intended to goad Saddam into providing an excuse for war. But he failed to mention that the bombing was merely Plan B, alongside Plan A that involved provoking Saddam to reject inspectors, so also providing a trigger for war. Once again, the real issue somehow just managed to escape his focus.

CONCLUSION

Anyone who wonders how Bush and Blair, clearly major war criminals, were able to remain in power, need look no further than to the corporate media performance above, which is all but uniform right across the media 'spectrum'. Only Smith, writing in the *Sunday Times*, managed to discuss honestly the significance of the documents leaked to him. Notice that this bizarre media response occurred despite the ready availability in the *Sunday Times*, and on the internet, of the key documents under discussion. Brazenly, in broad daylight, as it were, the media stole the truth out from under the public's nose.

Critics might object that this is an anomaly, a freak of timing; that a generally honest media system felt the public had simply had enough of Iraq. Thus, Freedland accepted that the memo story had been all but ignored. But he added: 'Journalists decided that voters were Iraq-ed out and so gave the memo much less coverage than it deserved.'[42] But, again, this misses the point. It was not merely that journalists decided that the public were 'Iraq-ed out'. The memo got plenty of coverage; the problem was that the coverage avoided the truth of what the memo revealed.

It is tempting to psychoanalyse mainstream journalists, to try to understand how highly educated professionals can behave as an intellectual herd in this way. Anyone who has read the material above carefully will feel a sense of awe at what is, in essence, a spectacular conjuring trick – the media caused the truth to vanish from sight. It really is an astonishing phenomenon. How *can* apparently civilised Western journalists so consistently subordinate the misery and despair of innocent people to the needs of power and profit? In the corporate media, putting the corporation first means not alienating centres of political and economic power that hold the keys to survival and success.

The crucial point is that, in the age of the internet, there is simply no longer any need to indulge the mainstream media's high-paid servility to power. Though they scoff at the notion, journalists really *do* have the blood of millions of innocent people on their hands. People who care about rational thought, who feel compassion for human suffering, will withdraw their support from the corporate media system. Readers will stop supporting it with their subscriptions, writers will stop supporting it with their words – and they will instead set about the vital work of building and supporting not-for-profit, internet-based media offering our only serious hope for compassionate change.

Why is it wrong for even well-meaning people to participate in fundamentally corrupt systems? Tolstoy explained:

> It is harmful because enlightened, good and honest people, by entering the ranks of the government, give it a moral authority which but for them it would not possess. If the government were made up entirely of that coarse element – the violators, self-seekers, and flatterers – who form its core, it could not continue to exist. The fact that honest and enlightened people are found who participate in the affairs of the government gives it whatever it possesses of moral prestige.[43]

We believe the observation generalises to the blood-soaked 'moral prestige' of today's corporate media.

6

Mind Your Methodology:
Killing the 2004 *Lancet* Report

BIG KILLING – BIG TEST

As a test of the honesty of the mass media, few tasks are more revealing than that of reporting our own government's responsibility for the mass killing of innocents abroad. In a 'post-historical' age of 'converged' political parties and globalised corporate control, few influential groups have any interest in seeing such horrors exposed, while many are strongly opposed to such exposure. Corporate journalists therefore face two competing pressures: 1) the moral, human imperative to report honestly our responsibility for mass killing; and 2) state-corporate inducements and flak rewarding servility and punishing dissent. The results, visible all around us, reveal much about the moral and political health of our media and our democracy.

On July 20, 2005 an article by Terry Kirby and Elizabeth Davies in the *Independent* noted that a November 2004 report in the *Lancet* had estimated Iraqi civilian deaths at nearly 100,000, but that the methodology 'was subsequently criticised'.[1] The report in question was produced by some of the world's leading research organisations – the Johns Hopkins Bloomberg School of Public Health, Columbia University and Baghdad's Al-Mustansiriya University – and was published in one of the world's most prestigious science journals – the *Lancet*. We were therefore keen to know which criticisms Kirby and Davies had in mind. We wrote to the *Independent* and Kirby replied on July 22: 'So far as I am aware, the *Lancet's* report was criticised by the Foreign Office.'[2] Also on July 20, an *Independent* editorial had claimed that the *Lancet* findings had been reached 'by extrapolating from a small sample ... While never completely discredited, those figures were widely doubted'.[3]

We wrote to the *Independent's* senior leader writer on foreign affairs, Mary Dejevsky: 'What is the basis for the claim that the sample was "small"? The report authors told me that the sample was standard for research of this kind, so that "we have the scientific strength to say what we have said with great certainty. I doubt any *Lancet* paper has gotten as much close inspection in recent years as this one has!"'.[4] Dejevsky responded on August 10:

> Personally, I think there was a problem with the extrapolation technique, because – while the sample may have been standard for that sort of thing – it seemed small from a lay perspective (I remember at the time) for the conclusions being drawn and there seemed too little account taken of the different levels of unrest in different regions. My main point, though, was less based on my impression than on the fact that this technique exposed the authors to the criticisms/dismissal that the govt duly made, and they had little to counter those criticisms with, bar the defence that their methods were standard for those sort of surveys.[5]

We wrote again on August 18:

> Thanks, Mary. You say that 'personally' you 'think there was a problem with the extrapolation technique' because while the sample was standard it was 'small from a lay perspective'. Your argument then is that the problem with the extrapolation technique was that people like you had a problem with it because the sample seemed too small. That's a deeply shocking response from a senior journalist writing in a serious newspaper about such an important report. We are talking about *our* responsibility for the mass death of civilians, after all.
>
> Should the methodology not be judged by the standards of science and reason rather than some ill-informed 'lay perspective'? Why on earth would we judge anything of importance by the standards of an ill-informed view?
>
> Your claim that the authors had little with which to counter criticism is flatly false. I can send you many powerful replies provided to us by the report authors in response to a range of (mostly trivial) criticisms we found in the media.

Dejevsky replied the same day:

> Thanks – I obviously sounded more off-hand than I intended. I just feel that extrapolation may be entirely sound when you can project over relatively uniform areas (subject, geographical whatever), but that – common sense suggests – it will be less reliable when the situation is so uneven, as in Iraq. This may be unjust and ill-informed, and maybe the arguments from the report's authors were not sufficiently aired because they were – in effect – suppressed. If you have some of the counter arguments I would be interested

to see them (beyond the defence that the methodology is standard, tried and tested, etc.).

Incidentally, I think it is absolutely legitimate, and right, for journalists to apply a common sense standard to scientific arguments and methods. We should have been far more exacting over the intelligence methodology that gave us Saddam's WMD.

The challenge to provide 'counter arguments' was one we were keen to accept. It was clear to us that, like most journalists, Dejevsky did not have a clue about epidemiology. (This sounds harsh, but in fact journalistic ignorance on these issues has been a phenomenon.) We contacted Les Roberts, lead author of the *Lancet* report. Roberts responded on August 22 with an email which he asked us to forward to the *Independent*:

Dear Mr. Kirby and Ms. Dejevsky,

I was disappointed to hear that you felt our study was in some way dismissed by Jack Straw's anemic response to our report in the *Lancet* last November. Serious reviews of our work and the criticisms of it were run in the *Financial Times*, the *Economist*, the *Chronicle of Higher Education* (attached above) and the WSJ [Wall Street Journal] Online on August 5th. Closer to home, John Rentoul of the *Independent* solicited a response to the Jack Straw letter last Nov. 21st and we responded with the attached letter [Not provided here]. I am told that it was printed by your paper.

Many people, like Ms. Dejevsky, have used the word extrapolation to describe what we did. When I hear people use that word they mean what is described in my Webster's Unabridged: '1. Statistics. to estimate the value of a variable outside its tabulated or observed range.' By this definition and the one I hear used by everyone on this side of the Atlantic, we did not extrapolate. We did sample. We drew conclusions from within the confines of that universe from which we sampled. Aside from a few homeless and transient households that did not appear in the 2002 [Iraqi] Ministry of Health figures or households who had been dissolved or killed since, every existing household in Iraq had an equal chance that we would visit them through our randomization process.

I understand that you feel that the sample was small: this is most puzzling. 142 post-invasion deaths in 988 households is a lot of deaths, and for the setting, a lot of interviews. There is no statistical doubt mortality is up, no doubt that violence is the main cause, and no doubt that the coalition forces have caused far more of these violent deaths than the insurgents (p<.0000001).

In essence this is an outbreak investigation. If your readers hear about a sample with 10 cases of mad cow disease in 1000 British citizens randomly tested, I am sure they would have no doubt there was an outbreak. In 1993, when the US Centers for Disease Control randomly called 613 households in Milwaukee and concluded that 403,000 people had developed Cryptosporidium in the largest outbreak ever recorded in the developed world, no one said that 613 households was not a big enough sample. It is odd that the logic of epidemiology embraced by the press every day regarding new drugs or health risks somehow changes when the mechanism of death is their armed forces.

The comments of Ms. Dejevsky regarding representativeness ... are also cause for concern because she seems to have not understood that this was a random sample.

By picking random neighborhoods proportional to population, we are likely to account for the natural variability of ethnicity, income, and violence. Her words above strongly suggest that the Falluja numbers should be included, rather than being used to temper the results from the other 32 neighborhoods. Please understand how extremely conservative we were: we did a survey estimating that ~285,000 people have died due to the first 18 months of invasion and occupation and we reported it as at least ~100,000.

Finally, there are now at least 8 independent estimates of the number or rate of deaths induced by the invasion of Iraq. The source most favored by the war proponents (Iraqbodycount.org) is the lowest. Our estimate is the third from highest. Four of the estimates place the death toll above 100,000. The studies measure different things. Some are surveys, some are based on surveillance which is always incomplete in times of war. The three lowest estimates are surveillance based.

The key issues are supported by all the estimates that attribute deaths to the various causes: violence is way up post-invasion and the Coalition is responsible for many times more deaths than are the insurgents. The exact number is less important than these two indisputable facts which helps us to understand why things are going badly and how to fix them.

I hope these thoughts are helpful.[6]

Perhaps most damning in Roberts' reply – in light of media criticism of the *Lancet*'s alleged exaggeration of civilian deaths – was his refutation of the claim that the uneven levels of violent unrest in Iraq compromised the accuracy of the figures. In fact, the study not only accounted for this variability, it erred on the side of caution by excluding data from Fallujah where deaths were unusually high. Moreover, other violent hotspots – such as Ramadi, Tallafar and Najaf – were all passed over in the sample by chance. This suggested that the actual total of civilian deaths was likely to be higher than 100,000. Indeed, it would have made far more sense for the media to be criticising the report authors for under-estimating the number of deaths.

We wrote to Dejevsky asking if she had received Roberts' response. She replied on September 1:

> Yes, and I understand the arguments. But I stick to my position that extrapolation, however scientific and well-thought through is no substitute for real figures. I know that the 'real' figures here do not exist, but I still think that extrapolation has obvious drawbacks which lay the resulting figures open to question – and therefore vulnerable to govt spokesmen who seek to discredit them. Incidentally, my view on extrapolation is really neither here nor there. My chief objection to it is, as I have just said, that it lays the figures themselves open to question by those who have an interest in discrediting them.

Dejevsky thus simply chose to ignore Roberts' point that he and his team had *not* extrapolated; they had sampled.

Edward Herman, co-author with Noam Chomsky of the classic media study, *Manufacturing Consent*, commented on this response: 'Massive incompetence in support of a war-apologetic agenda. Dejevsky objects to the figures because they are vulnerable to discrediting for reasons that make no sense. I wonder if she finds sampling discreditable in all cases.'[7] The last point was particularly interesting to us: had the *Independent* and other media voiced similar objections to earlier cases of sampling? It was easy enough to check.

THE PUZZLED EPIDEMIOLOGIST

It is understandable that Roberts found Kirby's and Dejevsky's responses 'puzzling'. After all, in 2000 Roberts began the first of three surveys in Congo for the International Rescue Committee (IRC) in which he used methods akin to those of the Iraq study. Roberts' first survey estimated that an astonishing 1.7 million people had died in Congo over 22 months of armed conflict – an average of 2,600 deaths per day. The IRC's president, Reynold Levy, put the figures in perspective: 'It's as if the entire population of Houston was wiped off the face of the Earth in a matter of months.'[8]

As Roberts commented in 2005, the reaction could not have been more different to that which followed the *Lancet* report: 'Tony Blair and Colin Powell quoted those results time and time again without any question as to the precision or validity.'[9] Indeed, within a month of Roberts' IRC report being published, the UN Security Council passed a resolution that all foreign armies must leave Congo, and later that year, the United Nations called for $140 million in aid to the country, more than doubling its previous annual request. Citing Roberts' study, the US State Department announced an additional $10 million for emergency programmes in Congo.

In his October 2001 speech to the Labour Party conference, Tony Blair said the international community could resolve many of the world's worst conflicts: 'It could, with our help, sort out the blight that is the continuing conflict in the Democratic Republic of the Congo, where three million people have died through war or famine in the last decade.'[10] The 3 million figure was taken straight from one of Roberts' studies using essentially the same methodology employed in Iraq. By contrast, in rejecting the *Lancet* report out of hand, Blair told parliament in December 2004: 'Figures from the Iraqi Ministry of Health, which are a survey from the hospitals there, are in our view the most accurate survey there is.'[11]

Foreign secretary Jack Straw said the government would examine the *Lancet* figures 'with very great care', adding, 'it is, however, an estimate that is not based on standard methodology for assessing casualties'.[12] Like so much else that Straw says, this was simply untrue. Blair's press spokesman said the government had a number of 'concerns and difficulties' about the methodology used, Patrick Wintour and Richard Norton-Taylor reported in the *Guardian*: '"The findings were based on extrapolation and treating Iraq as if it were all the same in terms of the level of the conflict", he said of the study published in the *Lancet*. "This is not the case."'[13] Then, in a classic example of media propaganda, Wintour and Norton-Taylor presented the government's concocted 'controversy' as genuine: 'The controversy about the study largely turns on whether the sample size of 7,800 people used by the team of US and Iraqi academics was sufficiently large, and whether the 33 neighbourhoods chosen were representative of the rest of the country.' This, again, was false. In reality, there was and is no 'controversy' about the size of the sample among scientists and serious commentators. Michael J. Toole, head of the Center for International Health at the Burnet Institute, an Australian research organisation, said: 'That's a classical sample size.' Researchers typically conduct surveys in 30 neighbourhoods, so the Iraq study's total of 33 strengthens its conclusions. 'I just don't see any evidence of significant exaggeration', Toole added.[14]

David R. Meddings, a medical officer with the Department of Injuries and Violence Prevention at the World Health Organization, said surveys of this kind always have uncertainty because of sampling and the possibility that people gave incorrect information about deaths in their households. However, Meddings added: 'I don't think the authors ignored that or understated. Those cautions I don't believe should be applied any more or any less stringently to a study that looks at a politically sensitive conflict than to a study that looks at a pill for heart disease.'[15]

The *Independent's* deep ignorance of the subject continued to fuel the idea of a controversially small sample: 'The *Lancet* said the research was based on a sample of fewer than 1,000 Iraqi households but said the findings were convincing.'[16] Much was made of a comment printed in the *Washington Post* by Marc E. Garlasco, a senior military analyst at Human Rights Watch, who said of Roberts' figures: 'These numbers seem to be inflated.'[17] This was reported in the British media. Unreported anywhere, as far as we can tell, is the fact that Garlasco subsequently admitted that he had not read the *Lancet* paper at the time and called his quote in the *Washington Post* 'really unfortunate'. Garlasco said he had told the reporter: 'I haven't read it. I haven't seen it. I don't know anything about it, so I shouldn't comment on it.' But 'like any good journalist, he got me to'.[18]

The large gap between the *Lancet* estimate and that of Iraq Body Count – a constant feature of press coverage – was also not surprising for reasons which we will examine in the following chapter.

Dr Bradley Woodruff, then a medical epidemiologist at the US Centers for Disease Control and Prevention said, 'Les [Roberts] has the most valid estimate.' Dr Toole agreed: 'If anything, the deaths may have been higher [than the *Lancet* study's estimate] because what they are unable to do is survey families where everyone has died.'[19] The media, however, knew better. Roger Alton, then editor of the *Observer*, gave us his view of the *Lancet* report: 'I find the methodology a bit doubtful...'.[20] David Aaronovitch, then of the *Guardian*, told us: 'I have a feeling (and I could be wrong) that the report may be a dud.'[21] Perhaps Aaronovitch's 'feeling' was a close relation of Dejevsky's when she wrote 'I just feel' the 'extrapolation technique' was unsuited to a situation as 'uneven' as Iraq.

'STUNNING' BUT 'SOUND': MEDIA RESPONSE TO THE CONGO METHODOLOGY AND NUMBERS

We learn some ugly truths when we compare the media response to Les Roberts' report on Iraq with the response to his earlier work in Congo. In our analysis we found that in both the US and the British press, news reports initially presented the estimates of 100,000 deaths in Iraq and initially 1.7 million, and later 3 million, deaths in Congo without critical comment. The difference lies in the days, weeks and months that followed. Whereas the Congo figures and methodology were accepted without challenge, the Iraq figures and methodology were subjected to steady, withering criticism by both politicians and journalists (with rare defences in comment pieces by, for example, Seumas Milne and Terry Jones in the *Guardian*).

Interestingly, we found that the right-wing British press appeared to have been marginally more accurate in its news reporting on the Iraq figures than the so-called liberal press. For example, *The Times* wrote of the *Lancet* report in November 2004: 'While doubts have been cast over some of the report's findings ... If anything, researchers appear to have erred on the side of caution, opting to omit all data from Fallujah, where the mortality rates were significantly higher.'[22] The *Financial Times* even managed to make the obvious point we are making in this chapter: 'This survey technique has been criticised as flawed, but the sampling method has been used by the same team in Darfur in Sudan and in the eastern Congo and produced credible results. An official at the World Health Organisation said the Iraq study "is very much in the league that the other studies are in ... You can't rubbish (the team) by saying they are incompetent".'[23] By comparison, reports in the 'liberal' press tended to be more sceptical of the *Lancet* estimates and more respectful of government criticism. For example, foreign correspondent Patrick Cockburn wrote in the *Independent on Sunday*:

> The Iraqi [*sic*] Body Count figure is probably much too low, because US military tactics ensure high civilian losses. American firepower, designed to combat the Soviet army, cannot be used in built-up areas without killing or injuring many civilians. Nevertheless a study published in the *Lancet*, estimating that 100,000 civilians had died in Iraq, appears to be too high.[24]

Consider the logic: one estimate is 'probably much too low' because the American army uses powerful weapons designed for Cold War combat – a complete non sequitur. That was considered a serious response by a major newspaper on a very serious issue. Another study 'appears to be too high', perhaps because American weapons are not *that* powerful. One can only feel for epidemiologists like Les Roberts who have to read these responses to their work.

On June 9, 2000, the *Washington Post* and *New York Times* both reported the initial figure of 1.7 million dead in Congo without challenge. The *Guardian* did the same on June 10. The *New York Times'* 'Quotation Of The Day' on June 9 read: '"Men with guns come and wreak havoc on a very regular basis. Those men cause more death by making people flee their homes than actually by shooting or slitting throats." Les Roberts, supervisor of a survey that attributes 1.7 million deaths in eastern Congo to two years of war.' The *Guardian* reported: 'a new survey by the International Rescue Committee (IRC) sheds light on what is happening across this vast country. The New York-based IRC estimates that 1.7m people have died from the war in the northern and eastern provinces alone in the past two years.'[25] On June 24, a *Washington Post* editorial observed: 'The Roberts estimate is, of course, a rough one. Nevertheless, the report deserves to be taken seriously as the first comprehensive attempt to establish the dimensions of the crisis.'[26]

In April 2001, Karl Vick of the *Washington Post* described updated IRC figures for Congo (approaching 3 million dead) as 'stunning' such that they 'beggar belief even among some war zone demographers'. Vick cited the reaction of Jeff Drumtra, a researcher for the US Committee for Refugees: 'One doesn't know what to do with that kind of estimate except reach down and pull your jaw up off the floor.'[27] Vick continued: 'Independent experts who have reviewed both IRC reports say the surveys appear to be sound.' He cited a Western medical epidemiologist with long experience in humanitarian emergencies: 'My personal belief is these numbers are the absolute best that could be done in the circumstances, and there's absolutely no reason to believe any bias of any kind has found its way in.'

On May 10, 2001, the *Washington Times* reported IRC estimates as fact and sympathetically interviewed Les Roberts, asking him questions such as: 'How does this disaster compare in scope and scale to other African crises?' and 'What can be done?'[28] The *New York Times* wrote in April 2002: 'To policy makers, humanitarian workers or journalists working in sub-Saharan Africa, one of the hardest things to find is a reliable number ... Because of the scarcity of numbers here, those that do exist tend to be more politicized and less scrutinized than they are elsewhere.'[29] Of Roberts' Congo figures, however, the *New York Times* concluded: 'The agency's figures have been well accepted.'

The *Guardian* reported updated IRC figures in April 2003: 'A total of 4.7 million people have died as a direct result of the Democratic Republic of Congo's civil war in the past four and a half years, according to a report released today by the International Rescue Committee, a leading aid agency.' The article added:

> With a margin for error of 1.6m – a standard proportion is applied to areas too dangerous for researchers to reach – IRC admits its estimate is approximate. Yet few aid workers in eastern Congo doubt that a total death toll of 4.7m is possible. 'With an almost complete lack of medical care, as well as food insecurity and violence over a vast area, this number does not seem exaggerated', said Noel Tsekouras, the UN humanitarian coordinator for eastern Congo.[30]

We found literally dozens of examples of this kind. Even though the estimates of death in Congo clearly astonished even experienced observers of the conflict, the media reported the figures with essentially zero mention of any concerns about the validity of either the numbers or the methodology.

'EGREGIOUS POLITICISATION': MEDIA RESPONSE TO THE IRAQ METHODOLOGY AND NUMBERS

Consider, by contrast, a June 23, 2005 editorial in the *Washington Times* in response to the 2004 *Lancet* report on mortality in Iraq. The paper lamented an instance of 'egregious politicization of what is supposed to be an objective and scientific journal'. The editors explained:

> We're referring to the *Lancet*'s role in trying to influence the U.S. presidential election with a cynical 'study' of deaths in the Iraq war in October. The study, led by Les Roberts of the Johns Hopkins Bloomberg School of Public Health, purported to show that nearly 100,000 deaths had resulted from the Iraq war. But as it turned out, Mr. Roberts used less-than-ideal methods and then overstated his results, possibly by a factor of two or three.

Echoing Mary Dejevsky's comments about the lack of 'real' figures, the editorial continued: 'The method for this study – looking at population figures and surveying a few thousand Iraqis to ask how many deaths they'd heard of – abstracted the question and avoided the hard work of actually documenting the deaths.'[31] Following the standard misrepresentation, the *Washington Times* added:

> In any event, the fine print showed the study didn't really even conclude 100,000 deaths occurred. It actually concluded that casualties were somewhere between 8,000 and 194,000. At the time, the British research group Iraq Body Count had placed the number of confirmed deaths reported in the media at around 15,000 – probably a low estimate, but not by a factor of six.

The conclusion was calculated to be as damning as possible: 'Does the publication of one politically motivated study mean the entire product of a journal is suspect? Of course not. But it rightly raised eyebrows on both sides of the Atlantic and showed that even the most esteemed and avowedly apolitical institutions can be susceptible to hijacking.' In December 2004, the *Washington Times* had written:

> Or how about the constantly cited figure of 100,000 Iraqis killed by Americans since the war began, a statistic that is thrown about with total and irresponsible abandon by opponents of the war. That number, which should be disputed at every turn by those who care about the truth of what is going on in Iraq was derived from a controversial study by the British journal of medicine the *Lancet*. It is five to six times higher than the highest estimates from other sources of all Iraqi deaths, be they military or civilian. The *Lancet* study relied on reporting of deaths self-reported by 998 families from clusters of 33 households throughout Iraq, a very limited sample from which to generalize.
>
> As the *Financial Times* reported on Nov. 19, even the *Lancet* study's authors are now having second thoughts.[32]

The *New York Times* quoted Michael E. O'Hanlon, a senior fellow in foreign policy studies at the Brookings Institution, who said the Iraq Body Count figures were within the realm of reason: 'We've used their data before. It's probably not too far off, and it's certainly a more serious work than the *Lancet* report.'[33] In Britain, the pro-war *Observer* noted that the *Lancet* study 'was published soon before the US election, bringing accusations that the respected journal had become politicised. Journalist Michael Fumenton [*sic*] of the US-based TCS [Tech Central Station] website called it "Al-Jazeera on the Thames".' Reporter Jamie Doward added, foolishly: 'The report's authors admit it drew heavily on the rebel stronghold of Falluja, which has been plagued by fierce fighting. Strip out Falluja, as the study itself acknowledged, and the mortality rate is reduced dramatically.'[34] This comment was corrected in a 97-word paragraph in the paper one week later,[35] which noted that Fallujah had, in fact, of course been stripped out. But the correction was low-profile and the damage had been done.

In the *Guardian*, professor of mathematics John Allen Paulos wrote: 'Given the conditions in Iraq, the sample clusters were not only small, but sometimes not random either ... So what's the real number? My personal assessment, and it's only that, is that the number is somewhat more than the IBC's confirmed total, but considerably less than the *Lancet* figure of 100,000.'[36] We were unable to find a single example anywhere in the British or US press of a commentator rejecting the Congo figures and offering their own 'personal assessment' in this way.

After we discussed Paulos' comments in a series of media alerts in September 2005, he wrote to us:

I liked your piece, MEDIA ALERT: BURYING THE *LANCET* – PARTS 1 AND 2. I regret making the comment in my *Guardian* piece that you cite: 'My personal assessment, and it's only that, is that the number is somewhat more than the IBC's confirmed total, but considerably less than the *Lancet* figure of 100,000.' I still have a few questions about the study (moot now), but mentioning a largely baseless 'personal assessment' was cavalier. I should simply have stated my doubts about the study's scientific neutrality given what seemed at the time like an expedient rush to publish it.[37]

In an article entitled, 'We should be counting the dead in Iraq, but let's not get the figures out of proportion like this', the *Independent on Sunday*'s chief political commentator and Blair biographer, John Rentoul, demonstrated standard media ignorance in discussing the *Lancet*'s 100,000 figure:

However, this number is only the central point of a range that extends from 8,000 to 194,000. This huge disparity was mocked ignorantly by one American commentator as 'not an estimate, it's a dartboard'. It was also defended, equally ignorantly, by the editor of the *Lancet*, who said: 'It's highly

probable the figure is 98,000. Anything more or less is much less probable.'
Both wrong. What the figures say is that there is a 95 per cent chance that the
true figure lies between 8,000 and 194,000 ... It is statistically respectable,
which is why the *Lancet* article passed its peer reviews, but it produces
estimates hedged about with great uncertainty.

And there are good reasons for thinking that the true figure is towards the
lower end of the *Lancet*'s range.[38]

And there are good reasons for questioning Rentoul's objectivity.
Writing in the wake of the July 7, 2005 London bombings, Rentoul
wrote: 'The worst succour that the anti-war left in Britain can give
to the terrorists, however, is to entertain the idea that there is a
moral equivalence between the deliberate killing of civilians and the
casualties of military action in Iraq.' He added that, 'even Iraq Body
Count, an anti-war campaign, puts the total attributable to coalition
forces at under 10,000, rather than the figure with an extra zero
that is the common misconception of anti-war propaganda'.[39] The
Johns Hopkins Bloomberg School, Columbia University, Baghdad's
Al-Mustansiriya University, and the *Lancet*, being, we must presume,
anti-war propagandists.

Writing in the *New Statesman*, Peter Wilby noted that Rentoul 'has
written a reverential biography of Tony Blair, and even the former
Guardian (now *Times*) columnist David Aaronovitch must concede
to him the palm for unstinting support of new Labour'.[40] No small
achievement.

How, then, are we to explain the respectful, unquestioning
acceptance of Les Roberts' Congo studies on the one hand, and
the fierce criticism based on fraudulent arguments and journalistic
ignorance in response to his Iraq studies using essentially the same
methodology, on the other? And how can we account for the near-
uniform difference in responses to the Congo and Iraq studies right
across the supposed media 'spectrum'? The answer, really, is obvious.
The corporate media system, while masquerading as an honest,
independent source of unbiased news and views, has in fact evolved
to protect the powerful corporate and political interests of which it is
a part. The corporate media is not owned by big business, as is often
claimed – it *is* big business. It does not watch over concentrated power
– it *is* power. The media system does not fail in its task of guarding
the people against power – it *succeeds* in its task of protecting power
at the expense of people and planet.

This is not corruption in the retail sense of dishonest people deliberately choosing to tell lies out of corrupt motives. This is deep, structural corruption rooted in the very nature of a profit-oriented media system operating within state-capitalist society. In considering the various arguments about methodology and results above, it is easy to lose sight of the real significance of the subject under discussion. The media was here responding to just about the most credible scientific evidence modern society is able to muster indicating that our government was responsible for the mass killing of innocent civilians as the result of an illegal, criminal war of aggression. And this is how even our best media reacted!

So how did our society perform in the moral test described at the beginning of this chapter? The results could hardly be more sobering. No doubt everyone will have their own reaction. Ours is to suggest that, if such a response is possible to the 2004 *Lancet* report, anything is possible. We suspect that there are literally no limits on the ability of our society to suppress and apologise for state crimes. It is a conclusion strongly supported by the political and media reaction to a second *Lancet* report on mortality in Iraq published in 2006 – the subject of our next chapter.

7
One Million Dead and Counting:
The 2006 *Lancet* Report and Beyond

655,000 EXCESS IRAQI DEATHS

On October 11, 2006, news organisations began reporting the results of an article published by the *Lancet* medical journal: 'Mortality after the 2003 invasion of Iraq: a cross-sectional cluster sample survey.' This second study was led by Gilbert Burnham of Johns Hopkins with Les Roberts named as a co-author. The survey itself was conducted by eight Iraqi doctors led by Riyadh Lafta of Al-Mustansiriya University, Baghdad. The doctors collected data from 1,849 households comprising 12,801 individuals in 47 population clusters across Iraq. The survey findings were staggering:

> We estimate that, as a consequence of the coalition invasion of March 18, 2003, about 655,000 Iraqis have died above the number that would be expected in a non-conflict situation, which is equivalent to about 2·5% of the population in the study area. About 601,000 of these excess deaths were due to violent causes. Our estimate of the post-invasion crude mortality rate represents a doubling of the baseline mortality rate, which ... constitutes a humanitarian emergency.[1]

The scientists estimated that the most probable number of excess deaths was 654,965. They also estimated, with 95 per cent certainty, that the actual number lay between 392,979 and 942,636.

It is important to note that the standard figure for Iraqi deaths offered by the mainstream media at that time was supplied by Iraq Body Count (IBC). The 'maximum' IBC figure in October 2006 stood at around 49,000. There was great confusion among journalists about exactly what this figure represented. Many believed it described the maximum possible total of Iraqi dead, or of all Iraqi civilians killed. In fact it was then the figure solely for Iraqi civilian victims of violence as reported by at least two (mostly Western) media as selected by IBC for use in their study. IBC eventually ditched their confusing use of 'maximum' and 'minimum' on their website. They now simply give a numerical range under the heading: 'Documented civilian deaths from violence.' After years of relying on doubly or multiply cited casualty reports, IBC began using single-sourced reports from December 2007.

So although the second *Lancet* study measured a much broader range of deaths, the difference from IBC's toll was nevertheless enormous, particularly for the many journalists who assumed the studies measured much the same thing. Likewise, the *Lancet* figures must have struck the public as astonishingly high given that they had repeatedly been reminded of IBC's 49,000 death toll and George Bush's claim that 30,000 had died.

Like the first, the *Lancet*'s second study had inherent credibility for reasons explained in a rare US press editorial on the matter in the *St. Louis Post-Dispatch* (Missouri): 'Here is one of the world's most respected medical journals publishing a peer-reviewed study by epidemiologists backed by Johns Hopkins University's School of Public Health, part of one of the world's most respected medical schools.'[2] A free press in a free society would simply have to have investigated this study in depth, if only to resolve the confusion of a bemused and concerned public in response to an inherently credible report.

THE FRONT PAGES

In the event, the story failed to appear on the front pages of most newspapers on October 12, 2006, the day after the results were published. We collected a pile of dailies that day and noted the following front pages:

Daily Mirror: 'Terror in the tower' and 'Sex swap Jacko? Showbiz exclusive.'
Daily Telegraph: 'The tagged prisoners freed to kill.'
Daily Mail: 'Britain's taxes soaring' and 'But landlord Hamza is doing very nicely out of this country.'
The Times: 'Race quotas "needed to end divide in schools"', and '10/11 – New York plane hits building.'
Daily Express: 'Oh no not again – Plane hits New York tower block.'
Daily Star: 'My BB date rape hell.'
Sun: 'Apauling.' [Relating to an England football match.]
Financial Times: 'Visa bows to pressure and unveils IPO move.'

Only the *Independent* – '655,000 the toll of war in Iraq' – and *Guardian* – 'One in 40 Iraqis killed since invasion' – made the report their front-page lead stories. *The Times* devoted a third of a page to the *Lancet* story on page 45. The *Daily Mail* had three-quarters of a page on page 2. The *Daily Express* had a two-inch wide column on page 6 dwarfed by the adjacent story: '"Ageist" birthday cards banned from the office.' The *Daily Telegraph* had 422 words on page 5. The *Financial Times* had 609 words on page 7. Of these newspapers, only one published any follow-up reporting or commentary in the week that followed – 35 words in the *Financial Times* as part of a round-up of the week's events on October 14. The *Observer* devoted 43 words in a single sentence in a comment piece by Mary Riddell (October 15) and a single sentence in a news piece on page 8. The *Independent on Sunday* referred to the story in one sceptical paragraph in a comment piece by John Rentoul on page 40 and in one sentence of an article by Patrick Cockburn (October 15). The *Daily Mirror* and *Daily Star* made no mention of the report at all. The *Independent* covered the story on October 12 in a news piece, an editorial, and in a brief examination of how *Lancet* editor Richard Horton 'has turned a once-staid academic journal into a publication at the centre of a string of controversies'.[3] The *Independent* then mentioned the story in two sentences on October 13 and October 18. The *Guardian* gave 930 words to the story on October 12 in a news piece and 214 words in a brief explanation of the methodology behind the study. The paper also published a comment piece defending the report by *Lancet* editor, Richard Horton. In the same paper, there was then Ben Rooney's 200-word round-up of web-based debate on the story (October 13) and a single sentence in an article by Simon Tisdall (October 17). The *Guardian* also mentioned the study in an October 12 leader – in a single sentence. This was an aside in a piece focusing on the 'chaotic travesty' of Saddam Hussein's trial:

> Judicial procedure and decorum may seem irrelevant in a country that is reeling under seemingly unstoppable sectarian violence. Even if the human toll since March 2003 is less than the horrific, if contentious, new estimate of 655,000, Iraq seems to be bleeding to death and falling apart. Still, when Saddam was captured in December 2004, trying him was seen...[4]

With the evidence of our own mass killing before their eyes – and clearly spelled out in the *Lancet* report – this reference to 'sectarian violence' was all the *Guardian* editors had to say. Instead, the focus of their concluding paragraph was elsewhere: 'The old tyrant may be getting a far better deal than anything that existed when he was in charge. But that is not saying much. And it is not nearly good enough.' So much for the progressive credentials of the country's 'leading liberal newspaper'.

A LexisNexis database search (October 18, 2006) found that the words 'Jack Straw' and 'veil' had been mentioned in 348 articles over the previous week (Straw had criticised the wearing of full veils by British Muslims). The words 'Madonna' and 'adoption' were mentioned in 219 articles. The words 'Iraq' and '*Lancet*' were mentioned in 44 articles. The words '*Lancet*' and '655,000' were mentioned in eight national newspaper articles.

GEORGE BUSH: EPIDEMIOLOGIST

The BBC linked to the story from the front page of its website. The BBC1 One O'Clock News on October 11 spent 19 seconds on the topic. On the Six O'Clock News, anchor Natasha Kaplinsky – of *Strictly Come Dancing* fame – described the figures as 'shocking and controversial'. Baghdad correspondent Andrew North reassured viewers: 'It is only an estimate.' On the News at Ten, anchor Huw Edwards – presenter of Trooping the Colour and the Festival of Remembrance – explained that while the report was serious the figures were 'controversial though'. Reporter David Shukman declared: 'We'll never know the figures, it's too dangerous [in Iraq].' The study, he added, had 'weaknesses', such as 'the margin of error'. Huw Edwards turned to world affairs editor John Simpson for his view. Simpson – presenter of the *Panorama* documentary 'Saddam Hussein: A Warning From History' – thought hard and commented that it was 'difficult to be certain' about the death toll. The figures were 'possible', he said, but 'nobody can tell'. This was the BBC's idea of insightful commentary on the *Lancet*'s supremely important and very credible report of mass death in Iraq. George Bush's comment on the report – 'The methodology is pretty well discredited' – was widely broadcast and printed. A great moment in TV history was missed when journalists failed to seek clarification from the president on the exact nature of his problem with the methodology.

In fact Bush's claim that the methodology had been discredited was a lie, as the people who told him what to say were no doubt well aware. Richard Brennan, head of health programmes at the New York-based International Rescue Committee, which has conducted similar projects in Kosovo, Uganda and Congo, told Associated Press: 'This is the most practical and appropriate methodology for sampling that we have in humanitarian conflict zones.' He added: 'While the results of this survey may startle people, it's hard to argue with the methodology at this point.'[5] Professor Mike Toole of the Centre for International Health, Melbourne, said:

> The methodology used is consistent with survey methodology that has long been standard practice in estimating mortality in populations affected by war. For example, the Burnet Institute and International Rescue Committee (IRC) used the same methods to estimate mortality in the Democratic Republic of Congo. The findings of this study received widespread media attention and were accepted without reservation by the US and British governments. The Macfarlane Burnet Institute for Medical Research and Public Health's Centre for International Health endorses this study.[6]

Richard Garfield, a public health professor at Columbia University who works closely with a number of the authors of the report (and who was a co-author of the 2004 *Lancet* study), told the *Christian Science Monitor*:

> I loved when President Bush said 'their methodology has been pretty well discredited'. That's exactly wrong. There is no discrediting of this methodology. I don't think there's anyone who's been involved in mortality research who thinks there's a better way to do it in unsecured areas. I have never heard of any argument in this field that says there's a better way to do it.[7]

John Zogby, whose New York-based polling agency, Zogby International, has done several surveys in Iraq since the war began, said: 'The sampling is solid. The methodology is as good as it gets. It is what people in the statistics business do.'[8] Zogby noted that similar survey methods had been used to estimate casualty figures in other conflicts, such as Darfur and the Congo. He pointed out that US critics commonly accept the method for opinion polls, which are based on interviews with around 1,000 Americans in a country of 300 million people.

Frank Harrell Jr, chair of the biostatistics department at Vanderbilt University, called the study design solid and said it included 'rigorous, well-justified analysis of the data'.[9] Steve Heeringa, director of the statistical design group at the Institute for Social Research at the University of Michigan, said: 'Given the conditions (in Iraq), it's actually quite a remarkable effort. I can't imagine them doing much more in a much more rigorous fashion.'[10] BBC *Newsnight* interviewed Sir Richard Peto, Professor of Medical Statistics at the University of Oxford, who described the study as 'statistically reliable'.[11] Professor Sheila Bird of the biostatistics unit at the Medical Research Council said: 'They have enhanced the precision this time around and it is the only scientifically based estimate that we have got where proper sampling has been done and where we get a proper measure of certainty about these results.'[12] Richard Horton, the editor of the *Lancet*, commented: 'It is worth emphasising the quality of this latest report, as judged by four expert peers who provided detailed comments to editors.'[13]

None of this matters to political and media commentators. Frederick Jones, a White House spokesman, commented that the *Lancet* 'seems to be a medical organization that has politicized itself'.[14] General George Casey, then commander of US forces in Iraq, commented: 'I have not seen the study. That 650,000 number seems way, way beyond any number that I have seen. I've not seen a number higher than 50,000. And so, I don't give that much credibility at all.' Asked about the source of his 50,000 figure, Casey replied: 'I don't remember, but I've seen it over time.'[15]

Any 'controversy' surrounding the study is clear, then – professional epidemiologists and other experts in the field consider the report credible while the politicians and generals responsible for the bloodbath detailed in the study dismiss it out of hand. No matter, BBC News online chose to focus on the 'controversy', and alleged 'huge gaps' in the study. We wrote to the BBC's world affairs correspondent Paul Reynolds, author of the article:

> I've read your report, 'Huge gaps in Iraq death estimates' (BBC News Online, October 12, 2006) with interest.
>
> You cite critics of this week's *Lancet* report and of the earlier 2004 report: Michael O'Hanlon, Frank Kaplan, Margaret Beckett, George Bush and Gen George Casey. You also mention that the 'IBC reaction to the *Lancet* report is awaited.'
>
> As BBC world affairs correspondent – a senior BBC journalist – what prevents you from approaching professional epidemiologists and other recognised experts in the field, such as Bradley Woodruff, Michael Toole, David Meddings, Richard Garfield and Patrick Ball? Why do you cite only the criticisms of non-experts in response to what is, after all, an extremely complex and involved field of scientific inquiry?[16]

Reynolds replied: 'I quoted those people because they are players'.[17] We sent Reynolds some of the expert opinion cited above and asked him: 'Do you honestly believe BBC Online readers would have found these views less important and credible than, say, those of General Casey and Fred Kaplan? If so, why? If not, why did you ignore them?' Reynolds responded that he had amended the article to include expert commentary 'from Prof Burnham of JH [Johns Hopkins] and another from Ronald Waldman, an epidemiologist at Columbia'. Reynolds added: 'If you send me Les Roberts' address I will question him direct.'[18]

SHAMEFUL AND COWARDLY DISSEMBLING

We now know from papers obtained by the BBC World Service's *Newshour* programme under the Freedom of Information Act in September 2006 that senior government officials lied when they dismissed the second *Lancet* study as flawed, with the Foreign Office commenting that it was a 'fairly small sample ... extrapolated across the country'.[19]

One of the documents obtained by the BBC is a memo by the Ministry of Defence's chief scientific adviser, Sir Roy Anderson, dated October 13, 2006, two days after the *Lancet* report was published. Anderson wrote: 'The study design is robust and employs methods that are regarded as close to "best practice" in this area, given the difficulties of data collection and verification in the present circumstances in Iraq.' When these recommendations were sent to Blair's advisers, they expressed their concern. One person briefing Blair wrote: 'are we really sure that the report is likely to be right? That is certainly what the brief implies?' A Foreign Office official was forced to conclude that the government 'should not be rubbishing the *Lancet*'.

The prime minister's adviser finally accepted the conclusion. He wrote: 'the survey methodology used here cannot be rubbished, it is a tried and tested way of measuring mortality in conflict zones'. And yet, speaking six days after Roy Anderson praised the study's methods, British Foreign Office minister Lord Triesman said: 'The way in which data are extrapolated from samples to a general outcome is a matter of deep concern.'[20]   In response to these revelations, the editor of the *Lancet*, Richard Horton, commented on Blair's 'shameful and cowardly dissembling' in rejecting the study when he had been told it was robust. Horton added: 'This Labour government, which includes Gordon Brown as much as it does Tony Blair, is party to a war crime of monstrous proportions. Yet our political consensus prevents any judicial or civil society response. Britain is paralysed by its own indifference.'[21]

To its credit, *Newsnight* interviewed Les Roberts – a rare chance for one of the report's co-authors to defend the study. On his BBC blog, then *Newsnight* editor Peter Barron revealed that internet-based activism had been a factor in *Newsnight*'s coverage of the story:

> When the story broke of the *Lancet* report into civilian deaths in Iraq it was accompanied by a rash of e-mails from anti-war groups urging us to run the story. Did that influence us? Well, yes in the sense that I learned of the story from an anti-war campaigner who e-mails me regularly. But also no. When I took the report into our morning meeting where none of the producers had yet seen it, there was instant and unanimous agreement that – while the claim was in some people's view not credible – it was easily the most significant development of the day...
>
> Are these unsolicited interventions helpful or unhelpful? The former, I think, as long as we read them with eyes wide open. You might argue that it would be purer to ignore the pressure from all quarters, but I think lobbying can actually improve our journalism, as long as it's not corrupt, that access to the editors of programmes is equally available to everyone (via e-mail it is) and that we question everything we're told.[22]

But *Newsnight*'s coverage was a rare departure from the norm of stunning media indifference. Where were the in-depth media analyses, expert interviews and investigations? Where were the leaders, documentaries and news specials comparing the different death tolls reported from Iraq? Where were the articles and programmes examining US–UK responsibility under international law, as occupying powers, for the catastrophe in Iraq? Where were the discussions of the abject failure of modern democracy to offer either the British or American people any semblance of meaningful choice on foreign policy?

We have been monitoring and reporting media performance for many years, particularly since 2001. The above media response to a credible report that our government was responsible for the deaths of 655,000 Iraqis remains the most shocking and outrageous example of media servility to power we have yet seen.

THE DISAPPEARING ORB STUDY

On September 14, 2007, a report by the British polling organisation, Opinion Research Business (ORB), revealed that 1.2 million Iraqi citizens 'have been murdered' since the March 2003 US–UK invasion.[23] After conducting additional research, ORB revised their figures and reported in January 2008 that 'the death toll between March 2003 and August 2007 is likely to have been of the order of 1,033,000'.[24] In February 2007, Les Roberts had argued that Britain and America might by then have triggered in Iraq 'an episode more deadly than the Rwandan genocide', in which 800,000 people were killed.[25] The importance of the ORB poll was that it provided strong supporting evidence for this claim, and for the findings of the 2006 *Lancet* study, which reported 655,000 deaths. Roberts sent this email in response to the ORB poll:

> The poll is 14 months later with deaths escalating over time. That alone accounts for most of the difference [between the October 2006 *Lancet* paper and the ORB poll]. There are confidence interval issues, there are reasons to assume the *Lancet* estimate is too low but the same motives for under-reporting should apply to ORB. Overall they seem very much to align (e.g. both conclude that: most commonly violent deaths are from gunshot wounds [in contradiction to IBC and the Iraqi Ministry of Health], most deaths are outside of Baghdad [in contradiction to the other passive monitoring sources which tallied ~3/4th of deaths in the first 4 years in Baghdad and have only recently attributed even 1/2 as being elsewhere], Diyala worse than Anbar...).[26]

And yet, despite its obvious significance, the ORB study was almost entirely blanked by the US–UK media. Four days after the findings were announced, the poll had been mentioned in just one national UK newspaper – ironically, the pro-war *Observer*. It had been ignored by the *Guardian* and the *Independent*. The BBC's *Newsnight* may have been alone in providing TV broadcast coverage. The programme devoted the first 28 minutes of its September 14 edition to the financial crisis at Northern Rock bank. At 28:53, anchor Gavin Esler said:

> More than a million Iraqis have been killed since the invasion in 2003, according to the British polling company ORB. The study is likely to fuel controversy over the true, human cost of the war. It's significantly up on the previous highest estimate of 650,000 deaths published by the *Lancet*

last October. At the time, the Iraqi government described *that* figure as 'ridiculously high'. The independent Iraqi [*sic*] Body Count group puts the current total at closer to 75,000.[27]

Esler's contribution ended after 34 seconds at 29:27.

Could it be that journalists were just too ill-informed to understand the importance of the ORB study? Not according to news presenter Jon Snow, who responded to one emailer asking why Channel 4 had not covered the new study:

> Anyone who reports Iraq is bound to be aware of every death toll assessment. Alas no one has the slightest idea exactly how many people have died. We are all certain that a very great many have. Obviously those of us who find the war most heinous want to pin the largest possible number on the people who did this. It is an unfulfilling exercise because by definition it is unprovable and therefore pointless. What we do try to do is to report the known deaths whenever they happen. Iraq Body Count, the *Lancet* extrapolated survey, the Red crescent are all estimates that help to give us a sense of numbers, but we shall never know for sure. What we also do is to report the four million people (minimum) who have been displaced by the war. The one and a half million in Jordan and in Syria respectively are largely counted numbers and reliable.[28]

Snow wrote: 'anyone who reports Iraq is bound to be aware of every death toll assessment'. We are to believe, then, that highly trained professional journalists have a solid grasp of these issues – members of the public need not worry on that score. But what is so striking is that journalists consistently exhibit an inability to grasp even the basic meaning of the figures involved. Consider Esler's comment above: 'The independent Iraqi Body Count group puts the current total at closer to 75,000.' Iraq Body Count does not at all offer a 'total' figure to be compared with the *Lancet* and ORB studies. John Sloboda, professor of music psychology at the University of Keele, and a co-founder of Iraq Body Count, said his team's efforts would inevitably lead to a count smaller than the actual figure because not every death was reported in the news media. By contrast, the *Lancet* studies provide figures for all deaths – violent and non-violent, civilian and military, reported and unreported.

The response we received from the *Newsnight* editor Peter Barron was a further case in point: 'I certainly think it was right to report the ORB findings, and to put them in context. The IBC figure is of course not offering a comprehensive estimate of the total number of deaths, but it has the virtue of being real data and therefore provides one end of the spectrum.'[29] The suggestion that the *Lancet* reports are not based on 'real data' was absurd. It was also wrong to suggest that IBC provides a different 'end of the spectrum' to the *Lancet* reports. Talk of a 'spectrum' presupposes that the same quantity is being measured in each case. But that is not the case.

Snow also comments: 'alas no one has the slightest idea exactly how many people have died'. In fact we do have a good idea of how many have died – the issue of exactness is a red herring. The point about the ORB study is that it provided strong supportive evidence for the findings of the earlier, far more detailed and rigorous 2006 *Lancet* study. The *Lancet* authors had been calling for exactly this kind of follow-up study to help confirm or refute their findings. It seems clear that the *Lancet* figure of 655,000 deaths, although now two years out of date, was accurate.

IRAQ BODY COUNT

For a long time, when the issue of civilian casualties was discussed in the mainstream media three words were invariably mentioned: Iraq Body Count. We suspect this has been less often the case in the last couple of years, but IBC remains highly influential. IBC describes itself as 'an ongoing human security project which maintains and updates the world's largest public database of violent civilian deaths during and since the 2003 invasion'.[30] In its press release, 'The state of knowledge on civilian casualties in Iraq', IBC explained 'What IBC does': 'Provides an irrefutable baseline figure'. Similarly in 2006, IBC wrote: 'We are providing a conservative cautious minimum.'[31]

These both described laudable objectives involving little more than accurate data collection. IBC co-founder John Sloboda made the point in a BBC interview in response to criticism from a leading professional epidemiologist that he and his colleagues were 'amateurs' in the field of mortality studies: 'Our position is, and always has been, that reading press reports, which is what this job is, requires nothing other than care and literacy. The whole point about it is that it doesn't require statistical analysis or extrapolations.'[32] And yet in their September 3, 2007 press release under the title, 'How plausible is 600,000 violent Iraqi deaths?', IBC devoted five pages to wide-ranging criticism of the 2006 *Lancet* study which, as discussed above, estimated 655,000 excess deaths in Iraq. IBC's conclusion: 'Our own view is that the current death toll *could* be around twice the numbers recorded by IBC and the various official sources in Iraq. We do not think it could possibly be 10 times higher.'[33] In similar vein, the *Toronto Star* quoted John Sloboda as saying: 'The death toll could be twice our number, but it could not possibly be 10 times higher.'[34] This last comment was reported less than a week after the publication of ORB's poll revealing 1.2 million Iraqi deaths.

Two questions arise: Why did IBC – which argues that it is in the business of providing an 'irrefutable baseline' based on data collection – choose to challenge the methodology and conclusions of the *Lancet*'s epidemiological studies which went far beyond data collection and which did not in any way challenge their baseline as a 'cautious minimum'? Second, while IBC's self-described task does indeed require only 'care and literacy', does not the task of challenging peer-reviewed science published by some of the world's leading epidemiologists require very much more? Does it not, in fact 'require statistical analysis or extrapolations', and much else besides?

In a 2006 addition to their website, IBC wowed visitors with scientific jargon:

> Our data is very rich, because it provides a large subset of what is happening. It has high spatiotemporal specificity. Post-event interviews are always hampered by the fact that people tend to move on, and may not remain in the area or even in the country. Our data is recorded as close to the time and place of death as possible, and so has 'forensic' elements.[35]

It seems that IBC used their credibility as data collectors to 'cross sell' their credibility as commentators on peer-reviewed epidemiology to the media community. But this second task is unrelated to their task as data collectors, and is an area in which, to our knowledge, none of the co-authors of their press releases have any research record or publication history in any relevant scientific discipline. In a 2006 BBC interview, Sloboda said of the 2004 *Lancet* study: 'Some critics of the *Lancet* study have said it's like a drunk throwing a dart at a dartboard. It's going to go somewhere, but who knows if that number is the bulls [*sic*] eye. Unfortunately many many people have decided to accept that that 98,000 figure is the truth – or the best approximation to the truth that we have.'[36] Sloboda was here endorsing one of the media's most foolish claims based on a failure to comprehend even the basic meaning of the *Lancet* study's range of figures – the 'drunk throwing a dart at a dartboard' analogy is a nonsense. No qualified epidemiologist would countenance making such a comment. But Sloboda is *not* a qualified epidemiologist – he is a professor of music psychology.

Unsurprisingly, most journalists reporting on international affairs appear unable to distinguish between the task of 'reading press reports' on the one hand, and engaging in 'statistical analysis or extrapolations' on the other. Reporters naturally assume that, given their data's 'high spatiotemporal specificity', IBC's credibility is on a par with the world's leading experts in the field published in the world's leading scientific journals and subject to an exacting system of peer review. Certainly IBC do nothing to discourage, and everything to encourage, such a view.

THE PROBLEM OF RELYING ON THE JOURNALISTIC RECORD

IBC also moved far beyond data collection with this addition to their website:

> Those who suggest that the IBC data-base is likely to contain only a tiny minority of actual deaths generally argue three things. First, they say that IBC only records deaths in areas where Western journalists are present; second they propose that there have been at least seven credible studies which suggest up to ten times as many deaths as we have recorded; and third they assert that an alternate media world exists containing a professional Arab-language press which continually reports far more deaths than the sources we monitor in English. We have dealt with the first two claims in detail on the public record and will be happy to answer questions about them in the discussion.[37]

IBC omitted to mention the most obvious and telling criticism: that the credibility of their database as an approximate guide to levels of violence in Iraq – specifically, their claim that 'The death toll could be twice our number, but it could not possibly be 10 times higher' – is undermined by the fact that conditions in Iraq are so lethal that journalists are unable to discover many violent deaths of civilians. Consider that a study of deaths in Guatemala from 1960 to 1996 by Patrick Ball et al. at the University of California, Berkeley, found that numbers of murders reported by the media in fact *decreased* as violence increased. Ball described the 'problem of relying on the journalistic record' in evaluating numbers of people killed in Guatemala: 'When the level of violence increased dramatically in the late 1970s and early 1980s, numbers of reported violations in the press stayed very low. In 1981, one of the worst years of state violence, the numbers fall towards zero. The press reported almost none of the rural violence.' Ball added: 'Throughout the 1980 to 1983 period newspapers documented only a fraction of the killings and disappearances committed by the State. The maximum monthly value on the graph is only 60 for a period when monthly extra-judicial murders regularly totaled in the thousands.' Ball explained that 'the press stopped reporting the violence beginning in September 1980. Perhaps not coincidentally, the database lists seven murders of journalists in July and August of that year.'[38]

The significance of the last point for the Iraq death toll is suggested by a Reporters Sans Frontières (RSF) report (September 7, 2007), which described how the number of journalists and media workers killed in Iraq since the start of the 2003 invasion had reached 200. According to RSF, 73 per cent of journalists killed had been directly targeted, a figure which was 'much higher than in previous wars'. RSF also reported that more journalists had been taken hostage in Iraq than anywhere else in the world. A total of 84 journalists and media workers had been kidnapped in the previous four years.[39]

The bureau chief of one of three Western media agencies providing a third of IBC's data from Iraq sent this email to a colleague in 2006 (the latter asked us to preserve the sender's anonymity): 'Iraq Body Count is I think a very misleading exercise. We know they must have been undercounting for at least the first two years because we know that we did not report anything like all the deaths we were aware of ... we are also well aware that we are not aware of many deaths on any given day.'[40] In December 2007, James Forsyth, online editor for the *Business* and the *Spectator* wrote in the *Guardian*: 'Iraq is the most difficult conflict in any of our lifetimes to report ... Much normal reporting is simply impossible.'[41] Colin Freeman, the *Sunday Telegraph*'s chief foreign correspondent, described it as a 'uniquely dangerous and chaotic environment' – 235 journalists and media assistants had so far been killed covering the war.[42] We also found good reasons for scepticism regarding IBC's figures. In January 2006, we searched the IBC database looking for incidents involving the mass killing of Iraqi civilians by 'coalition' forces between January and June 2005. We began by searching for incidents citing a minimum of 10 deaths and above. We found 58 such incidents. Of these just one was attributed to a US air strike. Of the other 57 incidents listed, 25 were attributed to suicide bombers and a further 29 were attributed to insurgent actions targeting Iraqi government troops, government officials, religious groups, and so on. The few remaining cases described individuals shot at close range, people blindfolded and shot, and executed victims whose bodies had been dumped.

In short, out of 58 incidents involving a minimum of 10 or more Iraqi civilian deaths, just one was attributed to the 'coalition'. We then searched for incidents citing less than a minimum of 10 deaths involving 'coalition' air strikes, helicopter gunfire and tank fire. We found three references in the six-month period we examined, totalling 15 civilians killed. And yet, in the December 2005 edition of the *New Yorker*, journalist Seymour Hersh reported a US Air Force press release indicating that, since the beginning of the conflict, the 3rd Marine Aircraft Wing alone had dropped more than 500,000 tons of ordnance on Iraq. In December 2005, Associated Press reported that the US Air Force, Navy and Marine Corps had 'flown thousands of missions in support of US ground troops in Iraq this fall with little attention back home, including attacks by unmanned Predator aircraft armed with Hellfire missiles, military records show'.[43] The aircraft included front-line attack planes. The number of air strikes increased in the weeks leading up to the December 2005 election, from a monthly average of 25 in the first half of the year to more than 60 in September and 120 or more in October and November. The monthly number of air missions grew from 1,111 in September to 1,492 in November. And yet, when we checked, the first 18 pages of the IBC database, covering the period between July 2005 and January 2006, contained just six references to helicopter attacks and air strikes killing civilians.

Jason Washburn, who served with the Marine Corps in Iraq, reported in March 2008: 'Most of the innocents that I actually saw get killed were behind the wheel of a vehicle, usually taxi drivers. I've been present when almost a dozen taxi drivers got killed just driving.'[44] Washburn served in Iraq in three periods between 2002 and 2006 in al-Hilla, Najaf and Haditha. In December 2008, we checked deaths of taxi drivers recorded in the IBC database. In the periods when Washburn was in Iraq, IBC recorded only three deaths of taxi drivers. Of these, only one (in Haditha) might have been among 'almost a dozen' taxi drivers that Washburn says he saw being killed.

This is unsurprising. As US veterans and others have commented, US forces have routinely covered up killings of civilians. Numerous veterans have described how they carried extra 'drop weapons', such as AK-47 rifles, because 'if we accidentally shot a civilian, we could just toss the weapon on the body, and make them look like an insurgent'.[45] Jason Lemieux, formerly of the Marine Corps, has testified that known shootings of civilians were not reported 'because marines did not want to send their brothers-in-arms to prison when all they were trying to do was protect themselves in a situation they'd been forced into'.[46]

WARS KILL MORE

In the only poll in which Americans were asked to estimate the number of Vietnamese deaths during the Vietnam war, the average estimate was 100,000, about 5 per cent of the official figure. According to Vietnamese accounting, the war cost them three million killed, 300,000 missing, 4.4 million wounded, and two million harmed by toxic chemicals.[47] The true number of people who died in Vietnam and other wars was re-evaluated in a study published in the June 20, 2008 online edition of the *British Medical Journal* (BMJ). The study compared data on war deaths from eyewitnesses and the media from 13 countries over the past 50 years with peacetime data in the United Nations World Health Surveys, which were collected after the end of the wars.

The researchers estimated that 5.4 million people died from 1955 to 2002 as a result of wars in 13 countries. These deaths range from 7,000 in the Democratic Republic of Congo to 3.8 million in Vietnam – close to the Vietnamese government estimate.[48] According to lead author Ziad Obermeyer, a public health researcher at the Institute for Health Metrics and Evaluation in Seattle, Washington, the estimates are three times higher than those of previous reports. Obermeyer commented: 'War kills more people than we had previously thought. And that has to be taken into account when we're looking historically, and it's important for people and policy makers to know when they're looking at the consequences of the war. It's important that there's an awareness of how many people actually die.'[49]

It is often claimed that war deaths have been declining in recent years. The decline is attributed to technological innovations like 'smart' bombs and different strategic priorities. Obermeyer challenged this view: 'This idea appears to be supported by media reports. But what we are finding is these reports are not a reflection of reality.'[50] On June 20, 2008, we wrote to Obermeyer: 'I'm wondering what your study tells us about the credibility of the categorical claim made by John Sloboda that the death toll in Iraq "could not possibly be" 10 times higher than his IBC count based primarily on media reports. Is it reasonable for him to be that certain?' Obermeyer replied: 'Based on these data, it is certainly not implausible that media reports could underestimate deaths by a factor of 10 in some conflicts, though of course I can't comment specifically on Iraq.'[51] Stephen Soldz, Director of the Center for Research, Evaluation, and Program Development at the Boston Graduate School of Psychoanalysis, commented to us:

> It is a far cry from saying that he [Sloboda] thinks the real number is around twice theirs and saying 'could not possibly be'. Of course, a better lower bound would be about 3 times … As a researcher, I think the preponderance of the evidence is that the figure is far higher. But I also know that there is great uncertainty. For Sloboda to express such certainty is to discredit him on the face of it.[52]

Obermeyer's co-author, Christopher Murray, commented to the media: 'There's almost no reason to believe the passive surveillance strategies should work.'[53] The BMJ study was yet further evidence pointing to a massive death toll in Iraq. It was not reported by any UK newspaper.

8
Bitter Harvest: Bombings in Britain, Spain and Iraq

UNITED IN VIOLENCE

Terrible ironies attend the use of violence for political ends. Despite their ostensible opposition, two warring factions are often united in their fundamental view of the world. Both insist that continued violence is the only realistic option. Both insist the enemy is the incarnation of mindless evil, completely beyond reason. Both reject as treasonous, rational analyses indicating their own responsibility for promoting violence and rejecting non-violent alternatives.

In other words, patriotic clichés and rousing rhetoric come at a high price. To the extent that rational thought and compassion for suffering are drowned out, the forces of violence are empowered. Writing in the immediate aftermath of the July 7, 2005 suicide bombings in London, a *Guardian* leader recalled the horrors of the Blitz: 'Just like their predecessors in the face of those earlier horrors, today's generation of Londoners responded to this latest unprovoked act of evil ... with a combination of calm and courage.'[1] The article concluded: 'In the end, as Mr Bush and Mr Blair each said, it is the contrast that counts. This is a conflict of values.' This brought to mind a 2001 *Guardian* editorial written in the aftermath of the September 11 attacks. The editors commented on a speech by Tony Blair: 'The core of the speech – intellectual as well as moral – came when he contrasted the west's commitment to do everything possible to avoid civilian casualties and the terrorists' proven wish to cause as many civilian casualties as possible ... Let them do their worst, we shall do our best, as Churchill put it. That is still a key difference.'[2]

Answers cannot be found in self-serving rhetoric of this kind. It is not as though outrage at the mass killing of civilians by the British and American governments – regimes absolutely determined to wage war in 2003, with all the risks that entailed for civilians – can be attenuated by patriotic editorials. The horrors in London were anything but 'unprovoked' from the point of view of those who closely identify with the very real victims of Western violence in Afghanistan, Palestine and Iraq.

In truth, there is no contradiction in accepting that our government's actions merit intense moral outrage, and in also rejecting utterly the actions of those who express their outrage through violence. On the contrary, to turn a blind eye to our own crimes while focusing on the crimes of others is to guarantee more of both.

AZNAR: A LIE TOO FAR

Other ironies are painful to contemplate. The July 7 attacks in London were the first suicide bombings ever seen in Britain. But before March 2003, there had also never been a suicide bomb attack in Iraq. That all changed with the catastrophic Bush–Blair invasion. It is estimated that half of the 135 car-bomb attacks in Iraq in April 2005 were suicide bombings. Major General William Webster, the US officer in charge of Baghdad, reported that car bombs in the capital had fallen from twice daily in June to about one a day in July 2005.

Writing in the *New York Times*, novelist Ian McEwan wrote of the London atrocities: 'How could we have forgotten that this was always going to happen? We have been savagely woken from a pleasant dream.'[3] But the British public had not been woken from a pleasant dream – instead, long-held fears were shown to have been well-founded. On February 15, 2003, as many as two million people had flooded London to protest the impending Bush–Blair war. They did so in part because they knew that invading Iraq would make them targets for terrorism. According to a YouGov survey that month, 79 per cent of Londoners felt that British involvement in an attack on Iraq 'would make a terrorist attack on London more likely'.[4] Also at that time, fully 72 per cent of the British population opposed Britain joining military action against Iraq, without United Nations approval. One year later, a poll showed that three-quarters of Britons continued to feel 'more vulnerable' to terrorist attack because of the government's decision to attack Iraq.[5] With his usual blend of deceitful rhetoric and amateur theatricality Blair simply dismissed the largest political demonstration in British history – he knew better.

In Spain, Aznar's Partido Popular government similarly waved away vast and repeated anti-war protests all across the country ahead of the war. Almost one year after the invasion, on March 12, 2004, 191 people were killed and 1,800 injured by ten bombs placed on trains at the height of the Madrid rush hour. In October 2003, Osama bin Laden had warned that Spain would be targeted for backing the Iraq war. *The Times* reported a senior Al Qaeda official as declaring: 'We must make maximum use of the proximity to the elections in Spain ... Spain can stand a maximum of two or three attacks before they will withdraw from Iraq.'[6] As with the London bombings, the political stakes were high. David Sharrock explained in the *Times*:

> Neither of Spain's main parties wants to say it too loudly, but the identity of the authors of the terrorist atrocity is a crucial factor in determining who will win tomorrow's general election.
>
> If ETA is responsible, as the Government of Jose Maria Aznar believes, then his People's Party (PP) could fully expect an increased vote which will guarantee its majority in government for four years.[7]

With remarkable cynicism, the Spanish government instantly blamed the Basque separatist group ETA. Spain's interior minister, Angel Acebes, said: 'The conclusion of this morning that pointed to the terrorist organisation [ETA] right now is still the main line of investigation ... [But] I have given the security forces instructions not to rule out anything.'[8] Despite the obvious interest of the Spanish government, the threats issued by Al Qaeda, and the fact that a van with seven detonators and Arabic language tapes with Koranic verses had been found in the town of Alcala de Henares outside Madrid, politicians, intelligence services and the media rushed to affirm the claims of the Spanish government. The *Guardian* reported how George Bush had offered his condolences: 'I appreciate so very much the Spanish government's fight against terror, their resolute stand against terrorist organisations like ETA. The United States stands with them.'[9] Leslie Crawford wrote in the *Financial Times*: 'With only three days to go before a general election, Spanish politicians presented a united front against ETA, the violent Basque separatist group that has been blamed for yesterday's Madrid bombs.'[10]

Bowing to the official version of events in their customary manner, the *Guardian* editors wrote: 'the assumption that ETA, or some faction of it, was planning an overwhelming strike on the eve of a general election is reasonable enough'.[11] As undeniable facts made a nonsense of this, the media began to hint at the grim implications of the truth. The *Daily Telegraph* warned: 'If al-Qa'eda has succeeded in spreading its Jihad to Europe, it will raise alarm in capitals across the world, especially all those with troops in Iraq.'[12] The *Observer* reported widely held sentiments in Spain when it quoted one mourner of the Madrid bombings. 'This was the fault of Bush and Blair. It's because of our involvement in Iraq. Aznar is Bush's shoe-shine boy. I will vote against the Partido Popular.'[13] A *Guardian* editorial commented: 'Many voters expressed anger against the ruling Popular party: first for making Spain a target for Islamist extremists by its support for the Iraq war; and second for rushing too quickly to accuse the armed Basque separatist group ETA of Madrid's bombing.'[14]

Curiously, the media did not denounce these rational observations as shameful apologetics for terror.

GEORGE GALLOWAY: BRITAIN'S NO. 1 TRAITOR

By contrast, after the London attacks, the suggestion that the same Londoners who opposed Blair's foreign policy had paid for his actions with their lives, was met with shrieks of outrage and denial. In an article entitled 'The twisted logic of Galloway', the *Daily Mail* reported Respect MP George Galloway's reaction to the London attacks:

> 'The loss of innocent lives, whether in this country or Iraq, is precisely the result of a world that has become a less safe and peaceful place in recent years. We have worked without rest to remove the causes of such violence from our world. We argued, as did the security services, that the attacks on Afghanistan and Iraq would increase the threat of terrorist attack in Britain. Tragically Londoners have now paid the price of the Government ignoring such warnings.'[15]

Several years later, this reads as an entirely common sense analysis. As discussed, this was pretty much what our own press had finally concluded in the aftermath of the Madrid atrocities – a conclusion accepted by virtually the entire Spanish population.

In response, Armed Forces Minister Adam Ingram described Galloway as a 'foul mouthed ... thug' who was 'dipping his poisonous tongue in a pool of blood'.[16] The *Sun* wrote: 'VILE George Galloway last night confirmed he is Britain's No1 TRAITOR after blaming Tony Blair for the terror bombings.'[17] Christopher Hitchens wrote in the *Mirror*: 'How can anyone bear to be so wicked and stupid? How can anyone bear to act as a megaphone for psychotic killers?'[18]

Interviewing Galloway on *Newsnight*, BBC presenter Gavin Esler asked in response to Galloway's statement: 'That was a pretty crass thing to say though, wasn't it, when bodies are not even buried or identified?'[19] Esler asked again: 'But don't you think you owe it to relatives of the bereaved to be more sensitive at this time than to tell them that they paid the price of a policy? Because it sounded as if you were playing the politics of the last atrocity.' For a third time, Esler asked: 'Do you not owe it to your constituents to speak more carefully about these subjects?' And yet, that very day, an article in the *New York Times* commented on the attacks: 'Perhaps the crudest lesson to be drawn was that, in adopting the stance he took after the Sept. 11 attacks, Mr. Blair had finally reaped the bitter harvest of the war on terrorism – so often forecast but never quite seeming real until the explosions boomed across London.'[20] A week later, the same newspaper reported:

Sanjay Dutt and his friends grappled Friday with why their friend Kakey, better known to the world as Shehzad Tanweer, had decided to become a suicide bomber. 'He was sick of it all, all the injustice and the way the world is going about it,' Mr. Dutt, 22, said. 'Why, for example, don't they ever take a moment of silence for all the Iraqi kids who die?' 'It's a double standard, that's why,' answered a friend, who called himself Shahroukh, also 22, wearing a baseball cap and basketball jersey, sitting nearby. 'I don't approve of what he did, but I understand it. You get driven to something like this, it doesn't just happen.'[21]

Robert Pape, author of *Dying to Win: Why Suicide Terrorists Do It*, commented a year later:

Researching my book, which covered all 462 suicide bombings around the globe, I had colleagues scour Lebanese sources to collect martyr videos, pictures and testimonials and biographies of the Hizbollah bombers. Of the 41, we identified the names, birth places and other personal data for 38. We were shocked to find that only eight were Islamic fundamentalists; 27 were from leftist political groups such as the Lebanese Communist Party and the Arab Socialist Union; three were Christians, including a female secondary school teacher with a college degree. All were born in Lebanon.
   What these suicide attackers – and their heirs today – shared was not a religious or political ideology but simply a commitment to resisting a foreign occupation.[22]

The influential think-tank Chatham House, formerly known as the Royal Institute of International Affairs, concluded there is 'no doubt' the invasion of Iraq has 'given a boost to the al-Qaida network' in 'propaganda, recruitment and fundraising', while providing an ideal targeting and training area for terrorists. 'Riding pillion with a powerful ally has proved costly in terms of British and US military lives, Iraqi lives, military expenditure and the damage caused to the counter-terrorism campaign.'[23]

A 2004 joint Home Office and Foreign Office dossier prepared for Tony Blair – 'Young Muslims and Extremism' – identified the Iraq war as a key cause of young Britons turning to terrorism. The analysis stated:

> It seems that a particularly strong cause of disillusionment among Muslims, including young Muslims, is a perceived 'double standard' in the foreign policy of western governments, in particular Britain and the US. The perception is that passive 'oppression', as demonstrated in British foreign policy, e.g. non-action on Kashmir and Chechnya, has given way to 'active oppression'. The war on terror, and in Iraq and Afghanistan, are all seen by a section of British Muslims as having been acts against Islam.[24]

The analysis identified Iraq as a 'recruiting sergeant' for extremism.

Earlier, an assessment prepared by the Joint Intelligence Committee five weeks before the invasion of Iraq (February 10, 2003) entitled 'International Terrorism: War with Iraq', had said: 'The JIC assessed that al-Qa'eda and associated groups continued to represent by far the greatest terrorist threat to Western interests, and that threat would be heightened by military action against Iraq.'[25] Robert Fisk provided a rare example of honesty in the aftermath of the London bombings:

> And it's no use Mr Blair telling us yesterday that 'they will never succeed in destroying what we hold dear'. 'They' are not trying to destroy 'what we hold dear'. They are trying to get public opinion to force Blair to withdraw from Iraq, from his alliance with the United States, and from his adherence to Bush's policies in the Middle East. The Spanish paid the price for their support for Bush – and Spain's subsequent retreat from Iraq proved that the Madrid bombings achieved their objectives – while the Australians were made to suffer in Bali.[26]

Understanding that the costs of wilful blindness are high, the *Financial Times* essentially echoed Galloway:

The uncomfortable truth is that the ambitions and capabilities of the jihadis cannot be divorced entirely from the bloodshed in Iraq. The toppling of Saddam Hussein did not cause Islamist extremism but the present insurgency serves both as recruiting agent and training ground for al-Qaeda's war against the west.

Whatever one thinks of the original decision to remove Mr Hussein, the hubris that preceded the invasion and the negligence that has followed it have given strength and succour to the Islamists. Culpability here lies largely with the Pentagon but Mr Blair carries guilt by association.[27]

The FT, needless to say, was not described as 'wicked', 'vile' or 'twisted'.

HANS VON SPONECK:
THE UN WAS MORE HUMANE WITH ITS DOGS

In a display of cynicism that easily rivals Aznar's performance, Blair instantly dismissed the idea that the London attacks were linked to British involvement in Iraq. Blair said on July 10: 'September 11 happened before Iraq, before Afghanistan, before any of these issues and that was the worst terrorist atrocity of all.'[28] This was a classic Blair deception. September 11 *did indeed* happen before the 2003 Iraq war, but it did not happen before the 1991 Iraq war, which devastated the country with the equivalent of seven Hiroshima-sized bombs. Eric Hoskins, a Canadian doctor and coordinator of a Harvard study team, reported in January 1992 that the allied bombardment 'effectively terminated everything vital to human survival in Iraq – electricity, water, sewage systems, agriculture, industry and health care'.[29] And September 11 did not happen before a decade of US–UK sanctions had killed Iraqi civilians in their hundreds of thousands.

In his book, *A Different Kind Of War: The UN Sanctions Regime In Iraq*, Hans von Sponeck, former UN Humanitarian Coordinator for Iraq, wrote: 'At no time during the years of comprehensive economic sanctions were there adequate resources to meet minimum needs for human physical or mental survival either before, or during, the Oil-For-Food programme.'[30] For example, during 'phase v' of the Oil-For-Food programme, from November 1998 to May 1999, each Iraqi received a food allocation worth $49, or 27 cents per day! Von Sponeck commented that 'the UN was more humane with its dogs than with the Iraqi people':[31] $160 was allocated for food for each UN dog over the same period. Also during 'phase v', $5.80 worth of health supplies were available per person, $1.60 for water and sanitation,

$4.10 for agriculture, $2.50 for electricity and $1.00 for education. Though it is rarely reported, this was in fact not humanitarian aid; it was funded through the sale of Iraqi oil (as was the dog food). Von Sponeck commented:

> Whoever the members of the UN security council were, as individuals and the countries they represented during the twelve years of sanctions, they – individually and collectively – had the knowledge of all the aspects of the human catastrophe that was unfolding in Iraq...
>
> The hard-line approach prevailed, with the result that practically an entire nation was subjected to poverty, death and destruction of its physical and mental foundations.[32]

In particular, von Sponeck blames Britain and the United States, who, as 'the main and permanent hardliners', were 'unable to strike a balance between their political objectives and humanitarian principles'.[33]

This is about as damning as it is possible for a career diplomat to be. It is easy to understand why his book has never been reviewed in the British press (published in 2006, it has been mentioned in a single paragraph in a single article by Robert Fisk in the *Independent* on January 20, 2007). Von Sponeck's central conclusion is simply too awful to be tolerated: 'The profound seriousness of the Iraqi tragedy is that it was not accidental nor the result of ignorance. The impact of sanctions and the inadequacy of the humanitarian exemption were known and documented.'[34] Von Sponeck's book is so important because it documents in meticulous detail the existence of a level of brutality and ruthlessness in US–UK politics that is almost beyond belief. We all have a desire to believe that the people who run our countries are motivated by benign intentions. We can easily persuade ourselves that they are doing their best within constraints that they are powerless to change. But von Sponeck points to a policy of voluntary, unnecessary brutality that was entirely avoidable.

A further implication, assuming that most people are not monsters, is that political power in foreign affairs is almost completely divorced from public influence. It is the plaything of a rich, ruthless elite essentially answerable to no one for their crimes. This is powerfully supported by an unwritten agreement between the corporate media and the major political parties that foreign policy issues will not be discussed at election time. American media analyst, Robert McChesney comments: 'If the elite, the upper 2 or 3 per cent of society who control most of the capital and rule the largest institutions, agree on an issue then it is off-limits to journalistic scrutiny.'[35] The point being that New Labour and Conservative, Republican and Democratic parties all agree on the fundamental means and goals of foreign policy.

As Blair knew very well, Osama bin Laden was clear about his motives for the September 11 attacks. In a September 19, 2001 appearance on the David Letterman show, ABC journalist John Miller described how bin Laden had told him in an interview that his top three issues were 'the US military presence in Saudi Arabia; US support for Israel; and US policy toward Iraq'. Attacking Iraq yet again in 2003, much less occupying the country, was an act of breathtaking stupidity for anyone concerned with promoting peace and reducing terror and war.

Behind the impassioned, Churchillian rhetoric, one overwhelming fact is clear – the protection of ordinary Western people is not, and never has been, the highest priority for the elites directing US–UK foreign policy.

9
Israel and Palestine:
An Eye for an Eyelash

IT'S ALL BANG BANG STUFF!

Hands up anyone who understands the Israel–Palestine conflict! If so, you belong to an exclusive, media-resistant minority. Glasgow University Media Group (GUMG) has analysed media coverage of the conflict and its impact on audience opinion. The researchers transcribed over 3,000 lines of text from TV bulletins broadcast between September 28 and October 16, 2000. Of these, just 17.5 lines referred to the history of the crisis. Viewers were also asked to write down what they knew about the conflict. The results were predictable:

> The lack of historical knowledge made it very difficult for people to understand key elements of the conflict. For example, some [viewers] had written that 'land' was an issue but there was a great deal of confusion over what this meant. Another participant described how his understanding included no sense of the Palestinian case that land had been taken from them.[1]

Lead researchers Greg Philo and Mike Berry commented:

> The emphasis here is on 'hot' live action and the immediacy of the report rather than any explanation of the underlying causes of the events. One BBC journalist who had reported on this conflict told us that his own editor had said to him that they did not want 'explainers' – as he put it: 'It's all bang bang stuff.' The driving force behind such news is to hold the attention of as many viewers as possible, but in practice ... it simply leaves very many people confused.[2]

A typical example of this confusion was provided by one viewer:

> The impression I got was that the Palestinians had lived around that area and now they were trying to come back and get some more land for themselves – I didn't realise they had been actually driven out, I just thought they didn't

want to live as part of Israel and that the places they were living in, they decided they wanted to make self-governed – I didn't realise they had been driven out of places in wars previously.[3]

In reality, huge numbers of Palestinians were forced from their land when the Israeli state was formed in 1948. The Israeli historian Ilan Pappé notes that more than half of Palestine's native population, close to 800,000 people, were uprooted and 531 villages were destroyed.[4] The intention of 'Plan Dalet', carried out by the military forces of what was to become Israel, was to ethnically cleanse a large part of Palestine of hostile 'Arab elements'. Numerous massacres occurred, including at Deir Yassin, Ayn Al-Zaytun, Tantura and elsewhere. Avi Shlaim, another Israeli historian, writes:

> The novelty and audacity of the plan lay in the orders to capture Arab villages and cities, something [the Jewish forces] had never attempted before ... Palestinian society disintegrated under the impact of the Jewish military offensive that got underway in April, and the exodus of the Palestinians was set in motion ... by ordering the capture of Arab cities and the destruction of villages, it both permitted and justified the forcible expulsion of Arab civilians.[5]

Speaking in 1955, prominent Israeli military leader and politician, Moshe Dayan, commented: 'What cause have we to complain about their fierce hatred for us? For eight years now they sit in their refugee camps in Gaza, and before their eyes we turn into our homestead the land and villages in which they and their forefathers have lived.'[6] The Palestinians were forced to live as refugees in Lebanon, Syria, Jordan, Iraq and on the West Bank (of the Jordan River) and the Gaza Strip. There followed a series of conflicts and, at times, outright war between Israel and its Arab neighbours. During the 1967 (Six Day) War, Israel occupied the West Bank and East Jerusalem (previously under Jordanian control), the Gaza Strip and the Sinai peninsula (Egypt) and the Golan Heights (Syria). This occupation brought many Palestinian refugees under Israeli military control.

Jerusalem, a religious centre for Muslims, Jews and Christians, became a major centre of conflict. The Israelis also built illegal settlements in the newly occupied areas of Gaza and the West Bank and exploited natural resources, in particular taking control of the vital resource of water. Shlaim writes that these settlements were part of a systematic policy intended to exert strategic and military control, which in this case involved 'surrounding the huge Greater Jerusalem area with two concentric circles of settlements with access roads and military positions'.[7] Some Israelis have defended the occupation arguing that they have religious claims (from the time of the Bible) on the land and Jerusalem. It was also argued that Israel's security needs could only be met by extending its borders, as for example when Israel expropriated a part of southern Lebanon in 1982–83 as a 'security zone'. This action led to an extended conflict with Hezbollah guerrillas from Lebanon, and Israel eventually withdrew in May 2000 after suffering serious losses.

The conflict with the Palestinians in the Occupied Territories resulted in two major Intifadas (or uprisings) beginning in 1987 and 2000. In the period between these there were a series of American-led 'peace efforts', notably the Oslo Agreements of 1993 and 1995, and the Wye Accords of 1998. These in practice gave the Palestinians limited self-rule in parts of the West Bank and Gaza. But the Israeli army still control roads and access and can effectively seal off the Palestinian areas, thus exerting a stranglehold on economic movement. They also continue to control and exploit water supplies as well as keeping a large army and undercover police presence.[8]

UNFRIENDLY FIRE: TIM LLEWELLYN ON THE BBC

In 2004, Tim Llewellyn, who was the BBC's Middle East correspondent for ten years, reflected on how awful the BBC had become at covering the conflict. He wrote:

> Watching a peculiarly crass, inaccurate and condescending programme about the endangered historical sites of 'Israel' – that is to say, the Israeli-occupied Palestinian Territories – on BBC2 in early June 2003, I determined to try to work out, as a former BBC Middle East correspondent, why the Corporation has in the past two and a half years been failing to report fairly the most central and lasting reason for the troubles of the region: the Palestinians' struggle for freedom.
>
> In the news reporting of the domestic BBC TV bulletins, 'balance', the BBC's crudely applied device for avoiding trouble, means that Israel's lethal modern army is one force, the Palestinians, with their rifles and home-made bombs, the other 'force': two sides equally strong and culpable in a difficult dispute, it is implied, that could easily be sorted out if extremists on both sides would see reason and the leaders do as instructed by Washington...

When suicide bombers attack inside Israel the shock is palpable. The BBC rarely reports the context, however. Many of these acts of killing and martyrdom are reprisals for assassinations by Israel's death squads, soldiers and agents who risk nothing as they shoot from helicopters or send death down a telephone line. I rarely see or hear any analysis of how many times the Israelis have deliberately shattered a period of Palestinian calm with an egregious attack or murder. 'Quiet' periods mean no Israelis died ... it is rarely shown that during these 'quiet' times Palestinians continued to be killed by the score.[9]

Philo and Berry have provided numerous examples of the false 'balance' identified by Llewellyn. In one ITV discussion, a journalist referred to 'the even-handedness which has characterised American diplomacy in the Middle East'. A second journalist responded, explaining that 'the Americans have long maintained that the only way they have any influence in the Middle East is to be a relatively neutral, honest broker'.[10] A BBC1 lunchtime news report in 2000 described then President Bill Clinton as 'the man who has spent eight years trying to bring permanent peace to the Middle East'.[11] The standard deception is 'that peace may be found in the comings and goings of world leaders and that their priority is to urgently secure peace, rather than to pursue more narrowly defined concerns such as national interests or political support at home'.[12] Other types of bias are even more glaring:

In our samples of news content, words such as 'mass murder', 'savage cold-blooded killing' and 'lynching' were used by journalists to describe Israeli deaths but not those of Palestinians/Arabs. The word 'terrorist' was used to describe Palestinians, but when an Israeli group was reported as trying to bomb a Palestinian school, they were referred to as 'extremists' or 'vigilantes'.[13]

One ITV news bulletin spoke of 'Israeli determination' in the 'fight against terror', a standard description used across corporate news.[14] No ITV correspondent or newsreader has ever talked of the 'determination of Palestinian fighters to defend their land against Israeli terror'. A BBC Radio 4 report described an Israeli air attack as 'sending the toughest possible message to the Palestinians'.[15] It is inconceivable that the BBC would describe a Palestinian attack as 'sending the toughest possible message to the Israelis to end military rule'.

As Philo and Berry note, there is 'a stronger tendency in the headlines to highlight Israeli statements, actions or perspectives', and it is 'hard to avoid the conclusion that one view of the conflict is being prioritised'.[16]

AN ISRAELI SOLDIER IS CAPTURED: AND THE TRUTH IS 'KIDNAPPED'

A good example of the consistent bias was provided in reporting of the June 25, 2006 capture of an Israeli soldier, Gilad Shalit, by Palestinian militants at an army post at Kerem Shalom near Gaza. The BBC and ITV news, the *Guardian*, the *Independent* and most other media described the action as a 'kidnapping'. *Guardian* journalist David Fickling wrote: 'Israeli troops arrested dozens of Hamas ministers and parliamentarians today as they stepped up their campaign to free a soldier kidnapped by militants in Gaza at the weekend.'[17] We asked Fickling why Israeli militants 'detain' and 'arrest', whereas Palestinian militants 'kidnap'.[18] Fickling replied: 'There is a well-attested distinction between arrest – an action carried out by a state as the first step of a well-defined legal process – and kidnap, which is an action carried out by private individuals with no defined outcome, enforceable purpose, or rights of review or release.'[19]

Israeli Air Force bombings of (empty) Hamas offices at the time were clearly intended to signal that Hamas leaders could and would be assassinated if Israel so desired. It was not even clear what their crimes were alleged to have been. And were we to believe that they had any rights of review or release? In reality, these 'arrests' occurred in occupied territory in violation of international law. The notion of a 'well-defined legal process' is therefore laughable; Israel has no legal jurisdiction in the territories.

The media represented the capture of Gilad Shalit as a key event responsible for escalating the conflict. Stephen Farrell reported in *The Times* 'a dramatic escalation of the conflict sparked by the abduction'.[20] The *Financial Times* wrote of 'the rapid escalation of the crisis sparked by last Sunday's kidnap'.[21] The BBC described the Palestinian attack as 'a major escalation in cross-border tensions'.[22] Most readers or viewers would have been unaware that the day before the 'kidnapping', Israeli commandos had entered the Gaza Strip and captured two Palestinians – a doctor and his brother.[23] Nor did the press report the one-sided nature of the violence in the weeks leading up to the 'kidnapping'. Consider some salient events not considered 'sparks' by the media:

On June 8, the Israeli army assassinated Jamal Abu Samhadana, the recently appointed Palestinian head of the security forces of the Interior Ministry, and three others. On June 9, Israeli shells killed seven members of the same Palestinian family picnicking on Beit Lahiya beach. Some 32 others were wounded, including 13 children. On June 13, an Israeli plane fired a missile into a busy Gaza City street, killing eleven people, including two children and two medics. On June 20, the Israeli army killed three Palestinian children and injured 15 others in Gaza with a missile attack. On June 21, the Israelis killed a 35-year-old pregnant woman, her brother, and injured eleven others, including six children. Then came the June 24 Israeli capture of two Palestinians, followed by the June 25 Palestinian capture of Shalit and the killing of two other soldiers. This sequence of events was completely ignored in news reporting.

Following the beach deaths on June 9, Hamas, then the ruling party in the Palestinian Authority, broke an 18-month ceasefire and joined other militant groups in firing Qassam rockets into Israel. Above, we cited Tim Llewellyn's observation that the media tend to present 'Israel's lethal modern army' and the Palestinians, 'with their rifles and home-made bombs', as 'two sides equally strong and culpable'. In a June 2006 interview, the political scientist Norman Finkelstein compared the lethality of Israeli and Palestinian attacks. He pointed out that since Israel's withdrawal from Gaza in September 2005, between 7,000 and 9,000 heavy artillery shells had been shot and fired into Gaza. By contrast, Palestinian forces had fired around 1,000 crude Qassam missiles into Israel. The ratio of missiles fired was thus between seven and nine to one. But Israel was also using far more destructive weaponry. Finkelstein noted that in the previous six months, approximately 80 Palestinians had been killed in Gaza as a result of Israeli artillery fire. But over the previous five *years*, eight Israelis had been killed by Qassam missiles. As Finkelstein commented, this represented 'a huge disproportion, a huge discrepancy' – one that is buried beneath the media's fraudulent 'balance'. Finkelstein also discussed the issue of hostage-taking. True, one Israeli soldier had been 'kidnapped'. But, Finkelstein noted:

Let's talk about those 9,000 Palestinians who are effectively hostages being held by Israel. 1,000 of them are administrative detainees ... who are being held without any charges or trial. And the other 8,000 are being held after military courts have convicted them, almost always on the basis of confessions which were extracted by torture. So if we're going to look simply at the numbers, we have one hostage on the Palestinian side, and effectively we have about 9,000 on the Israeli side.[24]

LEBANON: A SERIOUS ESCALATION

On July 12, 2006, in the immediate aftermath of the above events, Israel launched a massive assault on Lebanon. Israel had previously invaded its northern neighbour in 1978 and 1982, finally withdrawing in 2000. The 1982 invasion had cost some 20,000 civilian lives. The latest invasion would similarly end with appalling levels of civilian death and injury, international revulsion at Israel's actions (with shameful exceptions) and a humiliating retreat.

On July 16, a BBC radio report again talked in terms of a 'serious escalation'. But this was not a reference to the killing, by then, of 130 Lebanese as a result of 2,000 sorties by Israeli war planes smashing bridges, roads, airports and oil refineries, with half a million people driven from their homes. Instead, the BBC was describing a Hezbollah rocket attack that day that had killed eight Israelis in Haifa. Although a Channel 4 News report on the attack was titled 'Lebanon burns',[25] three minutes of the four-minute film focused on the Haifa attack. Ten seconds were devoted to Israel's subsequent killing of 16 people in Lebanon's southern city of Tyre in a building used by rescue workers. The Channel 4 News piece began by describing how Hezbollah leader Hassan Nasrallah had warned that the attack on Haifa was 'just the beginning'. Like the BBC, the *Financial Times*, the *Daily Mail* and other news outlets, Channel 4 failed to mention Nasrallah's caveat that Haifa was just the beginning 'if Israel continues its attacks'.[26]

A BBC online article covering the story was titled 'Deadly Hezbollah attack on Haifa'. As independent journalist Jonathan Cook observed, much milder language was used to describe the killing of Lebanese civilians: 'Those dead, many of them women and children, hardly get a mention, their lives apparently empty of meaning or significance in this confrontation.'[27] Sometimes there was no mention at all. A Media Lens reader posed a simple, powerful question to the BBC about a July 17 report: 'The closing headlines included the information that 24 Israelis have died in the current conflict. But no mention was made of the 200 Lebanese reported as killed and as reported by Ch4 News at 7pm. WHY EXACTLY IS THIS?'[28] Debby Moyse, Assistant Editor to the Head of BBC TV News, delivered a standard BBC response:

You are right to point out that the number of people killed, in the current conflict, in Lebanon was not in the closing headlines and it would have been better to have reflected both figures. However the reporting from Lebanon, seen in conjunction with the pictures of people fleeing the country, clearly reflected the impact of the six days of air strikes. Also taken in the context of the overall coverage, the effect of the conflict on each country was balanced.[29]

And so on...

But the indifference to the fate of Lebanese civilians was very real. As refugees from the border village of Marwaheen left in a convoy on July 15 on Israeli orders, Israeli jets attacked, killing 20 people, at least nine of them children. Robert Fisk wrote in the *Independent* of how the local fire brigade 'could not put out the fires as they all burned alive in the inferno'. Fisk noted dryly that another 'terrorist' target had thus been eliminated.[30] We found six mentions of Marwaheen in the UK national press. An *Observer* article was titled merely: 'Children die in convoy attack as Israel widens Lebanon assault.'[31] Predictably, there was minimal detectable outrage.

Amazingly, the BBC and other media described these and other killings as 'retaliation' for Haifa, even though Israel had been launching such strikes for four days before the Hezbollah attack. Indeed, with great consistency, the media describe Israel as 'responding' or 'retaliating'. In 2002, Greg Philo and Mike Berry provided a long list of similar examples stretching over several years: 'The trigger for the Israeli offensive was a massacre on the West Bank.'[32] 'Palestinian suicide attacks trigger more Israeli raids.'[33] The authors commented: 'On the news, Israeli actions tended to be explained and contextualised – they were often shown as merely "responding" to what had been done to them by Palestinians (in the 2001 samples they were six times as likely to be presented as "retaliating" or in some way responding than were the Palestinians).'[34] The reality is that journalists take their lead from Israeli actions in an almost child-like way. A *Guardian* editorial reported that the sixth day of Israeli aerial attacks on Lebanon had killed 47 people and wounded at least 53. But the editors added: 'It is also worth remembering that the weekend's chaos began three weeks ago, with the [June 25] provocative kidnapping of an Israeli soldier by allies of Hamas.'[35]

As we have seen, the June 24 kidnapping of a Palestinian doctor and his brother by Israeli forces, and the earlier Israeli killings, somehow have no place in the chain of cause and effect. The wrong kind of 'chaos' is ignored more generally. Above we described Israeli killings immediately prior to the June 25 'kidnapping' of an Israeli soldier. But according to the Palestinian Centre for Human Rights, from January to May 30, 2006, the Israeli military launched 18 assassinations, described as 'targeted assassinations of militants'. Between March 29 to May 30 that year, there were 77 air strikes on Palestinian population centres, government offices and other infrastructure, with nearly 4,000 artillery shells being fired by Israel over the same period. Between May 26 and June 21, more than 40 Palestinians were killed, 30 of them civilians, including 11 children and two pregnant women. None of these were deemed 'provocative' by our media. Only a wilfully skewed reading of recent history could allow the media to portray Israeli actions as being consistently in 'self-defence'.

Establishing an accurate death toll for Israel's attack on Lebanon was, as ever, no simple task. The United Nations Children's Fund estimated that 1,183 people had died in the attack, mostly civilians with about a third of them children. War dead counts did not include victims of exploding land mines or Israeli cluster bombs after the fighting ended.[36]

ATTACKING THE PRISONERS OF GAZA

In 2008, Israel again attracted international criticism; this time for its latest series of onslaughts against the prison of Gaza, the crowded home to around 1.5 million Palestinians. In just one week, over 120 Palestinians died under Israeli air attacks and what the media called 'incursions' by Israeli troops. Many women and children were among the dead, including four boys who had been out playing football, and babies killed in their homes. One day alone saw the deaths of 60 Palestinians as a result of Israeli attacks. Over a similar period, three Israelis died – one a civilian killed during a rocket attack by Hamas, and two Israeli soldiers.

Just before this escalation in violence, the newswire service Associated Press had briefly flagged up a new report on the Occupied Territories, commissioned by the UN.[37] The report, authored by UN Special Rapporteur John Dugard, concluded that Palestinian terrorism was the 'inevitable consequence' of Israeli occupation. While Palestinian terrorist acts were deplorable, 'they must be understood as being a painful but inevitable consequence of colonialism, apartheid or occupation'. Dugard, a South African law professor, accused the Israeli state of acts and policies consistent with all three.[38] The report noted that Israel had attempted to justify earlier attacks and incursions as 'defensive operations' aimed at preventing the launching of rockets into Israel. Dugard was clear that 'the firing of rockets into Israel by Palestinian militants without any military target, which has resulted in the killing and injury of Israelis, cannot be condoned and constitutes a war crime'. But he also noted that 'serious questions arise over the proportionality of Israel's military response and its failure to distinguish between military and civilian targets. It is highly arguable that Israel has violated the most fundamental rules of international humanitarian law, which constitute war crimes.'

Dugard pointed out that, 'above all', the Israeli government had violated the prohibition on collective punishment of an occupied people contained in article 33 of the Fourth Geneva Convention. In the days that followed, as killings and injuries rapidly rose under a massive Israeli assault, we could find not a single mention in any UK national newspaper of this important assessment by the UN Special Rapporteur on the Occupied Territories. The BBC News website did eventually mention the report, devoting 168 words at the bottom of a short news item. The article noted blandly that unspecified 'scheduling problems' meant that presentation of the report to the UN had been postponed by three months.[39]

That the Special Rapporteur's assessment had been shunted to one side by the 'international community', even as the slaughter in the Middle East continued, was horribly ironic. The possibility that power politics might have been at play in the alleged 'scheduling problems' apparently did not occur to the BBC.

THE ETERNAL BBC CLAIM:
'WE WILL NOT BE CHEERLEADERS FOR ANYBODY'

During this period, Jeremy Bowen, the BBC's Middle East news editor, defended the corporation's unbalanced news coverage from the region: 'The BBC's reporting will be as impartial as we can make it. We will not be cheerleaders for anybody.'[40] Israeli 'incursions' into Gaza continued; one week in April 2008 saw 22 Palestinian deaths, including five children. This time, the Israeli military 'operations' were, the media dutifully observed, 'sparked' by a Hamas ambush that had left three Israeli soldiers dead. Reporting followed the usual script that Israel's advanced weaponry was deployed as 'retaliation' for 'militant' Palestinian attacks. One of the dead was a Reuters cameraman, a 23-year-old Palestinian, killed by a shell fired from an

Israeli tank he was filming. Few details emerged about the numerous other victims of Israeli violence. We emailed Bowen:

> In the BBC's recent reports about the violence in Gaza, the only victim of Israeli firepower that I can recall the BBC naming is Fadel Shana, the Reuters cameraman.
>
> As you know, 22 people were killed, 5 of whom were children. Why are their names not provided by the BBC? Where are the further details that tell us something about them as individuals? Where are the interviews with their grieving families?
>
> If logistical problems make it difficult to do this, shouldn't you explain this clearly and prominently to your audience?
>
> Surely if 5 Israeli children had been killed, the BBC's news coverage would have been significantly different.[41]

Bowen responded on the same day:

> You imply that we have double standards in marking the deaths of Palestinian and Israeli children. I can assure you that we do not.
>
> After twenty years of reporting wars I believe strongly that it is important to humanise the victims. But we cannot broadcast long roll calls of the dead. News is often about death. If we read out the name of everyone whose death we covered, we would have no room for anything else, including a proper explanation of how and why they died.
>
> Our coverage yesterday did that I thought excellently ... There were no interviews yesterday with grieving families because as the death of the Reuters cameraman showed, it was very dangerous to move around. They may well surface in the next few days. Very little video came out of Gaza yesterday. In a piece I did the night before last I interviewed the father of an 11 year old boy, Riad al Uwasi from al Burej camp, who was killed last week. When he was killed it was impossible to get to al Burej, which is where the Reuters cameraman died. When things were calmer, it became possible, until the next incursion.[42]

We asked Jonathan Cook, an independent Israel-based journalist (www.jkcook.net), for his response to Bowen's email. Cook, whose honest and incisive reporting from Israel puts the corporate media to shame, told us:

> It is a terrible irony that, precisely because Israel has created an environment in the occupied territories in which it can unleash so much violence so

unpredictably, journalists are increasingly fearful of venturing there to tell the human stories of the Palestinian casualties behind the simple numbers. It is, of course, equally ironic that, because life inside Israel is relatively safe, journalists can easily humanise the stories of the far smaller number of Israeli casualties. Unfortunately, Bowen and most other journalists fail to appreciate this irony or to act in useful ways to counter its effects on their reporting.

When Bowen tells us that 'we cannot broadcast long roll calls of the dead', he's implicitly accepting a set of news priorities that mean the more Palestinians killed the less importance their deaths have to news organisations like his. Conversely, the fewer Israelis killed the more seriousness their deaths are accorded.[43]

We also contacted former BBC correspondent Tim Llewellyn for his view. He praised Bowen's impact on the BBC's performance:

My view of the BBC's Israel/Palestine coverage has changed a little, and mainly because Jeremy Bowen's presence on the ground and in London has brought some sense and balance to the operation. The standard of reporting from Palestine has also improved in the past couple of years or so, since Jeremy took over and especially since the departure of James Reynolds.

However, Llewellyn pointed to the deep constraints that preclude fair and balanced BBC reporting: 'The problem [of bias] is not with him [Bowen] and cannot be dealt with within his aegis.' Llewellyn explained:

Editors, producers, presenters, and their immediate bosses, live in the heated climate of London and very much still within their own cultural heritage: the politics of the day plus the memories of an English education. ... the story 'concept' in London is still, I am afraid, that Israelis are 'people like us', who should not be shelled every day while they drive their Polos to recognisable branches of Asda or whatever; while Arabs are 'tricky' and 'emotional' and if they weren't all firing rockets and hating Jews in the first place none of this would be happening. This is still the platform off which most Western journalists in London jump. To take a different tack is to run into that wall of 'anti-Semitic' or 'unbalanced' reportage that any of us who tries to explain the facts on the ground in the region runs into.[44]

John Pilger is one journalist who has been on the receiving end of such flak in his extensive reporting on Palestine over several decades. His award-winning 2002 television documentary, *Palestine is Still the*

Issue, is one of his most powerful, and most watched, films on the crisis.[45] We sent Pilger Bowen's email, highlighting the BBC editor's assertion that 'You imply that we have double standards in marking the deaths of Palestinian and Israeli children. I can assure you that we do not.' Pilger praised Bowen's own performance but replied: 'Jeremy Bowen's quote is indefensible.' Pilger then recounted an example of the BBC's institutional bias that systematically suppresses uncomfortably honest perspectives:

> A few years ago, [Bowen] invited me to take part in a BBC special about war correspondents, and we spent an enjoyable hour or so 'in conversation'. Although it was clear that tales of derring-do would have been preferred, I raised the unwelcome subject that the BBC was an extension and voice of the established order in Britain and its reporting on the Middle East and elsewhere reflected the prevailing wisdom – with honourable exceptions from time to time. My contribution was cut entirely from the programme. I emailed Bowen and sometime later received an unsatisfactory response that there wasn't 'time or space' in the film – something unsurprising like that. Censorship by omission is standard, if undeclared practice.[46]

Regular readers of our work will be familiar with the corporate media claim that lack of time or space accounts for the regular omission of honest reporting and critical analysis. As a result of this undeclared media censorship, public understanding of the Middle East remains limited, and challenges to Western support of brutal Israeli policy are easily diffused and minimised.

AN EYE FOR AN EYELASH

On March 24, 1999, an emotional Tony Blair appealed to the House of Commons and to the people of Britain: 'We must act to save thousands of innocent men, women and children from humanitarian catastrophe.' Blair described the emergency: 'Let me give the House an indication of the scale of what is happening: a quarter of a million Kosovars, more than 10 per cent of the population, are now homeless as a result of repression by Serb forces ... Since last summer 2000 people have died.'[47] In a BBC article, Blair added: 'It is no exaggeration to say what is happening in Kosovo is racial genocide. No exaggeration to brand the behaviour of Milosevic's forces as evil.'[48]

Not even Blair claimed all the killings had been on one side. George Robertson, the UK Defence Secretary at the time of the crisis, testified before the House of Commons that until mid-January 1999, 'the Kosovo Liberation Army [KLA] was responsible for more deaths in Kosovo than the Serbian authorities had been'.[49] The *Guardian* rallied to Blair's cause: 'The only honourable course for Europe and America is to use military force to try to protect the people of Kosovo ... If we do not act at all, or if there is a limited bombing campaign which still fails to change Milosevic's mind, what is likely to be Kosovo's future?'[50] The following day, NATO began its 78-day blitz of Serbia.

Ten years later and more than one-half of the 2,000 death toll that so horrified Blair and the *Guardian* in 1999 was reached by the Israeli Defence Forces (IDF) in the first three weeks of its Operation Cast Lead massacre of 1,000 Palestinians, beginning December 27, 2008. Some 4,200 had been wounded. This slaughter was far more one-sided than Kosovo. By mid-January, three Israeli civilians and ten soldiers had been killed: four of the latter were victims of their own 'friendly fire'. The KLA killed hundreds of Serbs. KLA attacks did nothing to temper media outrage at the spectacle of the Serbian state attacking tiny Kosovo. The focus was on Serbian 'massacres' and 'genocide'. The *Observer* wrote of the alleged killing of 45 Albanian civilians in Račak by Serb armed forces on January 16, 1999: 'History will judge that the defining moment for the international community took place on 16 January this year ... Albanians returning after an attack by Serb security forces discovered the bodies of men they had left behind to look after the houses.'[51] Serb forces, the *Observer* wrote, were 'pursuing their own version of a Balkan Final Solution'. With the NATO bombing of Serbia underway, Andrew Marr, now with the BBC, wrote in the *Observer*: 'I want to put the Macbeth option: which is that we're so steeped in blood we should go further. If we really believe [Serbian leader] Milosevic is this bad, dangerous and destabilising figure we must ratchet this up much further. We should now be saying that we intend to put in ground troops.'[52]

However extreme this sounds now, the fact is that British newspapers were full of this kind of call to action. That same month, David Aaronovitch wrote in the *Independent*: 'Is this cause, the cause of the Kosovar Albanians, a cause that is worth suffering for? ... Would I fight, or (more realistically) would I countenance the possibility that members of my family might die?' His answer: 'I think so.'[53] We wrote to Aaronovitch on January 14, 2009 and asked him if he would be willing to fight for the people of Gaza. He responded: 'If an international force was to be assembled to police a settlement to the Israel/Palestine mess which, for a minimum of 60 years has caused such loss of life, then I do think that would be worth fighting for.'[54]

In 1999, British and American media were full of talk of 'genocide' in Kosovo. A Nexis database search showed that between 1998 and 1999 the *Los Angeles Times*, the *New York Times*, the *Washington Post*, *Newsweek* and *Time* used 'genocide' 220 times to describe Serb actions in Kosovo.[55] In January 2009, we found no examples of a British journalist describing Israel's attack as 'genocidal'. *Daily Mail* columnist Melanie Phillips made rare use of the word on January 5: 'Many others also share the view that Israel is in the wrong. So why is a country [Israel] under attack from genocidal fanatics pilloried for defending its citizens against slaughter?'[56]

Israel's massacre was presented as a 'war', as a 'Gaza conflict' between two sides engaged in 'fighting'. This is the standard fiction. We note again Tim Llewellyn's comment that, for the BBC, 'Israel's lethal modern army is one force, the Palestinians, with their rifles and home-made bombs, the other "force": two sides equally strong and culpable in a difficult dispute, it is implied...'.[57] Norwegian doctor Mads Gilbert, one of two foreign doctors working at Gaza's biggest hospital, al-Shifa, told CBS News: 'I've seen one military person among the hundreds that we have seen and treated. So anyone who tries to portray this as sort of a clean war against another army are lying. This is an all-out war against the civilian Palestinian population in Gaza and we can prove that with the numbers.'[58]

Even the death toll cited above does little to communicate the true one-sidedness of the wider violence, injustice and cruelty. Largely unmentioned by the media, prior to the December 27, 2008 attack, 14 Israelis had been killed by mostly home-made rockets fired from Gaza over the last seven years as against 5,000 Palestinians killed in Israeli attacks.[59] Consider the response of Blair and the *Guardian* to Israel's mass killing. From Blair there was no longer talk of the need to send bombs and tanks to save a stricken population (Blair led calls for a ground war against Serbia). Instead:

I think the position is that there are circumstances in which we could get an immediate ceasefire and that's what people want to see. I think the circumstances focus very much around clear action to cut off the supply of arms and money from the tunnels that go from Egypt into Gaza. I think if there were strong, clear, definitive action on that, that would give us the best context to get an immediate ceasefire and to start to change the situation.[60]

No *Guardian* editorials proposed a massive military assault on Israel as the only 'honorable course for Europe and America'. The question was not asked: 'If we do not act at all ... what is likely to be Gaza's future?' Instead, the country's 'leading liberal newspaper' was content to contemplate a slap on the wrist: 'If Israel presses on regardless, it should face an immediate suspension of all arms from the EU, as Nick Clegg, the Liberal Democrat leader, proposes.'[61] As ever, Israeli politicians claimed to have been heroically restraining themselves and their capacity for violence (a manifest source of pride) in the face of endless provocation. And yet as recently as February–March 2008, 110 Palestinian civilians had been killed during 'Operation Winter Heat'.

This military violence was piled on the staggering economic violence of Israel's blockade of Gaza. Prior to the Operation Cast Lead offensive, John Ging, who runs the Gaza operations of UNRWA, the UN agency that looks after Palestinian refugees, told the BBC:

> There's one million on food aid, including 750,000 refugees. 80% are below the poverty line, meaning they live on less than $2 a day. Almost 100,000 jobs have gone in the last 18 months, since the total Israeli embargo came in. [Because that included most building materials] $93m of UNRWA construction projects, medical centres, houses for refugees, all are stopped. 3,200 out of 3,500 Gaza businesses have gone down in the siege.
>
> There's no ray of sunlight. It's all going in the wrong direction. It's all well documented and predictable.
>
> The Quartet [of the US, the UN, Russia and the EU] said a new approach was needed for Gaza. In fact there are even stricter sanctions.[62]

During the ceasefire, Israel placed severe restrictions on the number of trucks allowed to bring food, fuel, cooking-gas canisters, spare parts for water and sanitation plants, and medical supplies to Gaza. Israeli historian, Avi Shlaim, professor of international relations at the University of Oxford, wrote in the *Guardian*: 'It is difficult to see how starving and freezing the civilians of Gaza could protect the people on the Israeli side of the border. But even if it did, it would still be immoral, a form of collective punishment that is strictly forbidden by international humanitarian law.' He added: 'The Biblical injunction of an eye for an eye is savage enough. But Israel's insane offensive against Gaza seems to follow the logic of an eye for an eyelash.'[63]

It is the sheer cruelty of Israeli oppression that captures the world's imagination. Or, more accurately, defies it.

TARGETING HAMAS

The corporate media were happy to echo the claim that Israel was 'targeting Hamas' rather than the Palestinian people. In reality, the Palestinian people elected Hamas as its democratic government in 2006. And it was the Palestinian people who were paying the price. The state of the art, US-supplied missiles, bombs and artillery shells were not being aimed at the regular army targets for which they were designed: tanks, command posts, trenches and bunkers. They were being fired into residential areas in one of the world's most densely-populated strips of land.

The white phosphorus (WP) shells used were incendiary airburst weapons designed to incinerate a wide target area. As we noted in Chapter 3, the weapon has been used by US forces in their infamous 'shake 'n' bake' attacks on Iraqi insurgents in cities such as Fallujah. On the BBC's World News, correspondent Ben Brown said WP shells were being used merely to illuminate targets in Gaza.[64]

Israel consistently claimed that 80 per cent of those killed were Hamas 'militants'. Al Haq, a Palestinian legal rights group, reported that in fact 80 per cent of Palestinian fatalities were civilians. According to figures cited by the World Health Organization, at least 40 per cent were children.[65] *Independent Catholic News* provided details of a January 9, 2009 attack on a medical centre in Gaza belonging to Caritas Internationalis. The centre, along with $10,000 worth of medical equipment, was completely destroyed by a US-made, Israeli F-16 fighter. Fr Manuel Musallam, parish priest of Gaza, said on the telephone from Beit Hanoun in Gaza: 'There is extreme fear everywhere here. The bombs the Israelis are dropping are literally cutting through people and through homes.'[66] Musallam reported that there was no water, and almost no fuel for cooking. He added: 'The Israeli aggression has made these people live like animals and our school is the zoo. There are dead bodies lying on the streets. The clinics are carrying out operations on the floor. Women have no place to give birth. One pregnant woman was shot on her way to a clinic to give birth. They tried to save the baby but it too was dead.'[67]

One day after the Caritas attack, an Israeli jet destroyed a health clinic providing free care funded by Christian Aid. A spokesperson for the agency commented: 'So many mothers had brought their babies and children for treatment. Now the whole clinic lies in ruins.'[68] The destruction of the Caritas clinic was mentioned in a single UK newspaper article. The bombing of Christian Aid was mentioned in two articles.

A key deception promoted by Israel's National Information Directorate involved the claim that the cycle of violence after December 27, 2008 began when Hamas broke a four-month ceasefire agreed the previous June. In fact, Israel had broken the ceasefire when it launched a raid into Gaza on November 4, killing six people. On November 5, the *Guardian* reported:

> A four-month ceasefire between Israel and Palestinian militants in Gaza was in jeopardy today after Israeli troops killed six Hamas gunmen in a raid into the territory.
>
> Hamas responded by firing a wave of rockets into southern Israel, although no one was injured. The violence represented the most serious break in a ceasefire agreed in mid-June, yet both sides suggested they wanted to return to atmosphere of calm. ... Until now it had appeared both Israel and Hamas, which seized full control of Gaza last summer, had an interest in maintaining the ceasefire. For Israel it has meant an end to the daily barrage of rockets landing in southern towns, particularly Sderot.[69]

On December 27, at the start of the Operation Cast Lead attacks, Reuters reported that US Secretary of State Condoleezza Rice had 'blamed Hamas for breaking a cease-fire with Israel, which launched air strikes on Gaza killing more than 200 people'. Rice commented: 'The United States strongly condemns the repeated rocket and mortar attacks against Israel and holds Hamas responsible for breaking the ceasefire and for the renewal of violence in Gaza.'[70]

Alan Dershowitz wrote in the *Telegraph* on January 10, 2009: 'Hamas deliberately broke the ceasefire by firing rockets into southern Israel from densely populated cities, using the areas around schools and mosques as launching points.'[71] The BBC's version of events from January 9 was more subtly deceptive: 'The ceasefire, brokered by the Egyptians, was often broken in practice ... Events began to come to a climax after the Israelis raided southern Gaza on 4 November 2008 to destroy smuggling tunnels.'[72] No mention was made of the six human lives also destroyed in the attack. The same BBC article, 'Q&A: Gaza conflict', asked:

> What casualties have the Hamas rockets caused? Since 2001, when the rockets were first fired, more than 8,600 have hit southern Israel, nearly 6,000 of them since Israel withdrew from Gaza in August 2005. The rockets have killed 28 people and injured hundreds more. In the Israeli town of Sderot near Gaza, 90% of residents have had a missile exploding in their street or an adjacent one.

The article noted that 'Palestinian medical sources say that about 700 people have been killed in Gaza during Israel's current campaign there.' Again, curiously, despite mentioning that Hamas rockets had killed 28 Israelis since 2001, the BBC made no mention of the fact that 5,000 Palestinians had been killed by Israeli strikes over the same period prior to the current Israeli offensive – a figure that was then fast approaching 6,000.

THE LOGIC OF MASSACRE

Noam Chomsky noted that Israel's breaking of the ceasefire on November 4, 2008, killing six Palestinians, happened at a significant time. The attack came shortly before a key meeting in Cairo when Hamas and its political rival Fatah were to hold talks on 'reconciling their differences and creating a single, unified government', the *Guardian* reported. It would have been the first meeting at such a high level since the near civil war of 2007.[73] Chomsky wrote that the meeting 'would have been a significant step towards advancing diplomatic efforts. There is a long history of Israel provocations to deter the threat of diplomacy, some already mentioned. This may have been another one.'[74] The attack also came on the day of the US presidential elections. Israeli leaders knew the world would be focusing elsewhere – this would help obscure the fact that Israel, not Hamas, had broken the ceasefire. It would also help provide a rationale for the slaughter planned for later in the month and clearly timed to end just before Obama's inauguration. Chomsky summarised the appalling truth: 'The effort to delay political accommodation has always made perfect sense ... It is hard to think of another way to take over land where you are not wanted.'[75]

Israel, then, consistently shows a preference 'for expansion over security'.[76] Peace is actually a threat to a programme of illegal expansion that can be achieved only through violence under cover of conflict and war. And so, from this perspective, inflicting horrific violence on a defenceless civilian population makes perfect sense. When a high-tech military power demolishes schools, mosques and medical centres, it enrages, divides and demolishes the 'political threat' of peaceful negotiation. So while it is true that Israel's bombs were intended to destroy Hamas and to stop the rockets, they also had a much uglier aim. And although, as we have seen, there is serious evidence in support of this argument, it cannot be found in the mainstream press. During the December 2008–January 2009 crisis, the *Independent*'s Robert Fisk did not offer Chomsky's argument in any of his numerous articles on Gaza. Instead, he commented: 'Hamas is not Hizbollah. Jerusalem is not Beirut. And Israeli soldiers cannot take revenge for their 2006 defeat in Lebanon by attacking Hamas in Gaza – not even to help Ms Livni in the Israeli elections.'[77]

Similarly, the *Guardian*'s Seumas Milne cited Israeli journalist Amos Harel who commented that 'little or no weight was apparently devoted to the question of harming innocent civilians'.[78] Only John Pilger offered essentially the same argument as Chomsky in his January 8 article in the small circulation *New Statesman* magazine. Pilger wrote: 'Every subsequent "war" Israel has waged [since 1947] has had the same objective: the expulsion of the native people and the theft of more and more land.'[79]

In our introductory chapter we warned of the disproportionate impact of small gestures in the direction of truth. During Israel's January 2009 massacre in Gaza, several people commented to us on the high quality of mainstream coverage. There *was* concern, we were told; there was outrage. But we need only ask ourselves what the tone and depth of coverage would have been like if New York, rather than Gaza, had been the victim of such an onslaught. The answer is that it would have been almost completely unrecognisable, characterised by wall-to-wall outrage, all day, every day.

10
Real Men Go To Tehran:
Targeting Iran

But let's have some perspective, please: we're talking about a country with roughly the G.D.P. of Connecticut, and a government whose military budget is roughly the same as Sweden's.

Paul Krugman, *New York Times*[1]

WHAT WOULD *YOU* DO?

Okay, so you're a journalist. You've just seen your entire profession bamboozled (as you see it) into a disastrous war in Iraq by a bunch of mendacious fanatics clearly pursuing a hidden agenda. There were the more obvious lies: Saddam Hussein had sinister links with Al Qaeda – you know, now, they were sworn enemies. Iraq was involved in the 9/11 attacks on America – you know, now, there was not a scrap of evidence to support such a claim. And you know now that Iraq had retained not even a scrap of its weapons of mass destruction. If you've done a little bit of scratching around, you'll know that senior weapons inspectors had tried to point out that Iraq had been 'fundamentally disarmed' as far back as December 1998. You know that the whole Iraqi 'threat' was fabricated, hyped, and heaped on a British public that absolutely did not want to go to war in the spring of 2003.

So fine, what do you do when the same proven liars in government announce that Iraq's neighbour, *Iran* – a country with a military budget the size of Sweden's – is now threatening the world, just as Iraq was in 2002–03? Answer: you act as though 2002–03 never happened.

In 2005, Fred Halliday, Professor of International Relations at the London School of Economics, noted that in Washington in 2003 the fashionable phrase was, 'wimps go to Baghdad, real men go to Tehran'.[2] Writing in the *New Yorker* magazine in January 2005, the renowned investigative journalist Seymour Hersh reported that the 'real men' in question had itchy feet. A former high-level intelligence official told him:

This is a war against terrorism, and Iraq is just one campaign. The Bush Administration is looking at this as a huge war zone. Next, we're going to have the Iranian campaign. We've declared war and the bad guys, wherever they are, are the enemy. This is the last hurrah – we've got four years, and want to come out of this saying we won the war on terrorism.[3]

Hersh added: 'In my interviews, I was repeatedly told that the next strategic target was Iran.' In January 2005, on the BBC1 lunchtime news, diplomatic correspondent James Robbins declared that US relations with Iran were 'looking very murky because of the nuclear threat'.[4] Robbins should have said: the alleged, potential, future nuclear threat from Iran. On the BBC's Six O'Clock News five days later, Robbins again spoke of Iran 'where the President is confronting the nuclear threat'.[5] And yet, a week earlier, Ian Traynor had reported in the *Guardian* that Western concern over Iran's suspected nuclear programme had been growing since 2003: 'The International Atomic Energy Agency in Vienna has had inspectors in the country throughout the period. While finding much that is suspect, the inspectors have not found any proof of a clandestine nuclear bomb programme.'[6]

In November 2007, the US National Intelligence Estimate (NIE), which summarises the work of the 16 American intelligence agencies, disclosed that Iran had *not* been pursuing a nuclear weapons development programme for the previous four years: 'Tehran's decision to halt its nuclear weapons programme suggests it is less determined to develop nuclear weapons than we have been judging since 2005.'[7] The report concluded: 'We judge with high confidence that in fall 2003 Tehran halted its nuclear weapons programme.' The programme had not been restarted as of the middle of 2007.

This was not the first time James Robbins had boosted a bogus threat. On the BBC's September 17, 2002 lunchtime news, he reported that UN weapons inspectors were 'asked to leave' by the Iraqi government in 1998 after relations broke down. This claim was heavily promoted by the British and American governments to indicate that Iraq could not be disarmed through peaceful diplomacy. But it was a lie. In fact, weapons inspectors were advised to leave by the US government ahead of bombing (Operation Desert Fox) in December that year. On June 28, 2004, following the alleged 'handover of power' from the US occupation to the Iraqi interim government, Robbins declared the occupation of Iraq at an end, leaving the country 'sovereign and free'[8] – a comment that ought to have seemed as absurd then as it does now.

After complaints were sent by Media Lens readers to the BBC on the Iranian 'nuclear threat', Robbins replied: 'I accept that it would have been better to have said "alleged nuclear threat". I am sorry that my wording was not as precise as it could have been.'[9] But similar comments have been steadily percolating throughout the press and the public mind. Writing in the *Guardian* in January 2006, Timothy Garton Ash observed: 'Now we face the next big test of the west: after Iraq, Iran.' Garton Ash thus blithely ignored the fact that all the evidence coming out of Iraq indicated that Iraq's 'big test' was in reality the West's fraud. Iraq was offering a threat to no one outside its own borders. Nevertheless, Garton Ash warned: 'we in Europe and the United States have to respond. But how?'[10]

The *Guardian*'s Polly Toynbee joined the propaganda chorus: 'Now the mad mullahs of Iran will soon have nuclear bombs, are we all doomed? ... Do something, someone! But what and who?'[11] In providing the answer, Gerard Baker of *The Times* joined the Trevor Kavanagh (the *Sun*) and Con Coughlin (*Daily Telegraph*) school of responsible journalism: 'The unimaginable but ultimately inescapable truth is that we are going to have to get ready for war with Iran.'[12] As the distraught weatherman played by Bill Murray reported from Punxsutawney: 'It's Groundhog Day ... *again!*'

Why exactly did we have to prepare for war – again? Baker explained: 'If Iran gets safely and unmolested to nuclear status, it will be a threshold moment in the history of the world, up there with the Bolshevik Revolution and the coming of Hitler.' Baker made further fearsome predictions:

> Iran, of course, secure now behind its nuclear wall, will surely step up its campaign of terror around the world. It will become even more of a magnet and haven for terrorists ... Imagine how much more our freedoms will be curtailed if our governments fear we are just one telephone call or e-mail, one plane journey or truckload away from another Hiroshima.

This is the same Gerard Baker who crowed in the *Financial Times* in February 2003 that 'victory [in Iraq] will quickly vindicate US and British claims about the scale of the threat Saddam poses'. He was positively gleeful: 'I cannot wait to hear what the French, Russians and Germans have to say when the conquering troops begin to uncover the death factories Mr Hussein has been hiding from inspectors for 12 years ... And do not be shocked if allied liberators discover all kinds of connections between Baghdad and terrorism around the world.'[13] A year later and Baker quietly changed his story on the threat posed by Saddam Hussein: 'This threat lay not in vats of chemicals or nuclear centrifuges but in his ambitions.'[14] All along it was Saddam's 'ambitions', not his 'death factories' and 'all kinds of connections between Baghdad and terrorism', that were the threat. In his February 2003 article, Baker had predicted: 'it will become clear, even to the most rabid of anti-Americans just how much better off Iraqi people will be without their current president. The lifting of the yoke of Saddam Hussein will be an act of humanity far greater than the unseating of the Taliban.'

At time of writing (March 2009), the dictionary supplies few adequate words to describe Iraq sans 'yoke'. Words like 'cataclysm' and 'catastrophe' are inadequate to communicate the sheer scale of the suffering of the civilian population. Baker is a signatory to the Statement of Principles posted at the website of The Henry Jackson Society. Patrons include mild-mannered neo-conservatives like former US assistant secretary of defence, Richard 'Prince of Darkness' Perle, William Kristol, editor of the *Weekly Standard*, and James Woolsey, former director of the CIA. Other signatories include former head of MI6, Sir Richard Dearlove, Colonel Tim Collins, Oliver Kamm, Andrew Roberts and Jamie Shea. The Society declares that it '[s]upports a "forward strategy" to assist those countries that are not yet liberal and democratic to become so. This would involve the full spectrum of our "carrot" capacities, be they diplomatic, economic, cultural or political, but also, when necessary, those "sticks" of the military domain.'[15]

Serbia, Afghanistan and Iraq know all about the '"sticks" of the military domain'.

Four of the Society's eight 'Principles' refer to military intervention and military power – another notes that 'only modern liberal democratic states are truly legitimate'. Everyone else, we can presume – and see for ourselves – is fair game.

DESTINATION 'RATIONAL UNIVERSE'

In the *New York Times* in March 2007, Max Hastings – former editor of the *Daily Telegraph* and the *Evening Standard* – agreed with 'people in Washington' who described Iran as 'one of the most reckless and erratic regimes in the world', a country run by the 'wild men of Tehran', headed by 'the Holocaust-denying President Mahmoud Ahmadinejad'. With Iraq ablaze, Hastings was happy to repeat the kind of incendiary propaganda that set the fire: 'Iran represents a menace to the security of us all, not to mention what it must be like to live under that reprehensible regime.'[16]

Journalists have been demonising other countries for so long, it seems they cannot stop. Always it is the 1930s; always Hitler is plotting our destruction; always we need to recoil in fear, disgust and horror. Is this the real world? Or is it journalism as pathology?

Objectivity and balance are not serious concerns. The realities of career progression demand that journalists side with 'us' against 'them'. Thus Hastings observed of the latest 'them': 'The game they [the Iranians] play with considerable skill is to project themselves at once as assertive Islamic crusaders, and also as victims of imperialism.'

This recalled reporter James Mates' comments on ITN when he observed that Saddam Hussein was again 'playing his favourite role of defender of the Arab people'.[17] Which news reporter would ever describe Barack Obama or Gordon Brown as 'playing his favourite role of defender of the free world'? This is how we are trained to feel contempt for the official enemy, to distrust their motives and sneer at their 'values'. As for the idea that the Iranians are portraying themselves as 'victims of imperialism' as a kind of 'game', we need only recall how Amnesty International described the regime brought to power in Iran by the US–UK military coup of 1953. This was a state, Amnesty reported, that had the 'highest rate of death penalties in the world, no valid system of civilian courts and a history of torture' which was 'beyond belief'. It was a society in which 'the entire population was subjected to a constant, all-pervasive terror'.[18] The motive behind US–UK violence was, very simply, control of Iranian oil. None of this exists for Western journalists, for whom Iranian history began with the 1979 hostage crisis.

Hastings continued his account of the Iranian regime: 'They crave respect and influence. Their only claims to these things rest upon their capacity for menacing the West, whether through international terrorism, support for Palestinian extremists, or the promise of building atomic weapons.' That's 'them' – the 'bad guys', craving glory and power at any cost (as 'bad guys' do). As for 'us': 'We must keep talking to the Iranians, offering carrots even when these are contemptuously tossed into the gutter, because there is no credible alternative. Even threats of economic sanctions must be considered cautiously.' That's 'us' – the 'good guys'. Our 'carrots' include ringing Iran with military bases, sending nuclear-armed aircraft carrier battle groups to the Gulf to conduct 'war games', and broadcasting open threats to bomb Iranian nuclear facilities.

Hastings suggested that 'even' the use of sanctions 'must be considered cautiously' – not because the 1990–2003 sanctions on Iraq resulted in the deaths of one million human beings, but because the most likely consequence would be 'to strengthen the hand of Tehran's extremists'. The perennial obsession is with 'us', 'our' needs, 'our' costs. The portion of the brain that deals with empathy for the suffering we might cause 'them' – real, live, loving human beings like us – is inert, silent, a slab of dead grey meat in the skulls of mainstream journalists. And who actually makes up this alliance labelled 'we', referred to when Hastings writes: 'We must keep talking to the Iranians'?

Obviously, he had in mind the British and American governments. But he was also proposing a further component – himself, a journalist – as well as inviting the readers of the *New York Times* to identify themselves as 'us'. One could hardly find a clearer example of how professional journalism openly allies itself with elite power. Nobody notices this bias when it endorses the view of an establishment pulling together in time of crisis. Why? Because the establishment media determine the full range of relevant opinions worth discussing. What could be more balanced than affirming what everyone (who matters) believes? There might be odd squeaks and squawks sounding from beyond the establishment spectrum, but they can be ignored. Why? Because they are 'silly'. Why are they 'silly'? Because they are voiced by people without influence. As Channel 4 News presenter Jon Snow told a reader: 'I am relieved to see that media lens ... [is] "growing up" ... I have not been bombarded with adolescent look-alike emails now for more than six months!'[19]

For the mainstream media, an opinion barely exists if it doesn't matter, and it doesn't matter if it is not voiced by people who matter. The full range of opinion, then, represents the full range of power. In that sense the mainstream media is indeed balanced.

There was not even a glimmer in Hastings' article of journalism's ostensible duty of holding power to account, of promoting scepticism of government claims, of military warnings and alleged threats. That, in itself, is reprehensible. And this despite everything that Hastings, like the rest of us, had witnessed concerning Iraq over the previous five years. Of this, he merely commented: 'The United States and Britain have suffered a disastrous erosion of moral authority in consequence of the Iraq war.'

He made clear that he meant by this that many nations now had little sympathy for the US and British position in the Gulf region. But what he was careful not to suggest was that this opinion reflected an *actual* erosion of US–UK morality (or that they had no moral authority to erode) – that would not do. Instead, his view was made very clear: 'It is not the American way, but only patience, statesmanship and a refusal to respond in kind to outrageous behavior offer a chance of eventually persuading this dangerous nation to join a rational universe.' Hastings meant, of course, the 'rational universe' inhabited by the West, with Britain and America very much at the hub.

But anyone who has been analysing politics over the last few years knows that Britain and America invaded Iraq on a set of spectacular lies. This is the 'rational universe' for Hastings, beyond which Iran threatens as the 'dangerous nation', the 'rogue state'.

SHOULD WE BOMB THE UNITED STATES?

At the top of the emailed version of the June 21, 2007 edition of the *New York Times*, this 'advertisement' appeared in large red letters: 'Should We Bomb Iran? Vote in This Urgent Poll'. Questions for American readers to fill in over their ham and eggs included:

'Do you believe Iran poses a greater threat than Saddam Hussein did before the Iraq War?' 'Who should undertake military action against Iran first? U.S. Israel. Neither country.' We can guess the reaction in Washington if the *Tehran Times* published a poll asking: 'Should We Bomb The United States?' Another actual question asked: 'Do you believe U.S. efforts to contain Iran's nuclear weapons program are working?' In fact there was, and is, no evidence that Iran has a nuclear weapons programme.

After completing the questionnaire, readers were automatically directed to a special offer for an 'emergency radio':

Homeland Security Alert. Dear NewsMax Reader: The Department of Homeland Security advises all Americans to have an emergency radio. An emergency radio should work on battery or hand power. Emergency radio is a vital link to keep you informed during power outages, hurricanes, tornadoes, earthquakes, terrorism events and other disasters.

In November 2007, George Monbiot wrote in the *Guardian*: 'I believe that Iran is trying to acquire the bomb.' He added: 'Yes, Iran under Mahmoud Ahmadinejad is a dangerous and unpredictable state involved in acts of terror abroad.'[20] We wrote to Monbiot on the same day:

> In your latest *Guardian* article, you write: 'I believe that Iran is trying to acquire the bomb.' What is the basis for your belief, please? You also write: 'Yes, Iran under Mahmoud Ahmadinejad is a dangerous and unpredictable state involved in acts of terror abroad. The president is a Holocaust denier opposed to the existence of Israel.'
>
> Is it your understanding that Ahmadinejad, rather than Khamenei, is the supreme ruler of Iran? If so, why? And which 'acts of terror abroad' do you have in mind? Do you include the claims that Iran has supplied EFPs [Explosively-Formed Penetrators] to blow up US–UK tanks and troops in Iraq, for example?
>
> Finally, what is the basis for your belief that Ahmadinejad is 'opposed to the existence of Israel'?

We wrote a further two times but received no reply.

On December 18, 2007, we analysed the UK national press over the previous 20 years searching for 'gay rights' and 'Iran'. We found 79 mentions – 56 of these had been since the March 2003 invasion of Iraq:

2007 – 14
2006 – 9
2005 – 9
2004 – 19
2003 – 6 (5 post-invasion, 1 pre-invasion)
2002 – 2
2001 – 3
2000 – 1
1999 – 1
1998 – 2
1997 – 2
1996 – 1
1995 – 1
1994 – 5
1992 – 1
1989 – 1
1988 – 2

We found a similar pattern when searching for the terms 'Taliban' and 'women's rights'. Between February 1995 and December 2007, there were 56 mentions in the *Guardian*. Of these, 36 appeared after the 9/11 attacks. Following those attacks, there was the same number of mentions (nine) in the last three and a half months of that year as there had been in the previous three years combined. Ninety per cent of the mentions in 2001 occurred after 9/11.

It is clear that, following the invasion, Iran took the place of Iraq as the West's enemy of choice – it was an ideal scapegoat for the catastrophic occupation and a suitable device for maintaining the traditional fear of foreign 'threats'.

PENTAGON PROPAGANDA OCCUPIES THE *GUARDIAN*'S FRONT PAGE

In May 2007, the *Guardian* editor Alan Rusbridger told it like it is: 'The *Guardian*'s vision is to offer independent, agenda-setting content that positions us as the modern, progressive, exciting challenger to the status-quo.'[21] The reality is rather less glorious. Consider the *Guardian*'s May 22, 2007 front-page story: 'Iran's secret plan for summer offensive to force US out of Iraq', by Simon Tisdall.[22] Tisdall's high-profile piece claimed that Iran had secret plans to do nothing less than wage war on, and defeat, American forces in Iraq by August 2007.

Iran, it seemed, was 'forging ties with al-Qaida elements and Sunni Arab militias in Iraq in preparation for a summer showdown with coalition forces intended to tip a wavering US Congress into voting for full military withdrawal'.[23] The claim was based almost entirely on unsupported assertions made by anonymous US officials. Indeed 22 of the 23 paragraphs in the story relayed official US claims: over 95 per cent of the story. The compilation below indicates the levels of balance and objectivity:

> 'US officials say'; 'a senior US official in Baghdad warned'; 'The official said'; 'the official said'; 'the official said'; 'US officials now say'; 'the senior official in Baghdad said' 'he [the senior official in Baghdad] added'; 'the official said'; 'the official said'; 'he [the official] indicated; 'he [the official] cited'; 'a senior administration official in Washington said'; 'The administration official also claimed'; 'he [the administration official] said'; 'US officials say'; 'the senior official in Baghdad said'; 'he [the senior official in Baghdad] said'; 'the senior administration official said'; 'he [the senior administration official] said'; 'the official claimed'; 'he [the official] said'; 'Gen Petraeus's report to the White

House and Congress'; 'a former Bush administration official said'; 'A senior adviser to Gen Petraeus reported'; 'the adviser admitted'.

No less than 26 references to official pronouncements formed the basis for a *Guardian* story presented with no scrutiny, no balance, no counter-evidence. Remove the verbiage above and the *Guardian*'s front-page news report becomes a straight Pentagon press release. Tisdall quoted 'a senior official in Baghdad' as saying: 'Iran is fighting a proxy war in Iraq and it's a very dangerous course for them to be following. They are already committing daily acts of war against US and British forces.' And: 'We expect that al-Qaida and Iran will both attempt to increase the propaganda and increase the violence prior to Petraeus's report in September' – when the then US commander, General David Petraeus, was to report to Congress on the 'surge' of 30,000 troop reinforcements. The anonymous official added:

> Iran is perpetuating the cycle of sectarian violence through support for extra-judicial killing and murder cells. They bring Iraqi militia members and insurgent groups into Iran for training and then help infiltrate them back into the country. We have plenty of evidence from a variety of sources. There's no argument about that. That's just a fact.

Tisdall included the most pitiful of disclaimers in the final paragraph of a long (1,200-word) piece: 'Iranian officials flatly deny US and British allegations of involvement in internal violence in Iraq or in attacks on coalition forces.

THE *GUARDIAN* BRACES ITSELF

Edward Herman commented on Tisdall's piece:

> I saw that story and was amazed that what we call here the 'Judy Miller syndrome' has caught on in the UK 'liberal media.' Pretty amazing, after the overwhelming evidence of the past five years that the U.S.–Bush government is in the very business of disinformation, and their steady and obvious desire to demonize the Iranians, that this unconfirmed propaganda is treated as news (and not news pathology).[24]

Readers will recall that the *New York Times* journalist Judith Miller's 'syndrome' presented as an extreme willingness to accept the claims of government sources at face value. In the wake of its disastrous pre-war reporting on Iraq, the *New York Times* published a humbling apology:

> Editors at several levels who should have been challenging reporters and pressing for more skepticism were perhaps too intent on rushing scoops into the paper. Accounts of Iraqi defectors were not always weighed against their strong desire to have Saddam Hussein ousted. Articles based on dire claims about Iraq tended to get prominent display, while follow-up articles that called the original ones into question were sometimes buried. In some cases, there was no follow-up at all.[25]

In response, the paper implemented new rules governing its use of unnamed sources: 'When we use such sources, we accept an obligation not only to convince a reader of their reliability but also to convey what we can learn of their motivation – as much as we can supply to let a reader know whether the sources have a clear point of view on the issue under discussion.' The rules go on to advise:

> In any situation when we cite anonymous sources, at least some readers may suspect that the newspaper is being used to convey tainted information or special pleading. If the impetus for anonymity has originated with the source, further reporting is essential to satisfy the reporter and the reader that the paper has sought the whole story.[26]

Journalists at the *New York Times* have done a splendid job of ignoring these rules ever since. The *Guardian* – which did not apologise for its equally awful pre-war reporting – claims to observe similar rules. Its February 2003 'Editorial Code' actually leads with a discussion of 'Anonymous quotations'. The code states: 'The *New York Times* policy on pejorative quotes is worth bearing in mind: "The vivid language of direct quotation confers an unfair advantage on a speaker or writer who hides behind the newspaper, and turns of phrase are valueless to a reader who cannot assess the source."'[27] And yet Tisdall appeared to feel no obligation to convince readers of the reliability of his sources, as the *New York Times* recommends – not a shred of evidence was supplied in support of their claims. Likewise, there was no sense that Tisdall had 'sought the whole story'; the version supplied by the anonymous US official was deemed sufficient – again.

Juan Cole, Professor of Modern Middle East and South Asian History at the University of Michigan, dismissed Tisdall's 'silly article', describing the anonymous sources as 'looney in positing a coming offensive jointly sponsored by Iran, the Mahdi Army and al-Qaeda'.[28] He concluded: 'US military spokesmen have been trying to push implausible articles about Shiite Iran supporting Sunni insurgents for a couple of years now, and with virtually the sole exception of the *New York Times*, no one in the journalistic community has taken these wild charges seriously. But the *Guardian*?'

The *Guardian* was soon bracing itself for the fallout from Tisdall's story. Murray Armstrong, an associate editor, noted in his blog that the article had 'led the discussion' at that morning's editorial conference. He added: 'Simon noted that several readers had already accused him of peddling US propaganda.'[29] It is fair to describe readers' responses to Armstrong's defence on his blog as devastating and close to 100 per cent critical. Tisdall responded to one challenger via email:

> Today's article was based on statements made by several senior US officials who are intimately familiar with the problems facing coalition forces in Iraq. I requested the interviews, not the other way round. These officials asked not to be identified. I am confident that they were telling the truth as they see it, on the basis of information received from a variety of sources.[30]

It seems readers were to be reassured by Tisdall's defence that he actively sought out US propaganda, rather than acted as a passive conduit. To the *Guardian*'s credit, two critical pieces soon appeared on their online section, Comment is Free. D.D. Guttenplan, London correspondent for *The Nation* magazine, wrote: 'History really does repeat itself. Either that or the Bush administration has decided to show its commitment to the environment by recycling lies. Those are the only firm conclusions to be drawn from the *Guardian*'s front page story this morning.'[31] Middle East analyst Dilip Hiro warned that the official briefings given to the *Guardian* were driven by a US political agenda. The timing was crucial: Ryan Crocker, the US ambassador in Iraq, was about to meet Iran's envoy Hassan Kazerni Qomi in Baghdad to discuss Iraqi security. Hiro also pointed out obvious inconsistencies in the story: the claim of a link-up between the virulently anti-Shia Al Qaeda in Mesopotamia and the largely Shia Iranians was 'beyond belief'.[32] Why, then, would such an implausible claim be made? Hiro explained: '[T]here is no more potent phrase than "al-Qaida" to draw the attention, even alarm, of Americans and other westerners. And when it is bracketed with Iran, the combination can set alarm bells ringing in most western capitals.'

Noam Chomsky described the *Guardian* cover story as: 'Disgusting, but not far from the norm', adding that, in any case, 'the whole debate is utterly mad'. He expanded:

> Would we have had a debate in 1943 about whether the Allies were really guilty of aiding terrorist partisans in occupied Europe? The absurdity of the whole discussion was highlighted by a marvellous statement by Condi Rice a few days ago. She was asked what the solution is in Iraq, and said something like this: 'It's obvious. Withdraw all foreign forces and foreign weapons.' I was waiting to see if one commentator would notice that there happen to be some foreign troops and weapons in Iraq apart from the Iranian ones she was of course referring to. Couldn't find a hint.
>
> The basic assumption, so deeply rooted as to be invisible, is that the US owns the world (and Britain must toddle obediently behind), so US forces and weapons cannot be foreign anywhere, by definition. If they were to 'liberate' England, they'd be indigenous. I doubt if any religion or totalitarian state could command such fanatic obedience. Maybe North Korea, or some crazed religious cult.[33]

The internet-based response to Tisdall's piece was fierce and widespread. It suggested that the long years when the elite media could boost official propaganda without challenge, and without cost, are at last coming to an end. Comments left on the *Guardian* website, for example, were overwhelmingly sceptical. One reader posed two questions:

> 1 – How did a White House press release find its way on to the *Guardian* front page?
> 2 – Why hasn't it been replaced with an apology and the article that should have been there? You know, the one written by a journalist with some functioning brain cells and at least a vestige of a critical faculty.[34]

Another reader asked:

> why are the US/UK/western strategies never reported by 'journalists' like Tisdall? Perhaps we could even have similar reports about US strategy based on unnamed Iranian sources, spinning and confabulating in order to further their own hidden plans, on the front page of the *Guardian*. I simply can't remember ever reading a print article that discussed the USA's long-term geo-

political strategies (except from people it is easy to dismiss as 'extremists'), or come to that, any serious examination of Iranian strategies that aren't framed by the US's view of the matter.[35]

Many readers felt the *Guardian* had simply been used as a booster for crude US propaganda. The reputation of the paper surely paid the price.

11
Iran in Iraq

TONY BLAIR TAKES REFUGE

The Roman historian Tacitus observed: 'Crime once exposed has no refuge but in audacity.' What better example than Tony Blair's declaration at an October 7, 2005 press conference: 'There is no justification for Iran or any other country interfering in Iraq'?[1] In a sane society, Blair's audacity would have been denounced far and wide. But out of more than 70 mentions we saw in the British press, there were just two published letters and one editorial, in the *Daily Mirror*, indicating the obvious. And this was all the *Mirror* had to say: 'Tony Blair says he doesn't want other nations interfering in Iraq. That sounds familiar. It is exactly what America and the UK were accused of after invading that country.'[2]

America and the UK had been, were, and are, accused of rather more than 'interfering in Iraq', as Noam Chomsky pointed out in his book *Imperial Ambitions*: 'It's as open an act of aggression as there has been in modern history, a major war crime. This is the crime for which the Nazis were hanged at Nuremberg, the act of aggression. Everything else was secondary. And here's a clear and open example.'[3] As so often, we had to turn to the internet to find honest analysis of Blair's comments. Craig Murray, former British ambassador to the central Asian republic of Uzbekistan, wrote on his blog:

Last week Tony Blair finally shifted to displaying the kind of lack of self-knowledge that marks the truly delusional leader. He warned that Iran had 'No right' to interfere in the internal affairs of Iraq.

Apparently his mind was undisturbed by any visions of pots and kettles. The risible, monstrous hypocrisy of his statement had no effect on the studied earnest look he has adopted.[4]

The *Mirror* noted that Blair insisted five times in his press conference that he was just telling journalists 'exactly what I know'. This should have resurrected painful memories of the claims he made about Iraqi WMD. In a February 2003 interview with the BBC, Blair had said: 'I mean this is what our intelligence services are telling us and it's difficult because, you know, either they're simply making the whole thing up or this is what they are telling me, as the prime minister.'[5] When Blair described Iraq as 'a current and serious threat to the UK national interest', John Morrison, an adviser to the parliamentary intelligence and security committee, recalled: 'I could almost hear the collective raspberry going up around Whitehall.'[6]

Blair's reference to Iran at the October 7 press conference was made the day after an anonymous British official had accused Tehran of supplying Iraqi insurgents with sophisticated roadside bombs that had allegedly killed eight British soldiers and two security guards since May 2005. The official claimed the bombs were designed and manufactured by the Tehran-backed guerrilla group Hezbollah, based in Lebanon, and smuggled to Iraq via Iran. He blamed the smuggling of the bombs on the Iranian Revolutionary Guard Corps, answerable to Iran's highest executive body, the national security council. He also suggested that the Iranian government's motives were 'to tie down the "coalition" in Iraq'.[7]

Despite the obvious grounds for scepticism, much of the media was happy to take Blair at his word in the usual manner. Anton La Guardia commented in the *Daily Telegraph*: 'The best guess is that Iran has adopted a "ballots and bullets" policy: helping the insurgency to sap America's strength while supporting political allies to take power in Baghdad. So far, the policy has been highly successful.'[8] Channel 4 News observed: 'It's clear the government doesn't want to talk openly about it and so make it into a full-blooded diplomatic incident, yet at the same time they want Iran to know that they know.'[9] After everything that had happened in Iraq, that simply had to read: 'they want Iran to know what they *claim* they know'.

On the BBC News website, Paul Reynolds noted that the British accusation had come 'after months of frustration' for diplomats. Reynolds explained that William Patey, the British ambassador to Baghdad, 'has time and again complained to his Iranian counterpart that there is a traceable link' between the bombs that have killed British soldiers 'and devices used by Hezbollah in southern Lebanon, which is backed by Iran'.[10]

Again, we were to believe the frustration was real, not another propaganda concoction.

Britain's most popular tabloid, the *Sun*, fed its readers the usual dose of poison. Political editor Trevor Kavanagh commented: 'We are now to all intents and purposes at war with Iran. It may still be a war of words – and worried Western leaders will do their best to keep it like that. But if oil-hungry Teheran has its way, this is doomed to turn to bloody conflict.' As for Tony Blair: 'If he has sleepless nights, it is the prospect of an expansionary and merciless Iran that keeps him awake. His nightmare is fuelled by certain knowledge that nothing – apart from unimaginable military action – can stop the mullahs acquiring nuclear power and then nuclear weapons.'[11] Kavanagh thereby, in effect, did a cut and paste of his own commentary from 2002–03, replacing 'Iraq' with 'Iran' and 'Saddam Hussein' with 'the mullahs'. In a piece entitled 'He's bang to rights – Saddam's lies exposed', Kavanagh wrote in February 2003:

> Saddam Hussein was finally nailed as a massive threat to mankind yesterday. US Secretary of State Colin Powell unveiled PROOF the Iraqi tyrant has weapons of mass destruction – and PROOF he has links with al-Qa'ida terrorists.
>
> In a powerful speech to the UN Security Council, General Powell used evidence from satellite photos and tapped phone calls to make the case for war against Saddam. He told how an Osama Bin Laden lieutenant sheltered by Iraq was linked to the ricin poison factory found in North London and the murder of DC Stephen Oake in Manchester.[12]

The prevailing myth would have us believe that journalists are hard-headed, seen-it-all cynics. But in fact it is Kavanagh's job to affect child-like innocence; to pretend to fail to learn even the most obvious lessons from even the immediate past as he pushes a merciless, realpolitik version of the world at his readers.

The 'coalition' is, of course, only too keen to paint the insurgency in Iraq as an illegitimate campaign instigated by foreign fanatics against the wishes of ordinary Iraqis. But in September 2005 the Center for Strategic and International Studies reported that foreign elements made up some 4 to 10 per cent of the total Iraqi insurgence, which was estimated to be around 30,000. The study concluded: 'There are strong indications that the largest component of the insurgency is composed of Iraqis.'[13] Two years later, the Iraq Study Group Report observed:

> Most attacks on Americans still come from the Sunni Arab insurgency. The insurgency comprises former elements of the Saddam Hussein regime, disaffected Sunni Arab Iraqis, and common criminals. It has significant support within the Sunni Arab community ... Al Qaeda is responsible for a small portion of the violence in Iraq, but that includes some of the more

spectacular acts: suicide attacks, large truck bombs, and attacks on significant religious or political targets.[14]

A poll in September 2007 conducted by the BBC found that seven out of ten Iraqis believed the US troop 'surge' in Baghdad and Anbar province had made security worse in those areas – nearly half wanted coalition forces to leave immediately. Nearly 60 per cent saw attacks on US-led forces as justified.[15] In their book, *Winter Soldier*, Iraq Veterans Against the War wrote: 'Tailors, barbers, and car mechanics joined militias that attacked US forces. Every Iraqi was a potential insurgent.'[16] This cannot be accepted by our press because it suggests that the insurgency is a war of national resistance against an occupation as illegal as any in imperial history. Iraq veteran Jason Hurd commented: 'If a foreign occupying force came here to the United States, whether they told us they were here to liberate us or to give us democracy, do you not think that every person who owns a shotgun would not come out of the hills and fight for their right to self-determination?'[17]

DEMONISING FOR VICTORY

Despite the media view, according to military experts it was not at all clear who made or supplied the Basra bombs in 2005. 'We can't be definite about this one', a senior officer told the *Sunday Herald*. 'The force of the explosions is so great that there's very little left in the way of clues to let us know the weapons' provenance. In any case, you can find all you want to know about how to build them on the internet.'[18]

This indeed is a constant theme of expert commentary – the technology is 'out there'; Iraqis do not need Iranian help to build even the most powerful roadside bombs. According to defence sources, basic armour-piercing weapons are easy to manufacture, relying on principles discovered more than a century ago and in use since the Second World War. Military officials said there was 'so much expertise in Iraq the bombs could have been made by former members of Saddam Hussein's security forces'.[19] The *Guardian* reported the same sources as suggesting that blaming the Iranian Revolutionary Guard for supplying the bombs was 'going too far'.[20] Even if the technology had originated in Iran there was no certainty that this was the result of deliberate Iranian government policy. The long and porous border between Iran and Iraq made policing extremely difficult.

Asked if there was any official Iranian involvement in arms supplies to Iraq, Pentagon spokesman Lawrence DiRita replied: 'That I am not aware of.'[21] When asked the same question, Brigadier General Carter Ham, US deputy director for regional operations, replied that bomb-making equipment was probably being smuggled into Iraq, but denied knowledge of any Iranian complicity in the operations: 'It's not known to the best of my understanding.'[22] Trevor Royle commented in the *Sunday Herald*:

> It is difficult to find any reason why Iran would want to foster violence ahead of this week's constitutional referendum in Iraq and there is no evidence to suggest that Iran is intent on destabilising the present interim administration. A victory for the Shia factions would be likely to lead to the new government building friendly links with its near neighbour and there would be nothing to gain by souring that relationship.
>
> It is possible that Iran might want to draw attention away from its nuclear weapons programme by causing trouble in Iraq but, again, it is not easy to see what might be gained by following that course of action at a time when they are under such intense international scrutiny.[23]

THE ART OF INSTANT FORGETTING

On February 16, 2007, the US media watchdog, FAIR, recalled how, as discussed in the previous chapter, the *New York Times* had implemented new rules governing its use of unnamed sources in the wake of its disastrous pre-war reporting on Iraq. And yet, the *Times'* lead story on February 10, promoting US government charges against Iran, trashed these rules completely. FAIR commented:

> Repeatedly citing the likes of 'administration officials', 'American intelligence' and 'Western officials', the article used unnamed sources four times as often as named ones. Only one source in ... [the] report challenged the official claims: Iranian United Nations ambassador Javad Zarif, who was allowed a one-sentence denial of Iranian government involvement.[24]

A January 16, 2007 leader in the *Telegraph* – which did not apologise for its own catastrophic pre-war reporting or implement new rules – was bolder still:

> It has been clear for many months that Iran has been actively involved in the Iraqi insurgency: by supplying arms and manpower to the militias who target

American and British forces, and inciting sectarian violence, it has helped to maintain the state of chaotic instability which has persisted in spite of all attempts to bring order to the country...[25]

The direct involvement of Iran's leadership was also not in doubt:

as those in charge of our forces on the ground in Basra are clearly aware, Iran is not simply a delinquent state indulging in gratuitously destructive terrorism. However absurd and nihilistic the posturing of its president may seem, his country is committed to an orchestrated political plan [in Iraq] which will require systematic opposition.[26]

On BBC's *Newsnight* (February 12, 2007), the *Telegraph's* Con Coughlin declared that military action was looming now that 'diplomacy is almost at an end'. By contrast, a week earlier, the *Los Angeles Times* had cited an ironic comment from a British officer stationed in Iraq:

'We do have intelligence which suggests that weapons and ammunition are being smuggled in from Iran', Maj. David Gell, a spokesman for British forces in Basra, said last week. 'We don't always manage to find any.'

US military officials in Diyala have had the same experience. No munitions or personnel have been seized at the border, officers said.[27]

An analysis for the Inter Press News Agency by investigative journalist Gareth Porter, an expert in US national security policy, noted that:

The [US] administration suggested that there could be no other explanation for the presence of Iranian-made weapons than official government sponsorship of smuggling them into Iraq. But in doing so, they had to ignore a well-known reality: most weapons, including armor-piercing projectiles, can be purchased by anyone through intermediaries in the Middle East.[28]

Porter cited Michael Knights, chief of analysis for the Olive Group, a private security consulting firm, who presented evidence in *Jane's Intelligence Review* that Iraqi Shiites have manufactured both the components for 'explosively formed penetrators' (EFPs) and the complete EFPs. Knights claimed that the equipment required to make EFPs 'can easily be found in Iraqi metalworking shops and garages', and that all EFPs exploded thus far could have been manufactured in one or at most two simple workshops with one or two specialists in each – one in the Baghdad area and one in southern Iraq. Knights commented of US–UK forces: 'I'm surprised that they haven't found evidence of making EFPs in Iraq. That doesn't ring true for me.' Indeed, after Porter's article appeared, the *New York Times* included this comment at the end of one news report: 'An Iraqi unit, aided by American advisers, caught militants in the act of constructing devices known as explosively formed projectiles in a house in Hilla, south of Baghdad, on Saturday, according to the American military.'[29]

Knights said he believed there was a time when whole EFPs were imported from outside, but that by February 2007 most, if not all, were manufactured by Iraqis. Certainly the idea that only Iran possesses the necessary lathes and operators trained in the manufacture of EFPs is outlandish. Writer Milan Rai observed that no evidence had been produced that Iraq lacked the means to produce EFPs – there was no shortage of metal tubes or explosives. Indeed, an independent assessment of Improvised Explosive Devices (IEDs) in Iraq, obtained by *Defense News* in 2006 and based on British military intelligence, said: 'Based on current usage, there are enough stocks of illegal explosives to continue the same level of attack for 274 years without re-supply.'[30]

Writing in the *Independent*, Patrick Cockburn noted the wretched irony of US–UK government claims:

> The US stance on the military capabilities of Iraqis today is the exact opposite of its position four years ago. Then, President Bush and Tony Blair claimed that Iraqis were technically advanced enough to produce long-range missiles and to be close to producing a nuclear device. Washington is now saying that Iraqis are too backward to produce an effective roadside bomb and must seek Iranian help.[31]

Anthony Cordesman, a US military analyst at the Center for Strategic and International Studies in Washington DC, observed that Iraq's insurgents were probably just tapping a pool of common bomb-making technology, none of which required special expertise: 'There's no evidence that these are supplied by Iran. A lot of this is just technology that is leaked into an informal network. What works in one country gets known elsewhere.'[32] Even US Marine General Peter Pace, Chairman of the Joint Chiefs of Staff, noted that while some of the material used in explosive devices had been made in Iran that 'does not translate that the Iranian government per se, for sure, is directly involved in doing this'.[33]

To their credit, some journalists failed to toe the propaganda line. On January 23, 2007, the *Los Angeles Times* reported that, despite the aggressive rhetoric, the Bush administration had 'provided scant evidence to support these claims. Nor have reporters traveling with US troops seen extensive signs of Iranian involvement.'[34] The *Times* report cited senator John Rockefeller, head of the US Senate Intelligence Committee, who said: 'To be quite honest, I'm a little concerned that it's Iraq again', referring to the false claims made ahead of the March 2003 invasion.[35] The *Independent's* Patrick Cockburn also voiced his scepticism: 'The allegations against Iran are similar in tone and credibility to those made four years ago by the US government about Iraq possessing weapons of mass destruction in order to justify the invasion of 2003.'[36]

In October 2007, Gareth Porter described on Inter Press Service how the US military command had accused Iran in January of that year of providing EFPs despite knowing that Iraqi machine shops had been producing their own EFPs for years. By late 2005, the British military had found clear evidence that Iraqi Shiites were manufacturing their own EFPs. The US command also had substantial evidence that the Iraqi Mahdi army had received EFP technology and training on how to use it from Hezbollah rather than Iran. In November 2006, a senior intelligence official told the *New York Times* and CNN that Hezbollah had trained as many as 2,000 Mahdi army fighters in Lebanon. According to Michael Knights, writing in *Jane's Intelligence Review* in 2007, the earliest EFPs appearing in Iraq in 2004 were probably constructed by Hezbollah specialists. Porter noted that British and US officials have long known that the EFPs being used in Iraq closely resemble weapons used by Hezbollah against Israeli forces in Southern Lebanon.

Despite all of this, Porter observed, the US command, operating under close White House supervision, 'chose to deny these facts in making the dramatic accusation that became the main rationale for the present aggressive US stance toward Iran'.[37]

HARD EVIDENCE = RESPONSIBLE JOURNALISM

Falling in line with the official propaganda described above, on February 11, 2007, the BBC's flagship News at Ten led with claims made by anonymous US officials in Baghdad that the Iranian government had supplied advanced roadside bombs in Iraq, killing more than 170 US troops since June 2004.

BBC correspondent Andrew North's headlining boost for these unsubstantiated claims concluded with the briefest of disclaimers: 'But given the past history of intelligence dossiers on Iraq, it may take an uphill struggle convincing people that tougher action should follow this one.' That constituted nine seconds out of a report lasting nearly three minutes. On February 12, we emailed Helen Boaden, director of BBC news, asking what had become of her earlier firm insistence that the BBC would report controversial claims as news only on the basis of 'hard evidence'. We asked: 'Why does your approach now differ so markedly from that adopted previously [in 2005] when the BBC failed to report the mounting evidence of white phosphorus weapons, cluster bombs, modified napalm and depleted uranium munitions in Fallujah and elsewhere in Iraq?' Two years earlier, the BBC had repeatedly rejected numerous credible reports from Iraqi doctors, refugees, humanitarian NGOs and other sources. Boaden wrote at the time: 'BBC News will continue to do what we can to find independent verification of these claims. However, it would not be responsible journalism for the BBC to report such claims without having found hard evidence that they are correct.'[38]

And yet 'hard evidence' was apparently not required when the BBC reported claims made by shadowy US officials, 'speaking off camera on condition of anonymity'. It was enough that they were official spokespeople. We asked Boaden:

> What documented, publicly available editorial BBC guidelines exist for deciding whether to repeat controversial claims; and, just as significant, how to report them in a balanced, fair and responsible manner?
>
> Why have your reports been so credulous and unbalanced? Why did you only show the briefest of interviews with the Iranian ambassador in Baghdad, rejecting the US claims? Where are the sceptical commentators, such as western intelligence and military experts, who have also previously rejected such claims?

We concluded our email to Boaden: 'What lessons has the BBC learned from its reporting on Iraq back then? On the evidence of recent BBC reports on these anonymous, warmongering US claims about Iran, véry few indeed.'[39] We received no reply.

Meanwhile that same month, Iran presented evidence of US involvement in a February 14 bomb blast against Iran's Islamic Revolutionary Guard Corps (IRGC) in Zahedan, southeastern

Iran, which claimed 13 lives. Agence France-Press reported on February 17:

Local officials said the unrest bore suspicious hallmarks of involvement by the United States and Britain, reiterating previous allegations of Western trouble-making in the southeastern Sistuan-Baluchestan province ... State television showed footage of a substantial arms cache of bullets, explosives and machine guns seized at a militant hideout. One image showed a packet of 20 bullets with the inscription 'Made in the USA'.

'It is interesting that the weapons are made by the United States and the United Kingdom', said the director of the province's political affairs office Soltan Ali Mir, according to the Mehr agency.

'The terrorists (detained) revealed some meetings in some neighbouring countries for their financial support. They indicate that the United States and the United Kingdom were involved in the recent incidents.'[40]

Stratfor, a research institute made up of former US security officials, claimed that 'this latest attack against IRGC guards was likely carried out by armed Baloch nationalists who have received a boost in support from Western intelligence agencies'.[41] Stratfor added: 'the United States has likely ramped up support for Iran's variety of oppressed minorities in an attempt to push the Iranian regime toward a negotiated settlement over Iraq'.[42] And yet when we checked that month (February 21, 2007), claims of US involvement in the Zahedan attack had been mentioned in a single sentence in a single article in one national UK newspaper.[43] Presumably it would not have been 'responsible journalism' for the media to report such claims 'without having found hard evidence that they are correct'.

THE BRITISH SAILORS: CASE STUDY IN BIAS

News that British schoolteacher Gillian Gibbons had been jailed in Sudan after allowing her pupils to call a teddy bear 'Mohammed' fed straight into the UK media's hate factory and its 'war for civilisation'. *Daily Mail* columnist Melanie Phillips wrote of how the teddy bear incident was 'yet another symptom of the great onslaught being mounted against our civilisation and towards which not one inch of ground must be given if that civilisation is to survive'.[44] Such preposterous hype belongs in the same category as Hitler's description of Czechoslovakia as 'a dagger pointed at the heart of Germany'.[45]

Phillips was similarly outraged when 15 British sailors were 'kidnapped' by an Iranian warship on March 23, 2007 while on patrol in the Shatt al-Arab waterway between Iran and Iraq. She raged at 'a military debacle for Britain – a self-inflicted humiliation at the hands of Iran, at a time when the mortal danger posed to the free world by this rogue state is increasing by the day'.[46]

Iran was, of course, 'steadily advancing towards its goal of obtaining nuclear weapons with which it is threatening to bring about the apocalypse it has been working towards for the past three decades'. Like the rest of the media, Phillips later fell silent when evidence emerged suggesting that the British sailors had in fact strayed into Iranian waters, and had therefore not been 'kidnapped' at all. On July 22, 2007, the UK Foreign Affairs Committee reported: 'We conclude that there is evidence to suggest that the map of the Shatt al-Arab waterway provided by the Government was less clear than it ought to have been. The Government was fortunate that it was not in Iran's interests to contest the accuracy of the map.'[47]

Martin Pratt, Director of Research at the International Boundaries Research Unit at Durham University, pointed out that the British government's map was 'certainly an oversimplification ... it could reasonably be argued that it was deliberately misleading'.[48] In April 2008, *The Times* reported:

Fifteen British sailors and Marines were seized by Iran in internationally disputed waters and not in Iraq's maritime territory as Parliament was told, according to new official documents released to *The Times*.

The Britons were seized because the US-led coalition designated a sea boundary for Iran's territorial waters without telling the Iranians where it was, internal Ministry of Defence briefing papers reveal.[49]

And yet, Des Browne, the Defence Secretary, told the House of Commons on June 16, 2007 that the personnel were seized in Iraqi waters:

There is no doubt that HMS Cornwall was operating in Iraqi waters and that the incident itself took place in Iraqi waters ... In the early days the Iranians provided us with a set of co-ordinates, and asserted that was where the event took place, but when we told them the co-ordinates were in Iraqi waters they changed that set and found one in their own waters. I do not think that even they sustain the position that the incident took place anywhere other than in Iraqi waters.[50]

The Ministry of Defence, in a televised briefing by Vice-Admiral Charles Style, the Deputy Chief of the Defence Staff, produced a map showing a line in the sea called 'Iraq/Iran Territorial Water Boundary'. A location was given for the capture of the Britons inside what the chart said were 'Iraq territorial waters'. But a subsequently released top-level internal briefing accepted that no such border exists:

> Since the outset of the Iraq–Iran War there has been no formal ratified TTW [territorial waters] agreement in force between Iraq and Iran ... In the absence of any formal agreement, the coalition tactical demarcation [the Op Line] is used as a notional TTW boundary. It is a US NAVCENT [US Naval Forces Central Command] construct based on an extension of the Algiers accord demarcation line beyond the mouth of the Shatt al-Arab [waterway] into the NAG [northern Arabian Gulf]. While it may be assumed that the Iranians must be aware of some form of operational boundary, the exact co-ordinates to the Op Line have not been published to Iran.[51]

Professor Robert Springborg, of the School of Oriental and African Studies, said that it was negligent to fail to clarify with the Iranians where the notional boundary was. Two articles covering this exposé appeared in *The Times* – no other newspaper covered the story.

12
Venezuela:
Dousing the 'Firebrand'

RISE OF THE ECONOMIC HIT MEN

In his book, *Confessions Of An Economic Hit Man*, John Perkins described the role he played in the West's devastation of the Third World for profit. Perkins compared himself to the slave traders of colonial times: 'I had been the heir of those slavers who had marched into African jungles and hauled men and women off to waiting ships. Mine had been a more modern approach, subtler – I never had to see the dying bodies, smell the rotting flesh, or hear the screams of agony.'[1]

In January 1971, Perkins was hired by American big business to forecast economic growth in developing countries. These forecasts were used to justify massive international loans which funded engineering and construction projects, so funnelling money back to US corporations while enriching a small Third World elite. Perkins explained that his real task, rarely discussed but always understood in high government and business circles, had been to deliberately exaggerate growth forecasts in countries like Peru, Ecuador, Indonesia and Saudi Arabia. The goal was for these countries to *fail* to achieve their inflated targets and so be unable to repay their loans. The intention was that leaders in those nations would then 'become ensnared in a web of debt that ensures their loyalty [to the United States]'. As a result, American interests 'can draw on them whenever we desire – to satisfy our political, economic, or military needs. In turn, they bolster their political positions by bringing industrial parks, power plants, and airports to their people. The owners of US engineering and construction companies become fabulously wealthy.'[2]

The 'needs' include military bases, votes at the United Nations, cheap access to oil and other human and natural resources. Perkins describes this as a non-military means for achieving 'the most subtle and effective form of imperialism the world has ever known'.[3] Bankrupt debtor countries have thus been forced to spend much of their national wealth simply repaying huge debts, even as their people sicken and die from malnutrition and poverty. For example, international banks dominated by Washington loaned Ecuador billions of dollars from the 1970s onwards so that the country could hire engineering and construction firms to improve life for the rich. In the space of 30 years, poverty grew from 50 to 60 per cent, under-employment or unemployment increased from 15 to 70 per cent, public debt increased from $240 million to $16 billion, and the share of national resources allocated to the poor fell from 20 per cent to 6 per cent. Today, Ecuador is required to devote nearly 50 per cent of its national budget to debt repayment, leaving almost no resources for millions of citizens classified as 'dangerously impoverished'. Out of every $100 worth of oil pumped from the Amazon, less than $3 goes to Ecuadorian people, dying from lack of food and potable water.

Perkins made it clear that waiting in the wings should the economic hit men (EHMs) fail, were the real hit men – 'the jackals'. He wrote of Jaime Roldós, president of Ecuador, and Omar Torrijos, president of Panama, who both died in plane crashes: 'Their deaths were not accidental. They were assassinated because they opposed that fraternity of corporate, government, and banking heads whose goal is global empire. We EHMs failed to bring Roldós and Torrijos around, and the other type of hit men, the CIA-sanctioned jackals who were always right behind us, stepped in.'[4] Perkins wrote of Roldós' death in May 1981:

> It had all the markings of a CIA-orchestrated assassination. I understood that it had been executed so blatantly in order to send a message. The new Reagan administration, complete with its fast-draw Hollywood cowboy image, was the ideal vehicle for delivering such a message. The jackals were back, and they wanted Omar Torrijos and everyone else who might consider joining an anti-corporate crusade to know it.[5]

Torrijos was killed just two months later.

Despite his book achieving bestseller status by word of mouth, Perkins' account of corporate imperialism has been all but ignored by the mainstream British press since its publication in 2005, receiving mentions in just four articles. In one of these, a *Sunday Times* reviewer wrote: 'One measure of the success of an author is whether his book passes the "laugh out loud" test. John Perkins's had me in stitches. The problem is, it is not meant to.'[6] Cynically ignoring the issues and evidence, David Charters dismissed the book as 'ridiculous': 'If it was not so laughable, it could be depressing.' The book has received similar treatment in the US press.

The last 50 years have seen a vast bloodbath in Latin America as Washington has funnelled money, weapons and supplies to client dictators and right-wing death squads battling independent nationalism across the region. Britain's only left-wing daily newspaper, the *Morning Star*, with a small circulation of around 14,000, is virtually a lone voice describing these horrors. In the November 22, 2005 edition, Dr Francisco Dominguez, head of the Centre for Brazilian and Latin American Studies at Middlesex University, observed:

> Military dictatorship, death squads, torture, assassination, economic blockade, economic genocide, military intervention, wanton repression, corruption and every other means intrinsic to capitalist and imperialist 'management techniques' have been utilised to secure the profits of primarily US multinationals and the wealth of the privileged few. Mass unemployment and mass poverty are just two extra means with which to obtain compliance with the economic and political pillage of the continent.[7]

With Venezuela increasingly in the crosshairs of US power, John Pilger added:

> In the US media in the 1980s, the 'threat' of tiny Nicaragua was seriously debated until it was crushed. Venezuela is clearly being 'softened up' for something similar. A US army publication, Doctrine for Asymmetric War against Venezuela, describes Chávez and the Bolivarian revolution as the 'largest threat since the Soviet Union and Communism'.[8]

We should be under no illusions. The corporate media oppose leftist leaders in Latin America, notably Venezuela's Hugo Chávez, because the corporate system is viscerally opposed to policies that are unleashing democratic hopes in that part of the globe. It takes a moment's thought to understand that greater democracy, equality, justice and popular empowerment are *not* in the interests of a system built on exploitation. As John Perkins commented of the media:

> Things are not as they appear ... Our media is part of the corporatocracy. The officers and directors who control nearly all our communications outlets know their places; they are taught throughout life that one of their most important jobs is to perpetuate, strengthen, and expand the system they have inherited. They are very efficient at doing so, and when opposed, they can be ruthless.[9]

CONTROVERSIAL AMERICAN PRESIDENT?

For the *Independent on Sunday*, Chávez is 'Venezuela's outspoken President'.[10] For the *Independent*'s Washington editor, Rupert Cornwell, he is 'the Venezuelan strongman, Hugo Chávez'.[11] He is a 'firebrand leader' who is 'virulently anti-American' and whose 'attachment to democracy [has] a temporary and improvised feel'.[12] He is a 'demagogue' who wields a 'brand of aggressive socialism'; a 'high priest of political theatre'; 'the new mouthpiece of the anti-American fervour' and a 'divisive force in Latin America'.[13] The *Independent* even resorted to quoting Chávez's psychiatrist: 'Chávez's character is unpredictable and disconcerting – He is a dreamer of impossible dreams.'[14]

To the *Daily Mirror*, Chávez is a 'controversial leader' known as '"the Crackers from Caracas" by his own supporters'.[15] He is an 'aggressively populist left-wing leader', *The Times* writes.[16] He is a 'Left wing firebrand' according to the *Evening Standard*,[17] and according to the *Observer*, an 'international revolutionary firebrand'.[18] The *Guardian*, the UK's proud vanguard of liberal journalism, described Chávez as 'the scourge of the United States'.[19] Although this was a news report, not a comment piece, the title adopted the required tone of mockery during Chávez's visit to London: 'Revolution in the Camden air as Chávez – with amigo Ken – gets a hero's welcome'. A *Daily Telegraph* comment piece continued the pan-media smearing: 'Now the anticipation is over, and today, flush with six trillion dollars worth of oil reserves, Hugo Chávez, president of Venezuela, flies in to fill the despot-of-the-month slot at London mayor Ken Livingstone's lunch table.'[20] The *Financial Times* wrote of how 'the populist militaristic strongman has irked Washington with his anti-US rhetoric'.[21] The *Independent on Sunday* wrote: 'Mr Chávez's brand of aggressive socialism is taken seriously because of his country's vast oil resources.'[22]

We wait in vain for an *Independent on Sunday* news report referring to Bush, Obama, Blair and Brown's 'brand' of 'aggressive', indeed 'militant', capitalism: that would be biased news reporting, after all. And imagine the suggestion that Bush and Blair's aggressive support for 'democracy' in the Middle East was taken seriously only because of their economic and military power.

The *Observer* noted that Chávez has a 'growing regional profile' which is 'built on a mix of populist rhetoric and his country's oil wealth'. The report added that Chávez 'has been publicly feuding with Bush, whom he has likened to Adolf Hitler – with Tony Blair dismissed as "the main ally of Hitler"'.[23] In responding to similarly disparaging comments in *The Times*, Julia Buxton of the University of Bradford was all but alone in providing some relevant background: 'To place this statement in context, Chávez was compared to Adolf Hitler by the US Secretary of State for Defence, Donald Rumsfeld, during a visit to Paraguay. President Chávez rejected the comparison and countered that if any individual were comparable to Hitler, it would be President Bush.'[24]

Channel 4 News asked of Chávez: 'Is he a hero of the left or a villain in disguise?' For the media, of course, a 'hero of the left' *is* a 'villain in disguise' – so viewers were actually being asked if Chávez was a villain or a villain. Like many other media, Channel 4 News patronised the Venezuelan president as 'a global poster boy for the left'. The same programme later asked if he was 'a hero of the left or a scoundrel of all democrats?' (We consider a case study from Channel 4 News in more detail below.) In similar vein, Daniel Howden, deputy foreign editor of the *Independent*, observed:

> Not surprisingly for a man who divides the world, Hugo Chávez is greeted as a saviour or a saboteur wherever he goes. The Venezuelan President seems immune to nuance and perfectly able to reduce the world to Chavistas or to Descualdos, the 'squalid ones' as his supporters dismiss those who try to depose him.[25]

Immunity to 'nuance' is a perennial problem on the left. Steve Crawshaw, then of the *Independent* and now with Human Rights Watch, once reviewed a book by Noam Chomsky under the title: 'Furious ideas with no room for nuance.' 'Chomsky knows so much,' Crawshaw wrote, 'but seems impervious to any idea of nuance.'[26] A BBC manager, then Acting Europe Region Editor of the BBC's World Service, once wrote to us: 'If your language was more nuanced it would get a better reception.'[27]

The American media watchdog, Fairness and Accuracy In Reporting (FAIR), reported that 95 per cent of the nearly 100 US press commentaries covering Venezuelan politics during the first six months of 2005 expressed clear hostility to Chávez. The *Wall Street Journal* labelled Chávez a 'tyrant' and 'strongman', claiming he had presided over 'the collapse of democracy'. Three *Journal* editorials also referred to Chávez as a 'strongman', while the editorial board suggested that Chávez should be placed on a list of the world's worst dictators. The *Los Angeles Times* called Chávez a 'would-be dictator' who engaged in 'undemocratic tactics'.[28]

It might be argued that media reporting simply reflects a dismal reality; perhaps Chávez *is* irresponsible. But such media smears reveal more about power relations in Britain and the United States than they do about politics in Venezuela. In 1992, FAIR's Jeff Cohen described media coverage afforded to one important Western ally:

> During that whole period when the United States was helping build up the military and economic might of Saddam Hussein in Iraq, the issue of his human rights abuses was off the media agenda. There was this classic in the *New York Post*, a tabloid in New York. After the [1990] crisis began, they had a picture of Saddam Hussein patting the British kid on the head and their banner headline was 'Child Abuser'. That was very important to us and very ironic, because Amnesty International and other human rights groups had released studies in 1984 and 1985 which showed that Saddam Hussein's regime regularly tortured children to get information about their parents' views. That just didn't get the coverage.
>
> It shows one of the points FAIR has made constantly: that when a foreign government is in favour with the United States, with the White House, its human rights record is basically off the mainstream media agenda, and when they do something that puts them out of favour with the US government, the foreign government's human rights abuses are, all of a sudden, major news.[29]

In a review of press reporting on Iran under the mass-murdering Shah, a Western ally installed and armed by Britain and America, William A. Dorman and Ehsan Omad noted: 'We have been unable to find a single example of a news and feature story in the American mainstream press that uses the label "dictator".'[30] British media performance is close to identical, as we have documented many times.

In fact, in all the voluminous coverage of the 'threat' of 'firebrand' socialism 'sweeping across' Latin America, there has been close to zero analysis of why so many Latin Americans living in resource-rich countries have been so poor for so long. The press has barely hinted at the unimaginable horror and desperate hopes buried beneath the mocking of Chávez; namely, the suffering of Latin American people under very real Western economic and military violence. The *Independent on Sunday* managed this vague mention: 'Mr Morales [the Bolivian president] was, the Venezuelan President said, a direct descendant of an indigenous Latin American people, adding: "These are oppressed people who are rising. They are rising with peace, not weapons. Europe should listen to that."'[31] The tragedy out of which these people are rising, and how their hopes of a better life have been systematically crushed by Western force in the past, was of course not explored by the *Independent on Sunday*.

The *Guardian* also managed a tiny reference to the reality: Chávez's 'unabashed opposition to US foreign policy, and the pressure it has produced from Washington, tap into the deep vein of suspicion and resentment that two centuries of US invasions, coups, and economic domination have aroused in Latin America and the Caribbean'.[32] But that was that. As the *Guardian* writers must know full well, these comments appear in a context of almost complete public ignorance of just what the United States has done to Latin America. Quite simply, the British and American press do not cover the West's mass killing of Latin Americans.

DOING SOMETHING FOR THE POOR

First elected in 1998, Chávez launched massive campaigns, described as Bolivarian Missions (named after the Venezuelan revolutionary, Simon Bolivar) to combat disease, illiteracy, malnutrition, poverty and other social ills. Eighteen months after taking office, in a country of 25 million people, 1.4 million had been taught to read and write, while three million previously excluded from education due to poverty had enrolled in the education system. Seventy per cent of the population now enjoy access to free health care while 45 per cent receive subsidised food. Julia Buxton argued that the Chávez government 'has brought marginalised and excluded people into the political process and democratised power'.[33] Chomsky commented on Chávez: 'The wealthy and the privileged hate him. On the other hand, the great majority of the population is very impoverished and has always been kept out of the country's enormous wealth. This Bolivarian Revolution, whatever you and I may think about it, is actually doing something for the poor and apparently they are reacting.'[34]

Radical attempts to raise the living standards of the poor are not welcomed by US elites. Such reforms risk creating 'the threat of a good example', unleashing demands for greater equality and justice among impoverished people across the region. The potential cost to Western corporations exploiting this poverty is incalculable. Thomas

Carothers, a former Reagan State Department official, has described US policy in Latin America as being driven by the need to maintain 'the basic order of ... quite undemocratic societies' and to avoid 'populist-based change' that might upset 'established economic and political orders' and open 'a leftist direction'.[35]

The Venezuelan government and its programme of change have been repeatedly ratified by the Venezuelan electorate in eleven out of twelve elections and referenda during the period 1998 to 2008. In 2006, FAIR noted that, in spite of the fact that polls indicated that Chávez's domestic approval rating was above 70 per cent, 'almost all commentaries about Venezuela represent the views of a small minority of the country, led by a traditional economic elite that has repeatedly attempted to overthrow the government in clearly anti-democratic ways'.[36]

Many people in Venezuela, including Chávez himself, fear that America is planning to invade the country. Chomsky argues that this would probably already have happened, but for the disastrous turn of events in Iraq. Some kind of military action is certainly an option for US policy makers. In an April 2002 article titled, 'US "gave the nod" to Venezuelan coup', the *Guardian* reported US involvement in the coup that temporarily removed Chávez from office earlier that month. A few weeks before the coup attempt, US administration officials had met business leaders who took over the interim government after Chávez was arrested. The US Defense Department also confirmed that the Venezuelan army's chief of staff, General Rincon, visited the Pentagon the previous December and met senior officials.

Although the Organization of American States denounced the coup attempt, as did all Venezuela's neighbours, Washington was eager to acknowledge the new, short-lived government, declaring: 'A transitional civilian government has been installed. This government has promised early elections.'[37] In 2006, Tony Blair tried to preach ethics to Venezuela: 'It is rather important that the government of Venezuela realise that if they want to be respected members of the international community they should abide by the rules of the international community.' In his response, Chávez made the point that mattered: 'You, Mr Blair, do not have the morality to call on anyone to respect the rules of the international community. You are precisely the one who has flouted international law the most ... siding with Mr Danger [George Bush] to trample the people in Iraq.'[38]

CARTOON TIME: CHANNEL 4 NEWS SMEARS CHÁVEZ

Jonathan Rugman, Washington correspondent for Channel 4 News, has a particularly impressive track record as an apologist for Western power. Rugman's March 27, 2006 report relentlessly smeared Chávez.[39] The piece was described by John Pilger as 'one of the worst, most distorted pieces of journalism I have ever seen'.[40] Channel 4 News presenter Jon Snow introduced the film:

> Now, he's the president with his own television show and a stream of semi-humorous invective hurled at America and George Bush. Venezuela's president, Hugo Chávez, accuses the US of planning to invade his country to take control of its vast oil reserves. And last night he invoked the ultimate deterrent – the bow and arrow dipped in Indian poison. 'If we have to put a few arrows into the invading gringo, then you'll be done in thirty seconds.'

Snow is well-known for his humorous take on politics. But in the context of Rugman's report, and of wider political commentary, his introduction promoted the cartoonisation of Chávez. Cartoon 'bad guys' are, of course, traditionally depicted as absurd and wicked, and as absurdly delighted by their wickedness. Tapping into these stereotypes, journalists portray enemies of the West as both menacing and foolish. Western leaders, on the other hand, are presented as sober, dignified and rational – serious people who have ascended (with a little divine inspiration, and perhaps even intervention) to the summit of a meritocratic and benevolent social order. Thus, Snow followed his comical portrait of Chávez by noting the mature and rational concerns of sensible people in the West:

> Venezuela is the world's fifth largest oil exporter, and a major supplier to America itself – that causes jitters in Washington, where Chávez is seen as a demagogue who could spearhead a regional shift to the left. Chávez is undoubtedly popular at home, where he's spent billions on health and education programmes to improve the lives of the country's poor, although his critics point to an increasingly authoritarian streak.

The opening moments of Rugman's report recalled the *Guardian*'s infamous October 2005 smear of Noam Chomsky (see Chapter 14) in which Chomsky was pictured with various monsters: Fidel Castro, John Pilger, and 'en route to Hanoi to give a speech to the North Vietnamese'. Rugman's film similarly showed footage of Chávez with the likes of Fidel Castro, Saddam Hussein and Gaddafi. Rugman's voiceover, strident and dramatic, hammered the point home: 'He supplies 15 per cent of America's oil, yet America's enemies are his friends. Hugo Chávez, in danger of joining a rogue's gallery of dictators and despots – Washington's latest Latin nightmare.' The film repeatedly depicted Chávez as a dictatorial menace, referring to his 'personality cult' and to factories run as 'Soviet-style collectives'. Rugman asked: 'Is Chávez on the way to becoming a dictator?' If so, what species of monster might we be contemplating? Rugman told us:

He's no Saddam, but what's happening here does feel eerily familiar. A strongman buoyed up by oil defying the United States, using oil wealth to rearm and consolidate his own power. Setting off alarm bells in Washington where securing energy is a key foreign policy goal. A petro-state heading for a showdown with its northern neighbour.

'Rearm' is a media trigger word intended to suggest a resurgent menace: Hitler rearmed after the First World War; Saddam was said to be rearming prior to the West's 2003 invasion. So when exactly did mighty Venezuela *disarm*? Rugman did not explain. Instead, Washington's goal, he continued, is merely 'securing energy' – a reasonable enough priority, one might think, for any modern, high-tech state. But there was not a word in Rugman's report about the barbaric corporate greed that has led the United States to exploit, terrorise and devastate its southern neighbours for decades.

Rugman interviewed Maria Corina Machado, describing her as a 'civil rights activist'. In fact, she was a leader of Sumate, an extreme right-wing organisation that was deeply involved in the 2002 coup that temporarily ousted Chávez. Machado met Bush in the White House shortly before the coup. The *New York Times* reported:

Ms. Machado does not hide her close relations with Washington, which has provided financial aid to Sumate, the anti-Chávez, election-monitoring organization she helps run. In May, she infuriated the [Venezuelan] government when she met with President Bush at the White House, and she further antagonized officials in September by announcing that Sumate had received a fresh infusion of $107,000 from Washington.[41]

John Pilger sent a letter to Channel 4 News complaining of Rugman's report:

This was a piece seemingly written by the US State Department, although Channel 4's Washington correspondent, Jonathan Rugman, appeared on screen. It was one of the worst, most distorted pieces of journalism I have ever seen, qualifying as crude propaganda. I have been in Venezuela lately and almost nothing in Rugman's rant coincides with reality. Factories are like 'Soviet collectives'; a dictatorship is on the rise; Chávez is like Hitler (Rumsfeld); and the media is under government attack. The inversion of the truth throughout this travesty is demonstrated in the 'coverage' of a cowed media. Venezuela is a country in which 95 per cent of the press and TV and radio are owned by the far-right, who mount unrelenting daily attacks on the government unhindered. The Latin American Murdoch, Cisneros, unfettered, controls much of it. Indeed, it is probably the most concentrated, reactionary media on earth – but that was not worthy of a single word from Rugman.[42]

CHÁVEZ AND RCTV

No surprise, then, that Chávez's decision not to renew the licence of Radio Caracas Television (RCTV) in 2007 elicited outrage across Britain and America. In an article titled, '"He is losing the country's respect"', Catherine Philp wrote in *The Times*: 'The move has fuelled accusations that Mr Chávez is moving towards an increasingly authoritarian rule and is quashing dissent against his "socialist revolution".'[43] The *Washington Post* described the action as an attempt to silence opponents, supplying further 'proof' that Chávez is a 'dictator'.[44]

One might think from these comments that Chávez was indeed behaving like a stereotypical 'strongman'. So why was he refusing to renew the licence? According to CNN reporter T. J. Holmes, the motive lay in the fact that RCTV 'has been critical of his government'.[45] The Associated Press also stressed that RCTV 'has been critical of Chávez'.[46] A *Guardian* headline carried the same emphasis: 'Chávez silences critical TV station – and robs the people of their soaps.'[47] A *Financial Times* news report was titled: 'Chávez pulls plug on dissenting TV station'.[48] These and similar claims gave the impression that Chávez was simply crushing dissent. An *Independent* leader came closer to the truth: 'President Chávez has long detested RCTV, accusing it of helping to incite a coup against him in 2002.'[49] As this suggested, the problem with RCTV did not revolve around political differences with Chávez, but around RCTV's attempts to overthrow the democratically elected government of Venezuela. A consistent theme of media reporting was to ascribe this 'accusation' to Chávez personally. Thus the *Independent* wrote of the 'station, which Mr Chávez believes was plotting against him'.[50] *The Times* reported: 'President Chávez withdrew its licence, accusing the network of "coup plotting".'[51] Likewise the *Financial Times*: 'Chávez has repeatedly alleged that it supported the [2002] coup.'[52] And the BBC: 'He [Chávez] says they were involved in a coup that nearly toppled him five years ago.'[53]

These media reports thus all distorted the truth by attributing a mere 'claim' to Chávez, someone they had all previously demonised as an authoritarian 'strongman'. This earlier demonisation acted to undermine the credibility of the charge against RCTV in readers' minds, so reinforcing the bias of ostensibly balanced reporting. Robert McChesney and Mark Weisbrot explained: 'This is a common means of distorting the news: a fact is reported as accusation, and then attributed to a source that the press has done everything to discredit.'[54] It is a simple fact, not a claim, that RCTV was deeply complicit in the 2002 military coup – and the 'claims' of the West's Venezuelan bête noire should have been placed front and centre only if we were content for media demonisation to undermine this truth.

A CLIMATE OF TRANSITION: OVERTHROWING CHÁVEZ

In a rare example of media honesty, the *Los Angeles Times* reported that RCTV had initially been focused on providing entertainment: 'But after Chávez was elected president in 1998, RCTV shifted to another endeavour: ousting a democratically elected leader from office.'[55] Controlled by members of the country's ruling elite, including station chief Marcel Granier, the channel saw Chávez's 'Bolivarian Revolution' in defence of Venezuela's poor as a threat to established privilege and wealth.

Thus, for two days before the April 11, 2002 coup, RCTV cancelled regular programming and instead ran constant coverage of a general strike aimed at ousting Chávez. A stream of commentators delivered fierce criticism of the president with no response allowed from the government. RCTV also ran non-stop adverts encouraging people to attend an April 11 march aimed at toppling the government and broadcast blanket coverage of the event. When the march ended in violence, RCTV ran manipulated video footage falsely blaming Chávez supporters for the many deaths and injuries. On the same day, RCTV allowed leading coup plotter Carlos Ortega to call for demonstrators to march on the presidential palace. After the overthrow appeared to have succeeded, another coup leader, Vice-Admiral Victor Ramírez Pérez, told a journalist: 'We had a deadly weapon: the media. And now that I have the opportunity, let me congratulate you.' Another grateful leader remarked: 'I must thank Venevisión and RCTV.'[56] RCTV news director Andres Izarra later testified at National Assembly hearings on the coup attempt that he had received clear orders from superiors at the station: 'Zero pro-Chávez, nothing related to Chávez or his supporters ... The idea was to create a climate of transition and to start to promote the dawn of a new country.'[57]

While the streets of Caracas erupted with public outrage against the coup, RCTV turned a blind eye and showed soap operas, cartoons and old movies instead. On April 13, 2002, RCTV's Marcel Granier and other media moguls met in the Miraflores palace to offer their support to the country's new dictator, Pedro Carmona who, at a stroke, demolished Venezuela's democratic institutions – eliminating the Supreme Court, the National Assembly and the Constitution. Finally, when Chávez returned to power later the same day, the commercial stations again refused to cover the news.

In a leader titled 'Chávez clampdown: Closing TV station is part of pattern of authoritarianism', the *Financial Times* observed: 'The closure limits freedom of expression and reflects the arbitrary and authoritarian approach that has come to characterise Mr Chávez's government. In a region where the media have been becoming more open in recent years after the dark period of military rule in the 1970s and 1980s, this is a backward and worrying step.'[58] The irony was bitter indeed. It was a 'backward and worrying step' of exactly this kind that RCTV had attempted to impose on Venezuela by means of a military coup. As the coup appeared to have succeeded in April 2002, the *Financial Times* helped create 'a climate of transition' for British readers:

> But while the Chávez administration was hobbled by inefficiency, a lack of support across class lines and an inability to tackle the country's economic problems and rising crime rate, it was Mr Chávez's overbearing and authoritarian style that analysts said transformed the public's resigned acceptance of an ineffectual government into an active desire among a majority to see it removed.[59]

As for the Venezuelan media's involvement in this 'backward and worrying step', the *Financial Times* had no complaints, other than to comment:

> An example of Mr Chávez's militaristic style has been his confrontational relationship with the local media, particularly television. On Tuesday, when

the business sector and union confederation began what was then a 24-hour strike, the state began interrupting broadcasts that showed the success of the work stoppage with turgid interviews with ministers and old video footage of oil wells operating normally.[60]

The liberal media – often considered great bastions of democracy and honest reporting – queued up to present the overthrow of Chávez as an inevitable response to his alienating authoritarianism and multiple failures. With Chávez apparently gone for good, Alex Bellos wrote in the *Guardian* of 'the leftwing firebrand': 'Mr Chávez was elected in 1998 on a wave of popular support and quickly established a reputation as Latin America's most charismatic leader. But his popularity plummeted as he antagonised almost every sector of society and failed to improve the lot of the poor.' Bellos concluded: 'Mr Chávez polarised the country by his attacks on the media and Roman Catholic church leaders, his refusal to consult with business chiefs and his failed attempt to assert control on the unions. The US accused his government of provoking the crisis by ordering its supporters to fire on peaceful demonstrators.'[61]

In fact it turned out that the US had conspired with the coup plotters to overthrow the government. Likewise, Chávez supporters had been *defending* themselves against sniper attack. The Venezuelan media had misrepresented film footage to present the required version of events. In similar vein, the *Independent on Sunday* wrote of Chávez:

> His authoritarian style, his friendship with Fidel Castro and his inability to reverse Venezuela's 20-year slide into poverty and corruption, took their toll on his popularity ratings ... Convinced he was embarked on a 'Bolivarian revolution', inspired by the ideals of his hero, independence leader Simon Bolivar, Mr Chávez was messianic in his fervour. He alienated every organised group from the former leftist guerrillas of Bandera Roja to the employers' federation, Fedecamaras.[62]

And the *Observer* weighed in: 'In almost four years in office Chávez alienated most sections of Venezuelan society and was fast becoming as much of an irritant to the US as Fidel Castro, the Cuban leader.' The conclusion: 'His popularity waned in recent months as he became more autocratic, pushing through constitutional changes and alienating former supporters. He exasperated many Venezuelans by implementing economic policies by decree, and accused the news media and Roman Catholic leaders of conspiring to overthrow him.'[63]

Even after days of non-stop media broadcasts had succeeded in working for the overthrow of Chávez, for this *Observer* journalist talk of a media conspiracy remained merely Chávez's accusation.

The opinions of these ostensibly well-informed, highly-trained professional journalists were instantly rubbished by the vast popular uprising that restored Chávez to power, and in the longer term by Chávez's eleven election and referendum wins in ten years. In truth, the coup was a class-based revolt by and for privileged elites, led by Pedro Carmona who, as the BBC reported, was 'head of Venezuela's biggest business organisation, Fedecamaras'. Carmona, it was, who 'marshalled business and trade union opposition to Mr. Chávez's economic policies'.[64]

GENUINE ATTACKS ON FREE SPEECH THAT GO UNNOTICED

A May 30, 2007 *Independent* leader declared: 'RCTV was the sole opposition-aligned station with a national reach. Now it has gone. All governments need media opposition to keep them honest. But it appears that President Chávez does not have much time for this concept.'[65] Refusing to renew the licence of a TV channel complicit in the demolition of democracy described above was somehow 'a show of intolerance' for the *Independent*. In fact, RCTV had not 'gone' – it was allowed to continue operating by satellite and cable. The Venezuela Information Centre (VIC) noted:

> In Britain, TV and radio must adhere to the Broadcasting Code which embodies objectives that Parliament set down in the Communications Act of 2003. This states that 'Material likely to encourage or incite the commission of crime or to lead to disorder must not be included in television or radio services' and that 'Broadcasters must use their best endeavours so as not to broadcast material that could endanger lives.' RCTV's role in the coup would have clearly violated these laws.[66]

FAIR also made the obvious point: 'Were a similar event to happen in the U.S., and TV journalists and executives were caught conspiring with coup plotters, it's doubtful they would stay out of jail, let alone be allowed to continue to run television stations, as they have in Venezuela.'[67] The BBC reported: 'The decision to close RCTV has received international condemnation, including from the EU, press freedom groups, Chile and the US, which urged Mr Chávez to reverse the closure.'[68]

Almost unmentioned anywhere in the media were the statements of support made by a number of countries and leaders, such as Rafael Correa in Ecuador, Daniel Ortega in Nicaragua, Evo Morales in Bolivia and Luiz Inacio Lula da Silva in Brazil. The BBC report cited RCTV's general manager Marcel Granier who described the 'closure' as 'abusive' and 'arbitrary' – not a word was written of Granier's role in the 2002 coup. In a letter published in the *Guardian* (May 26, 2007), Gordon Hutchinson of VIC noted that despite claims made by opponents of Chávez, there was no censorship in Venezuela, where 95 per cent of the media was fiercely opposed to the government. This included five privately owned TV channels controlling 90 per cent of the market. All of the country's 118 newspaper companies, both regional and national, were held in private hands, as were 706 out of 709 radio stations.

While the British and American press focused intensely on the alleged crushing of free speech in Venezuela, little was written about comparable actions elsewhere. A report on 21 countries, including the US and in Europe, by J. David Carracedo, published in the magazine *Diagonal*, found that there had been at least 236 closures, revocations, and non-renewals of radio and TV licences.[69] There was also little media interest in genuine attacks on media freedom in Latin America.

In Honduras, beginning May 28, 2007, President Manuel Zelaya ordered all TV and radio stations to broadcast daily one-hour prime-time programmes for ten days to counteract what he called 'misinformation' on his administration provided by the press.[70] The BBC reported Zelaya's planned actions on May 25.[71] A June 11 media database search found that in the previous two weeks the US press had mentioned Zelaya's actions in four articles – the highest-profile outlet being the *Miami Herald*. Over the same period, the US press had mentioned the words 'Chávez' and 'RCTV' in 207 articles. The British press had not mentioned Zelaya's actions at all – Chávez and RCTV had been mentioned in 23 articles. In Colombia, President Álvaro Uribe was asked if he would have refused to renew RCTV's licence. Uribe replied: 'I would not do that to anybody.' The Inter Press Service News Agency commented wryly: 'But the rightwing Uribe cannot shut down opposition TV stations for the simple reason that there aren't any.'[72] In October 2004, Uribe closed the public Instituto de Radio y Televisión (Inravisión). The Colombian government argued that Inravisión was 'inefficient'. But the underlying problem 'was the strength of the union' of Inravisión employees, according to

Milciades Vizcaíno, a sociologist who worked for nearly 27 years in educational programming for the channel.[73] In Nicaragua in 2002, La Poderosa radio station lost its licence and had its equipment seized without any legal proceedings by the Enrique Bolaños administration. La Poderosa was an outspoken critic of the government.

These and many other attacks on free speech across the region did not make the front pages of the British and American press. As usual, alleged concerns for democracy and human rights mask deeper priorities: protecting governments that toe the line dictated by Western power, and undermining those that do not. In other words, despite all that has happened in Iraq, the British liberal media can *still* be relied upon to support Washington and London's agenda of demonising the next potential victims of Western power, whether in Iran, Syria or Latin America.

13
Liberal Press Gang:
Behind the Scenes at the
Independent and the *Guardian*

OF CRITICAL THOUGHT AND ROBERT FISK

In March 2005, the *Independent*'s star foreign correspondent, Robert Fisk, stuck out his jaw and told the *Democracy Now!* website: 'I don't work for Colin Powell, I work for a British newspaper called the *Independent*; if you read it, you'll find that we are.'[1] This comment locates the point where Fisk's capacity for critical thought capitulates to corporate groupthink. Imagine John Pilger boosting the bona fides of the *New Statesman* in similar fashion. Or imagine Noam Chomsky lauding the independence of the *New York Times*, which has syndicated his articles. We sent Chomsky a standard example of the *Independent*'s reporting on Iraq before the 2003 invasion. We received this evaluation of the paper's journalism in response:

> It's worth remembering that no matter how much they try, they are part of the British educated elite, that is, ideological fanatics who have long ago lost the capacity to think on any issue of human significance, and entirely in the grip of the state religion. They can concede errors or failures [by Western leaders], but anything more is, literally, inconceivable.[2]

Chomsky was not, it should be noted, referring to Fisk's work, which he holds in high regard. But a chasm separates this analysis from Fisk's. Indeed it is a thing of wonder that someone as astute as Fisk can view his own employer with an eye so blinded by professional pride. We might not normally turn to His Holiness the Dalai Lama for commentary on media matters, but the exiled Tibetan leader certainly shines a light on this discussion:

> When I talk to people of various professional backgrounds, particularly from the West, they seem to have a tremendous amount of attachment to their own profession. One could say that many people have an enormous personal

investment in their profession, they identify with it, so much so that they feel as if their profession is so vital for the world's well-being that if it were to degenerate the whole world would suffer. This suggests to me that their level of attachment is inappropriate.[3]

Professional attachment also explains Fisk's dismal view of internet-based media, in reality a source of tremendous hope for progressive change:

The *New York Times*, *Los Angeles Times*, *Washington Post* version of events doesn't satisfy millions of people. So more and more people are trying to find a different and more accurate narrative of events in the Middle East. It is a tribute to their intelligence that instead of searching for blog-o-bots or whatever, they are looking to the European 'mainstream' newspapers like the *Independent*, the *Guardian*, the *Financial Times*.[4]

Fisk's view of the *Independent* is shared by others on the paper, of course, but also by the press industry more generally. In receiving a gong at the 2004 British Press Awards, 'the Oscars of the newspaper industry', Simon Kelner, editor-in-chief of the *Independent* and the *Independent on Sunday*, promised 'no retreat from the qualities that have underpinned the *Independent* since its launch ... the role for an independent paper, one that is not driven by proprietorial agenda and that has no party allegiance, is as great as ever'.[5] The judging panel heaped praise on the paper's 'heroic decision' to transform into a compact (tabloid) version, declaring: 'thanks to the *Independent*, the face of British national newspapers has been changed for ever'. The panel added that 'the paper had also excelled in its journalism ... The *Independent*'s approach to the war in Iraq meant it was already having a good year even before its mould-breaking revamp.'[6]

In truth, the *Independent*'s 'approach to the war' meant it was having a terrible year, although not as terrible as the people of Iraq. It says much about the corporate media mind-set that the issue of tabloidisation and war reporting could be roped together in this way.

FLEXIBLE FRIENDS: ROGER ALTON AND SIMON KELNER

Former *New Statesman* editor Peter Wilby is no Chomskyite radical. But he does on occasion use his column to light a candle for truth in the deep industrial murk that is *MediaGuardian*. Consider Fisk's view in light of Wilby's analysis:

[T]he *Independent*'s founders never intended it to be a left-wing paper. Their preference, in the late 80s, was for Thatcherism with a human face. They expected to gain most readers from the *Telegraph* and *Times*. As it turned out, they found leftwing journalists more willing to join their venture and acquired more readers from the *Guardian* than from other papers. The editorial line remained pro-market and generally pro-foreign intervention, but compassionate towards the poor (in a vague sort of way) and leftish on social issues such as race, crime and smacking. Its position, in many respects, anticipated Blairism.[7]

It was in fact no surprise, Wilby wrote, that Roger Alton, the pro-Iraq war editor of the *Observer* had taken over editorship of the *Independent* from Simon Kelner, a close friend:

Both have political views that may be described as flexible or undogmatic, depending on how you look at it.

True, one committed his paper to supporting the Iraq invasion, the other to opposing it. But given different circumstances, it is easy to imagine either of them deciding on the opposite course. Many friendships were ruptured by Iraq. That between Alton and Kelner survived – another example of how similar they are.

True, also, Wilby added, that in 2006 Alton described hostility to Blair as 'quite baffling', but he 'could claim to echo the founders' views more closely' than Kelner had done.[8] This was a quietly devastating analysis for anyone who saw the *Independent* as a rare source of mainstream hope. It certainly drove a stake through the heart of Fisk's view of his employer. Yes, technically the *Independent* is independent of certain forms of external control. But it is, itself, a money-grubbing corporation! It is not independent of its own greed, its own goals, of its allotted place in the profit-driven state-corporate system – a system with almost limitless power to punish even small glimmers of dissent.

I MAXIMALIST! ANTHONY O'REILLY AND THE *INDEPENDENT*

Until May 2009, the *Independent* was owned by Irish billionaire Sir Anthony O'Reilly. That month, he stepped down as chief executive of Independent News & Media Plc (INM), the multinational company that publishes the *Independent* and *Independent on Sunday*. The reins of power were handed on to his son Gavin, while O'Reilly Sr. was bestowed by the INM board with the grand title 'president emeritus'. He remained the largest shareholder.[9]

O'Reilly is a former chairman, president and CEO of HJ Heinz, the leading food company. He is also a former member of the board of the New York Stock Exchange. His personal fortune has been estimated at £1.3 billion, which makes him one of the richest men in Ireland. He earns £15 million a year in salary and dividends. The personal fortune of his wife, Chryss Goulandris, a Greek shipping heiress, has been estimated at £442 million. O'Reilly has a controlling 72 per cent share in Arcon, the zinc mining operation, and he has interests in oil and gas exploration. He also owns Fitzwilton, a large industrial group with core activities in food retail and light manufacturing. The list goes on...

According to a report in the US press, 'O'Reilly counts among his friends and acquaintances a veritable who's who of world leaders and notables. His castle wall has a photo of him playing tennis at the White House with former President George Bush [Sr.], signed "Tony, greetings from the White House Field of Combat – George Bush."'[10] We read further: 'Entertaining celebrity friends on a grand scale is often done at one of O'Reilly's five residences around the world.' As well as an Irish castle 'overlooking 1,000 verdant acres that include a stud farm', O'Reilly 'owns a Georgian townhouse on fashionable Fitzwilliam Square in Dublin, a seaside home in Glandore, Ireland, a Deauville, France, chateau built on the ruins of the castle where William the Conqueror plotted his 1066 invasion of England' and 'an island retreat with a private beach in Lyford Cay, Bahamas'.[11]

O'Reilly's philosophy is simple: 'I am a maximalist. I want more of everything.'[12] Not just more wealth, but more power. O'Reilly's 1998 acquisition of a full stake in the *Independent* 'gave him complete control of the British broadsheet and the attendant clout and respectability that he had craved'.[13] Long-time Media Lens sparring partner and former *Independent* editor, Andrew Marr, commented:

[O'Reilly's] country house in Kildare, where the Liffey is just a stream, is Castlemartin, a beautiful home, warmer in style and furnishing than one imagines any Protestant ascendancy house would have been, with a constant stream of petitioning Irish politicians at the gate and rolling acres for the expensive horseflesh to frolic in all around. I mention this only because in the history of relations between proprietors and editors, the sheer gloss and glitter of great wealth, and its effect on middle-class British tradesmen, which is what journalists are, should not be underestimated.[14]

But surely, as editor of the *Independent*, Marr was immune to the gloss and glitter? In his book, *My Trade*, Marr conducted a fingertip soul-search of his motives for becoming editor: 'So, why had I done it?' His conclusions:

There were, looking back, two crucial factors in my mind. The first was vanity. The second was greed. To be a national newspaper editor is a grand thing. Even at the poor-mouse *Independent*, though I didn't have a chauffeur, I was driven to and from work in a limousine, barking orders down my mobile phone. Even as the poorest-paid of my contemporary national editors, I was soon on £175,000, which was much more than I was worth. One is not supposed to admit those things matter but they do, of course. In the office, I was the commander. Eyes swivelled when I arrived and people at least pretended to listen when I spoke. The Indy might be small, but she was mine. It was a little like one of those naval novels, where the officer gets command of his first ship and doesn't care that it has only two masts...[15]

In 2007, O'Reilly's chief executive of INM in the UK, Ivan Fallon, earned 1.2m euros. Fallon was also chief executive of mobile phone content company iTouch until May 2005. He stepped down after INM sold its 37 per cent stake in the company to Japanese firm For-side.com for a £51 million profit. The non-executive directors on the board of INM are selected for their 'clout and respectability'. They include Ken Clarke, former Tory chancellor of the exchequer and deputy chairman of British American Tobacco; Brian Hillery, chairman of UniCredito Italiano Bank (Ireland) Plc and Providence Resources Plc; Baroness Margaret Jay, a former member of Tony Blair's cabinet and leader of the House of Lords; and Brian Mulroney, a former prime minister of Canada and now a senior partner at the Montreal law firm of Ogilvy Renault.

INM has described itself as 'a leading international newspaper and communications group, with its main interests in Australia, India, Ireland, New Zealand, South Africa and the United Kingdom'.[16] The group publishes over 200 newspaper and magazine titles with a combined weekly circulation in excess of 32 million copies, and a weekly audience of over 100 million consumers. In Australasia, INM is the largest radio operator (over 130 stations and an audience of almost six million people) and outdoor advertising operator. It also has leading outdoor advertising operations in Hong Kong, Malaysia, India, Indonesia and across Africa.

The group notes that 'it has grown consistently over the last 15 years by building a geographically unique and diverse portfolio of market-leading brands'.[17] It manages gross assets of 4.7 billion euros, revenue of over 1.9 billion euros and employs approximately 9,600 people worldwide. And this, of course, is the prime focus: consistent growth of 'market-leading brands' generating 'gross assets' of billions of euros. It is commonly thought that newspapers like the *Independent* tailor their brand to target particular readers. This is true, of course, but more importantly they target readers who appeal to the big business advertisers who supply around 75 per cent of the paper's revenue.[18] The *Independent*'s primary business, in fact, is selling wealthy audiences to wealthy advertisers. As discussed, O'Reilly has commented: 'For the advertiser, the newspaper remains the most effective mechanism to convey to the potential consumer the virtue, value, colour and style of any new product, service or offering that he has.'[19] Writing in the *Guardian*, Stephen Brook noted that Simon Kelner, now the *Independent*'s managing director and editor-in-chief, 'has basically outsourced the *Independent*'s marketing department to Freud Communications, run by the well-connected Matthew Freud': 'Freud will help to fashion the message that it connects directly with brand-conscious, upscale, young, high-earning readers.'[20]

Corporate realpolitik places advertising revenues, attracted by 'high-earning readers', above the grave problems that afflict and threaten the needs, welfare and rights of the general population. This, then, is the actual and metaphorical bottom line for the media and its flexible friends.

MYTHICAL FIREWALL:
KICKING THE PEOPLE WHO WRITE THE CHEQUES

It is not that newspapers like the *Independent* and the *Guardian* are merely cautious in dealing with other businesses; they have evolved to become an integral part of the business system. James Twitchell, author of *Adcult USA*, explains:

> You name it: the appearance of ads throughout the pages, the 'jump' or continuation of a story from page to page, the rise of sectionalisation (as with news, cartoons, sports, financial, living, real estate), common page size, halftone images, process engraving, the use of black-and-white photography, then colour, sweepstakes, and finally discounted subscriptions were all forced on publishers by advertisers hoping to find target audiences.[21]

In November 2001, the press reported that the *Daily Telegraph* had lost 100,000 readers over the previous year. Richard Ingrams commented in the *Observer*: 'No doubt this alarming fall explains a recent meeting between *Telegraph* executives and advertising agency J. Walter Thompson, at which the admen attacked the poor old *Telegraph* editor Charles Moore for his outdated Little England attitudes coupled with homophobia.'[22] Ignoring these obvious realities, the *Guardian*'s Emily Bell insists that advertisers have the right to spend, or not spend, money where they like. However, 'there is nothing ethical about seeking to derail freedom of expression', she adds. Her conclusion: 'If an advertiser is stupid enough to ask for editorial favours in return for advertising money, and a publisher craven enough to give it, then the advertiser-funded model for news media is in serious trouble.'[23]

These are surreal comments when we consider Twitchell's description of how newspapers are not merely influenced by, but are creatures *born* of, advertiser power.

Indeed there is a schizophrenic quality to media discussions on this issue. On the one hand, journalists know that media businesses bend over backwards to attract and please advertisers. Sometimes it is conscious, sometimes reflexive, but the basic trend is not in doubt. In *My Trade*, Andrew Marr wrote: 'But the biggest question is whether advertising limits and reshapes the news agenda. It does, of course. It's hard to make the sums add up when you are kicking the people who write the cheques.'[24] Note the curious contradiction: the 'biggest question' remains a question even though the answer is declared obvious. So why the mind games? Because corporate journalists must be seen to be devoted to the exalted values of Accuracy, Honesty and Balance; even as their companies carefully shape their product to suit the all-important advertisers.

In April 2006, the US-based watchdog Fairness and Accuracy in Reporting (FAIR) commented on the link between the media and advertising: 'Most people are aware that news media rely on corporate advertising dollars – though the fact is rarely discussed, and when it is, editors and producers will generally insist that there's no connection between the companies that buy ads and the content of the news.'[25] In October 2006, Guy Keleny provided a good example of this insistence in the *Independent*:

A free press, run commercially, has to set a firewall between the journalistic writing and the advertising that pays the bills. ... The journalists do not allow their reporting to be muffled by the interests of advertisers, and the advertisers are free to say what they like in the space they have bought (subject to the law and industry codes) without regard to the newspaper's editorial opinions.[26]

We wrote to Keleny and suggested that, in reality, the firewall was a sham. We asked if he was aware that BP and Morgan Stanley had issued directives in the previous year demanding that their adverts be pulled from any publication that included 'objectionable' content. BP had demanded advance notice of any stories mentioning the company, a competitor of the company, or the oil and energy industry in general. We quoted FAIR: 'While these demands may seem like an egregious intervention into the editorial process, the truth is, as one anonymous editor told [trade journal] *Advertising Age* (May 16, 2005), there's "a fairly lengthy list of companies that have instructions like this".'[27]

We also quoted Keleny's former editor, Andrew Marr, on the difficulty of 'kicking the people who write the cheques'. We suggested that it was absurd to claim that these pressures had no impact on newspaper content. Keleny responded: 'I didn't know that about BP and Morgan Stanley. But threats by advertisers to boycott publications that print things they don't like are nothing new. Every local weekly newspaper gets them from time to time. The question is whether or not the editor gives in to them. I imagine some do and some don't.'[28] This was the sound of a firewall sputtering. Had Keleny not boldly declared in his article that 'journalists do not allow their reporting to be muffled by the interests of advertisers'? Once again, we find that journalists have one opinion for public consumption and another for sensible discussion.

FAIR's report pointed out that powerful advertisers also like to ensure that they are associated with positive spin. The October 31, 2005 issue of *Time* magazine featured a section titled 'The Future of Energy'. This focused on attempts to find alternatives to oil and to make oil production more efficient. FAIR provided a summary: 'Throughout the feature were full-page ads for BP, with taglines like "investing in our energy future," explaining how the company is pursuing alternatives to oil. BP is also mentioned by a source in *Time*'s feature article as one of the more innovative energy companies. That, presumably, was free.'[29] Around the time that we wrote to Keleny, prominent BP advertising was also appearing regularly in the *Independent*. This included full-page ads in the print edition as well as BP 'Target neutral' ads online. These presented an image of the oil giant working tirelessly to protect the world by replacing fossil fuels and moving to a greener future.

The *Independent on Sunday* made a rare effort to broach the advertising issue that same year when its readers' editor, Michael Williams, dismissed readers protesting the paper's climate-killing adverts as 'a curmudgeonly lot of puritans, miseries, killjoys, Stalinists and glooms'.[30] The loony 'Stalinists' hoping for a sane media reaction to the climate crisis were clearly beyond the pale for Williams, whose piece was titled: 'Welcome to Mars (or North Korea)!' This recalled Channel 4 newscaster, Jon Snow's equally foolish comments to us: 'You want to produce a bland, boring, under-financed bloody media, which has no adverts, and which prattles on about events that occurred 30 years ago.'[31]

Guardian editor Alan Rusbridger has also warned against creating a 'joyless' paper: 'If you had nothing to do with any form of consumption, your circulation would take a big dip and reading the *Guardian* would become a duty rather than a pleasure.'[32] It is marvellous that senior journalists are devoted to filling their readers with joy. On the other hand, many readers, internet browsers and TV viewers would chew off a limb if it meant they could avoid having to wade through the endless advertising junk, advertorials and infotainment. This is unlikely to happen. The *Economist* once reported how media projects 'unsuitable for corporate sponsorship tend to die on the vine' because 'stations have learned to be sympathetic to the most delicate sympathies of corporations'.[33]

Michael Williams did not respond to the totalitarian 'glooms' who continued to fear for the future of the planet and who continued to email him politely and cogently. Two years later, however, he forced himself to revisit the depressing subject, commenting truculently: 'The advertisers don't interfere with the views of commentators and the newspaper doesn't meddle with them.' He added: 'we believe "IoS" readers are intelligent enough to make up their own minds. And there's one reader offer we won't be making. A free hair shirt with every edition.'[34]

THE *GUARDIAN*: FILLING UP WITH CHILDISH EXCITEMENT

Like the *Independent*, the *Guardian* is part of a major media empire. Consider the $1.35 billion Trader Media Group (TMG) in which the Guardian Media Group (GMG) has a majority stake. TMG owns over

70 weekly publications. In February 2007, the *Guardian* demanded that there should be 'No more excuses' on climate change: 'What we do know is simple: that climate change is most likely caused by carbon emissions. The answer is to cut those emissions. The time to do so is now. Even if there is nothing that can be done for the damage already taking place, that should only cause policy makers to redouble their efforts.'[35]

The newspaper that published these fine words was, and is, part of a corporate giant that publishes *Auto Trader*, *Bike Trader*, *Truck Trader* and *Top Marques*. TMG owns the UK's busiest automotive web site, autotrader.co.uk, which attracts some 2.3 million unique users per month. TMG also offers interactive services on digital television and mobile phones. The vital statistics are impressive: 'With an annual turnover in excess of £280 million, TMG employs over 4,000 employees, located over 35 locations throughout the UK and Ireland. TMG also has three international operations located in Holland, Italy and South Africa.'[36]

The people who have graced the GMG Board and/or the Scott Trust (a non-profit organisation which owns Guardian Media Group, including the *Guardian* and the *Observer*) link the corporate media, the Labour Party, Cadbury Schweppes, Tesco, KPMG Corporate Finance, the chemicals company Hickson International Plc, Fenner Plc, the investment management company Rathbone Brothers Plc, erstwhile global investment company Lehman Brothers, global financial services firm Morgan Stanley and the Bank of England. We are to believe that a newspaper embedded in these establishment and corporate networks and, as discussed, dependent on corporate advertisers for 75 per cent of its revenues, is not compromised in its ability or motivation to provide honest, challenging coverage of a world dominated by these same powerful interests.

In June 2005, a *Guardian* article extolled the virtues of the latest model of 'over-powered invalid carriage' (to use George Monbiot's evocative phrase) to be launched by Lexus cars. Reporter Leo Hickman wrote:

'Display. Climate. Info.' On a vast acreage of dashboard, these three words are embossed on large, adjacent buttons. They could have been lost against their more showy neighbours – the large sat-nav screen, the media player that shuffles six CDs and shows DVDs on the screens built into headrests, the moveable steering column that politely retreats to allow you to step out of the car gracefully – but it's the buttons that leap out. I feel a little ashamed for filling up with such childish excitement...

Hickman continued:

If you read the motoring press then you might believe that the RX400h, with its part electric/part petrol 'hybrid' engine, has been sent from above to single-handedly slay climate change ... A breathless review in *Automobile* magazine talks of a car that 'accelerates with V-8 gusto and cradles its occupants in leather-lined luxury'. The hyperbolic review ends: 'The Lexus RX400h provides the well-to-do with a sacrifice-free ride to social responsibility.'[37]

The front cover of the *Guardian*'s G2 supplement had a full-page picture of the Lexus RX400h against a green background with the headline: 'Can this car save the planet?' The previous week, *Guardian* advertising correspondent Stephen Brook had reported on the Lexus. He cited Clive Baker, a regional account director with the advertising agency Saatchi & Saatchi: 'When we are looking at something like Lexus ... our media money is nowhere near the amount of our competitors ... We really want to make a noise. It's such a change for the motor industry, it's very different to what's out there.'[38] The *Guardian* had previously carried major advertising for Lexus cars. For example, page 18 of the October 1, 2003 edition featured an article on the catastrophic effects of climate change. It also featured a large advert for Lexus cars spread across two pages. Is it possible that the *Guardian*'s decision to publish the Hickman and Brook articles was influenced, either consciously or unconsciously, by Lexus advertising revenue? After all, the former chief executive of the *New York Times*, Arthur Sulzberger, once admitted that he had leaned on his editors to present the car industry's position on a range of issues because it 'would affect advertising'.[39]

In an interview, writer and broadcaster David Barsamian asked US activist and three-time presidential candidate Ralph Nader about the media: 'Wouldn't it be irrational for them to even discuss corporate power, since their underwriting and sponsors come from very large corporations?' Nader replied: 'Very irrational ... [There are] a few instances almost every year where there's some sort of criticism of auto dealers, and the auto dealers just pull their ads openly from radio and TV stations.'[40]

Leo Hickman's piece did contain critical comments about the RX400h. The article quoted Emily Armistead, a climate campaigner for Greenpeace who was 'enraged' by the claim that the RX400h was a 'Green' SUV: 'It has marginally less impact on the climate, but it is demonstrably not a green car ... You're still driving two tonnes around unnecessarily to do the shopping.' But the article contained a far greater number of positive comments. Would the *Guardian* be as willing to publish an article that was truly damning of the Lexus car in a way that risked alienating the company as an advertiser? As we saw in the first chapter, history suggests otherwise.

Guardian editor Alan Rusbridger responded with customary media civility to some questions we put to him about his paper and Lexus:

> Can we be told how much money the *Guardian* has received from Lexus advertising in recent years?
> 'NO'
> Did this money influence the decision to publish today's article by Leo Hickman?
> 'NO'
> Have discussions taken place in recent weeks between *Guardian* executives and Lexus on plans for the promotion of the new car?
> 'NO'[41]

We checked with Lexus and were told that both the *Guardian* and the *Observer* were included as part of their advertising campaign for the RX400h through to September that year, 2005. How this was agreed without discussions between the *Guardian* and Lexus 'in recent weeks' was not clear to us, so we asked Rusbridger. He replied the same day: 'I assumed you were addressing me as editor. I have no idea what discussions have or haven't taken place between Lexus and the commercial side of the paper. Why don't you ask them?'[42] G2 editor Ian Katz also responded to the same questions:

> That's an intriguing conspiracy theory David but just that I'm afraid. To answer your questions:
> 1) I have absolutely no idea how much money the *Guardian* has received from Lexus advertising in recent years (or when, or what, Lexus last advertised, for that matter). You could ask our press office that question (try Anna Sinfield or Isabel Milner) but I suspect that is commercially sensitive information that they won't release. (Would you?) 2) The piece had nothing to do with any advertising. Like I say I had no idea about any Lexus advertising. In any case, I don't know how you do things at the [New] Statesman [for which

Media Lens wrote a monthly column at the time] but I have never in seven years as *Guardian* features editor known any piece to be commissioned to please an advertiser. We don't work that way. In fact Leo's piece was originally commissioned as a look at green motoring options (specifically lpg) and it was tilted towards the new Lexus when Leo reported back to us that the launch of the Lexus was the latest development in greener car technologies. You also neglect to quote from the end of his piece where he questions Lexus's claims about the model's green credentials – a scepticism which we reflected in the cover line by using the word green in quotes.[43]

Katz wrote of a 'conspiracy theory' – an alternative description might be 'free market economics'. Katz commented: 'I have never in seven years as *Guardian* features editor known any piece to be commissioned to please an advertiser. We don't work that way.'

We accepted that Katz's answers were given in good faith. And yet in February 2004, the *Guardian* launched its *Spark* magazine in association with Toyota Prius. Five of the magazine's 36 pages were taken up in advertising Toyota's car. In their introduction, the editors wrote: 'Welcome to Spark, a new magazine about the positive things that are going on all over the world, and the people working to create a brighter future for us all.' Opposite these words could be seen a full-page advert for the Toyota Prius with the banner: 'The future starts now.' The text on the front cover of the magazine read: 'Positive thinking for a better tomorrow.' Toyota's website informed visitors that Prius means 'ahead of its time'.

We wrote to *Spark* magazine editor, Nick Taylor: 'Surely the needs and preferences of advertisers were central considerations in deciding the format and focus of the [Spark] magazine.'[44] Taylor responded: 'Your point is valid. But certainly not unique to my product. Ever worked on a magazine launch? The first and only real questions are: who will advertise with in [*sic*] product? Will it be read by people whom advertisers want to reach?'[45] Of course, we cannot know that the timing of the appearance on the G2 cover of the Lexus, one week after a major multimedia campaign for precisely that vehicle had been announced, was anything more than a coincidence. Likewise, the G2 front-page headline, 'Can this car save the world?', may simply have been deemed the most appropriate regardless of the impact on advertising. We asked Andrew Rowell, a contributor to the *Guardian* on environmental issues and author of the book *Green Backlash*,[46] what he thought of the G2 cover. He replied: 'The concept of a 4 x 4 saving the planet is a complete contradiction – it is the ultimate example of greenwash.'[47] On the face of it our questions to the

Guardian editor were pretty outrageous. We were asking if money from advertisers had influenced the appearance of a major article in the paper. Were we suggesting a kind of corruption – that money through advertising was being traded for space in the paper? Really we were trying to make a different point that renders all of this irrelevant and in fact absurd.

Rusbridger and Katz both firmly, and doubtless with great sincerity, rejected the possibility of advertiser influence. And yet the fact remains that every last detail of the *Guardian*, and of every other newspaper, is *designed* to attract the advertisers on which it depends for its survival. If the very layout, structure and format of a paper are shaped by advertiser needs, then how can the words filling this layout not also be shaped by these same pressures, if only unconsciously? In other words, Rusbridger and Katz rejected the suggestion that advertisers influence content. And yet both know perfectly well that success depends on their attracting, not alienating, advertisers. This ability to embrace two conflicting ideas, without being aware of the contradiction, is a key factor facilitating journalistic self-deception and its remarkable result – 'brainwashing under freedom'.

GEORGE MONBIOT CHALLENGES HIS OWN PAPER

We have had an on-off relationship with George Monbiot over the years. When we started Media Lens in July 2001, he was strongly supportive of our project. After we criticised his reporting on Iraq in November 2002, he wrote to us:

> I have viewed your mailings over the past few months with growing concern. Rather than offering a clear, objective analysis of why the media works the way it does, who pulls the strings, how journalists are manipulated, knowingly or otherwise, you appear to have decided instead to use your platform merely to attack those who do not accept your narrow and particular doctrine. Whenever a journalist takes a line at variance to your own, your automatic assumption is that he has stopped thinking for himself, and has been, wittingly or otherwise, coerced by dark forces. As a result, you are in danger of reproducing the very problems you criticise. You appear to me to be confronting one form of bias and intolerance with another.[48]

This view had softened (perhaps temporarily) by February 2005: 'If, as I think you have, you have begun to force people working for newspapers and broadcasters to look over their left shoulders as well as their right, and worry about being held to account for the untruths they disseminate, then you have already performed a major service to democracy.'[49] In 2007, *Guardian* online hosted a live public debate with Monbiot. We posted the following contribution for him to answer:

> The *Guardian* website today proudly boasts: 'Over the last 12 months, the GNM [Guardian News and Media] total audience accounted for: 20% of all champagne drunk. One in six of all city breaks taken. One in five Acorn 'Urban Prosperity'. £1 in every £7 spent on computer hardware or software. 1/6 of all MP3 player expenditure.'
>
> Andy Pietrasik, the Travel editor, also writes: 'The section is designed to address the way we travel now: Weekend – for the budget airline generation that takes more short breaks than ever before at home and abroad. On Location – for the new generation of jetsetters, who have been inspired to travel to a destination because of a film they have seen.'
>
> Doesn't this make a mockery of the *Guardian*'s claims to be responding to climate change? Is it really credible to expect a newspaper dependent on corporate advertising for 75 per cent of its revenue to seriously challenge the corporate system of which it's a part and on which it depends? Why don't you discuss this inherent contradiction in your journalism?[50]

In response, Monbiot selected a particular snippet for his answer: '"Doesn't this make a mockery of the *Guardian*'s claims to be responding to climate change?" Yes, it does.' Monbiot's candour was welcome, but his response was incomplete. We followed up a few minutes later with a further question:

> Thanks, George, but you failed to answer our third question: 'Why don't you discuss this inherent contradiction in your journalism?' Isn't it vitally important that this structural problem of the corporate mass media system be exposed? Doesn't your silence on this issue indicate the very real limits of free speech in our 'free press'?

We received no further response during the live Q&A session and assumed our relationship with George had taken another step back. To our surprise, however, we received this gracious email a few days later:

> Dear David and David,
>
> I am taking your request seriously and looking into the implications of the newspapers not carrying ads for cars, air travel and oil companies. Like you,

I believe this is necessary if we are to have a chance of preventing runaway climate change. But if this call is to carry weight, I must be able to present an alternative: to demonstrate to news organisations, including the *Guardian*, that they can keep their heads above water while refusing this advertising. Assuming, as I think I will find, that they account for a large proportion of a newspaper's income, and assuming that all newspapers are in financial trouble (all the former broadsheets are, I think, now cross-subsidised by proprietors or other commercial outlets) what alternative funding models would you suggest?

If you wish to ask for ideas from other people, please do so.

With best wishes, George[51]

In responding, we pointed out that slave owners had for years insisted that abolition was an economic impossibility, indeed that slavery was in the best interests of the slaves (who were, it was claimed, at least treated as valuable property). That turned out to be nonsense, of course, as well as being morally unsustainable. Newspapers, as well as the motor racing industry, also shrieked about the impossibility of doing without tobacco advertising. But both appear to have survived intact despite the loss. Why could the media not survive the loss of fossil-fuel advertising?

Perhaps, we asked Monbiot, the *Guardian* could, with his prompting, open a debate with 'liberal' media rivals like the *Independent* to seek a consensus on the way forward. Could such papers perhaps seek out replacement advertisers in the growing renewables market? Could they consult with readers to discuss replacing fossil-fuel advertising with a higher cover price? There is, after all, a precedent – the *Guardian* already charges for an advert-free online service. Could newspapers begin by refusing the worst fossil-fuel advertising – gas-guzzling SUVs and short-haul air flights, for example?

We advised caution in focusing exclusively on the issue of funding. Monbiot had asked: 'what alternative funding models would you suggest?' This, in effect, asked: How can a psychopathic corporate media system be funded in a way that makes it less destructive? The corporate media subordinate people and planet to profit as a matter of legal obligation (as discussed earlier, they are legally required to seek to maximise profits for shareholders). They will not reverse these priorities as a result of altered funding. It would no doubt be preferable if Hannibal Lecter changed to a diet of nut cutlets, but he would remain a major nutcase.

We suggested to Monbiot that, as a highly respected journalist, he was arguably one of the most powerful supports for the delusion that the corporate media are willing to tell the truth that matters in a way that can lead to the change we need. Many of his articles on climate change, for example, are excellent and proclaim a loud message of honesty, action and hope. But the news reports, comment pieces and adverts that surround his work reinforce powerfully a 'pathology of normalcy' and prevent people from seeing the pathology for what it is.

Monbiot clearly gave these issues some thought. A subsequent column courageously challenged the press, including the *Guardian*, to cut fossil-fuel advertising. He wrote:

Newspaper editors make decisions every day about which stories to run and which angles to take. Why can they not also make decisions about the ads they carry? While it is true that readers can make up their own minds, advertising helps to generate behavioural norms. These advertisements make the destruction of the biosphere seem socially acceptable.[52]

He added: 'why could the newspapers not ban ads for cars which produce more than 150g of CO_2 per kilometre? Why could they not drop all direct advertisements for flights?' Three months later, the *Guardian*'s readers' editor, Siobhain Butterworth, wrote in her weekly column about 'the contradiction between what the *Guardian* has to say about environmental issues and what it advertises'.[53] Butterworth supplied *Guardian* editor Alan Rusbridger's comments on the issue: 'It is always useful to ask your critics what economic model they would choose for running an independent organisation that can cover the world as widely and fully with the kind of journalism we offer.'

Readers of our previous book, may recall Rusbridger bowling us this very same googly. It is often, of course, useful to discuss solutions. However, we have noticed that the question, 'Well, what's your alternative?', is often a fallback position after sheer weight of evidence has forced someone to abandon their attempts to deny the existence of a problem. We call such debaters the Free Press Faithful (FPF). They insist that, in the UK, we have a broad spectrum of news, analysis and commentary. This may be their firm belief – or at least, what they are firmly resolved to believe. On occasions when this position becomes untenable in debate, the FPF will appear to agree and move on to alternatives. Superficially, this looks like progress. But, all too often, the underlying conviction that no credible alternatives exist remains. The implication is that a problem without a solution is not a problem; it is a fact of life. Rusbridger had asked us:

> I'd be interested to know what alternative business model you propose for newspapers which would sustain a large, knowledgeable and experienced staff of writers and editors, here and abroad, in print as well as on the web. Do you prefer no advertising lest journalists are corrupted or influenced in the way you imagine? If so, what cover price do you propose? Or, in the absence of advertising, what other source of revenue would you prefer?
>
> These are all interesting debates, and I wish you well. I can only answer as to my experience.[54]

Alas, this was not a precursor of vibrant discussion. In the several years since, Rusbridger has refused to respond to our emails. Our 2006 book, *Guardians Of Power*, discussing these and related issues, has never been mentioned by the paper, much less reviewed. This could, of course, simply reflect the worthlessness of what we have to say. George Monbiot, however – one of the most respected commentators on the paper – appears not to share this view. More to the point, Monbiot's intervention aside, there has been essentially no discussion of issues that we and many readers (and many excellent writers and media analysts) have sought to raise over many years.

EPILOGUE: THE *GUARDIAN* EDITOR HAS A THINK

In December 2000, six months before Media Lens was born, David Edwards conducted a series of telephone interviews with leading editors and journalists. The following section from the interview with *Guardian* editor Alan Rusbridger is of particular interest:[55]

> David Edwards (DE): 'There's a radical analysis of the media which says that wealthy owners, parent companies, advertisers, and the profit orientation of the media, act as filters that tend to remove facts and ideas that are damaging to powerful corporate and state interests. Is that an argument you're aware of? Is it something you'd agree with?'
>
> Alan Rusbridger (AR): 'Say it again.'
>
> DE: 'Basically, one radical analysis of the media is that the pressures of advertising, of wealthy owners and parent companies, have an effect similar to filtering, so that facts and ideas that are damaging to powerful

advertisers and powerful parent companies, and so on, tend to be filtered from press reporting.'

[7 second pause]

AR: 'Um, I'm sure there is a ... [6 second pause] that the pressures of ownership on newspapers is, is pretty important, and it works in all kinds of subtle ways – I suppose "filter" is as good a word as any; the whole thing works by a kind of osmosis. If you ask anybody who works in newspapers, they will quite rightly say, "Rupert Murdoch", or whoever, "never tells me what to write", which is beside the point: they don't have to be told what to write.'

DE: 'That's right, it's just understood.'

AR: 'It's understood. I think that does work, and obviously the general interests of most of the people who own newspapers are going to be fairly conventional, pro-business, interests. So, you know, I'm sure that is broadly true, yes.'

DE: 'Does this then explain why this analysis hasn't appeared in the press? Have you ever seen a systemic analysis...?'

AR: 'There was an awful lot of that stuff published in the 80s and early 90s.'

DE: 'Really?'

AR: 'Well I think it was written about so widely that it's almost standard in any media studies course now.'

DE: 'Because I've never seen it in the mainstream press myself.'

AR: 'It doesn't get written about a lot in the mainstream press, but I mean, you know, for obvious reasons. But there's a lot of it in books...'

DE: 'Isn't it astonishing, given the importance of the issue – the pressure of advertisers, wealthy owners and parent companies – shouldn't that be a fundamental point of discussion where the media is concerned in the mainstream press?'

AR: 'Yes, but, I mean, I agree, but you can sort of understand the reasons why, why it doesn't happen.'

DE: 'So it's not able to be discussed?'

[8–9 second pause]

AR: 'Um...'

DE: 'I mean could you discuss it if you wanted to?'

AR: 'Oh yes. I would say it's something we do fairly regularly. But then we're not owned by a ... We're owned by a trust; we haven't got a proprietor. So we're in a sort of unique position of being able to discuss this kind of stuff.'

DE: 'Right. But otherwise you think that's the reason it's not discussed?'

AR: 'Yeah.'

Edwards later pushed the point that he had never seen such a discussion in the press, not even in the *Guardian*:

> DE: 'I've been a *Guardian* reader for probably 15 years, and there were a couple of discussions on press freedom about 5 or 6 years ago, but even those criticised the press for being too cynical, or too sensationalist, but the actual problem of a corporate press in a world dominated by corporations...'
>
> AR: 'Perhaps it's because it's such a sort of old problem. It's like female circumcision: how many times can people get round to writing about it? Maybe it's time to do it again.'
>
> DE: 'Yes, and actually look at the performance of the media system in a logical way and ask, well how does it stack up? And especially in the age of globalisation, I mean the power of corporations has increased dramatically; it seems an obvious thing...'
>
> AR: 'I will, I will think about it.'

Rusbridger may well have thought about it – if so, that is all he did. Nothing has appeared in the *Guardian* to seriously examine these issues. This remains a non-issue, in fact a taboo, for the press.

14

Brilliant Fools:
Snarls, Smears and the
Dark Art of Willy-Waving

'And to all my many enemies on the Left, and in various organisations like the pernicious Media Lens, I commend a splendid review by our vastly experienced foreign affairs editor, Peter Beaumont, of the new Noam Chomsky book about America, Failed States ... this is a superb demolition of Chomsky.'

Roger Alton, *Observer* editor[1]

'WHO DOES "JOHN LE CARRÉ" THINK HE IS'

The task of propaganda is to apply power-friendly labels and make them stick. The labelling factory par excellence, the machine that applies the right labels in the right way over and over again, is the mass media.

Dissidents have denounced the crimes of the powerful for decades, but they are swimming against a relentless tide. As has been so clearly demonstrated in Iraq, governments and big business can do pretty much what they like so long as the media factory is on hand to label it better: to label away the crimes, the lies, the suffering, the desperate need for change.

No surprise, then, that high-profile dissidents tend to attract negative media labels to the extent that they are honest in exposing the crimes of power. This labelling involves more than simple disagreement. As teachers of meditation have instructed for thousands of years, the mind is most effectively trained by constant repetition reinforced by emotional affect. If a smear is to be successful, revulsion must also be generated in the public mind. This ensures that the labelling is fixed both intellectually and emotionally, and recalled every time the target individual is remembered, seen or heard.

The impact becomes particularly striking when well-known individuals choose to focus on political dissent. Then, suddenly, the brilliant become brilliant fools; celebrated wordsmiths become childish scribblers; sophisticated storytellers become gauche and witless. Even world-renowned scientists are suddenly unable to grasp the most elementary principles of their own discipline.

Consider the abuse heaped on the novelist David Cornwell, who writes under the pseudonym John Le Carré. For decades, Le Carré received lavish praise for his spy novels – until he started to direct fierce criticism at US–UK foreign policy. In reviewing Le Carré's novel *Absolute Friends*, the *Sunday Telegraph* wrote:

> The poor fellow harangues us about globalisation, about George Bush, about Washington neo-conservatives ... With small sense of the ridiculous, he gives us a popular novel which nods gravely at the names of such as Noam Chomsky ... including, yes, John Pilger.
>
> What turned this much-loved entertainer into a cosmic prophet? What's eating him? Who does 'John Le Carré' think he is?[2]

The reviewer concluded: 'It is sad, but scarcely tragic ... *The Spy Who Came in From the Cold* will be read when most of today's polemics, including those of angry old David Cornwell, are quite forgotten.' The *Sunday Times* commented:

> Le Carré's anger comes across as a bit too raw to work as fiction, its rhetoric more in line with a Harold Pinter column than a Graham Greene novel.
>
> I finished *Absolute Friends* hoping that this greatest of all spy novelists writes for decades more, not only so he can keep creating characters like Mundy and Sasha, but also so that he can gain a more incisive perspective on our troubling times.[3]

SWALLOWING PINTER'S BILE

Another example is the late British playwright Harold Pinter, who was awarded the 2005 Nobel Prize for literature. Pinter had long been equally admired for his dramatic work and reviled for his political activism. Introducing his Nobel acceptance speech, playwright David Hare said: 'The theatre is what the British have always been good at. And nobody has so come to represent the theatre's strengths, its rigours, and its glories, as Harold Pinter.'[4] Reviewers write in near-mystical terms of Pinter's brilliance. Leading theatre critic Michael Billington observed in the *Guardian*: 'Although he is best known as a dramatist and screenwriter, Harold Pinter is an equally remarkable director ... As an actor, Pinter also possesses weight, authority and presence ... Pinter's production of Joyce's Exiles was a masterpiece of psychological insight and dramatic timing.'[5]

Pinter's use of sparse, menacing language in his drama is deemed the stuff of genius. Different labels are applied to his anti-war poems. These are deemed 'ludicrous, crass, offensive, second-rate, obscure-to-the-point-of-meaninglessness'. Daniel Finkelstein commented in *The Times*: 'The great dramatist has the right to intervene in politics, just as anyone else has. But he doesn't have the right to be taken seriously. Pinter simply has nothing interesting to say.'[6] Poet Don Paterson dismissed Pinter in the *Guardian*: 'To take a risk in a poem is not to write a big sweary outburst about how crap the war in Iraq is, even if you are the world's greatest living playwright. Because anyone can do that.'[7]

We cannot say if it is true that Pinter's talent deserted him when he wrote anti-war poetry. But caution is certainly advised. We recall, after all, the treatment meted out to Les Roberts of the Johns Hopkins School of Public Health. Journalists everywhere deferred utterly to Roberts as one of the world's most highly regarded epidemiologists when he estimated millions of deaths in the Congo in 2000 and 2001. But he was judged (by the powers that be) to be guilty of schoolboy errors when estimating 100,000 (in 2004) and then 655,000 (in 2006) civilian deaths in Iraq since the March 2003 US–UK invasion. To sample only one example, a *Wall Street Journal* editorial commented on the 2006 *Lancet* study: 'We know that number was wildly exaggerated. The news is that now we know why. It turns out the *Lancet* study was funded by anti-Bush partisans and conducted by antiwar activists posing as objective researchers. It also turns out the timing was no accident.'[8] As we (and many others) described at the time, every last word of that was false.

Simon Heffer wrote in the *Daily Mail* of Pinter: 'I don't begrudge Harold Pinter his Nobel Prize. I have never seen why someone's political views – which in Pinter's case are verging on the barking – should disqualify them from acclaim in any field of the arts.'[9] In the *New York Times*, James Traub declared: 'Pinter's politics are so extreme ... they are almost impossible to parody.'[10] Traub added, 'it is hard to think of anyone save Noam Chomsky and Gore Vidal who would not choke on Pinter's bile'. Tony Allen-Mills lamented in the *Sunday Times*: 'Among this year's Nobel laureates are several American scientists who are being rewarded for brilliant work. Yet their achievements appear destined to be overshadowed by a rant from a bolshie Brit.'[11] The *Mirror* reported Pinter's Nobel Prize speech with the headline: 'Pinter rant at "brutal" US policy.'[12] In the *Independent*, Johann Hari wrote an article with the wretched title: 'Pinter does not deserve the Nobel Prize – the only response to his Nobel rant (and does anyone doubt it will be a rant?) will be a long, long pause.'[13]

It is significant that Hari described Pinter's speech as a 'rant' before it had even been delivered – the label exists independently of the work, indeed of the author, in question. To subject power to serious, rational challenge is by definition to 'rant'. Hari commented: 'Ever since Pinter was a teenager, he has been relentlessly contrarian, kicking out violently against anything that might trigger his rage that day.' This was the standard, Soviet-style assertion that critics of power are afflicted by a psychological disorder, with the concocted 'sins' of power randomly selected as a focus for neurotic ire.

We have cited numerous examples to make a point: who, in all honesty, could come away from this apparently informed consensus without believing there was not something drastically wrong with Pinter and his politics? One of us (David Edwards) met Pinter a number of times in the 1990s, and conducted a lengthy interview with him in 1999. While it was obvious in these meetings that Pinter was a passionate individual, much of what he said was informed by an extremely sharp, if black, sense of humour.[14] Pinter came across as a highly intelligent, sincere and thoughtful individual – his compassion and sense of moral responsibility were real. Knowing this, it is staggering to read the many portrayals of Pinter as essentially a rage-driven idiot. Pinter's own comment from the interview offers a fitting response: 'That is actually bollocks.'

In truth, it is a brutal fact of modern media and politics that honesty and sincerity are not rewarded, but instead heavily punished, by powerful interests with plenty at stake. It does not matter how often the likes of Pinter, Le Carré, Noam Chomsky and John Pilger are shown to be right. It does not matter how often the likes of Bush, Brown and Blair are shown to have lied in the cause of power and profits. The job of mainstream journalism is to learn nothing from the past, to treat rare individuals motivated by compassion as rare fools deserving contempt. The benefits are clear enough: if even high-profile dissidents can be portrayed as wretched, sickly fools, then which reader or viewer would want to be associated with them? Then 'normal' – conforming, consuming, looking after 'number one' – can be made to seem healthy, balanced, sensible and sane. Historian Howard Zinn made the point well:

Realism is seductive because once you have accepted the reasonable notion that you should base your actions on reality, you are too often led to accept, without much questioning, someone else's version of what that reality is. It is a crucial act of independent thinking to be sceptical of someone else's description of reality.[15]

WHERE EGOS DARE: THE *GUARDIAN* SMEARS CHOMSKY

On October 31, 2005, the *Guardian* published an interview with Noam Chomsky by Emma Brockes, entitled 'The greatest intellectual?'[16] The article was ostensibly in response to the fact that Chomsky had been voted the world's top public intellectual by *Prospect* magazine the previous week. In reality, it was a carefully constructed smear. The article began thus:

> Despite his belief that most journalists are unwitting upholders of western imperialism, Noam Chomsky, the radical's radical, agrees to see me at his office in Boston. He works here as a professor of linguistics, a sort of Clark Kent alter ego to his activist Superman, in a nubbly old jumper, big white trainers and a grandad jacket with pockets designed to accommodate a Thermos. There is a half-finished packet of fig rolls on the desk. Such is the effect of an hour spent with Chomsky that, writing this, I wonder: is it wrong to mention the fig rolls when there is undocumented suffering going on in El Salvador?

The headline introduction to the article was:

> Q: Do you regret supporting those who say the Srebrenica massacre was exaggerated?
> A: My only regret is that I didn't do it strongly enough.

Remarkably, the answer attributed to Chomsky was actually in response to a different question posed during the interview. In a letter to the editor published in the *Guardian* on November 2, Chomsky explained:

> I did express my regret: namely, that I did not support Diana Johnstone's right to publish strongly enough when her book was withdrawn by the publisher after dishonest press attacks, which I reviewed in an open letter that any reporter could have easily discovered. The remainder of Brockes' report continues in the same vein. Even when the words attributed to me have

some resemblance to accuracy, I take no responsibility for them, because of the invented contexts in which they appear.

As for her personal opinions, interpretations and distortions, she is of course free to publish them, and I would, of course, support her right to do so, on grounds that she makes quite clear she does not understand.[17]

This is how Brockes presented the discussion in her article: 'Does he [Chomsky] regret signing it [a letter in support of Johnstone's work]? "No", he says indignantly. "It is outstanding. My only regret is that I didn't do it strongly enough. It may be wrong; but it is very careful and outstanding work."' The mis-matching of question and answer at the top of Brockes' article was a genuine scandal – it represented a depth of cynicism to which even mainstream journalism rarely sinks.

In the third paragraph of the article, Brockes wrote that Chomsky's 'conclusions remain controversial', namely:

that practically every US president since the second world war has been guilty of war crimes; that in the overall context of Cambodian history, the Khmer Rouge weren't as bad as everyone makes out; that during the Bosnian war the 'massacre' at Srebrenica was probably overstated. (Chomsky uses quotations marks to undermine things he disagrees with and, in print at least, it can come across less as academic than as witheringly teenage; like, Srebrenica was so not a massacre.)

We wrote to Brockes: 'What is the source for your claim that Chomsky has disagreed with the idea that there was a massacre at Srebrenica? Where, for example, has he used quotation marks in referring to the massacre?'[18] Chomsky was adamant that no such source existed. He wrote to us of Brockes:

her piece de resistance, the claim that I put the word 'massacre' in quotes. Sheer fabrication. She and the editors know perfectly well that there is nothing like that in print, or anywhere, certainly not in the interview: people don't speak with quotation marks. That's why they allowed her to refer vaguely to the phrase she invented, so as to insinuate that it is in print – which she knows, and the editors know, is a lie. Just ask them to produce the source.[19]

We received no reply from Brockes. It took just minutes searching the internet for us to find numerous quotes that contradicted Brockes' claims. In his January/February 2005 article, 'Imperial Presidency',

Chomsky described the November 2004 US assault on Fallujah as involving 'war crimes for which the political leadership could be sentenced to death under US law'. He added:

> One might mention at least some of the recent counterparts that immediately come to mind, like the Russian destruction of Grozny 10 years ago, a city of about the same size. Or Srebrenica, almost universally described as 'genocide' in the West. In that case, as we know in detail from the Dutch government report and other sources, the Muslim enclave in Serb territory, inadequately protected, was used as a base for attacks against Serb villages, and when the anticipated reaction took place, it was horrendous. The Serbs drove out all but military age men, and then moved in to kill them.[20]

Clearly, then, Chomsky considers Srebrenica nothing less than a counterpart to crimes 'for which the political leadership could be sentenced to death under US law'.

Similarly, on page 208 of his book *Hegemony or Survival*, Chomsky refers to the Srebrenica massacre[21] – no quotation marks were used either there or in the index. These are not the words of someone who insists in 'witheringly teenage' fashion: 'Srebrenica was so not a massacre.' They are not the words of someone who believes that the term massacre should be placed between quotation marks in describing Srebrenica. And yet this is what Brockes claimed in a national newspaper.

Chomsky's critics were everywhere in Brockes' piece, his admirers notably absent. The critics claimed that Chomsky 'plugs the gaps in his knowledge with ideology'. We learned that 'of all the intellectuals on the Prospect list, it is Chomsky who is most often accused of miring a debate in intellectual spam, what the writer Paul Berman calls his "customary blizzard of obscure sources"'. Book reviewer George Scialabba commented on Berman's reference to 'obscure sources' in *The Nation*:

> After the Indochina war, Berman writes, Chomsky had no way to explain the atrocities in Cambodia. He therefore set out, basing himself on his 'customary blizzard of ... obscure sources' (an ungracious remark, this, coming from the author of so lightly documented and empirically thin a book as *Terror and Liberalism*), to demonstrate that 'in Indochina, despite everything published in the newspapers ... genocide never occurred', or if it did, was all America's fault.

Scialabba explained that what Chomsky and Edward Herman actually set out to do in *The Political Economy of Human Rights* was

> to show how differently the crimes of official enemies are treated in mainstream American media and scholarship than are those of official allies or of America itself. Accepting without argument the existence of 'substantial and often gruesome atrocities' in postwar Cambodia, Chomsky and Herman reviewed the sources uncritically relied on in the mainstream, showed how inferior they were to sources that told a less convenient story and pointed out that equally credible sources that told of roughly equivalent atrocities within the American sphere of influence (for example, Indonesia's in East Timor) were generally ignored. Not the one-dimensional soundbite Berman alleges.[22]

But Berman was hardly alone in misrepresenting *The Political Economy of Human Rights*, Scialabba noted: 'Dealing fairly with the book's argument requires a modicum of discrimination, attention to detail and polemical scruple, courtesies rarely accorded Chomsky by his critics.' And certainly not by Brockes in the *Guardian*.

In reality, what is so impressive about Chomsky is that he relies on impeccable sources – recognised authorities in their fields, released government documents, establishment journals and the like – all meticulously referenced so that readers can check his accuracy for themselves. It cannot be any other way, as Chomsky has noted many times – dissidents challenging established power *must* provide far higher standards of evidence and argument than mainstream writers because they are guaranteed to be targeted for fierce attack.

Brockes asked Chomsky if he had a 'share portfolio'. Chomsky 'looks cross', we were told. From her lofty peak of wisdom and virtue, Brockes advised one of the world's most principled and tireless opponents of oppression: 'people don't like being told off about their lives by someone they consider a hypocrite'.

CAREFULLY PAIRED LETTERS

On November 1, 2005, the *Guardian* published two letters ostensibly sent in support of Chomsky's position. However, Chomsky commented:

> I have to say that these letters disturb me as much or more than the original deceit – which worked, as the letters show. Both writers assume that there

is a 'debate', as the editors falsely claimed, in which I question the massacre (or as they pretend, 'massacre') in Srebrenica. That is all fabrication, as the editors know well. They labored mightily to create the impression of a debate in which I take the position they assigned to me, and have succeeded. Now I'm stuck with that, even though it is a deceitful invention of theirs.[23]

As noted above, Chomsky was allowed a letter in response to Brockes' article a day later, on November 2. On the same day, the *Guardian* was fortunate to be able to publish an ideal letter from a survivor of Bosnia supporting Brockes' criticisms of Chomsky and praising the *Guardian*'s reporting.[24] We asked the editor and the comment editor if anyone associated with the *Guardian* had in any way solicited this letter – we received no reply. The paper also provided a link to an interactive guide titled 'Massacre at Srebrenica'.[25] Chomsky commented on the publication of his letter:

> Someone sent me the letter the *Guardian* printed [November 2], paired very carefully with a letter from a survivor from Bosnia, which, as the editors certainly know, is based entirely on lies in the faked 'interview' they published.
>
> Same with their title: 'Falling out over Srebrenica.' There was no Srebrenica debate, and they know it perfectly well. I never mentioned it, except to repeatedly try to explain to Brockes that I opposed the withdrawal of Johnstone's book under dishonest press attacks that were all lies, as I showed in the open letter I mentioned. And it had nothing to do with the scale of the Srebrenica massacre, as again they all know.
>
> As I think I wrote you, their legal department insisted that I delete the word 'fabrication' [from Chomsky's November 2 letter to the *Guardian*], and I agreed. Mistakenly I now realize, after seeing how low they can sink. I should have insisted on the word 'fabrication'...[26]

Although the *Prospect* poll was largely a joke, it did bring Chomsky's name to the attention of thousands of people who would otherwise never have heard of him. But anyone who read Emma Brockes' article in the *Guardian* can only have come away with one conclusion: Chomsky is an idiot – an angry, flaky fanatic given to denying obvious crimes against humanity. We spend our time well when we reflect that the source of this smear was not some rabid, right-wing, Murdoch organ but this country's 'leading liberal newspaper' – the *Guardian*.

THE *GUARDIAN* BACKS DOWN

On November 17, 2005, the *Guardian* published a 'correction and clarification' in regard to Brockes' piece by the paper's ombudsman at the time, Ian Mayes.[27] The *Guardian* editor also sent many readers a form letter advising of the paper's retraction and apology. The letter noted:

> The *Guardian* has a fully independent readers' editor, who has sole charge of a daily corrections and clarifications column on the most important page of the newspaper, alongside the leader columns. No other daily British paper has such an office or mechanism. It takes only one complaint to trigger his attention. The Chomsky case was highlighted by more than one website, some of which urged their own readers to write in and complain.
>
> While we welcome all correspondence, this had no bearing on the action of the Readers' Editor. It is, obviously, difficult to respond personally to such a quantity of email.[28]

This letter represented a significant change for the *Guardian*, which generally ignores emails from Media Lens readers as the work of a manipulative 'lobby' organising a robotic response (the *Guardian* editor, Alan Rusbridger, stopped replying to our emails after our media alerts in response to the Brockes smear). This would be reasonable if we were inaccurate or dishonest in representing the issues under discussion. It would also be reasonable if readers' letters were not overwhelmingly cogent and thoughtful.

Journalists and editors would do well to recognise that, while we *do* facilitate public criticism of the media, that criticism is nevertheless usually rational and sincere. In reality, the whole mass media system inclines readers to view what we write with scepticism. After all, we are not well-known professional journalists working in high-profile media companies, and we are often not in agreement with what most mainstream journalists are writing. We are also writing for an audience with little tradition of directly challenging often highly respected 'liberal' media from a left perspective. We believe that readers are therefore inclined *not* to respond unless they feel our arguments make rational sense – exactly the reverse of the *Guardian* view.

It is clear that the *Guardian*'s distortions were so obvious on this occasion – and so obviously damaging to its reputation – that the editors felt obliged to take the complaints seriously. We were willing to accept the *Guardian* claim that Mayes – who deserved real credit for the newspaper's apology – would have published his correction if just Chomsky had complained. But the editor's additional reply to readers clearly suggested that mass public engagement *did* raise the issue to a higher level of seriousness within the *Guardian*. For example, a number of correspondents wrote to the editor saying they had been buying the paper for many years – sometimes as long as 30 or 40 years – and would not be doing so again. This is something the *Guardian* could ill afford to ignore – a point worthy of consideration by all who aspire to a more honest and accountable media.

FERTILE FABRICATIONS: THE STORY UNFOLDS

On November 6, 2005, the *Independent on Sunday* published a short account of events up to that point:

> Noam Chomsky and the *Guardian* are still at loggerheads over an interview with him the newspaper published on Monday. The American academic and activist was incensed at what he calls 'fabrications' in the *Guardian* piece, and had a letter published on Wednesday in which he accused Emma Brockes of inventing 'contexts'. Chomsky denies saying that the massacre at Srebrenica has been overstated, as Brockes had claimed. But, to Chomsky's fury, the letter was printed next to one by a survivor of the massacre, both under the headline, 'Falling Out over Srebrenica'.
>
> Cue further letters to the *Guardian*'s ombudsman, Ian Mayes, protesting that such a juxtaposition was further misrepresentation and stimulating a false debate. 'As I presume you are aware, the "debate" was constructed by the editors on the basis of inventions in the article you published', Chomsky wrote.
>
> Mayes, who is also president of the international Organisation of News Ombudsmen, is no longer replying to Chomsky's emails. He was unavailable for comment.[29]

Predictably, the focus was on dissident fury and anger. This was reinforced by the observation that ongoing disagreement provoked 'further letters' from Chomsky to Mayes who was 'no longer replying to Chomsky's emails'. This suggested Mayes had given up on an irate, hectoring Chomsky. In fact, Chomsky told us that Mayes had not replied to *any* of his letters at the time the *Independent*'s piece appeared.

Meanwhile, the *Guardian* had published a piece by columnist Norman Johnson which also smeared Chomsky.[30] From the emails we received, it is clear that many readers were not in on the *Guardian*'s joke – they were unaware that Norman Johnson was a pseudonym, and that the column was intended as a spoof of the 'Cruise Missile Left': commentators such as David Aaronovitch, Nick Cohen, Johann Hari and Christopher Hitchens. Whatever the intention, Johnson's piece struck many people as yet another attack on Chomsky. Given that the paper was now under significant public pressure – having published its initial fabrications about Chomsky, and also the further smear pairing his letter with that of an understandably outraged Bosnian survivor – this 'spoof' was in extremely poor taste, to say the least.

Guardian comment editor Seumas Milne nevertheless responded to one Media Lens reader: 'As to the Norman Johnson article in today's paper, most readers take it to be a spoof column satirising a strand of liberal/former left thinking now in sympathy with the neocon project – so I hardly think it can seriously be regarded as an attack on Chomsky.'[31] Edward Herman, co-author with Chomsky of the book *Manufacturing Consent*, disagreed: 'Johnson obviously tries to be a wit as he writes, but the piece on [Chomsky] drips with venom and is larded with straightforward errors and misrepresentations that are in no way spoofing.' Herman added: 'Johnson has mastered the art of error or lie by implication, arguably more dishonest than a straightforward error or lie.'[32] For example, the Johnson article included this comment:

> It wasn't easy for me, either, when I realised the brilliant academic [Chomsky] whose linguistics lectures had once held me spellbound, that the political theorist I'd revered for his unsentimental computation of Mao Zedong's balance sheet, and firm evaluation of Pol Pot's achievement in creating modern Cambodia, had morphed into an unfeeling appeaser to whom the murder of Milosevic's victims could be assessed with an amoral sophistry that might have been lifted, with barely an adjustment, from the speeches of Douglas Hurd.

It seemed incredible that these words could have been published as a spoof just three days after the *Guardian* had published a letter by Chomsky strongly attacking the *Guardian*'s distortions about essentially the same charge of 'amoral sophistry', and after many emails had already arrived challenging the *Guardian* smear. After all, the charge was clearly taken seriously by senior figures within the *Guardian*. For example, on November 11, the following (badly translated) exchange between the Croatian journal *Globus* and leading *Guardian* columnist and former editor, Peter Preston, was published:

> Q: 'In an interview to [*sic*] the last week's *Guardian* Noam Chomsky stated his opinion about the crime against the Bosniaks in Srebrenica, supporting those who hold that that crime is exaggerated. What do you think of that?'
>
> A: 'I don't agree at all with Chomsky's opinion. I think it's impossible to rewrite history that way. After all, about Srebrenica speak mostly mass graves that were discovered and are still being discovered. I think to deny the crimes like that one in Srebrenica is in vain and wrong, because there is a clear position in the political and intellectual circles about them, to what, I must say, my colleagues from the *Guardian* have contributed a lot. That position is based on irrefutable facts and known scenes from Srebrenica.'
>
> Q: 'Why does Noam Chomsky has a need to revise those facts?'
>
> A: 'I have to admit I don't know. Perhaps it's his need to be controversial? I think the crime in Srebrenica has become part of planetary humanity, like Nazi crimes in the WWII, and it is really strange to draw the attention to oneself by denying that fact. I think that a much more important public duty would be to point out the fact that those who ordered that crime, Karadzic and Mladic, are still at large.'[33]

Preston thus accused Chomsky of 'denying' the crime in Srebrenica, but offered no evidence for this serious accusation. Was this also a spoof? One might have thought Preston would have been aware of the growing furore surrounding the *Guardian*'s fabrications at the time of his comments.

Two days later, Chomsky wrote that he had by then received a print copy of the *Guardian* interview. He responded in an open letter: 'the print version reveals a very impressive effort, which obviously took careful planning and work, to construct an exercise in defamation that is a model of the genre'. Chomsky described the photographs that accompanied the piece:

> One is a picture of me 'talking to journalist John Pilger'. The second is of me 'meeting Fidel Castro.' The third, and most interesting, is a picture of me 'in Laos en route to Hanoi to give a speech to the North Vietnamese.'
>
> That's my life: honoring commie-rats and the renegade who is the source of the word 'pilgerize' invented by journalists furious about his incisive and courageous reporting, and knowing that the only response they are capable of is ridicule.[34]

Chomsky's letter outlined the actual events and background behind the photographs used by the *Guardian*, adding:

> Quite apart from the deceit in the captions, simply note how much effort and care it must have taken to contrive these images to frame the answer to the question on the front page. [Q: Do you regret supporting those who say the Srebrenica massacre was exaggerated? A: My only regret is that I didn't do it strongly enough.]
>
> It is an impressive piece of work, and, as I said, provides a useful model for studies of defamation exercises, or for those who practice the craft. And also, perhaps, provides a useful lesson for those who may be approached for interviews by this journal.
>
> This is incidentally only a fragment. The rest is mostly what one might expect to find in the scandal sheets about movie stars, familiar from such sources, and of no further interest.

The front cover of the October 31, 2005 edition of the *Guardian's* G2 section containing Brockes' piece had an unflattering close-up photograph of Chomsky. This added to the very unpleasant impression that a team of journalists at the *Guardian* had set out to give Chomsky as rough a ride as possible.

BAD ARGUMENTS FOR GOOD FAITH

In its correction and retraction, the *Guardian* accepted that Chomsky had never denied that a massacre took place in Srebrenica. It noted that the headline answer printed at the top of the article was in response to a question that had not been posed to Chomsky in that form in the interview. It also accepted that the juxtaposition of a letter from a survivor of Omarska with Chomsky's letter exacerbated his original complaint.

While this was indeed an unusual and humbling apology from the *Guardian* – Mayes describes it as 'unprecedented in my experience in this job over the past eight years'[35] – it was seriously flawed. Note, for example, the following comment: 'Prof Chomsky has also objected to the juxtaposition of a letter from him ... with a letter from a survivor of Omarska ... At the time these letters were published ... no formal complaint had been received from him. The letters were published by the letters editor in good faith to reflect readers' views.' This was outrageous. In fact, the letters only added to overwhelming evidence that the whole affair was carefully planned and managed at the editorial level. How, after all, could a pair of letters be published under the title 'Falling out over Srebrenica' when one of the letters deplores the massacre and the other (Chomsky's) says nothing at all about it, asserting simply that the author takes no responsibility for anything written in the original interview, where everything relevant was 'fabricated' – the word the *Guardian* asked Chomsky to remove from his letter, but which they knew he had used? This is a logical impossibility, and the editors who paired the letters and wrote the headline are surely capable of elementary logic.

This, and much other evidence, gave the lie to editor Alan Rusbridger's astonishing claim to readers: 'I believe Professor Chomsky's concerns about a wider editorial motive behind the interview, suggested in an open letter, are wholly without foundation.'[36] Mayes also wrote in his correction:

> Both Prof Chomsky and Ms Johnstone, who has also written to the *Guardian*, have made it clear that Prof Chomsky's support for Ms Johnstone, made in the form of an open letter with other signatories, related entirely to her right to freedom of speech. The *Guardian* also accepts that and acknowledges that the headline was wrong and unjustified by the text.
>
> Ms Brockes' misrepresentation of Prof Chomsky's views on Srebrenica stemmed from her misunderstanding of his support for Ms Johnstone. Neither Prof Chomsky nor Ms Johnstone have ever denied the fact of the massacre.

Brockes' misinterpretation surely also stemmed from her 'misunderstanding' of Diana Johnstone's honest and courageous work. In an earlier response, Johnstone added a more general corrective that was missing from the *Guardian* apology:

> Neither I nor Professor Chomsky have ever denied that Muslims were the main victims of atrocities and massacres committed in Bosnia. But I insist that the tragedy of Yugoslav disintegration cannot be reduced to such massacres, and that there are other aspects of the story, historical and political, that deserve to be considered. However, any challenge to the mainstream media version of events is stigmatized as 'causing more suffering to the victims' – an accusation that makes no sense, but which works as a sort of emotional blackmail.[37]

The excellent American dissident David Peterson relished a subsequent, external ombudsman's report on the incident:

> My favorite section of all from the External Ombudsman's Report about his inquiry into the Chomsky affair at the *Guardian*? '17. The original interview

was tape recorded but unfortunately the tape has been partially recorded over. A transcript of sorts exists but the most contentious section of the interview was not available on tape. No one seems to doubt that this was genuine.'[38]

Would anyone dream of suggesting otherwise?

ARRESTING EBULLIENCE: BROCKES DOES KEARNEY

Emma Brockes subsequently interviewed another controversial political figure – *Newsnight's* political editor, Martha Kearney. In this case, there was no talk of compulsive revisionism, apologetics for war crimes, hypocritical personal investments and the like. There was no questioning of the BBC's role in facilitating the invasion and devastation of Iraq – the war was not mentioned. Brockes noted of Kearney: 'Her ebullient style is as arresting as Andrew Marr's and she has none of the self-importance that makes so much political broadcasting unwatchable.' But, like Chomsky, Kearney is not beyond criticism:

'When I ask other TV news hacks about Kearney, the only negative thing anyone says about her is that, while she is very good at contextualising stories, she doesn't always tell you anything you didn't already know.' This might seem unfortunate in a news reporter. Brockes was having none of it:

> This seems unfair, and dismissive of the fact that, for a while now, the public has been fed up of listening to political interviewers who bark so loudly you can't actually hear what they're saying. What Kearney does, by contrast, is widen the angle on a story and make viewers feel as if they are watching something slightly more nuanced than a cock fight between egos.[39]

Kearney read classics at Oxford. Brockes read English at Oxford. A report by the Sutton Trust in 2006 found that '45% of the leading journalists in 2006 – or 56% of those who went to university – attended Oxbridge'.[40]

In a guest media alert published by us, former *Guardian* and *Observer* journalist Jonathan Cook described how journalists are filtered as they rise up the media ranks:

> At the *Guardian*, where I worked for several years, it was seen as a mildly amusing idiosyncrasy that the newspaper recruited the odd trainee direct

from Oxbridge, and more usually from Cambridge. It was generally assumed that this was a legacy of the fact that the paper's editors had traditionally been Cambridge graduates. These journalists invariably worked their way up the paper's hierarchy rapidly.

This preference for untested Oxbridge graduates can probably be explained by the filtering process too. The selected graduates always came from the same predictable backgrounds, and were the product of lengthy filtering processes endured in the country's education system. The *Guardian* appeared to be more confident that such types could be relied on without the kind of 'quality control' needed with other applicants.[41]

It turns out that '54% of the top 100 newspaper editors, columnists, broadcasters and executives were educated privately, despite fee-paying schools catering for 7% of the school population'.[42] In a comment piece on the report, 'All you need to succeed in our meritocracy is privilege', former *New Statesman* editor, Peter Wilby, noted that journalism 'was once one of the most democratic occupations' but is now 'among the most elitist'. Wilby quoted Michael Young, author of *The Rise of the Meritocracy*: 'So assured have the elite become that there is almost no block on the rewards they arrogate to themselves.'[43] Luckily, the high standards of professional training within the industry mean that elite journalists were able to empathise equally with their Oxbridge peers and with the impoverished Iraqi children, mainly under-fives, dying in agony from extreme diarrhoea in Basra's hospitals, while 'no one is doing anything to help them', as local doctors reported in April 2006.[44]

'A TRAIN SPOTTERS' CLUB RUN BY UNCLE JOE STALIN': WELCOME TO OUR WORLD!

We at Media Lens have ourselves been subject to plenty of abuse. In October 2008, financial speculator and *Times* leader writer Oliver Kamm commented on Media Lens: 'That organisation, as my regular readers will recall, is among the most reliable conduits of antisemitism and genocide denial.'[45] This kind of smear may not be pleasant to read, but it is always flattering. After all, one simply has to ask why high-profile journalists would bother to attack a couple of writers writing on a tiny, barely funded website. The web offers a mind-boggling array of different sites, bloggers and vloggers seeking attention – why should we even be noticed by the mainstream? Presumably, if we were as awful as our critics claim, no one would even be aware of our existence. We have always felt that high-profile insults indicate that we are doing something right.

In June 2006, egged on by his editor Roger Alton, the *Observer*'s foreign affairs editor, Peter Beaumont, turned his formidable 'Microscope on Medialens'.[46] Beaumont's researches revealed some altogether unsavoury micro-organisms at the outer rim of media commentary. Media Lens, Beaumont told his readers, produced 'nasty emails', was 'run by a couple of acolytes of Noam Chomsky, and serviced by a couple of dozen die-hard supporters'. We ran an 'irritating site' given to 'hyper-ventilating' at journalists and 'anyone else who needs an email kicking'. As we have noted many times, it matters little how dissidents actually behave or what they argue; the mainstream will always focus on alleged anger, irrational hatred and other mania as a strategy of demonisation. Beaumont was unwilling to challenge even one of the thousands of arguments and facts at that time published in around 2,000 pages of media alerts and in our book *Guardians of Power* – instead, our supposed emotional flaws were the focus of attention. Even the alleged anger of members of the public who read and respond to our media alerts was used to discredit us. The reason is clear – Beaumont knows that we ourselves do *not* send angry abuse to journalists. Very few of our readers do either, if our inbox is any guide.

Beaumont's smear was so far-fetched that it descended into a kind of literary slapstick. He wrote of our website:

> there is no conversation between them and their victims. It is a closed and distorting little world that selects and twists its facts to suit its arguments, a curious willy-waving exercise where the regulars brag about the emails they've sent to people like poor Helen Boaden at the BBC – and the replies they have garnered. Think a train spotters' club run by Uncle Joe Stalin.

Ours is 'a deeply vicious little world as well'. What is so marked is the deep dislike of public participation in even the most urgent and serious political issues of our time. To write an email challenging a journalist's argument is to 'target' them. To encourage readers to send polite comments is to transform journalists into 'victims' of 'an email kicking'. But there is much here that just doesn't add up. What, after all, is the difference between individuals sending messages to the *Guardian*'s Comment is Free website and sending emails direct to media inboxes? Journalists are not compelled to read either the posts or the emails – both can be ignored or deleted. And if our practice of inviting comment is so despicable, why does the *Guardian* website do the same? ('The aim is to host an open-ended space for debate, dispute, argument and agreement and to invite users to comment on everything they read.'[47]) This is chilling stuff. Why does Beaumont not rage against his own newspaper for setting him up for 'an email kicking'?

In reality, journalists like Beaumont resent being subjected to the kind of rational challenges from which they have traditionally been protected. For decades, the mainstream media has wielded massive power with minimal accountability and right of reply. Responses have been limited to whichever letters the editors deigned to allow on the letters page. Because readers knew that serious criticism of media performance had little or no chance of being published, few went to the trouble of putting pen to paper. This is one reason why mainstream journalism is held in comparatively high esteem – there has simply been no means of exposing the superficiality, incompetence and deep structural bias of the media to a wide audience.

'The *Observer* is a conversation', Beaumont continued. 'It is not a commune, so some voices are louder than others, but it remains a conversation. Which is more than can be said for groups such as Medialens with their endless email campaigns. Because there is no conversation between them and their victims.' This could not be further from the truth. We have had profound disagreements with large numbers of journalists but a number of them – people like George Monbiot of the *Guardian*, Andrew Buncombe of the *Independent* and Peter Barron, formerly the BBC *Newsnight* editor – have subsequently expressed respect for, and even agreement with, what we are doing. That has been the result of rational conversation. And of course the *Observer* is not ultimately a 'conversation', in this sense; it is a business. All 'conversation' is required to step carefully around issues threatening the bottom line concern. And so we find no conversation about the impact of the profit motive on freedom of speech. There is no conversation about the *Observer*'s relationship with fossil-fuel advertisers in an age of catastrophic climate change. There is no conversation about the corporate domination of culture, economics, party politics and foreign policy.

The point about the conversation we encourage is that it is not constrained by the unwritten rules of corporate employment, where to be seen as overly critical of media companies or the government can damage, stall or wreck careers.

Beaumont concluded as damningly as possible: 'For journalists like myself, the voice of the disgruntled left we hear is not that of the silent hundreds of thousands I marched with against the war in 2003, but the small, shrill, squeaky voice of an extreme.'

Our experience has been very different. Time and again we have been dismayed to see sincere and reasonable emails from readers met with breathtaking arrogance and contempt. Beaumont's criticism of us, for example, could hardly be squeakier! As for 'shrill', in a 2003 *Observer* online debate, Beaumont advised questioners: 'now please piss off and let some serious posters ask questions'. Another questioner received personal counselling: 'get a life'.[48] 'Shrill' hardly seems adequate in describing the voice of Roger Alton, Beaumont's editor at the *Observer* at the time. Alton replied thus to one polite emailer: 'Have you just been told to write in by those cunts at medialens? Don't you have a mind of your own?'[49] But this earlier exchange between Alton and a restrained and rational reader writing from Seoul, South Korea, says it all for us:

Matey

This is utter bollocks – the piece wasn't compromised. It was fine. Please stop bothering people about such junk.

Roger Alton[50]

Our reader responded:

Thank you for taking the trouble to reply to the email I sent ... Unfortunately, it appears from the tone of your message that my comments are unwelcome and indeed have touched a raw nerve.

I am sorry that you seem to share Peter Beaumont's disdain for a genuine and open dialogue concerning the very real dangers of press impartiality. I feel that the points I raised are valid, and at the very least deserved a civil response. It is therefore disappointing to see the editor of a 'liberal' national newspaper such as the Observer succumb to this kind of anger and rudeness. Your reaction suggests to me that at heart you view your readers merely as passive consumers of knowledge rather than active thinkers struggling to make sense of a complex world.

I would ask you to reflect for a moment on your responsibilities and the contribution – or lack of one – that you are making to the kind of dialogue that would characterise a genuine democracy rather than a notional one.[51]

15
Compassion, Awareness
and Honest Journalism

BIASED IN FAVOUR OF COMPASSION

The mainstream media would have us believe that news reporting is an almost technical task. Journalists are depicted as collecting 'hard facts' on the ground much as a geologist collects rocks for research. Geologists have no emotional attachment to their rocks – journalists should be similarly disinterested. Historian Howard Zinn made the counter-argument: 'I understood early that what is presented as "history" or as "news" is inevitably a selection out of an infinite amount of information, and that what is selected depends on what the selector thinks is important.'[1] After all, 'behind any presented fact ... is a judgement – the judgement that this fact is important to put forward (and, by implication, other facts may be ignored). And any such judgement reflects the beliefs, the values of the historian [or journalist], however he or she pretends to "objectivity".'[2]

In this book, we have provided hundreds of examples of how the presented fact reflects the opinions of journalists. Psychologist Daniel Goleman has explained how even sights and sounds are not neutral perceptions by the time they reach the conscious mind – they have already been subjected to evaluation and value judgement. Researchers have measured the likes and dislikes created in the exact moment of perceiving a word, sound or picture. Goleman commented: 'The tests show that these evaluations are immediate and unconscious, and are applied even to things people have never encountered before, like nonsense words: "juvalamu" is intensely pleasing and "bargulum" moderately so, but "chakaka" is loathed by English-speakers.'[3] Dr Jonathan Bargh, a psychologist at New York University added: 'There's nothing that's neutral. We have yet to find something the mind regards with complete impartiality, without at least a mild judgment of liking or disliking.'[4]

Not only is journalistic 'objectivity' impossible, the attempt to achieve it is morally abhorrent. How can we remain neutral in a world afflicted by poverty and war? What does it mean to be 'impartial' in an age of catastrophic climate change? Is it even sane to declare oneself a disinterested spectator standing between taking action to avert disaster and doing nothing while the support systems of global life collapse? Zinn again made the point well: 'As I told my students at the start of my courses, "You can't be neutral on a moving train." The world is already moving in certain directions – many of them are horrifying. Children are going hungry, people are dying in wars. To be neutral in such a situation is to collaborate with what is going on.'[5] We should abandon, then, the fiction that journalists can or should be disinterested technicians standing neutrally between murderers and their victims, between torturers and the tortured.

But where does this awareness leave us? Does it mean we should be biased, prejudiced, even dishonest, in favour of the victims? Instead it means, first, that we should take the side of compassion against indifference, greed and hatred. Second, we should seek to identify the real causes of human and animal suffering with as much honesty as we are capable – we cannot hope to base real solutions on dishonest analysis and reporting. Third, by implication, compassionate journalism requires that we free ourselves from the root cause of dishonest, destructive journalism – self-serving bias. We will not perceive or expose the true causes of suffering if our primary motivation is to achieve our own welfare, or the welfare of a particular, favoured group – our focus of concern, quite simply, will be elsewhere. It is not possible to perceive or address the true causes of suffering in the Israel–Palestine conflict if we are devoted to the Zionist cause – of course we will see only what we want to see.

An honest journalist is someone who strongly reviles the notion that he should place his interests – his career, his security, his corporation, his class, his country – above the interests of others. She agonises about, feels actually pained by, the thought that she might be subordinating someone else's welfare to her own. The honest journalist does not merely believe, but *feels* that all happiness is of equal value. Thus we find that the best reporting is written out of a sincere motivation to relieve human suffering, impartially. Noam Chomsky and John Pilger do not love Iraqis or Palestinians more than they love Americans and Israelis. Their concern is to challenge policies rooted in greed and indifference that harm human beings. And if we reject the bias inspired by selfish concern, then we must also reject the bias inspired by its close relative – hatred. The problem is not subjectivity, which is unavoidable; it is subjectivity distorted by the lenses of self-centred greed and hatred.

This confronts journalists with a very real dilemma. They are required to report on a world controlled, and harmed, by the same powerful interests. The harm needs to be exposed; but the control implies a capacity to punish those who would do the exposing. Honest journalism, then, requires a deep commitment to the welfare of others – a shallow commitment will quickly vanish under the carrots of conformity and the brickbats of rebellion. This compassionate version of honest journalism is not based on hard science in the way of maths and physics (as the mainstream likes to pretend for its 'objective' version); it is based on ethical judgements, on human values. It is based on the assumption that it is our responsibility to relieve human and animal suffering, that violence is usually the worst solution and should always be the last (far down the list below self-restraint, generosity, forgiveness and tolerance). It rejects the idea that the most powerful should be unleashed to do what they will in the belief that 'survival of the fittest' benefits all. It rejects the idea that even the 'winners' benefit from their greed and violence. It is based on the belief that concern for all, universal compassion, delivers maximum benefits to all.

However reasonable and worthy this may sound, readers may find they have unanswered questions at the back of their minds. For example: 'Why should a journalist, why should any of us, give a damn about other people, actually? Why, in this short, hard life, should we not just take what we can get, fill our boots, and get away with what we can get away with?' These are very reasonable questions. If we are honest (as opposed to righteous), a more compassionate approach to journalism and life must begin here.

SO WHAT DO WE DO?

In an interview with David Barsamian, Noam Chomsky said:

> The question that comes up over and over again, and I don't really have an answer still – really, I don't know any other people who have answers to them – is, 'It's terrible, awful, getting worse. What do we do? Tell me the answer.' The trouble is, there has not in history ever been any answer other than, 'Get to work on it.' There are a thousand different ways to get to work on it.[6]

A subsequent comment by Chomsky suggested that he was aware that this response failed to address the real issue behind the question:

If there is a magic answer, I don't know it. But it sounds to me as if the tone of the questions and part of the disparity between listening and acting suggests – I'm sure this is unfair – 'Tell me something that's going to work pretty soon or else I'm not going to bother, because I've got other things to do.' Nothing is going to work pretty soon, at least if it's worth doing, nor has that ever been the case.[7]

This is exactly right; people are often reluctant to bother, but Chomsky appears not to perceive this as an issue with which to engage. Instead, he generally responds by offering the example of activists in the South facing terrible threats – threats which, he implies, are *real* problems. He has said of Haiti, for example:

Poor people, people in the slums, peasants in the hills, managed to create out of their own activity a very lively, vibrant civil society with grassroots movements and associations and unions and ideas and commitment and hope and enthusiasm and so on, which was astonishing in scale, so much so that without any resources, they were able to take over the political system...

Then you come to the U.S., the best imaginable conditions, and people simply haven't a clue as to how to respond. The idea that we have to go to Haiti to teach them about democracy ought to have everyone in stitches. We ought to go *there* and learn something about democracy. People are asking the question here, What do I do? Go ask some illiterate Haitian peasant. They seem to know what to do. That's what you should do...[8]

In other words, the solution to our lack of motivation, 'Tell me something that's going to work pretty soon or else I'm not going to bother', is to focus on examples that shock and shame us out of our passivity.

There is certainly merit in this approach, and the horrific physical threats faced by the people of Haiti and many other countries are very real. But it is not true that we in the West enjoy 'the best imaginable conditions' for engaging in dissent. As Chomsky has noted many times, we are subject to the most sophisticated and all-pervasive propaganda system the world has ever seen. Our problems are certainly different to those faced by the people of Haiti, but they are nevertheless real and need to be seriously addressed. It is not a sign of manky moral fibre that many of us find it difficult to be motivated to work for progressive change – it is the reality of where we are and how we are controlled. It is a reality we have to deal with.

The fact is that our society trains us every day of our lives to accept selfishness and indifference as the default positions of a 'balanced' individual. Consumer culture relentlessly persuades us to believe that everyone else is happier than we are and that we can be happier, too – *if* we just spend a little harder to buy 'the best a man can get' because 'you're worth it'. Endless films and TV series lampoon activists and altruists as social misfits, as sexual inadequates displacing their frustration; as naïve losers achieving either nothing or disaster. In science fiction films, the well-intentioned priests and hippies who seek dialogue with invading aliens are typically blasted to atoms. It is down to the military and hard-headed scientists to get 'payback' through force. In action films, high-profile individuals who talk in stirring terms of the need to defend the poor and confront the greed of capitalism, are crazed egotists using fine words to camouflage their lust for power and wealth. In one episode of the hugely popular BBC sitcom, *Only Fools And Horses*, young Rodney suddenly becomes obsessed with 'saving the planet'. His family and friends are aghast at this new found altruism until his much older brother, Del Boy, puts him right (to paraphrase): 'Can't you see what's happening? You're missing Cassandra [Rodney's ex-girlfriend] – you've got to get out there and get yourself another girl.' The scales drop from Rodney's eyes. He sees that his 'activism' was really displaced romantic and sexual frustration – he drops the whole nonsense.

Whereas selfishness is sold as young, modern and empowering, activism is sold as old, grim and futile. In response to what was, at the time (September 2002), the greatest anti-war march in a generation, the *Observer* wrote:

> It was back to the old days, too, in terms of types. All the oldies and goodies were there. The Socialist Workers' Party, leafleting outside Temple Tube station by 11 am. ('In this edition: Noam Chomsky in Socialist Worker!'). CND, and ex-Services CND. The Scottish Socialist Party. 'Scarborough Against War and Globalisation', which has a lovely ring of optimism to it, recalling the famous Irish provincial leader column in 1939: 'Let Herr Hitler be warned, the eyes of the Skibereen Eagle are upon him.'[9]

Working for progressive change means going against the social grain. It means taking time and energy out from serving our selves and working for the benefit of others. For many people that sounds about as inviting as a cold bath. The Tibetan Buddhist contemplative, Dilgo Khyentse Rinpoche, summarised our usual level of concern:

At present, when you feel happy yourself, you are probably quite satisfied. Other people may not be feeling happy, but you do not really consider that to be your problem. And when you yourself feel unhappy, you are too preoccupied with being rid of whatever it is that is upsetting you to care, or even remember, that others might be feeling unhappy, too.[10]

The Indian mystic Osho offered this shocking but surely accurate observation:

You don't give, even to those who are very intimate with you. You don't give, even to those who love you. You don't give to your father, your mother, your wife, your children; you simply don't give. You don't know the language of giving. You know only one language: how to get more, how to get more, how to get more from everybody else. You know only one way of thinking, and that is getting.[11]

We of course insist that we do give. We give at birthdays, Christmas, weddings – when we have to. But how many of us find ourselves railing at the thought of giving even twenty minutes of our precious time talking to a close relative on the phone? How agonising do we find it to help someone with a problem if it means *seriously* disrupting our cosy routine? How often do we really give in to the normal way of things? Giving runs so counter to society's prevailing ethos that 'unwarranted' giving arouses intense suspicion – 'What is he/she up to?'

Most of us strongly believe that we are, basically, kind, generous people. The reality is perhaps less glorious. We are, most of us, self-centred, obsessively focused on our own needs down to the smallest detail. As we will see, one of the problems in considering this issue is that it is precisely a function of the strongly egotistical mind to filter out inconvenient facts and ideas – we egotists will not *want* to see the truth of our selfishness. The point we are making is that the possibility of change begins with a recognition of the reality. If we underestimate our self-centredness, we will underestimate the difficulty of generating greater compassion in ourselves and in the society around us – we will be disappointed and disheartened. In our frustration, we may even reject concern for others as impotent and futile. We may even be seduced by the lethal notion that anger, hatred and violence are the most credible, powerful answers to injustice and exploitation. In his book, *The Art Of Loving*, Erich Fromm wrote:

This book ... wants to show that love is not a sentiment which can be easily indulged in by anyone, regardless of the level of maturity reached by him. It wants to convince the reader that all his attempts for love are bound to fail, unless he tries *most actively* to develop his total personality, so as to achieve a productive orientation; that satisfaction in individual love cannot be attained without the capacity to love one's neighbour, without true humility, courage, faith and discipline.[12]

In other words, the task of becoming a more compassionate person is a tremendous challenge. If we are serious, it is a task that needs to become a central focus of our lives over years and decades, just as self-concern has always been. This is nothing to be ashamed of; it is something to be accepted as the reality of who and where we are.

HAPPINESS IS EQUAL: SHANTIDEVA

The kind of compassionate journalist we have been advocating above will be greatly moved by the words of the eighth-century Buddhist sage Shantideva:

Mine and other's pain – how are they different?
Simply, then, since pain is pain, I will dispel it.
What grounds have you for all your strong distinctions?[13]

In his great poem, 'The Way of the Bodhisattva', Shantideva argued that sentient beings are fundamentally equal in one crucial respect: no individual's happiness is more important than any other's. All happiness is equal. All suffering is equal.

As we have discussed, self-centred habits of mind powerfully persuade us to believe that 'my' happiness is much more important than 'your' happiness. After all, is it not obvious that we do not actually feel the pain of others, whereas we do feel our own pain? How could our suffering not matter more to us? And yet Shantideva challenged all such arguments, both obvious and subtle, in proposing that the case for self-centredness cannot be rationally sustained. 'The Way of the Bodhisattva', indeed, is nothing less than a rationalist training manual intended to persuade us that the happiness of others is *more* important than our own happiness!

While we often imagine that the great religions are only too ready to indulge our wishful thinking – providing solace in a soulless universe – Shantideva's argument could hardly go more completely against the grain of what so many of us would like to believe. Shantideva's first proposition, then, is that it is not possible to defend the claim that 'my' happiness is more important than the happiness of any other individual. The second proposition, which follows, is that it is even less reasonable to claim that 'my' happiness is more important than the happiness of *many* others. As a purely mathematical proposition, the happiness of hundreds must be considered of greater importance than the happiness of any single individual. Again, we might like to believe otherwise, but from a purely rational perspective, we are guilty of bias. Additionally, Shantideva argued, we should recognise the debt we owe the other living beings we tend to view with such indifference. If we were to take away all that has been given to us by others, we would be left with nothing – not even our names, our bodies, our language, our ability to eat, walk and talk.

Everything we have, everything we consider so absolutely 'mine', is 'ours' in dependence on others. Any valued possession we happen to call 'mine' was made or grown by others, delivered by others, bought by money paid to us by others in response to work we did for labour they provided. True, the work was 'mine' – but the energy to do the work came from the bodies of animals and plants collected and supplied by others. And the knowledge of how to do the work was provided by numerous formal and informal teachers – in our case, of English language, grammar, writing, politics, philosophy, computer operation ... and so on.

How is it, then, that we can live as though we do not owe anything much to anyone; as though our great ego has done it all, independently, as an act of self-created genius? How is it that we can be so proud of 'our' achievements, as though we existed in a bubble?

It is possible to base our lives on an intellectual acceptance of the equality of self and other described above. We can simply decide that it is unjust, irrational, shameful to place our own needs above the needs of others. We can ignore the clamouring of the self-centred mind – 'It's my life. I want as much as I can possibly get for myself' – and choose to work for their benefit, rather than our own.

Noam Chomsky, we believe, is an example of someone who (independently of Buddhist thought) has based his political activism on the same belief in the equality of suffering. Chomsky argues that a rule of conduct applied to others must also be applied to ourselves. If it is wrong for terrorists to kill American civilians, then it is wrong for American state terrorism to kill Iraqi civilians. If suffering is equal, then it is wrong to benefit from exploitative systems that harm others, and so on.

Chomsky provides a supreme example of the power and dignity of a mind freed from self-centred bias, from preferential distortions that benefit 'me', 'my class', 'my country', 'my necessary illusions'. It is this that separates him from his mainstream critics who we would guess are driven by very different motives. But Shantideva went beyond advocating intellectual acceptance of the equality of self. Using a psychological and metaphysical analysis based on the teachings of the Buddha combined with years of his own intensive meditation, Shantideva rejected not just self-serving bias, but the very existence of the self, the ultimate root of self-centred concern.

THE SELF DELUSION

The Buddhist argument for 'selflessness', or 'sunyata', employed by Shantideva is tremendously sophisticated and challenging – only a brief outline can be attempted here.

His starting point is the observation that, while objects *do* exist, they do not exist in the way that we imagine:

Labelled continuities and aggregates,
Like strings of beads and armies, are like mirages.
Likewise, there is no one hurt by suffering,
For who is there to be oppressed by it?[14]

Thus, the word 'army', for example, is merely a label applied to a collection of soldiers and equipment – the 'army' itself does not exist as an inherently existent object or entity. Wherever we look, we find soldiers and tanks; we never find an army. 'Army', in fact, is just a label produced by our minds – it does not have an independent existence.

Shantideva's point (and this is where the difficulty begins) is that we normally do *not* perceive an army this way, as just a label of the mind. We believe it exists as something slightly more than a label, as something substantially existent in the world. This is an extremely subtle point: Buddhists claim that it can take intense and repeated reflection over a long period of time to identify accurately exactly how it is that we perceive objects as inherently real rather than as mere labels. And here's the real problem: everything is like the army.

To take another example: a forest is made up of trees. Wherever we look, we find only trees – the 'forest' is merely a label applied by the mind. But the same applies to an apparently solid 'car', which is made up of thousands of parts. We do not admire and feel attached to nuts and bolts; we admire our 'car'. Geshe Lhundub Sopa explored the point:

> We believe that a car absolutely exists. So long as we do not analyse it, there is something solid and identifiable as a car. However when we look in detail at the nature of the car, we find there is nothing actually real and independent. Our usual thought *car* is based on many things: a colour, door, floor, roof, engine, and so on. What is the real car? What is so special about *my* car that I care so much about it? The door is not the car. The floor is not the car. The roof is not the car. The steering wheel is not it either. Maybe the engine? But the engine has many parts – so where is the engine? We cannot find it in between the nuts and bolts. Maybe the shape? No. So where is the car? It disappears when we look for it. It is empty of truly, absolutely existing. This does not mean there is no car. The car exists phenomenally or relatively. It is nominally acceptable, understandable, and functional.[15]

Like an 'army' and a 'forest', the car to which we are attached exists only as a label in our minds – in reality it is a collection of parts (and the parts are also made up of parts). Just as an object produced by a mirage is unreal – an illusion produced by a combination of light and air – so objects are a combination of various parts that cause us to perceive a unity that is not actually there.

And when we break down the self into its constituent parts, we find a similar set of constantly changing physical and psychological elements. Nobody believes that his or her arm, eyebrow, or tooth is 'me'. We might assert that our mind is our self, in which case we might ask who possesses what when we talk of 'my mind'? In fact, what we call 'my mind' is a chain of thoughts, and none of these thoughts is 'me'. The thought 'I'm late', is not 'me'. Nor is the thought, 'I must phone.' A thought is a transient mental phenomenon, not a permanent self. And do we believe there is a 'me' that is somehow separate from, or behind, these thoughts? But, Shantideva asks, what would such a self distinct from thought be? How would it manifest itself? What would it do? The self, the 'I', then – like an army, a forest and a car – is a mere label applied to a transient collection of parts. And a label is a creation of the mind that does not exist as a concrete entity in the real world.

If Nietzsche declared 'God is dead!' in the nineteenth century, Shantideva, after the Buddha, declared 'Self is dead!' in the eighth. If modern atheists like to believe that God is a version of the human ego projected on a vast, cosmic canvas, Shantideva showed how atheists make their own impossibly self-directed, independent, God-like, illusory ego the centre of their own universe. For Buddhists, the self is the god that got away!

THE WATCHER

We flit between different notions of self-identity without noticing. If someone hits us, we say 'He hurt me.' At this moment we are identifying our self with our body. If someone tells us we are stupid, we say 'She insulted me.' At this moment we are identifying our self with our mind, not with our body. When we say, 'I saw Susan', we are not talking about her mind, just as we are not talking about her body when we say, 'She's so friendly.'

When an angry thought arises, we embrace it and pretty soon declare 'I'm furious.' At this moment, we are identifying our self not with the body, or the mind, but with a moment of anger in the mind. We tend to think that our mind is made up solely of thoughts; many of us believe that, in fact, we *are* these thoughts – the 'little voice' in our head that is 'me'. On closer inspection, we will find that our thoughts are observed by a watcher, a witnessing consciousness. It is this awareness that notices when a desire arises in our mind, when the fiery pain of desire fills our chest. It notices as the desire wanes and disappears. This watcher is not thought; it is also not a self. It is a capacity for awareness that is able to *observe* external and internal phenomena, including the thoughts and physical parts that we normally believe make up our self.

Consider, for example that, trained by society, tricked by greed, we are convinced that desire makes us happy. We hurriedly chase after desire; we even work hard to stimulate it in the belief that doing so will make us feel good. But Buddhism suggests that if we strengthen our awareness, our capacity to observe thoughts and emotions, we can gain greater insight into our true situation. We will discover, for example, that to desire is to suffer. Osho commented:

> Each desire brings its own misery. You are passing down the road and you see a beautiful car just passing by – a flash – and a desire arises to possess this car. Now you become miserable. Just a moment before you were perfectly okay,

there was no misery, and here this car passes and misery arises. Buddha says, 'Watch.' Just a moment before, you were humming a song and going for a morning walk, and everything was beautiful. The birds were singing and the trees were green, and the morning breeze was cool and the sun was fantastic – everything was beautiful. You were in a poetic world full of joy and verve and gusto, and you were juicy and you were part of this beautiful morning. Everything was simply just as it should be ... And here comes a car ...

Just watch, Buddha says simply watch. Stand by the side of the road and watch – what has happened? Just a small desire arising and you are thrown into hell, and you were almost in heaven. You can change from heaven to hell so many times in twenty-four hours, and you don't watch.[16]

We have powerful assumptions about what makes us happy and unhappy, but we are often utterly mistaken because we simply 'don't watch'. By increasing awareness of what is actually taking place in our heads and our hearts we can gain the capacity for greater freedom and compassion. Why? Because greater awareness reveals that we suffer intensely when we desire and hate. On the other hand, we learn that we experience tranquillity, bliss, when we feel love, compassion and friendliness.

Readers might like to carry out their own personal experiment. Try to cultivate awareness of how you feel when you are angry, greedy, loving, friendly and generous. Rather than chasing thoughts in the usual way, focus on the impact of the thoughts on your mind and happiness. It is this awareness, this personal experience, that has the power to dissolve our entrenched selfish habits – we can come to realise that what we thought was in our own best interests is not. This is not a question of repression, of responding out of guilt or shame; we simply drop what is worthless and adopt what is beneficial as a result of increased awareness. We can realise the great irony of human happiness – that self-centredness takes us *away* from happiness into claustrophobic misery. Our thoughts – heavily propagandised by society – would have us believe otherwise. But our internal watcher, our direct experience, has the power to see through the propaganda.

Why are we focusing on such an apparently esoteric issue at the end of a book about politics? The answer is that we passionately believe that without recognising the psychological depth of self-concern, progressive movements have little real hope of challenging the deeply entrenched forces of greed and hatred in *ourselves* and in the world around us. The novelist Norman Mailer once commented that 'the only way socialism can work is if there is ... some larger sense of things'. Otherwise, socialism becomes just 'the play of egos'.[17] This certainly has been our experience. In the absence of serious analysis of the psychology of self-concern – greed, pride, jealousy and hatred – progressive movements tend to create and collapse; to build out of love and destroy out of anger and egotism. It is the precious self that is so determined to appear 'lefter than thou', so desperate for the limelight. Moreover, to try to force other people to be more compassionate out a sense of moral duty and shame is to inspire great defensiveness, or worse, repression. Greater compassion does not arise out of guilt or shame; it arises out of awareness – specifically, out of the awareness that egotism is a painful prison and concern for others is the path to genuine freedom and happiness.

It takes something truly radical, something that goes to the heart of existence, to shift our self-concern. The kind of evidence we have offered in this book – awareness of the truth of the crimes for which our society is responsible – is not enough. We all know any number of people who have had access to political activism and who have casually shrugged it off. It is precisely the nature of the self-centred mind to filter out facts and ideas that obstruct self-indulgence. It is not enough to address ignorance with political argument, because anger and greed are an *active* form of ignorance – they *repel* counter-arguments. If we are to open minds, we must also open hearts.

A REMOTE DOT ON THE X-AXIS:
ALTRUISM AND HUMAN HAPPINESS

As we discussed in our earlier book, *Guardians of Power*, current research suggests that Buddhist monks who have seen through the lies of selfishness and so reinforced their capacity for compassion, are almost literally 'off the chart' in terms of psychological well-being. This can be dismissed as yet more 'New Age' nonsense, if we like, but the science is serious and credible.

In experiments conducted at the University of Wisconsin, brainwave activity was found to increase 1,200 per cent in Buddhist practitioners meditating on compassion while it barely changed in a control group also attempting to generate compassion.[18] There was a particularly large increase in activity in an area of the brain identified as a centre for emotions associated with well-being. High levels of activity in the left prefrontal cortex have been found in people who simultaneously report feelings of happiness, enthusiasm, joy, high energy and alertness. On the other hand, high levels of activity in a parallel site on the other side of the brain – in the right prefrontal cortex – correlate with reports of distressing emotions such as sadness, anxiety and depression.

The *Independent on Sunday* commented on results scored by French Buddhist monk, Matthieu Ricard:

> out of hundreds of volunteers whose scores ranged from +0.3 (what you might call the [depressed] zone) to –0.3 (beatific) the Frenchman [Ricard] scored –0.45. He shows me the chart of volunteers' results, on his laptop. To find Ricard, you have to keep scrolling left, away from the main curve, until you eventually find him – a remote dot at the beginning of the x-axis.[19]

In her book, *Train Your Mind Change Your Brain*, Sharon Begley, science columnist for the *Wall Street Journal*, noted that in the last 30 years there have been some 46,000 scientific papers studying depression and 400 on the subject of joy. Begley cited Buddhist meditation teacher Alan Wallace:

> Western scientists have an underlying assumption that normal is absolutely as good as it gets ... We in the modern West have grown accustomed to the assumption that the 'normal' mind, in the sense of one free from clinical mental illness, is a healthy one. But a 'normal mind' is still subject to many types of mental distress, including anxiety, frustration, restlessness, boredom, and resentment.[20]

Begley commented that science is now probing the minds of people 'whose powers of attention are far above the norm, whose wellsprings of compassion dwarf those of most people, who have successfully set their happiness baseline at a point that most mortals achieve only transiently before tumbling down to something comfortably above depression but far from what may be possible'. What we learn from these outliers 'may provide the key to raising everyone – or at least everyone who chooses to engage in the necessary mental training – to that level'.[21] Serious exploration of these claims should be part of the progressive response to the horrors that we have documented in this book.

To a greater or lesser extent, we all tend to subordinate the interests of others to self-concern because we believe this is the rational route to happiness. The irony is that the goal we are seeking is found in exactly the opposite direction.

POLISHING THE MEDITATIONAL CROWN JEWELS: TONGLEN

For about twelve years, one of us (Edwards) has been practising a Tibetan Buddhist meditation called tonglen (literally 'giving and taking'), considered one of 'the crown jewels' of Tibetan meditation. Tonglen involves imagining the suffering and happiness of others in order to strengthen our capacity for compassion and love. If this sounds other-worldly or pointless, consider that this, in fact, is what many of us spend much of our time doing anyway.

Who among us, dear reader, does not know the intensity of desire that can be generated by imagining ourselves in the arms of some absent lover? The visualisation involves mere imagination, but the desire is very real. And the more we practise this lusty form of meditation, the stronger our desire becomes. Similarly, we are all experts when it comes to meditating on moments when we have received wounding, vicious insults. Who has not thrashed around the bed at night, sleep a far distant prospect, as a result of this kind of meditation? Over and over again we recall the hurtful comment, visualise the hateful face – the anger that burns in our hearts is, again, very real.

Tonglen works on the same principle. Here is one way to approach this meditation:

1) Imagine that someone very close to you, perhaps someone who has been tremendously kind – a parent, partner or close friend – is in a terrible, suffering situation. Imagine that they are afflicted by unbearable agonies on their death bed (we know it sounds awful, bear with us!). Imagine that they are holding their loved ones for the last time, that they can't bear the thought of never seeing them again. Or imagine that, newly bereaved, they are returning to an empty house, grief-stricken, utterly alone. Imagine that they are filled with suffering and despair. Visualise this misery as a cloud of black smoke surrounding them, and imagine breathing that smoke into your own heart. There, it mingles with another cloud of dense black smoke that represents your own suffering and anxiety, all your problems. Imagine that as the two clouds of smoke meet they are instantly annihilated and replaced by an intense bright light that fills you with peace and happiness. Imagine that as you do this, your loved one is relieved of all suffering – they are suddenly peaceful and calm.

Next, imagine sending your happiness to your loved one as a beam of bright white light that fills their body and mind with peace and inexpressible happiness. Visualise them smiling with joy as they are flooded with happy feelings. Imagine that they have everything they need to make them happy – all health problems are completely relieved; all mental anguish is replaced by complete ease of mind and contentment. If they have always wanted children, imagine their delight at holding their own children for the first time. Whatever it is they want, imagine them receiving it in great happiness. Imagine them living in perfect comfort and security. Above all, imagine them filled with perfect peace and bliss.

2) The second step is to choose someone for whom you have no strong feelings, in either a positive or a negative sense. It could be your bus driver, a local shopkeeper, anyone who stirs no great emotions in you. Do the same visualisation – perhaps imagine them grieving at the hospital beside their lifelong partner, going home to an empty house, grieving alone through the night. Go through the same process as step one. Again imagine breathing in all their unhappiness so that they are instantly relieved. And imagine sending a blissful white light into their heart that fills every pore with happiness satisfying their heart's every desire. Imagine them beaming with happiness, surrounded by loved ones, totally overjoyed and at peace.

3) For step three, think of someone you really dislike, someone annoying, ideally someone who would actually be pleased if something unpleasant happened to you. Again, imagine this person alone, in tears, in some desperate situation – perhaps grieving someone's death, perhaps in agony on their own deathbed. As before, visualise that you absorb their suffering and then send them intense delight and joy. Imagine you are also sending them all good qualities – if they were angry and miserly, they are now beaming with friendliness and generosity of spirit.

Approach this third category with care. It can sometimes be beyond us to feel compassion for someone who has harmed us – the mind finds it unacceptable that we should even try. If that's the case, stoke your compassionate fires by going back to the earlier step of visualising a loved one – and then try again, or perhaps try someone else.

When you attempt these visualisations, you may be dismayed to find that you seem to have no great feelings of care or concern for *anyone*! After a bruising day at work, it may seem that your heart is made of stone. You may even decide that you are a heartless monster and give up. The key thing is not to be deterred, not to take this resistance too seriously. Try to find a chink in the armour of your tough, self-centred mind. Don't try too hard, just maintain a gentle effort every day – try to visualise a loved one who is suffering and try sending them happiness. Then try someone else. Can you think of someone you know who has a terrible problem? Try to imagine how they are feeling; try taking that suffering into yourself and sending them happiness.

As you continue with this, you may be surprised to find that you warm up a bit – you start to feel a glimmer of compassion, of happiness at the thought of someone else's happiness. Generous thoughts may appear in your head for someone you would normally see as a huge pain in the neck. You may also find that any gloom or unhappiness that surrounded you pre-tonglen has been replaced by feelings of happiness, even intense happiness. A despondent mood that a hundred songs, DVDs, phone calls and chocolates failed to shift, may suddenly have been dissipated just by doing this. Sometimes you will not feel much at all. As discussed, this is indeed 'the crown jewel' of meditations – the important thing is to continue with gentle persistence.

Again, it is understandable if this all sounds a bit quaint or even absurd. As discussed, all our lives we have been trained to believe that happiness can be achieved only by getting the good things 'out there'. We have to buy it, swallow it, chase it, grab it, medicate it. And here we are feeling happy simply as the result of sitting and thinking! It seems outrageous – we must be imagining it, making it up. On the other hand, we know only too well that we have never managed to simply make up happiness before – would that we could! As we know, in reality, much of the time happiness has seemed completely out of reach.

Also, we are encouraged to sneer at altruism and concern for others. Even the words 'love' and 'compassion' may elicit a painful cringe of embarrassment (particularly among hardened leftists). But this is an ancient meditation technique that has been practised for more than two thousand years. And it is one of the practices that have so measurably altered the minds of the Buddhist practitioners tested at the University of Wisconsin described above. As mentioned, one of these is the French Buddhist monk, Matthieu Ricard. He has commented on his experience of meditation:

> I have ... come to understand that although some people are naturally happier than others, their happiness is still vulnerable and incomplete, and that achieving durable happiness as a way of being is a skill. It requires sustained

effort in training the mind and developing a set of human qualities, such as inner peace, mindfulness, and altruistic love.[22]

Ricard explains how tonglen can promote these qualities: 'You simply have to do it again and again', Ricard insists. 'It's not so sophisticated.' Imagine someone you already love, wish for her well-being and gradually extend that feeling to others. This should include people you may think of as enemies. As noted in an article in *Psychology Today* magazine:

> The next step is to extend that feeling of compassion to all beings, letting the feeling 'grow and grow and invade your mind so that every single atom of your self is loving kindness and compassion and benevolence', Ricard says. 'You let that linger and linger and become more and more part of your mindstream, and you do it again and again. Eventually it becomes easier, faster and stronger the rest of the time too, not just when you're meditating. It's like riding a horse. In the beginning you have to be very careful not to fall off, but pretty soon you even forget you're on a horse.'[23]

TO ACCOMPLISH THE BENEFIT OF OTHERS

We can continue on our current course, if we like, with the usual personally and politically disastrous results. Alternatively, we can set out on an adventure of intellectual and ethical exploration. It is said that just before he achieved enlightenment, the Buddha saw a leaf floating *upstream*! This is nicely symbolic of the adventure we are advocating – one that goes against the tide of self-centredness, against the apparently irresistible forces of greed and hatred, of violence and retaliation. Greed and hatred may seem all-conquering, but their weakness is that they do not deliver solutions; they do not lead to genuine happiness.

It is not that a self-centred focus is evil, that we should become hair-shirted fanatics denying ourselves all pleasure. It is that we can experiment with a different direction. We can train our minds to focus on the suffering of others; to imagine taking that unhappiness from them and replacing it with intense happiness and peace of mind. How curious, how ironic – the result, extraordinarily, is that we become happier; very much happier if we are willing to make the effort.

As Ricard says, this really is not so sophisticated; it is not rocket science – it is a mundane, straightforward exercise. It does not take great intelligence or will power. We can then begin to use this awareness of the benefits of kindness and compassion to motivate our actions in everyday life. Not just by getting involved in activism, but by changing the whole direction of our lives – away from serving ourselves (through serving greed-driven corporations) and towards helping others.

The real meaning, and real motivation, for engaging in political dissent could not be clearer. Khenpo Karthar Rinpoche has commented:

> Come to an understanding that no matter how it may seem, the root of all suffering is in actuality the desire to accomplish our own benefit and our own aims, and the root of all happiness is the relinquishment of that concern and the desire to accomplish the benefit of others.[24]

Notes

1 NO CONSPIRACY: SOLVING THE PROPAGANDA PUZZLE

1. Channel 4 News presenter, Jon Snow, interviewed by David Edwards, January 9, 2001; http://www.medialens.org/articles/interviews/jon_snow. php
2. http://timesonline.typepad.com/oliver_kamm/2008/12/conflicts-of-in.html
3. Jonathan Cook, 'Intellectual Cleansing – Part 2', media alert, October 7, 2008; http://www.medialens.org/alerts/08/081007_intellectual_cleansing_part2.php
4. Nick Davies, *Flat Earth News*, Chatto & Windus, 2008, p. 111.
5. Manchester *Guardian*, May 5, 1921.
6. Andrew Marr, 'Politicians aren't as loathsome as we think: discuss', *Daily Telegraph*, January 10, 2001.
7. Ralph Nader, interview, RealNews.com, November 4, 2008; http://therealnews.com/t/index.php?option=com_content&task=view&id=31&Itemid=74&jumival=2718
8. Davies, *Flat Earth News*, p. 350.
9. Gideon Spanier, 'In the air', *Evening Standard*, September 6, 2006.
10. Email to Ed Vulliamy, February 27, 2008.
11. Stephen Glover, 'Colourful – and that's not just the Observer editor's language', *Independent*, January 16, 2006.
12. Michael D. Shear, 'Ex-press aide writes that Bush misled U.S. on Iraq', *Washington Post*, May 28, 2008; http://www.washingtonpost.com/wp-dyn/content/article/2008/05/27/AR2008052703679.html
13. Michael Tomasky, 'McClellan's other villain', *Guardian*, May 30, 2008.
14. http://transcripts.cnn.com/TRANSCRIPTS/0805/28/sitroom.01.html
15. Ibid.
16. http://www.salon.com/opinion/greenwald/2008/05/29/yellin
17. Ibid.
18. Ibid.
19. http://www.medialens.org/bookshop/review_herald.php
20. Jon Snow, interview with David Edwards, January 9, 2001; http://www.medialens.org/articles/interviews/jon_snow.php
21. *The Big Idea*, BBC2, broadcast February 14, 1996; http://www.aithne.net/index.php?e=news&id=4&lang=0
22. Barbara Ehrenreich, *Going To Extremes*, Granta, 2008.
23. Email to Media Lens from Ken Waldron, September 25, 2008.
24. Ibid.
25. Email from Tierney to Media Lens, October 1, 2008.
26. Tierney told us his review was published – with the unamusing mention of the US supermarket, and all references to it, removed – on August 16, 2008 (email from Tierney to Media Lens, September 30, 2008).

27. http://www.pressgazette.co.uk/story.asp?sectioncode=1&storycode=420 95&
28. James Erlichman, 'Threat of boycotts "turns firms green"', *Guardian*, October 27, 1988.
29. Email to Media Lens, June 14, 2005.
30. http://www.medialens.org/forum/viewtopic.php?p=9838#9838
31. Email from Greg Philo to Media Lens, September 30, 2008.
32. http://www.guardian.co.uk/commentisfree/2008/oct/01/cherieblair. women
33. Email to Media Lens, June 28, 2008.
34. Email to Media Lens, July 8, 2008.
35. http://www.guardian.co.uk/media/2008/jul/07/pressandpublishing. advertising1
36. Ibid.
37. George Monbiot, 'See you in court, Tony', *Guardian*, November 26, 2002.
38. Email to Monbiot, November 26, 2002. See our series of media alerts, beginning with: http://www.medialens.org/alerts/02/021202_Monbiot_ Iraq.HTM
39. Email to Media Lens, November 26, 2002.
40. David Edwards, 'Unthinkable Thoughts – An Interview With Harold Pinter', Media Lens, January 2000; http://www.medialens.org/articles/ the_articles/articles_2001/de_Pinter.htm
41. Email to Media Lens, November 27, 2002.
42. Email to Media Lens, December 3, 2002.
43. Daniel Goleman, *Vital Lies, Simple Truths: The Psychology of Self-Deception*, Bloomsbury, 1997, p. 158.
44. Quoted in ibid., p. 107.
45. Quoted in ibid., p. 186.
46. Ibid., p. 148.
47. Norman Mailer, *The Time of Our Time*, Little Brown, 1998, p. 457.

2   BBC BALANCE: THE MAGNIFICENT FICTION

1. BBC, Editorial Guidelines; http://www.bbc.co.uk/guidelines/editorial guidelines/edguide/impariality [*sic*].
2. Charlie Courtauld, 'Richard Sambrook: "War coverage has changed for ever. We might end up with a death live on TV"', *Independent*, March 31, 2003.
3. Quoted, Walter J. Rockler, 'War crimes law applies to U.S. too', *Chicago Tribune*, May 23, 1999.
4. Andrew Marr, BBC1, News at Ten, April 9, 2003.
5. Andrew Marr, *My Trade: A Short History of British Journalism*, Macmillan, 2004, p. 279.
6. 'Bush begins tour of Middle East', BBC News online, May 14, 2008.
7. Norman G. Finkelstein, 'First the carrot, then the stick: behind the carnage in Palestine', ZNet, April 18, 2002; http://www.normanfinkelstein.com/ article.php?pg=4&ar=12

8. Forwarded email, Helen Boaden, December 2, 2004.
9. Johann Hari, 'Why the BBC-bashers must not be allowed to destroy public broadcasting', *Independent*, January 30, 2004.
10. ITN News at 6:30, January 31, 2003.
11. Justin Webb, 'Feedback', BBC Radio 4, May 18, 2007.
12. Justin Webb, 'Death to America', BBC Radio 4 series, part three, first broadcast on April 30, 2007; http://www.bbc.co.uk/radio4/deathamerica
13. Email from Peter Barron, forwarded, May 5, 2007.
14. Interview with David Edwards, December 22, 2000, http://www.medialens.org/articles/the_articles/articles_2001/de_Rusbridger_interview.html
15. Interview with David Edwards, January 9, 2001; http://www.medialens.org/articles/interviews/jon_snow.php
16. Sarah Ryle, 'A chief tuned in to financial realities', *Observer*, September 23, 2001.
17. Richard Ingrams, 'We don't need Tony's cronies at the BBC', *Observer*, September 23, 2001.
18. Steve Barnett, 'Right man, right time, for all the right reasons', *Observer*, September 23, 2001.
19. BBC online, 'BBC Trust members'; http://www.bbc.co.uk/bbctrust/about/bbc_trust_members/index.html; accessed March 23, 2009.
20. James Curran and Jean Seaton, *Power Without Responsibility*, fifth edition, 1997, p. 122.
21. Ibid., p. 142.
22. John Pilger, *Hidden Agendas*, Vintage, 1998, p. 496.
23. Email to Media Lens, March 14, 2003.
24. David Miller, 'Media Apologies?', ZNet, June 15, 2004; http://www.zmag.org/znet/viewArticle/8359
25. John Pilger, 'The real first casualty of war', *New Statesman*, April 24, 2006.
26. Paul Reynolds, 'Kosovo: Clinton's greatest foreign test', April 4, 1999; http://news.bbc.co.uk/1/hi/programmes/from_our_own_correspondent/311438.stm
27. Email to Media Lens, September 5, 2005.
28. Forwarded to Media Lens, October 22, 2005.
29. Paul Wood, defence correspondent, BBC1, News at Ten, December 22, 2005.
30. Email to Media Lens, January 5, 2006.
31. Cited by Noam Chomsky, interview with Michael Albert, 'Iraq: yesterday, today, and tomorrow', ZNet, December 27, 2006; http://www.zmag.org/znet/viewArticle/2449
32. Email to Media Lens, January 20, 2006.
33. Email to Helen Boaden, January 20, 2006.
34. Email to Media Lens, January 31, 2006.
35. Matt Frei, BBC1, *Panorama*, April 13, 2003.
36. Email to Media Lens, April 14, 2005.
37. Email to Media Lens, December 21, 2006.
38. Email to Media Lens, September 9, 2007.

39. Reply from Roger Hermiston, Assistant Editor, *Today*; forwarded to Media Lens, November 19, 2006.
40. 'Lambasting for the "trendy Left-wing bias" of BBC bosses', *Daily Mail*, June 18, 2007.
41. Ibid.
42. Ibid.
43. Ibid.
44. Quoted in Nicole Martin, 'BBC viewers angered by its "innate liberal bias"', *Daily Telegraph*, June 19, 2007.
45. Tim Luckhurst, 'As John Humphrys announces his retirement. The giant the BBC hasn't got the guts to replace', *Daily Mail*, May 3, 2005.
46. Andrew Marr, 'Hail to the chief. Sorry, Bill, but this time we're talking about Tony', *Observer*, May 16, 1999.
47. '"The media is a feral beast, tearing people to pieces," the full speech', *Independent*, June 13, 2007.
48. http://www.monbiot.com/archives/2004/10/06/no-longer-obeying-orders
49. Danny Schechter, 'Why the latest news about online news ain't so good', March 29, 2000; http://www.mediachannel.org/views/dissector/lessnews.shtml

3 BACK-TO-BACK BIAS: AN A–Z OF BBC PROPAGANDA

1. Andrew Marr, BBC1, News at Ten, April 9, 2003.
2. http://en.wikipedia.org/wiki/Andrew_Marr#Politics_and_bias
3. 'No charges over Iraq video riots', BBC News online, January 4, 2007; http://news.bbc.co.uk/1/hi/uk/6230711.stm
4. http://www.youtube.com/results?search_query=british+troops+beating
5. '2001, Prescott punches protestor', BBC News online; http://news.bbc.co.uk/onthisday/hi/dates/stories/may/16/newsid_4098000/4098929.stm
6. Adam Curtis, Email to Editors, June 18, 2002.
7. Ilan Pappé, 'The Geneva bubble', *London Review of Books*, January 8, 2004; http://www.lrb.co.uk/v26/n01/papp01_.html
8. Bertrand Russell, January 31, 1970, http://en.wikipedia.org/wiki/Bertrand_Russell#Final_years_and_death
9. Mark Urban, '"Can-do" spirit of US troops in Baghdad', BBC News online, May 17, 2007; http://news.bbc.co.uk/go/pr/fr/-/1/hi/programmes/from_our_own_correspondent/6663513.stm
10. Ibid.
11. Aaron Glantz and Iraq Veterans Against the War, *Winter Soldier Iraq And Afghanistan: Eyewitness Accounts of the Occupations*, Haymarket Books, 2008, p. 61.
12. Ibid., p. 26.
13. Email forwarded by numerous Media Lens readers, July 13 onwards, 2005.
14. Gabriele Zamparini, 'BBC and Fallujah: war crimes, lies and omerta', November 10, 2005; http://www.thecatsdream.com/blog/2005/11/

bbc-and-fallujah-war-crimes-lies-and.htm. And 'The BBC, of course!', November 16, 2005; http://www.thecatsdream.com/blog/2005/11/bbc-of-course.htm

15. James Hider, 'US soldiers set to move in on martyrs' land', *The Times*, November 12, 2004.

16. Kim Sengupta, 'Iraq in crisis: unarmed civilians killed, say Iraqis', *Independent*, November 24, 2004. See also the archived journalism of Dahr Jamail at http://dahrjamailiraq.com, as well as Dahr Jamail's excellent book, *Beyond the Green Zone: Dispatches From an Unembedded Journalist in Occupied Iraq*, Haymarket Books, 2007.

17. Dahr Jamail, '800 civilians feared dead in Fallujah', Inter Press Service, November 16, 2004.

18. IRINnews.org, 'Death toll in Fallujah rising, doctors say', January 4, 2005; http://www.irinnews.org/report.asp?ReportID=44904&SelectRegion=Middle_East&SelectCountry=IRAQ

19. Paul Wood, 'Heated debate over white phosphorus', BBC News online, November 17, 2005; http://news.bbc.co.uk/newswatch/ukfs/hi/newsid_4440000/newsid_4441700/4441798.stm

20. 'Did BBC ignore weapons claim?', BBC News online, April 14, 2005; http://news.bbc.co.uk/newswatch/ukfs/hi/newsid_4390000/newsid_4396600/4396641.stm

21. Email to Media Lens, March 21, 2005.

22. Paul Wood, Fallujah, BBC Radio 4, May 6, 2008; http://www.bbc.co.uk/radio4/news/pip/m7a8j

23. Email to Media Lens, May 12, 2008.

24. Peter Beaumont, 'Gaza desperately short of food after Israel destroys farmland', *Observer*, February 1, 2009; http://www.guardian.co.uk/world/2009/feb/01/gaza-food-crisis

25. 'BBC defends Gaza appeal decision', BBC News online, January 22, 2009; http://news.bbc.co.uk/1/hi/uk/7846150.stm

26. 'UK millions pour in to Kosovo appeal', BBC News online, April 6, 1999. See David Bracewell's excellent work on this in our forum: http://www.medialens.org/forum/viewtopic.php?t=2934

27. 'Blair promises to help refugees', BBC News online, April 5, 1999; http://news.bbc.co.uk/1/hi/uk_politics/312024.stm

28. 'Hiroshima remembers atomic bomb', BBC News online, August 6, 2005; http://news.bbc.co.uk/1/hi/world/asia-pacific/4748027.stm

29. Radiation Effects Research Foundation, A Cooperative Japan–US Research Organisation, Frequently Asked Questions; http://www.rerf.or.jp/general/qa_e/qa1.html

30. Gar Alperovitz, *The Decision to Use the Atomic Bomb*, Vintage Books, 1996. Alperovitz first advanced his argument in his 1965 book, *Atomic Diplomacy*, Simon & Schuster.

31. Tsuyoshi Hasegawa, *Racing the Enemy: Stalin, Truman, and the Surrender of Japan*, Harvard University Press, 2005, p. 99.

32. Ibid., pp. 299–300.

33. 'Mid-East executions are condemned', BBC News online, April 20, 2006; http://news.bbc.co.uk/go/pr/fr/-/1/hi/world/middle_east/4925922.stm

34. 'US death toll in Iraq hits 2,000', October 26, 2005; http://news.bbc. co.uk/1/hi/world/middle_east/4376812.stm
35. Email to Media Lens from BBC complaints personnel, October 27, 2005.
36. Email forwarded to Media Lens, October 31, 2005.
37. Radiation Effects Research Foundation; http://www.rerf.or.jp/general/ qa_e/qa1.html
38. '"World backs Lebanon offensive"', BBC News online, July 27, 2006.
39. BBC News 24, August 1, 2006.
40. BBC1, Six O'Clock News, December 21, 2006.
41. Thom Shanker, Eric Schmitt and Richard A. Oppel Jr., 'Military expected to report marines killed Iraqi civilians', *New York Times*, May 25, 2006.
42. Tony Perry and Julian E. Barnes, 'Photos indicate civilians slain execution-style', *Los Angeles Times*, May 27, 2006. See media alert: http://www. medialens.org/alerts/06/060530_silence_in_the.php
43. Suzanne Goldenberg, 'Marines may face trial over Iraq massacre', *Guardian*, May 27, 2006; http://www.guardian.co.uk/world/2006/may/27/ iraq.topstories3
44. 'US Marine captain to face Haditha charges – lawyer', Reuters, December 19, 2006.
45. Matt Frei, BBC1, Six O'Clock News, December 21, 2006.
46. Glantz and Veterans, *Winter Soldier*, p. 100.
47. 'Prospects for Thursday 11th September', BBC News online, September 11, 2008; http://www.bbc.co.uk/blogs/newsnight/fromthewebteam/2008/09/ prospects_for_thursday_11th_se.html
48. Robert Plummer, 'Little progress on halting Iraq's decay', BBC News online, September 6, 2007; http://news.bbc.co.uk/1/hi/business/6977728. stm
49. Email from Media Lens to Robert Plummer, September 6, 2007.
50. www.platformlondon.org
51. Email from Robert Plummer, September 7, 2007.
52. Email to Robert Plummer, September 7, 2007.
53. 'Chile's general dies', BBC News online, December 10, 2006; http://search. bbc.co.uk/cgi-bin/search/results.pl?q=pinochet+and+kendall&scope=all &edition=d&tab=all&recipe=all
54. 'Obituary: Augusto Pinochet', BBC News online, December 10, 2006; http://news.bbc.co.uk/go/pr/fr/-/1/hi/world/americas/472707.stm
55. Dan Sabbagh, 'Wanted: new BBC Rottweiler to strike fear into political classes', *The Times*, February 11, 2008.
56. Broadcast BBC Election Night Special, May 6, 2005; video and transcript available at: http://www.informationclearinghouse.info/article8763. htm
57. Jeremy Paxman, 'Tuesday, 26 September, 2006', BBC News online; http:// news.bbc.co.uk/1/hi/programmes/newsnight/5382748.stm
58. 'On American imperialism and British me too-ism: Noam Chomsky interviewed by Jeremy Paxman', BBC *Newsnight*, May 19, 2004; http:// news.bbc.co.uk/1/hi/programmes/newsnight/3732345.stm

59. Quoted in John Pilger, 'The truths they never tell us: behind the jargon about failed states and humanitarian interventions lie thousands of dead', *New Statesman*, November 26, 2001.
60. Jonathan Head, 'The lasting legacy of Suharto', BBC News online, January 27, 2008; http://news.bbc.co.uk/go/pr/fr/-/2/hi/asia-pacific/7183191. stm
61. Email forwarded to Media Lens, January 28, 2008.
62. BBC News online, November 5, 2006.
63. Sabrina Tavernise, *New York Times*, November 6, 2006.
64. BBC1, Six O'Clock News, April 9, 2003.
65. Glantz and Veterans, *Winter Soldier*, p. 20.
66. 'Red cross horrified by number of dead civilians', April 3, 2003; http://www.ctv.ca/servlet/ArticleNews/story/CTVNews/1049413227648_10
67. 'Breakfast TV host Kaplinsky weds', BBC News online, August 22, 2005; http://news.bbc.co.uk/1/hi/entertainment/4172110.stm
68. BBC1, Six O'Clock News, October 1, 2004.
69. Mark Urban, 'Embedded with US surge troops', *Newsnight*; http://news.bbc.co.uk/player/nol/newsid_6650000/newsid_6655700/6655705. stm?bw=bb&mp=rm
70. Media alert, 'Newsnight diplomatic editor responds', May 31, 2007; http://www.medialens.org/alerts/07/070531_exchange_with_bbc.php
71. Media alert, 'Illegal, immoral, unwinnable: a British Army officer replies to Mark Urban', June 1, 2007; http://www.medialens.org/alerts/07/070601_ illegal_immoral_unwinnable.php
72. BBC1, Six O'Clock News, August 15, 2007.
73. BBC News online, 'US surge "failure" says Iraq poll', September 10, 2007; http://news.bbc.co.uk/1/hi/world/middle_east/6983841.stm
74. http://news.bbc.co.uk/1/hi/business/6977728.stm
75. Patrick Cockburn, 'Al-Sadr ceasefire allows troops to enter Shia slum', *Independent*, May 13, 2008; http://www.independent.co.uk/news/world/ middle-east/alsadr-ceasefire-allows-troops-to-enter-shia-slum-827012. html
76. BBC1, Lunchtime News, May 14, 2006.
77. BBC1, Six O'Clock News, May 12, 2006.
78. 'BBC's Grade wants Humphrys report', September 3, 2005; http://news. bbc.co.uk/1/hi/entertainment/tv_and_radio/4212016.stm
79. Owen Gibson and Sophie Kirkham, 'BBC reprimands "misguided" John Humphrys', *Guardian*, September 7, 2005.
80. Tom Baldwin, Andrew Pierce and Rhiannon James, 'The BBC got it right over sexed-up Iraq documents', *The Times*, September 3, 2005.
81. Matt Born, 'Humphrys "smears" and the link to Campbell's former aide', *Daily Mail*, September 6, 2005.
82. Baldwin et al., 'The BBC got it right over sexed-up Iraq documents'.
83. Ibid.
84. John Kampfner, 'A very corporate loss of nerve', *New Statesman*, October 10, 2005.
85. Gibson and Kirkham, 'BBC reprimands "misguided" John Humphrys'.
86. Kampfner, 'A very corporate loss of nerve'.

87. 'Journalists banned from poking fun at politicians', *Daily Mail*, May 31, 2006.
88. Ibid.
89. http://www.amazon.co.uk/gp/product/product-description/190602152X/ref=dp_proddesc_0?ie=UTF8&n=266239&s=books
90. Jeremy Bowen, 'Middle East on the road to change', BBC News online, January 2, 2006; http://news.bbc.co.uk/go/pr/fr/-/1/hi/world/middle_east/4551726.stm
91. Stephen Mawhinney, email forwarded to Media Lens, January 24, 2005.
92. Jonathan Beale, 'US nurtures key South Asia ties', BBC News online, March 2, 2006; http://news.bbc.co.uk/1/hi/world/south_asia/4759378.stm
93. David Aaronovitch, 'A few inconvenient facts about Saddam', *Guardian*, January 8, 2003.
94. David Aaronovitch, 'Dear marcher, please answer a few questions', *Guardian*, February 18, 2003.
95. Peter Wilby, 'To judge from my e-mails', *New Statesman*, September 5, 2005.
96. Mark Lawson, 'The Blair Years: economical with the candour', *Guardian*, November 17, 2007.
97. Helen Boaden, email forwarded to Media Lens, July 27, 2007.
98. Francis Elliott, 'Media Diary – Helen the hidden', *Independent*, November 26, 2006; http://www.independent.co.uk/news/media/the-tossers-who-could-win-for-the-tories-425799.html

4 CLIMATE CHAOS: KEEPING MADNESS MAINSTREAM

1. Erich Fromm, *The Sane Society*, Routledge, 1955, pp. 14–15.
2. Paul Rincon, 'Greenland ice swells ocean rise', BBC News online, February 16, 2006; http://news.bbc.co.uk/1/hi/sci/tech/4720536.stm
3. H.J. Schellnhuber, ed., *Avoiding Dangerous Climate Change*, Cambridge University Press, 2006.
4. IPCC 4th Assessment Report, Working Group 1 report, summary for policymakers, published 2 February 2007; http://www.ipcc.ch/SPM2feb07.pdf
5. Ibid., p. 10, italics in original.
6. James Hansen et al., 'Climate change and trace gases', *Philosophical Transactions of the Royal Society A*, 365, 1925–54, 2007.
7. James Hansen, 'Global Warming Twenty Years Later: Tipping Points Near', presentation at the National Press Club, and briefing to the House Select Committee on Energy Independence & Global Warming, June 23, 2008; http://www.columbia.edu/~jeh1/2008/TwentyYearsLater_20080623.pdf
8. Maxine Frith, 'In the middle of the desert: a monument to ecological folly', *Independent*, December 3, 2005.

9. FoE, 'Government and industry must do more on greener cars', November 10, 2005; http://www.foe.co.uk/resource/press_releases/government_and_industry_mu_09112005.html
10. Andy Rowell, Speech to Climate Change Action Meeting, London, May 2007.
11. Interview with Media Lens, December 13, 2005.
12. Marcus Fairs, 'Travel special: Roman holidays', *Independent on Sunday*, February 4, 2007.
13. Oliver James, *Affluenza*, Vermillion, 2007, p. 284.
14. Juliet Eilperin, 'Climate shift tied to 150,000 fatalities', *Washington Post*, November 17, 2005; http://www.washingtonpost.com/wp-dyn/content/article/2005/11/16/AR2005111602197.html
15. Christopher Booker, 'A turning point in climate change', *Sunday Telegraph*, March 11, 2007.
16. Melanie Phillips, 'The emperor's green new clothes', March 9, 2007; http://www.melaniephillips.com/diary/?p=1467
17. 'Slaughterhouse three', *Financial Times*, March 10, 2007.
18. '"Global warming is lies" claims documentary', *Life Style Extra*, March 4, 2007; http://www.lse.co.uk/ShowStory.asp?story=CZ434669U&news_headline=global_warming_is_lies_ claims_documentary
19. Carl Wunsch's website; http://ocean.mit.edu/~cwunsch/papersonline/channel4response
20. Geoffrey Lean, 'Climate change: an inconvenient truth ... for C4', *Independent*, March 11, 2007; http://news.independent.co.uk/environment/climate_change/article2347526.ece
21. Steve Connor, 'The real global warming swindle', *Independent*, March 14, 2007.
22. Real Climate, March 9, 2007; http://www.realclimate.org/index.php/archives/2007/03/swindled
23. Anjana Ahuja, 'It's hot, but don't blame the Sun', *The Times*, September 25, 2006.
24. Wunsch; http://ocean.mit.edu/~cwunsch/papersonline/channel4response
25. Tony Jones, 'Journalist puts global warming sceptics under the spotlight', Australian Broadcasting Corporation, March 7, 2005; http://www.abc.net.au/lateline/content/2005/s1318067.htm
26. George Monbiot, 'Beware the fossil fools', *Guardian*, April 27, 2004; http://environment.guardian.co.uk/climatechange/story/0,,1829315,00.html
27. Ofcom Swindle Complaint website, http://www.ofcomswindlecomplaint.net
28. Ofcom Broadcast Bulletin, Issue 114, p. 14, July 21, 2008; http://www.ofcom.org.uk/tv/obb/prog_cb/obb114/issue114.pdf
29. Hamish Mykura, 'It's not we who make the public sceptical on climate change', *Guardian*, July 22, 2008.
30. Press release, 'Royal Society response to OFCOM decision on "The Great Global Warming Swindle"', July 21, 2008; http://royalsociety.org/news.asp?id=7901
31. See George Monbiot, 'The revolution has been televised', *Guardian*, December 18, 1997; http://www.monbiot.com/archives/1997/12/18/the-revolution-has-been-televised

32. Lean, 'Climate change: an inconvenient truth ... for C4'.
33. Paul McCann, 'Channel 4 told to apologise to Greens', *Independent*, April 2, 1998.
34. Quoted in Sharon Beder, *Global Spin: The Corporate Assault on Environmentalism*, Green Books, 1997, p. 92.
35. Juliette Jowett, 'Poll: most Britons doubt cause of climate change', *Observer*, June 22, 2008.
36. Mark Lynas, 'Climate change is no longer just a middle class issue', *Guardian*, July 2, 2008.
37. Martin Hickman, 'Earth's ecological debt crisis: mankind's "borrowing" from nature hits new record', *Independent*, October 9, 2006.
38. Harry Shutt, *The Decline of Capitalism*, Zed Books, 2005, p. 7.
39. Ibid., p. 114.
40. Martin Luther King, 'On racism, poverty, capitalism, and other big questions', The Southern Christian Leadership Conference Presidential Address, 16 August 1967; http://www.hartford-hwp.com/archives/45a/628.html
41. Quoted in Paul Street, 'Martin Luther King, Jr., Democratic Socialist', ZNet commentary, January 14, 2006; http://www.zmag.org/Sustainers/Content/2006-01/14street.cfm
42. Franz Broswimmer, *Ecocide*, Pluto Press, 2002, p. 57.
43. Ibid., quoted p. 81.
44. Michael McCarthy, 'Global warming: your chance to change the climate', *Independent*, March 28, 2006.
45. Colin Challen, 'We must think the unthinkable, and take voters with us', *Independent*, March 28, 2006.
46. Mick Hume, 'Today's militants – a cream-puff army out for a jolly ideological picnic', *The Times*, March 31, 2006.
47. Quoted by Ian Mayes, 'Flying in the face of the facts', *Guardian*, January 24, 2004.
48. Leader, 'Climate change: hot air but no action', *Guardian*, March 29, 2006.
49. 'Archbishop blasts "unchristian" Bush', *Evening Standard*, March 28, 2006.
50. George Monbiot, 'In this age of diamond saucepans, only a recession makes sense', *Guardian*, October 9, 2007.
51. John Willman and Kate Burgess, 'Climate change "not a business priority"', *Financial Times*, June 4, 2007.
52. Email to Tim Lewis, February 12, 2007.
53. Independent News & Media website, http://www.inmplc.com/main.php?menu=menu2&mb=cp
54. Anthony O'Reilly, Independent News & Media Plc Annual Report 2004, p. 3.
55. Joel Bakan, *The Corporation*, Constable, 2004, p. 50.
56. Quoted in *The Oxford Dictionary of Political Quotations*, Oxford University Press, 2001, p. 350.
57. Greg King, email to Tim Lewis, February 8, 2007.

5   PLAN A/PLAN B: THE DOWNING STREET MEMO

1. Article 6, Charter of the International Military Tribunal, August 8, 1945; http://www.law.umkc.edu/faculty/projects/ftrials/nuremberg/NurembergIndictments.html
2. http://www.independent.co.uk/news/world/americas/bushs-fury-as-exspokesman-twists-the-knife-837678.html
3. Michael D. Shear, 'Ex-press aide writes that Bush misled U.S. on Iraq', *Washington Post*, May 28, 2008; http://www.washingtonpost.com/wp-dyn/content/article/2008/05/27/AR2008052703679_pf.html
4. 'Gen. Wesley Clark weighs presidential bid: "I think about it everyday"', *Democracy Now!*, March 2, 2007; http://www.democracynow.org/article.pl?sid=07/03/02/1440234
5. Richard Norton-Taylor, 'WMD claims were "totally implausible"', *Guardian*, June 20, 2005.
6. Michael Smith, 'Blair planned Iraq war from start', *Sunday Times*, May 1, 2005.
7. Ibid.
8. Ibid.
9. Ibid.
10. Michael Smith, 'Ministers were told of need for Gulf war "excuse"', *Sunday Times*, June 12, 2005.
11. Ibid., our emphasis.
12. Michael Smith, 'RAF bombing raids tried to goad Saddam into war', *Sunday Times*, May 29, 2005.
13. Ibid.
14. Michael Smith, 'The real news in the Downing Street memos', *Los Angeles Times*, June 23, 2005; http://www.latimes.com/news/opinion/commentary/la-oe-smith23jun23,0,1838831.story
15. 'War with Iraq not inevitable – Straw', January 6, 2003; http://news.bbc.co.uk/1/hi/uk_politics/2630155.stm
16. Ibid.
17. Jonathan Freedland, 'Campaign 05: It won't be the names that matter', *Guardian*, May 3, 2005.
18. Smith, 'Blair planned Iraq war', our emphasis.
19. Ibid.
20. Cited on *Panorama*, 'Iraq: Tony and the Truth', BBC1, 10.15 p.m., March 20, 2005; http://www.informationclearinghouse.info/article8579.htm
21. David Cracknell and Sarah Baxter, 'Allies set date for Iraq war', *Sunday Times*, February 23, 2003.
22. 'Blair speech – key quotes', February 15, 2003; http://news.bbc.co.uk/1/hi/uk_politics/2765763.stm
23. Cited on *Panorama*, 'Iraq: Tony and the Truth'.
24. Ibid.
25. Cited on *Panorama*, 'Iraq: Tony and the Truth'.
26. Smith, 'The real news in the Downing Street memos'.
27. Ibid.
28. Sidney Blumenthal, 'Blinded by the light at the end of the tunnel', *Guardian*, June 23, 2005.

29. Rupert Cornwell, 'Bush policies blocked as US mood on Iraq sours', *Independent*, June 17, 2005.
30. Andrew Gumbel, 'Americans turn against Bush and a war on Iraq that is getting nowhere', *Independent*, June 9, 2005.
31. 'In the air', *Evening Standard*, May 4, 2005.
32. 'PM hid truth on ousting Saddam', *Express*, May 2, 2005.
33. Ibid.
34. Christopher Adams and Ben Hall, 'Labour targets key marginals', *Financial Times*, May 2, 2005.
35. Christopher Adams, 'Blair defends decision for war with Iraq', *Financial Times*, May 2, 2005.
36. Ibid.
37. Richard Norton-Taylor and Patrick Wintour, 'Election 2005: Papers reveal commitment to war', *Guardian*, May 2, 2005.
38. Raymond Whitaker, '05.05.05 Election Special: evidence reveals Blair's true intention for war', *Independent on Sunday*, May 1, 2005.
39. Ibid.
40. Melissa Kite and Sean Rayment, 'If the political context is right, people will support "regime change", said Blair', *Sunday Telegraph*, May 1, 2005.
41. Jonathan Freedland, 'Yes, they did lie to us', *Guardian*, June 22, 2005.
42. Ibid.
43. L. Tolstoy, 'Letters to the liberals', *Writings On Civil Disobedience and Non-Violence*, New Society, 1987, p. 192.

6   MIND YOUR METHODOLOGY:
KILLING THE 2004 *LANCET* REPORT

1. Terry Kirby and Elizabeth Davies, 'Iraq conflict claims 34 civilian lives each day as "anarchy" beckons', *Independent*, July 20, 2005.
2. Terry Kirby, email to David Edwards, July 22, 2005.
3. Leader, 'The true measure of the US and British failure', *Independent*, July 20, 2005.
4. David Edwards to Mary Dejevsky, July 21, 2005.
5. Mary Dejevsky to David Edwards, August 10, 2005.
6. Les Roberts, email to Media Lens, August 22, 2005.
7. Email to Media Lens, September 1, 2005.
8. Hrvoje Hranjski and Victoria Brittain, '2,600 a day dying in Congolese war', *Guardian*, June 10, 2000.
9. Quoted in Lila Guterman, 'Researchers who rushed into print a study of Iraqi civilian deaths now wonder why it was ignored', *The Chronicle of Higher Education*, January 27, 2005; http://chronicle.com/free/2005/01/2005012701n.htm
10. 'Part one of the speech by prime minister, Tony Blair, at the Labour Party conference', *Guardian*, October 2, 2001.
11. David Hughes, 'No inquiry into Iraq death toll, says Blair', *Daily Mail*, December 9, 2004.
12. 'This week's big issues: new attack on Blair's Iraq policy', *Independent*, December 5, 2004.

13. Patrick Wintour and Richard Norton-Taylor, 'No 10 challenges civilian death toll', *Guardian*, October 30, 2004.
14. Cited in Guterman, 'Researchers who rushed into print'.
15. Ibid.
16. Colin Brown, 'Blair petitioned to set up inquiry into Iraqi war dead', *Independent*, December 8, 2004.
17. Guterman, 'Researchers who rushed into print'.
18. Ibid.
19. Ibid.
20. Email to Media Lens, November 1, 2004.
21. Email to Media Lens, October 30, 2004.
22. Sam Lister, 'Body-count report makes a mockery of Labour's "passion" for statistical analysis', *The Times*, November 23, 2004.
23. Stephen Fidler, 'Lies, damned lies and statistics', *Financial Times*, November 19, 2004.
24. Patrick Cockburn, 'Terrified US soldiers are still killing civilians with impunity', *Independent on Sunday*, April 24, 2005.
25. Hranjski and Brittain, '2,600 a day dying in Congolese war'.
26. Leader, 'Catastrophe in Congo', *Washington Post*, June 24, 2000.
27. Karl Vick, 'Death toll in Congo war may approach 3 million', *Washington Post*, April 30, 2001.
28. Didi Schanche, 'War deaths on "horrifying" rise, IRC says', *Washington Times*, May 10, 2001.
29. Norimitsu Onishi, 'African numbers, problems and number problems', *New York Times*, April 18, 2002.
30. James Astill, 'Away from the world's gaze 4.7m die in Congo', *Guardian*, April 8, 2003.
31. Leader, 'The *Lancet*'s Politics', *Washington Times*, June 23, 2005.
32. Helle Dale, 'Biased coverage in Iraq', *Washington Times*, December 1, 2004.
33. Hassan M. Fattah, 'Civilian toll in Iraq is placed at nearly 25,000', *New York Times*, July 20, 2005.
34. Jamie Doward, 'Death in the desert: why I was right on the 100,000 dead', *Observer*, November 7, 2004.
35. 'For the record', *Observer*, November 14, 2004.
36. John Allen Paulos, 'The vital statistics of war', *Guardian*, December 16, 2004.
37. John Allen Paulos, email to Media Lens, September 7, 2005.
38. John Rentoul, 'We should be counting the dead in Iraq, but let's not get the figures out of proportion like this', *Independent*, December 10, 2004.
39. John Rentoul, 'Islam, blood and grievance', *Independent*, July 24, 2005.
40. Peter Wilby, 'To judge from my e-mails', *New Statesman*, September 5, 2005.

7   ONE MILLION DEAD AND COUNTING: THE 2006 *LANCET* REPORT AND BEYOND

1. Gilbert Burnham, Riyadh Lafta, Shannon Doocy, Les Roberts, 'Mortality after the 2003 invasion of Iraq: a cross-sectional cluster

sample survey', http://www.thelancet.com/journals/lancet/article/PIIS0140673606694919/fulltext

2. 'Methodology in madness', *St. Louis Post-Dispatch*, October 15, 2006.
3. Ben Russell, 'Lancet back at centre of controversy', *Independent*, October 12, 2006.
4. Leader, 'Trials and errors', *Guardian*, October 12, 2006.
5. Malcolm Ritter, 'Bush dismisses Iraq death toll study', Associated Press Online, October 12, 2006.
6. Mike Toole, *The Age* (Melbourne), letters to the editor, October 14, 2006.
7. Dan Murphy, 'Iraq casualty figures open up new battleground', *Christian Science Monitor*, October 13, 2006.
8. Anna Badkhen, 'Critics say 600,000 Iraqi dead doesn't tally', *San Francisco Chronicle*, October 12, 2006.
9. Ritter, 'Bush dismisses Iraq death toll study'.
10. Ibid.
11. BBC *Newsnight*, October 11, 2006.
12. Channel 4 News, October 11, 2006.
13. Clive Cookson and Steve Negus, 'Survey says 600,000 have died in Iraq war', *Financial Times*, October 11, 2006.
14. Julie Hirschfeld Davis, 'Bush disputes estimates of Iraqi deaths', *Baltimore Sun*, October 12, 2006.
15. 'Co-author of medical study estimating 650,000 Iraqi deaths defends research in the face of White House dismissal', *Democracy Now!*, October 13, 2006; http://www.democracynow.org/article.pl?sid=06/10/12/145222
16. Email to Paul Reynolds, October 12, 2006.
17. Email to Media Lens, October 13, 2006.
18. Email to Media Lens, October 13, 2006.
19. Sarah Boseley, 'One in 40 Iraqis "killed since invasion"', *Guardian*, October 12, 2006; http://www.guardian.co.uk/Iraq/Story/0,,1920166,00.html
20. Owen Bennett-Jones, 'Iraqi deaths survey "was robust"', BBC News online, March 26, 2007; http://news.bbc.co.uk/1/hi/uk_politics/6495753.stm
21. Richard Horton, 'A monstrous war crime', *Guardian*, March 28, 2007; http://www.guardian.co.uk/comment/story/0,,2044157,00.html
22. http://www.bbc.co.uk/blogs/theeditors/2006/10/600000_killed_is_that_a_story.html
23. http://www.opinion.co.uk/Newsroom_details.aspx?NewsId=78
24. http://www.opinion.co.uk/Newsroom_details.aspx?NewsId=88
25. Les Roberts, 'Iraq's death toll is far worse than our leaders admit', *Independent*, February 14, 2007; http://comment.independent.co.uk/commentators/article2268067.ece
26. Email to Media Lens and others, September 14, 2007.
27. BBC *Newsnight*, September 14, 2007.
28. http://www.medialens.org/forum/viewtopic.php?p=8904#8904
29. Email to Media Lens, September 17, 2007.
30. http://www.iraqbodycount.org
31. http://www.iraqbodycount.org/analysis/qa/ibc-in-context
32. http://news.bbc.co.uk/2/hi/programmes/newsnight/4950254.stm
33. http://www.iraqbodycount.org/analysis/beyond/state-of-knowledge/7

34. Haroon Siddiqui, 'How many civilians have died?', *Toronto Star*, September 20, 2007; http://www.thestar.com/columnists/article/258511
35. http://www.iraqbodycount.org/analysis/qa/ibc-in-context/10
36. http://news.bbc.co.uk/2/hi/programmes/newsnight/4950254.stm
37. IBC in Context (Feb 2006); http://www.iraqbodycount.org/analysis/beyond/state-of-knowledge
38. Patrick Ball, Paul Kobrak, and Herbert F. Spirer, 'State violence in Guatemala, 1960–1996: a quantitative reflection', 1999; http://shr.aaas.org/guatemala/ciidh/qr/english/chap7.html
39. http://electroniciraq.net/news/themedia/Media_Worker_Death_Toll_Reaches_200-3197.shtml
40. Email sent October 25, 2006.
41. James Forsyth, 'The land the press forgot', *Guardian*, December 10, 2007; http://www.guardian.co.uk/media/2007/dec/10/iraqandthemedia.iraq
42. Ibid.
43. 'Air power strikes Iraq targets daily', Associated Press, December 20, 2005.
44. Aaron Glantz and Veterans Against the War, *Winter Soldier Iraq And Afghanistan: Eyewitness Accounts of the Occupations*, Haymarket Books, 2008, p. 20.
45. Ibid., p. 20.
46. Ibid., p. 19.
47. Cited in Edward Herman and Noam Chomsky, new Introduction to *Manufacturing Consent*, Pantheon Books, 1988.
48. http://www.bmj.com/cgi/content/full/bmj.a137
49. http://www.abcnews.go.com/Health/Healthday/story?id=5207645&page=1
50. http://www.forbes.com/forbeslife/health/feeds/hscout/2008/06/19/hscout616694.html
51. Email to Media Lens, June 22, 2008.
52. Email to Media Lens, July 2, 2008.
53. Daniel Cressey, 'War survey points to millions more dead', *Nature*, June 19, 2008; http://www.nature.com/news/2008/080619/full/news.2008.901.html

8   BITTER HARVEST:
BOMBINGS IN BRITAIN, SPAIN AND IRAQ

1. Leader, 'In the face of danger', *Guardian*, July 8, 2005.
2. Leader, 'Blair plays it cooler – A new tone, but few new answers', *Guardian*, October 31, 2001.
3. Ian McEwan, 'The surprise we expected', *New York Times*, July 8, 2005.
4. http://www.cnduk.org/pages/press/190504.html
5. George Wright and agencies, 'London attack "inevitable", says police chief', *Guardian*, March 16, 2004.
6. Matthew Campbell and Christine Toomey, 'Muslims held over Madrid massacre', *Sunday Times*, March 14, 2004.
7. David Sharrock, 'How terrorists can influence poll outcome', *The Times*, March 13, 2004.

8. Giles Tremlett, 'Massacre in Madrid: ETA or al-Qaida?', *Guardian*, March 12, 2004.
9. Ibid.
10. Leslie Crawford, 'Parties cancel rallies as mourning begins', *Financial Times*, March 12, 2004.
11. Leader, 'To die in Madrid', *Guardian*, March 12, 2004.
12. Isambard Wilkinson and Anton La Guardia, 'Millions rally in anger at Madrid bombers', *Daily Telegraph*, March 13, 2004.
13. Sandra Jordan, Giles Tremlett, John Hooper, Martin Bright and Jason Burke, 'Massacre in Madrid', *Observer*, March 14, 2004.
14. Leader, 'Europe responds', *Guardian*, March 15, 2004.
15. Graeme Wilson, 'The twisted logic of Galloway', *Daily Mail*, July 8, 2005.
16. Kirsty Walker, 'Galloway "poison" triggers outrage', *Daily Express*, July 8, 2005.
17. George Pascoe-Watson, 'The PM is to blame says sick Galloway', *Sun*, July 8, 2005.
18. Christopher Hitchens, '07/07: War on Britain: we cannot surrender', *Daily Mirror*, July 8, 2005.
19. Gavin Esler, BBC *Newsnight*, July 8, 2005.
20. Alan Cowell, 'Blair's rising star runs into a treacherous future', *New York Times*, July 8, 2005.
21. Hassan M. Fattah, 'Anger burns on the fringe of Britain's Muslims', *New York Times*, July 16, 2005.
22. Robert Pape, 'What we still don't understand about Hizbollah', *Observer*, August 6, 2006.
23. David Hencke, 'Tube bombs "linked to Iraq conflict"', *Guardian*, July 18, 2005.
24. Robert Winnett and David Leppard, 'Terror in London – leaked No 10 dossier reveals Al-Qaeda's British recruits', *Sunday Times*, July 10, 2005.
25. George Jones, 'Blair rejected terror warnings', *Daily Telegraph*, September 12, 2003.
26. Robert Fisk, 'Terror in London – the reality of this barbaric bombing', *Independent*, July 8, 2005.
27. Leader, 'The urgent need to end terror in Iraq', *Financial Times*, July 12, 2005.
28. Winnett and Leppard, 'Terror in London – leaked No 10 dossier reveals Al-Qaeda's British recruits'.
29. Eric Hoskins, 'Killing is killing – not kindness', *New Statesman*, January 17, 1992.
30. Hans von Sponeck, *A Different Kind Of War: The UN Sanctions Regime In Iraq*, Bergahn Books, 2006, p. 144.
31. Ibid., p. 38.
32. Ibid., pp. 160–1.
33. Ibid., p. 161.
34. Ibid., p. 270.
35. Robert McChesney, in Kristina Borjesson, ed., *Into The Buzzsaw: Leading Journalists Expose The Myth Of A Free Press*, Prometheus Books, 2002, p. 369.

9   ISRAEL AND PALESTINE: AN EYE FOR AN EYELASH

1. Greg Philo and Mike Berry, *Bad News From Israel*, Pluto, 2004, p. 216; see also http://www.gla.ac.uk/centres/mediagroup/media/israel_excerpt2.pdf
2. Ibid., p. 102.
3. Ibid., p. 216.
4. Ilan Pappé, *The Ethnic Cleansing of Palestine*, Oneworld Publications, 2006.
5. Avi Shlaim, *The Iron Wall: Israel and the Arab World*, W. W. Norton & Company, 2000, p. 31.
6. Quoted in ibid., p. 101.
7. Ibid., p. 582.
8. A useful and concise introduction is Mike Berry and Greg Philo, *Israel–Palestine: Competing Histories*, Pluto, 2006.
9. Tim Llewellyn, 'Why the BBC ducks the Palestinian Story – Part 1', Media Lens, January 15, 2004; http://www.medialens.org/alerts/04/040115_Ducking_Palestine_1.HTM
10. ITV Early Evening News, October 12, 2000, cited in Philo and Berry, *Bad News From Israel*, pp. 105–6.
11. BBC1 Lunchtime News, October 16, 2000, cited in Philo and Berry, *Bad News From Israel*, p. 105.
12. Philo and Berry, *Bad News From Israel*, p. 139.
13. Ibid., p. 259.
14. ITV Early Evening News, 8 March 2002, cited in ibid., pp. 187–8.
15. Philo and Berry, *Bad News From Israel*, p. 188.
16. Ibid., p. 144.
17. 'Israel detains Hamas ministers', *Guardian*, June 29, 2006.
18. Email from Media Lens to David Fickling, June 29, 2006.
19. Email from David Fickling to Media Lens, June 29, 2006.
20. Stephen Farrell, 'Tanks go into Gaza as Jewish settler is murdered', *The Times*, June 29, 2006.
21. Ferry Biedermann and Roula Khalaf, 'Abbas appeals to UN over arrests', *Financial Times*, June 30, 2006.
22. BBC World News, June 25, 2006.
23. Jonathan Cook, 'Kidnapped by Israel', Media Lens guest media alert, June 30, 2006; http://www.medialens.org/alerts/06/060630_kidnapped_by_israel.php
24. 'AIPAC v. Norman Finkelstein: A debate on Israel's assault on Gaza', *Democracy Now!*, June 29, 2006; http://www.democracynow.org/article.pl?sid=06/06/29/1420258
25. http://www.channel4.com/news/articles/world/lebanon+burns/166835
26. Jonathan Cook, 'Israelis are dying – it must be an escalation', ZNet, July 17, 2006; http://www.zmag.org/content/showarticle.cfm?ItemID=10591.
27. Ibid.
28. Email copied to Media Lens, July 26, 2006.
29. Ibid.
30. Robert Fisk, 'Hizbollah's response reveals months of planning', *Independent*, July 16, 2006.

31. Inigo Gilmore, Patrick Wintour and Tracy McVeigh, *Observer*, July 16, 2006.
32. ITV Early Evening News, December 13, 2001.
33. BBC 1, Late News, January 5, 2002.
34. http://www.gla.ac.uk/centres/mediagroup/badnews.htm
35. Leader, 'Middle East: on the brink of chaos', *Guardian*, July 17, 2006.
36. Sam F. Ghattas, Associated Press, 'Lebanon sees more than 1,000 war deaths', *Washington Post*, December 28, 2006; http://www.washingtonpost.com/wp-dyn/content/article/2006/12/28/AR2006122800594.html
37. Bradley S. Klapper, 'Report: Israeli occupation causes terror', Associated Press, February 26, 2008, published on Yahoo news website, http://news.yahoo.com/s/ap/20080226/ap_on_re_mi_ea/un_israel&printer=1
38. 'Human Rights Situation in Palestine and Other Occupied Arab Territories', Report of the Special Rapporteur on the situation of human rights in the Palestinian territories occupied since 1967, John Dugard, United Nations Human Rights Council, A/HRC/7/17; http://www.unhcr.org/cgi-bin/texis/vtx/refworld/rwmain?docid=47baaa262
39. BBC News online, 'UN alarm at Gaza-Israel violence', March 6, 2008; http://news.bbc.co.uk/1/hi/world/middle_east/7281711.stm
40. Email to Media Lens, March 6, 2008.
41. Email to Jeremy Bowen, April 17, 2008.
42. Email to Media Lens, April 17, 2008.
43. Email to Media Lens, April 21, 2008.
44. Email to Media Lens, April 18, 2008.
45. http://video.google.co.uk/videoplay?docid=1259454859593416473
46. Email to Media Lens, April 18, 2008.
47. Tony Blair: 'We must act – to save thousands of innocent men, women and children', *Guardian*, March 23, 1999; http://www.guardian.co.uk/Kosovo/Story/0,,209876,00.html
48. Tony Blair, 'Blair: My pledge to the refugees', BBC News online, May 14, 1999; http://news.bbc.co.uk/1/hi/uk_politics/343739.stm
49. Quoted in Noam Chomsky, *Hegemony or Survival*, Routledge, 2003, p. 56.
50. Leader, 'The sad need for force, Kosovo must be saved', *Guardian*, March 23, 1999.
51. Peter Beaumont, Justin Brown, John Hooper, Helena Smith and Ed Vulliamy, 'Hi-tech war and primitive slaughter – Slobodan Milosevic is fighting on two fronts', *Observer*, March 28, 1999.
52. Andrew Marr, 'Do we give war a chance?', *Observer*, April 18, 1999.
53. David Aaronovitch, 'My country needs me', *Independent*, April 6, 1999.
54. Email to Media Lens, January 14, 2009.
55. Email from Edward Herman to Media Lens, August 27, 2002.
56. Melanie Phillips, 'Yes, this war is terrible. But the alternative was worse – for us all', *Daily Mail*, January 5, 2009.
57. Tim Llewellyn, 'Why the BBC ducks the Palestinian Story – Part 1'.
58. CBS News, January 5, 2009; http://uk.youtube.com/watch?v=Ev6ojm62qwA
59. Seumas Milne, 'Israel's onslaught on Gaza is a crime that cannot succeed', *Guardian*, December 30, 2008; http://www.guardian.co.uk/commentisfree/2008/dec/30/israel-and-the-palestinians-middle-east

60. Andrew Sparrow, 'Immediate Gaza ceasefire is possible, says Tony Blair', *Guardian*, January 6, 2009; http://www.guardian.co.uk/world/2009/jan/06/israelandthepalestinians-middleeast
61. Leader, 'Gaza: no shelter', *Guardian*, January 7, 2009.
62. BBC News online, 'Bowen diary: the days before war', January 10, 2009; http://news.bbc.co.uk/1/hi/world/middle_east/7822048.stm
63. Avi Shlaim, 'How Israel brought Gaza to the brink of humanitarian catastrophe', *Guardian*, January 7, 2009; http://www.guardian.co.uk/world/2009/jan/07/gaza-israel-palestine
64. Ben Brown, BBC World News, January 9, 2009.
65. Jonathan Cook, 'Civilian death toll spurs legal action', *The National*, January 9, 2009; http://www.thenational.ae/article/20090109/FOREIGN/417838381/1002
66. 'Caritas clinic in Gaza destroyed by Israeli jet attack', *Independent Catholic News*, January 13, 2009; http://www.indcatholicnews.com/clinc435.html
67. Ibid.
68. 'Gaza clinic destroyed in strike', BBC News online, January 13, 2009; http://news.bbc.co.uk/1/hi/world/middle_east/7825215.stm
69. Rory McCarthy, 'Gaza truce broken as Israeli raid kills six Hamas gunmen', *Guardian*, November 5, 2008; http://www.guardian.co.uk/world/2008/nov/05/israelandthepalestinians
70. Tabassum Zakaria, 'Rice: Hamas broke cease-fire', News24, December 27, 2008; http://www.news24.com/News24/World/News/0,,2-10-1462_2446278,00.html
71. Alan Dershowitz, 'Don't play into the hands of Hamas', *Daily Telegraph*, January 10, 2009.
72. BBC News online, January 9, 2009; http://news.bbc.co.uk/1/hi/world/middle_east/7818022.stm
73. http://www.guardian.co.uk/world/2008/nov/05/israelandthepalestinians
74. Noam Chomsky, '"Exterminate all the Brutes": Gaza 2009', ZNet, January 19, 2009; http://www.zcommunications.org/znet/viewArticle/20316
75. Ibid.
76. Ibid.
77. Robert Fisk, 'The self delusion that plagues both sides in this bloody conflict', *Independent*, December 31, 2008.
78. Seumas Milne, 'Israel's onslaught on Gaza is a crime that cannot succeed', *Guardian*, December 30, 2008.
79. John Pilger, 'Gaza under fire', *New Statesman*, January 8, 2009; http://www.newstatesman.com/middle-east/2009/01/pilger-israel-gaza-palestine

10   REAL MEN GO TO TEHRAN: TARGETING IRAN

1. Paul Krugman on Iran, 'Fearing Fear Itself', *New York Times*, October 29, 2007.
2. http://www.thetruthseeker.co.uk/article.asp?ID=3689, October 12, 2005.
3. Seymour Hersh, 'The coming wars', *New Yorker*, January 17, 2005.
4. BBC1, One O'Clock News, January 20, 2005.

5. BBC1, Six O'Clock News, January 25, 2005.
6. Ian Traynor, 'Special forces "on the ground" in Iran', *Guardian*, January 17, 2005.
7. Ewen MacAskill, 'US spies give shock verdict on Iran threat: intelligence agencies say Tehran halted weapons programme in 2003', *Guardian*, December 4, 2007.
8. BBC1, One O'Clock News, June 28, 2004.
9. Forwarded to Media Lens, January 24, 2005.
10. Timothy Garton Ash, 'Let's make sure we do better with Iran than we did with Iraq', *Guardian*, January 12, 2006.
11. Polly Toynbee, 'No more fantasy diplomacy: cut a deal with the mullahs', *Guardian*, February 7, 2006.
12. Gerard Baker, 'Prepare yourself for the unthinkable: war against Iran may be a necessity', *The Times*, January 27, 2006.
13. Gerard Baker, 'Defeating prejudice with persuasion', *Financial Times*, February 20, 2003.
14. Gerard Baker, 'Freedom from fear is a worthy goal', *Financial Times*, March 18, 2004.
15. http://www.henryjacksonsociety.org
16. Max Hastings, 'Iran, the vicious victim', *New York Times*, March 30, 2007; http://www.nytimes.com/2007/03/30/opinion/30hastings.html?th=&em c=th&pagewanted=print
17. James Mates, ITN, Ten O'Clock News, February 16, 1998.
18. Martin Ennals, Secretary General of Amnesty International, cited in *Matchbox*, Autumn 1976.
19. Jon Snow, email forwarded to Media Lens, April 3, 2007.
20. George Monbiot, 'The Middle East has had a secretive nuclear power in its midst for years', *Guardian*, November 20, 2007; http://www.guardian. co.uk/israel/comment/0,,2213812,00.html
21. *Guardian* editor, Alan Rusbridger; Guardian Adinfo, Guardian Unlimited, May 24, 2007; http://adinfo-guardian.co.uk/the-guardian/index.shtml
22. You can see the front page here: http://www.medialens.org/alerts/07/ screenshots/guardian_070522_cover.jpg
23. http://www.guardian.co.uk/frontpage/story/0,,2085195,00.html
24. Email to Media Lens, May 22, 2007.
25. From the Editors, 'The Times and Iraq', *New York Times*, May 26, 2004.
26. Confidential News Sources, *New York Times*, February 25, 2004; http:// www.nytco.com/company-properties-times-sources.html
27. http://image.guardian.co.uk/sys-files/*Guardian*/documents/2005/02/25/ code2005.pdf
28. Juan Cole, Informed Comment blog, May 22, 2007; http://www.juancole. com/2007/05/parliament-building-shelled-iraqi.html
29. Murray Armstrong, 'Iran, Iraq and sources of information', May 22, 2007; http://commentisfree.guardian.co.uk/murray_armstrong/2007/05/iran_ iraq_and_sources_of_infor.html
30. Email to Ian Thomas, May 22, 2007.
31. D.D. Guttenplan, 'Don't get fooled again', Comment is Free, May 22, 2007; http://commentisfree.guardian.co.uk/dd_guttenplan/2007/05/ dont_get_fooled_again.html

32. Dilip Hiro, 'Briefing Encounter', Comment is Free, May 22, 2007; http://commentisfree.guardian.co.uk/dilip_hiro/2007/05/briefing_encounter.html
33. Email to Media Lens, May 24, 2007.
34. Comment posted at http://commentisfree.guardian.co.uk/dd_guttenplan/2007/05/dont_get_fooled_again.html.
35. Ibid.

11   IRAN IN IRAQ

1. Adrian Blomfield and Anton La Guardia, 'Stop meddling in Iraq, Blair tells Teheran', *Daily Telegraph*, October 7, 2005.
2. Leader, 'Drifting to war in Iran', *Daily Mirror*, October 7, 2005.
3. Noam Chomsky and David Barsamian, *Imperial Ambitions*, Hamish Hamilton, 2005, p. 35.
4. Craig Murray, 'Beyond parody, way beyond a joke', http://www.craigmurray.co.uk/weblog.html, October 9, 2005.
5. Blair On Iraq: A *Newsnight* Special, February 6, 2003.
6. 'Full text of Tony Blair's foreword to the dossier on Iraq', *Guardian*, September 24, 2002, and Richard Norton-Taylor, 'Official sacked over TV remarks on Iraq', *Guardian*, July 26, 2004.
7. Ewen MacAskill, Simon Tisdall and Richard Norton-Taylor, 'UK accuses Iran over killings of soldiers', *Guardian*, October 6, 2005.
8. Anton La Guardia, 'Troops are pawns in vicious Iran game', *Daily Telegraph*, October 6, 2005.
9. Channel 4 News, Snowmail, October 5, 2005.
10. Paul Reynolds, 'Hardball diplomacy goes public', http://news.bbc.co.uk/1/hi/world/middle_east/4314032.stm, October 5, 2005.
11. Trevor Kavanagh, 'Why West is paying for going soft on Iran', *Sun*, October 12, 2005.
12. Trevor Kavanagh, 'He's bang to rights', *Sun*, February 6, 2003.
13. http://www.csis.org/press/wf_2005_0919.pdf, September 19, 2005.
14. The Iraq Study Group Report, December 6, 2006; http://www.usip.org/isg/iraq_study_group_report/report/1206/iraq_study_group_report.pdf
15. http://news.bbc.co.uk/1/hi/world/middle_east/6451841.stm
16. Aaron Glantz and Iraq Veterans Against the War, *Winter Soldier Iraq And Afghanistan: Eyewitness Accounts of the Occupations*, Haymarket Books, 2008, p. 14.
17. Ibid., p. 41.
18. Trevor Royle, 'Bombings: confusion and contradiction over Iran's role', *Sunday Herald*, October 9, 2005.
19. MacAskill et al., 'UK accuses Iran over killings of soldiers'.
20. Ibid.
21. Royle, 'Bombings: confusion and contradiction over Iran's role'.
22. Ibid.
23. Ibid.
24. Fair Action Alert, 'NYT breaks own anonymity rules', February 16, 2007; http://www.fair.org/index.php?page=3042

25. Leader, 'The threat from Iran', *Daily Telegraph*, January 16, 2007.
26. Ibid.
27. Alexandra Zavis and Greg Miller, 'Scant evidence found of Iran-Iraq arms link', *Los Angeles Times*, January 23, 2007.
28. Gareth Porter, 'US briefing on Iran discredits the official line', February 13, 2007; http://ipsnews.net/news.asp?idnews=36547
29. Marc Santora, 'Iraqi militants launch attack on U.S. outpost', *New York Times*, February 20, 2007.
30. Milan Rai, 'IED lies', February 12, 2007; http://www.j-n-v.org/AW_briefings/IED_Lies.htm
31. Patrick Cockburn, 'Washington accuses Tehran, and sets stage for a new confrontation', *Independent*, February 12, 2007.
32. Ibid.
33. 'US officer doubts Iran arms claim', *Morning Star*, February 14, 2007.
34. Zavis and Miller, 'Scant evidence found of Iran-Iraq arms link'.
35. Ibid.
36. Cockburn, 'Washington accuses Tehran'.
37. Gareth Porter, 'U.S. Military Ignored Evidence of Iraqi-Made EFPs', IPS, October 25, 2007; http://ipsnews.net/news.asp?idnews=39810
38. 'Did BBC ignore weapons claim', BBC NewsWatch, April 14, 2005; http://news.bbc.co.uk/newswatch/ukfs/hi/newsid_4390000/newsid_4396600/4396641.stm
39. Email to Helen Boaden, February 12, 2007.
40. Stuart Williams, 'Iran chases militants behind new bomb blast', Agence France-Presse, February 17, 2007.
41. 'Iran: Bombing in Zahedan', Stratfor, February 14, 2007; http://www.stratfor.com/products/premium/read_article.php?id=284341
42. Ibid.
43. *The Times*, February 15, 2007.
44. Melanie Phillips, 'The teddy-bear teacher and Labour's spineless response to a rogue state that threatens us all...', *Daily Mail*, December 3, 2007.
45. Quoted in Noam Chomsky, *On Power And Ideology: The Managua Lectures*, South End Press, 1987, p. 33.
46. Melanie Phillips, 'The real issue isn't Mr Bean selling his story. It's our utter humiliation by Iran', *Daily Mail*, April 16, 2007.
47. http://www.publications.parliament.uk/pa/cm200607/cmselect/cmfaff/880/880.pdf
48. Ibid.
49. Dominic Kennedy, 'Britons were captured in disputed waters: allies drew a border but failed to tell Iran', *The Times*, April 17, 2008.
50. Ibid.
51. MoD report to the Chief of the Defence Staff under the heading: 'Why the incident occurred', dated April 13, 2007, released to *The Times* under the FoI.

12 VENEZUELA: DOUSING THE 'FIREBRAND'

1. John Perkins, *Confessions Of An Economic Hit Man*, Ebury Press, 2005, p. 148; www.johnperkins.org

2. Ibid., p. xi.
3. Ibid., p. 139.
4. Ibid., p. ix.
5. Ibid., p. 158.
6. David Charters, 'A miss not a hit', *Sunday Times*, March 5, 2006.
7. Francisco Dominguez, 'Latin America takes centre stage', *Morning Star*, November 22, 2005.
8. John Pilger, 'Chávez is a threat because he offers the alternative of a decent society', *Guardian*, May 13, 2006.
9. Perkins, *Confessions Of An Economic Hit Man*, p. 221.
10. Stephen Castle and Raymond Whitaker, 'Heralding the end of US imperialism', *Independent on Sunday*, May 14, 2006.
11. 'The 5-minute briefing: South America's struggle towards democracy', *Independent*, April 22, 2005.
12. Leader, *Independent*, June 6, 2006.
13. *Independent*, May 14 and 13, and June 6, 2006.
14. *Independent*, May 13, 2006.
15. Rosa Prince, 'He calls Bush "Hitler" and Blair "the pawn"', *Daily Mirror*, May 16, 2006.
16. Richard Owen, 'Pope tells Chávez to mend his ways', *The Times*, May 12, 2006.
17. Pippa Crerar, 'Chávez to meet the Mayor', *Evening Standard*, May 12, 2006.
18. Peter Beaumont, 'The new kid in the barrio', *Observer*, May 7, 2006.
19. Duncan Campbell and Jonathan Steele, 'Revolution in the Camden air as Chávez – with amigo Ken – gets a hero's welcome', *Guardian*, May 15, 2006.
20. William Langley, 'Welcome to the El Presidente show', *Daily Telegraph*, May 14, 2006.
21. Andy Webb-Vidal, 'US softens its stance on Venezuela in belief Chávez will hang on to power', *Financial Times*, August 6, 2004.
22. Stephen Castle and Raymond Whitaker, 'Chávez on tour', *Independent on Sunday*, May 14, 2006.
23. 'Chávez offers oil to Europe's poor', *Observer*, May 14, 2006.
24. See Buxton's excellent analysis here: http://www.vicuk.org/index.php?option=com_content&task=view&id=85&Itemid=29
25. Daniel Howden, 'Hugo Chávez: Venezualean [*sic*] leader divides world opinion. But who is he, and what is he up to in Britain?' *Independent*, May 13, 2006.
26. Steve Crawshaw, *Independent*, February 21, 2001.
27. http://www.medialens.org/alerts/02/021119_BBC_Panorama_Response2.HTM
28. Justin Delacour (FAIR), 'The Op-ed assassination of Hugo Chávez', February 13, 2006; http://www.venezuelanalysis.com/articles.php?artno=1670
29. Quoted in David Barsamian, *Stenographers To Power*, Common Courage Press, 1992, p. 142.
30. William A. Dorman and Ehsan Omad, 'Reporting Iran the Shah's way', *Columbia Journalism Review*, January–February 1979.
31. Castle and Whitaker, 'Chávez on tour'.

32. Jonathan Steele and Duncan Campbell, 'The world according to Chávez', *Guardian*, May 16, 2006.

33. Julia Buxton, 'Resisting confusion: pundit Michael Shifter and Venezuela', April 23, 2005; http://www.venezuelanalysis.com/articles. php?artno=1428

34. Chomsky interviewed by Steven Durel, 'Toward freedom', *Social Change Today*, November 7, 2005; http://www.chomsky.info/interviews/20051107. htm

35. Quoted in Neil Lewis, 'What can the US really do about Haiti?', *New York Times*, December 6, 1987.

36. Delacour, 'The Op-ed assassination of Hugo Chávez'.

37. Julian Borger and Alex Bellos, 'US "gave the nod" to Venezuelan coup', *Guardian*, April 17, 2002.

38. 'Chávez rejects "attack" by Blair', BBC News online, February 9, 2006; http://www.news.bbc.co.uk/1/hi/world/americas/4695482.stm

39. Channel 4 News, 'Hugo to go?', March 27, 2006.

40. John Pilger, email to Channel 4 News, copied to Media Lens, March 27, 2006.

41. Juan Forero, 'Venezuela's best-loved, or maybe most-hated, citizen', *New York Times*, November 19, 2005.

42. Pilger, email to Channel 4 News.

43. Catherine Philp, '"He is losing the country's respect"', *The Times*, May 29, 2007.

44. FAIR, Media Advisory, 'Coup co-conspirators as free-speech martyrs – distorting the Venezuelan media story', May 25, 2007; http://www. fair.org/index.php?page=3107

45. Ibid.

46. Ibid.

47. Rory Carroll, *Guardian*, May 23, 2007.

48. Benedict Mander, *Financial Times*, May 9, 2007.

49. Leader, 'A show of intolerance', *Independent*, May 30, 2007.

50. 'Anti-Chávez protesters clash with police', *Independent*, May 29, 2007.

51. Philp, '"He is losing the country's respect"'.

52. Richard Lapper, 'TV channel axed in latest Chávez drama', *Financial Times*, May 26, 2007.

53. James Ingham, 'Venezuelans protest over TV issue', BBC News online, May 27, 2007; http://news.bbc.co.uk/go/pr/fr/-/1/hi/world/americas/6695769. stm

54. Robert McChesney and Mark Weisbrot, 'Venezuela and the media: fact and fiction', *Common Dreams*, June 1, 2007; http://www.commondreams. org/archive/2007/06/01/1607

55. Bart Jones, 'Hugo Chávez versus RCTV – Venezuela's oldest private TV network played a major role in a failed 2002 coup', *Los Angeles Times*, May 30, 2007; http://www.latimes.com/news/opinion/commentary/la-oe-jones30may30,1,5553603.story?ctrack=1&cset=true

56. FAIR, 'Coup co-conspirators as free-speech martyrs'.

57. Jones, 'Hugo Chávez versus RCTV'.

58. Leader, *Financial Times*, May 29, 2007.

59. Richard Lapper and Andy Webb-Vidal, 'Militaristic president falls victim to military revolt', *Financial Times*, April 13, 2002.
60. Andy Webb-Vidal, 'Chávez tests limits of nation's patience', *Financial Times*, April 12, 2002.
61. Alex Bellos, 'Ousted Chávez detained by army', *Guardian*, April 13, 2002.
62. Phil Gunson, 'Deposed Chávez to be exiled as anti-coup rebels speak out', *Independent on Sunday*, April 14, 2002.
63. Faisal Islam, 'Venezuelan civil war fears as ousted president leaves', *Observer*, April 14, 2002.
64. 'Profile: Pedro Carmona', BBC News online, May 27, 2002; http://news.bbc.co.uk/1/hi/world/americas/1927678.stm
65. Leader, 'A show of intolerance', *Independent*, May 30, 2007.
66. 'The truth about RCTV – a VIC briefing'; http://www.vicuk.org/index.php?option=com_content&task=view&id=186&Itemid=29
67. FAIR, 'Coup co-conspirators as free-speech martyrs'.
68. 'Venezuela head in new TV warning', BBC News online, May 29, 2007; http://news.bbc.co.uk/go/pr/fr/-/1/hi/world/americas/6702965.stm
69. See 'The truth about RCTV'.
70. Ibid.
71. Will Grant, 'Honduras TV gets government order', BBC News online, May 25, 2007; http://news.bbc.co.uk/1/hi/world/americas/6690217.stm
72. Diana Cariboni, 'Easy to See the Speck in the Other's Eye', May 30, 2007; http://ipsnews.net/news.asp?idnews=37957
73. Ibid.

13   LIBERAL PRESS GANG: BEHIND THE SCENES AT THE *INDEPENDENT* AND THE *GUARDIAN*

1. 'Live from Iraq, an un-embedded journalist: Robert Fisk on Washington's "quagmire" in Iraq, civilian deaths and the fallacy of Bush's "war of liberation"', by Robert Fisk, Amy Goodman and Jeremy Scahill, *Democracy Now!*, March 25, 2003.
2. Email to David Cromwell, February 24, 2001.
3. HH Dalai Lama, *Transforming the Mind: Eight Verses on Generating Compassion and Transforming your Life*, Thorsons, 2000, pp. 64–5.
4. Justin Podur, 'Fisk: war is the total failure of the human spirit', December 5, 2005; http://www.rabble.ca/rabble_interview.shtml?sh_itm=a37c84dbd62690c4c1abb1a898a77047&rXn=1
5. Simon Kelner, 'The Independent: a new look for the original quality compact newspaper', *Independent*, April 12, 2005.
6. Ian Burrell, '"Mould-breaking" Independent named Newspaper of the Year at press awards', *Independent*, March 18, 2004; http://www.independent.co.uk/news/media/mouldbreaking-independent-named-newspaper-of-the-year-at-press-awards-566613.html
7. Peter Wilby, 'It is. Is he?', *Guardian*, April 14, 2008; http://www.guardian.co.uk/media/2008/apr/14/theindependent.pressandpublishing
8. Ibid.

9. Leigh Holmwood, 'Sir Anthony O'Reilly leaves INM to be replaced by his son Gavin', *Guardian*, March 13, 2009; http://www.guardian.co.uk/media/2009/mar/13/anthony-oreilly-resigns-independent-news-and-media

10. Cristina Rouvalis, 'Living large; Anthony O'Reilly rules a global business empire, enchants all those in his sphere and is now addressed as "Sir"', *Pittsburgh Post-Gazette*, July 22, 2001.

11. Ibid.

12. Richard Siklos, '"I want more of everything"', *Business Week*, December 20, 1999.

13. 'O'Reilly's global empire is still built on print', *Sunday Business Post*, April 29, 2001.

14. Andrew Marr, *My Trade: A Short History of British Journalism*, Macmillan, 2004, pp. 241–2.

15. Ibid., pp. 190–1.

16. Independent News and Media website, October 2005.

17. Ibid.

18. Peter Preston, 'War, what is it good for?', *Observer*, October 7, 2001.

19. Anthony O'Reilly, Independent News and Media Plc Annual Report, 2004, p. 3.

20. Stephen Brook, 'Upward and onward for the Independent's revolutionary', *Guardian*, April 13, 2008.

21. James Twitchell, quoted in Sharon Beder, *Global Spin*, Green Books, 1997, p. 181.

22. 'Richard Ingrams's week', *Observer*, November 4, 2001.

23. Emily Bell, 'Advertisers pile on the pressure', *Guardian*, June 13, 2005.

24. Marr, *My Trade*, p. 112.

25. 'Fear and Favor – FAIR's Sixth Annual Report', *Extra!*, March/April 2006; http://www.fair.org/index.php?page=2848

26. Guy Keleny, 'Errors & Omissions', *Independent*, October 7, 2006.

27. 'Fear and Favor – FAIR's Sixth Annual Report'.

28. Email from Guy Keleny to Media Lens, October 10, 2006.

29. 'Fear and Favor – FAIR's Sixth Annual Report'.

30. Michael Williams, 'A bottle of bubbly for the best way to fly', *Independent on Sunday*, January 22, 2006.

31. Jon Snow, interview with David Edwards, January 9, 2001; http://www.medialens.org/articles/interviews/jon_snow.php

32. Siobhain Butterworth, 'Open door: the readers' editor on … the contradiction between what we say and the ads we run', *Guardian*, October 29, 2007; http://www.guardian.co.uk/comment/story/0,,2200887,00.html

33. 'Castor oil or Camelot?', *Economist*, December 5, 1987, p. 101.

34. Michael Williams, 'Travel ads fund our freedom to talk green', *Independent*, March 30, 2008; http://www.independent.co.uk/opinion/commentators/michael-williams-readers-editor-802543.html

35. Leader, 'Climate change – no more excuses', *Guardian*, February 3, 2007.

36. Guardian website, August 2007.

37. Leo Hickman, 'A clean set of wheels', *Guardian*, June 13, 2005; http://www.guardian.co.uk/g2/story/0,,1504967,00.html

38. Stephen Brook, 'Lexus advertises its own adverts', *Guardian*, June 6, 2005.

39. Quoted in Beder, *Global Spin*, p. 181.

40. David Barsamian, 'An Interview with Ralph Nader', *Z Magazine*, February 1995.

41. Alan Rusbridger, email to Media Lens, June 13, 2005.

42. Email to Media Lens, June 17, 2005.

43. Ian Katz, email to Media Lens, June 14, 2005.

44. Email to Nick Taylor, April 6, 2004.

45. Email to Media Lens, April 6, 2004.

46. Andrew Rowell, *Green Backlash*, Routledge, 1996.

47. Andrew Rowell, interview with Media Lens, June 14, 2005.

48. George Monbiot, email to Media Lens, December 3, 2002.

49. George Monbiot, email to Media Lens, February 2, 2005.

50. 'Live online: Q&A with George Monbiot, June 20', Guardian Unlimited, June 20, 2007; http://environmenttalk.guardian.co.uk/WebX?128@147.djq7ckKAUVO@.775eaab4

51. George Monbiot, email to Media Lens, June 25, 2007.

52. George Monbiot, 'The editorials urge us to cut emissions, but the ads tell a very different story', *Guardian*, August 14, 2007; http://www.guardian.co.uk/commentisfree/2007/aug/14/comment.media

53. Siobhain Butterworth, 'Open door: the readers' editor on ... the contradiction between what we say and the ads we run', *Guardian*, October 29, 2007; http://www.guardian.co.uk/comment/story/0,,2200887,00.html

54. Email to Media Lens, February 6, 2004.

55. David Edwards interview with Alan Rusbridger, December 22, 2000; http://www.medialens.org/articles/the_articles/articles_2001/de_Rusbridger_interview.html

14 BRILLIANT FOOLS:
SNARLS, SMEARS AND THE DARK ART OF WILLY-WAVING

1. Observermail, June 16, 2006; http://observer.guardian.co.uk/observermail/story/0,,1799272,00.html

2. 'Unsmiley person – a new book shows the skilled thriller-writer slipping still further into the slough of gravitas', *Sunday Telegraph*, December 7, 2003.

3. Stephen Amidon, 'Dispatches from an angry old man', *Sunday Times*, December 14, 2003.

4. Harold Pinter, Nobel Prize speech, broadcast on More4, December 10, 2005; http://www.democracynow.org/2008/12/30/harold_pinter_1930_2008_on_art and http://www.democracynow.org/2008/12/31/harold_pinter_1930_2008_part_2

5. Michael Billington, 'High-octane Harold', *Guardian*, February 5, 2005.

6. Daniel Finkelstein, 'Warning: what you are about to read is f****** poetic', *The Times*, March 9, 2005.
7. Charlotte Higgins, 'Pinter's poetry? Anyone can do it', *Guardian*, October 30, 2004.
8. 'The Lancet's Political Hit', *Wall Street Journal*, January 8, 2008; http://online.wsj.com/article/SB119984087808076475.html
9. Simon Heffer, 'David, don't be scared of the truth', *Daily Mail*, October 15, 2005.
10. James Traub, 'Their highbrow hatred of us', *New York Times*, October 30, 2005.
11. Tony Allen-Mills, 'This Pinter guy could turn into a pain', *Sunday Times*, November 6, 2005.
12. *Daily Mirror*, December 8, 2005.
13. Johann Hari, *Independent*, December 6, 2005.
14. This is clearly discernible in the interview transcript. See http://www.medialens.org/articles/the_articles/articles_2001/de_Pinter.htm
15. Howard Zinn, *The Zinn Reader*, Seven Stories Press, 1997, p. 338.
16. *Guardian*, October 31, 2005; http://www.chomsky.info/interviews/20051031.htm
17. 'Falling out over Srebrenica', *Guardian*, November 2, 2005.
18. Email to Brockes, November 2, 2005.
19. Email to Media Lens, November 2, 2005.
20. Noam Chomsky, 'Imperial Presidency', *Canadian Dimension*, January/February 2005.
21. Noam Chomsky, *Hegemony or Survival*, Hamish Hamilton, 2003.
22. George Scialabba, 'Clash of Visualizations', *The Nation*, April 28, 2003.
23. Email copied to Media Lens, November 3, 2005.
24. http://www.guardian.co.uk/letters/story/0,3604,1606321,00.html
25. http://www.guardian.co.uk/flash/0,5860,474564,00.html
26. Email to Media Lens, November 2, 2005.
27. 'Corrections and clarifications. The *Guardian* and Noam Chomsky', *Guardian*, November 17, 2005.
28. Alan Rusbridger, email forwarded to Media Lens, November 17, 2005.
29. Media Diary, *Independent on Sunday*, November 6, 2005.
30. Norman Johnson, 'Yes, this appeaser was once my hero', *Guardian*, November 5, 2005.
31. Email forwarded to Media Lens, November 5, 2005.
32. Email to David Cromwell, November 7, 2005.
33. Globus, November 11, 2005; http://www.globus.com.hr/Default.aspx?BrojID=133
34. 'Chomsky answers *Guardian*', November 13, 2005; http://www.zmag.org/znet/viewArticle/5029
35. Email forwarded to Media Lens, November 19, 2005.
36. Rusbridger, email forwarded to Media Lens, November 17, 2005.
37. Diana Johnstone, 'Johnstone Reply', November 9, 2005; http://www.zmag.org/znet/viewArticle/5059
38. Email from David Peterson, May 26, 2006; John Willis, External Ombudsman Report, May 8, 2006, as posted to the *Guardian*, May 25,

2006, http://www.guardian.co.uk/readerseditor/story/0,,1782133,00.
html
39. Emma Brockes, 'You have to smile', *Guardian*, May 19, 2006; http://www.
guardian.co.uk/g2/story/0,,1778471,00.html
40. http://image.guardian.co.uk/sys-files/Media/documents/2006/06/14/
Journalistsbackgroundsfinal.pdf
41. Jonathan Cook, media alert, Intellectual Cleansing: Part 2, October 7,
2008; http://www.medialens.org/alerts/08/081007_intellectual_
cleansing_part2.php
42. Owen Gibson, 'Most leading journalists went to private schools, says
study', *Guardian*, June 15, 2006; http://education.guardian.co.uk/
publicschools/story/0,,1797567,00.html
43. Peter Wilby, 'All you need to succeed in our meritocracy is privilege',
Guardian, June 17, 2006; http://www.guardian.co.uk/comment/
story/0,,1799649,00.html
44. IRIN, 'Doctors, NGOs warn of high infant mortality in Basra', April 11,
2006; http://www.reliefweb.int/rw/RWB.NSF/db900SID/LSGZ-6NRGZK
?OpenDocument&rc=3&emid=ACOS-635P5D
45. http://timesonline.typepad.com/oliver_kamm/2008/10/free-speech-and.
html?cid=133247409#comments
46. Peter Beaumont, June 18, 2006; http://observer.guardian.co.uk/comment/
story/0,,1800328,00.html
47. http://commentisfree.guardian.co.uk/about.html
48. *Observer* foreign editor Peter Beaumont, *Observer* online debate, June
12, 2003; http://talk.guardian.co.uk/WebX?128@110.uTFNcgZTe3I.1@.
4a914425
49. Email forwarded to Media Lens, June 1, 2006.
50. Email forwarded to Media Lens, May 11, 2006.
51. Email forwarded to Media Lens, May 11, 2006.

15   COMPASSION, AWARENESS AND HONEST JOURNALISM

1. Howard Zinn, *The Zinn Reader: Writings on Disobedience and Democracy*,
Seven Stories Press, 1997, p. 16.
2. Ibid.
3. Daniel Goleman, 'Brain may tag all perceptions with a value', *New York
Times*, August 8, 1995; http://query.nytimes.com/gst/fullpage.html?res
=990CEFD91339F93BA3575BC0A963958260)
4. Quoted in ibid.
5. Zinn, *The Zinn Reader*, p. 17.
6. 'Looking for the magic answer?', Noam Chomsky interviewed by David
Barsamian, excerpted from *Class Warfare*, 1995, http://www.chomsky.
info/books/warfare03.htm
7. Ibid.
8. Ibid.
9. Euan Ferguson, 'A big day out in Leftistan', *Observer*, September 29,
2002.

10. Dilgo Khyentse Rinpoche, *The Heart of Compassion*, Shambhala, 2007, p. 107.
11. Osho, *The Buddha Said...*, Watkins Publishing, 2007, p. 418.
12. Erich Fromm, *The Art of Loving*, Thorsons, 1995, p. vii, our emphasis.
13. Shantideva, *The Way of the Bodhisattva*, Shambhala, 1997, p. 124.
14. *Ibid.*, p. 124.
15. Geshe Lhundub Sopa, *Steps on the Path to Enlightenment*, Volume 3, Wisdom Publications, 2008, p. 125.
16. Osho, *The Buddha Said...*, p. 317.
17. Alex Bellos, 'Fighting talk from a literary heavyweight', *Guardian*, September 23, 1997.
18. See Matthieu Ricard, 'Change Your Mind Change Your Brain'; http://video.google.com/videoplay?docid=-1424079446171087119&q=user%3A%22Google+engEDU%22&hl=en)
19. Robert Chalmers, 'Matthieu Ricard: Meet Mr Happy', *Independent*, February 18, 2007; http://news.independent.co.uk/people/profiles/article2276190.ece
20. Sharon Begley, *Train Your Mind Change Your Brain*, Ballantine, 2007, p. 250.
21. *Ibid.*, p. 251.
22. Matthieu Ricard, *Happiness: A Guide to Developing Life's Most Important Skill*, Atlantic Books, 2007, pp. 7–8.
23. Katherine Ellison, 'Mastering your own mind', *Psychology Today* magazine, Sept/Oct 2006; http://psychologytoday.com/articles/index.php?term=pto-20060828-000001&print=1
24. Khenpo Karthar Rinpoche, *The Instructions of Gampopa: A Precious Garland of the Supreme Path*, Snow Lion, 1996, p. 67.

Index

Compiled by Sue Carlton